# CREATING
# COLETTE

□□□□

# CREATING
# COLETTE

□□□□

VOLUME TWO

FROM BARONESS TO
WOMAN OF LETTERS
1 9 1 2 ⁄ 1 9 5 4

□□□□

CLAUDE FRANCIS &
FERNANDE GONTIER

STEERFORTH PRESS

SOUTH ROYALTON, VERMONT

For information about permission to reproduce selections
from this book, write to: Steerforth Press L.C.,
P.O. Box 70, South Royalton, Vermont 05068.

First published in France under the title *Colette* by Librairie Académique Perrin.

Library of Congress Cataloging-in-Publication Data
is available from the Library of Congress

ISBN 1–883642–76–0

Manufactured in the United States of America

FIRST EDITION

# CONTENTS

---

FOREWORD

---

$\mathcal{I}$N 1913 COLETTE entered her forties, prepared to reap the best of life. She opted for respectability, a husband, and a title. She became baronne de Jouvenel in spite of her mother's warnings against marriage. "You have given yourself a master, poor darling!" She had a daughter whom she entrusted first to an English nurse, later to her husband's mistress, Germaine Patat, the haute-couture maverick, and rival of Coco Chanel. Colette bade farewell to the music hall, and became reporter at large for *Le Matin* and later its drama critic as well as its literary editor. During World War I she managed several visits to her husband stationed near the front, but her articles were censured. After the war, the salon of Colette, baronne de Jouvenel was the meeting place of cosmopolitan Paris, of high-society lesbians and homosexuals such as the composer Francis Poulenc who came with his lover, a taxi driver, or the Spanish infante who startled *Tout-Paris* by coming to a ball naked but entirely painted blue.

Colette herself in her blazing summer years renounced nothing. She had heterosexual and homosexual lovers, among them the film star Musidora, and a five-year-long affair with her sixteen-year-old stepson, Bertrand de Jouvenel.

For brief interludes she tried to cover up her past and her present indiscretions by destroying entire correspondences or by plugging leaks in the press in order to protect the career of her husband, a rising left-wing politician for whom the presidency seemed within reach. But Colette felt fettered and decided to divorce Jouvenel and to end her relationship with her stepson. Like Sido she had a need to escape from everything and from all, "to soar toward a law written by herself for herself."

In 1925 she met a very Parisian Dutch-born dealer in diamonds and pearls, Maurice Goudeket, fifteen years her junior. It was the turning point in her life. She had found a love that would last till her death. This lover, whom she called "my best friend," became her third husband in 1935. He encouraged her to quit journalism and to write what have come to be known as her major works: *The Break of Day (La Naissance du Jour), Sido,* and *The Pure and the Impure (Le Pur et l'Impur),* in which she expounded on her Fourierist principles. Love is at the epicenter of her philosophy, "love food of my life and of my pen," asserted Colette.

In search of herself, she turned to her mother and transformed Sido into her literary self. She came to realize that Sido had immersed Colette into her own ethic that rejected "the old poisonous virtues" and had reshaped for her "the whole chart of human feelings."

Colette felt nostalgic for that paradise lost, for a time "when good and evil were mixed like two beverages blended into a single one," when sexuality had no boundaries. For, according to Fourier, Nature conceived of love in order to multiply infinitely people's social bonds, but in patriarchal societies sexuality was derailed from its natural course and became the root of all evil. For him marriage was enslaved monogamy and Colette called it "this jail that one calls life together." She shuddered at the thought of what it would have been like "to be confined to a single man." For her, heterosexuality, homosexuality, and bisexuality were natural forms of love. It was in her nature, she wrote, "to see in homosexuality a kind of legitimacy and to acknowledge its eternal character."

Colette asserted that any form of love is "pure;" what is "impure" is "what you do without pleasure" or out of imaginary duties. She gave herself as the example of one of the rare complete beings: the androgyne, part man, part woman. She put into practice in her life, as well as in her literature, Fourier's basic principle of "pivotal love." A pivotal or essential love welcomes other loves in an ever expanding circle of loves and friendships. For her, the most despicable lover is the traditional Don Juan, not because he goes from woman to woman, not because he is unfaithful, but because he drops his lovers and forgets them in his progress. Colette's ideal lover is one with an ever growing circle of loves who, in turn, each have their own circle of loves in the perfect harmony of an ever expanding, benign "amorous world." She gives herself as the model of the good Don Juan as she never willingly let go of any of her lovers — male or female. She turned them into friends and welcomed their own lovers into her charmed circle.

She thought that age had nothing to do with love, even as the hair turns white love carries on "with the priceless pain of loving." For her, the age gap did not exist — "the perversity of gratifying an adolescent does not devastate a woman, quite to the opposite." She speaks of "the season of sensuous devotion" and sees the mature woman or man as a "missionary" who has to shelter and nurture his or her young lovers. "To Colette it did not seem easy to distinguish between good and evil . . . It has been said that she loved scandal . . . It was merely that she had personal ideas about what was scandalous," asserted Goudeket.

Love was to bring to the sixty-eight-year-old Colette the anguish she had never known. During World War II, the Germans took away Maurice Goudeket, who was Jewish, and detained him in a concentration camp near Paris for transport to Auschwitz. Colette did not relent until she had him freed with the help of her powerful friends. He had to spend the rest of the war in hiding. Drained by her emotional turmoils, her health began to fail. Yet her last years were a long celebration mixed with more scandals. She was showered with honors, treated like royalty by the queen of Belgium, the prince of Monaco and the president of France. When she died at the age of eighty-one, she was the first woman writer to be granted a state funeral with full military honors. Her friend Jean Cocteau marveled at the extraordinary life of this extraordinary woman: "Colette's life. One scandal after another, then everything turns upside-down and she becomes an idol."

# I

## THE DEATH OF A MOTHER

SIDO'S HEALTH WAS FAILING. She was seventy-six years old in 1911; she had had a double mastectomy and she was afraid to die without seeing Colette. She felt that her daughter was so taken up by her life that she no longer needed Sido's advice, her support, that she had nothing to share with her anymore. She felt betrayed. For over a year in almost every letter she begged Colette to come to Châtillon. Colette would promise to come, then change her plans. Sido felt that someone was upsetting Colette's life. For the first time she did not get straight answers to her direct questions. Delays were followed by excuses and promises were not kept. Sido showed some impatience: "So you are putting me off until April — and then only to grant me a few hours!" What was happening to Missy? Quoting Voltaire, she suggested that she and Missy should "cultivate their garden," because that was the only way to live in peace.

April went by and Colette did not come. Sido asked ironically if she had postponed her visit indefinitely. She waited patiently through May, convincing herself that a letter announcing Colette's visit was on the way. It never came. In June she hoped to receive a letter announcing Colette's arrival. She did not come. Sido was now so deeply hurt that she asked her if she had decided never to come to Châtillon again. She wrote that she was very sad and that if she were to see Colette no more, she would rather die. Colette promised to come. By June she had not yet appeared; she was in Geneva — with whom? Sido was so anxious to know what was going on that she would sit in her small drawing room all morning, watching for the postman from the window. She received a postcard; Colette was not coming. The news upset her so much that she went into her garden and pulled up weeds to stop thinking — exercise keeps the imagination from spinning. She had learned at last why her daughter had no time for her, for Colette had written about her sudden and absorbing love affair with Henry de Jouvenel and sent her a letter from Jouvenel himself. "He writes penetrating letters, if I may say so,"[1] commented Sido, but what about Auguste Hériot? Was he in Geneva also?

Now that the secret was out, she hoped that Colette would show up. Sido was relieved to know the truth, and decided to go to Paris since her daughter would not come to her. She stayed three days. Colette was taken aback to see her so thin, so frail, and so cheerful, for her cheerfulness seemed feverish. Sido bought some pansy seeds to plant back in Châtillon; she went to the Opéra Comique and visited a special collection at the Louvre Museum. She had brought a gift for her daughter, rosebuds wrapped in a damp cloth. She eagerly asked about Colette's work — what was she writing? What was she planning to write? Colette took Sido to the station and put her on the train, which returned her to Achille less than two hours later. After leaving her, Colette felt the need to sit at her table, pick up her pen, and resume her work as a writer.

On July 22, Sido begged Colette to come for a few days, even a few hours. She needed to have a serious discussion with her because she felt things were falling apart. What about Missy? What about her beautiful manor, Rozven? What about Hériot, so rich, so devoted? So Colette was going to the Corrèze with Jouvenel? As she wrote these words Sido felt a sudden rush of fever, "God, how hot the weather is! Come my treasure, come, as soon as you can!"[2] Her anguish became pathetic. What could prevent Colette from coming? From writing to her? She feared an accident or sickness. She complained about a strange sadness that had seized her the previous morning and would not let go. Was it a foreboding of something unfortunate? She was so worried that she asked Colette to answer by telegram, reminding her of her promise to come at the end of July.

The last day of July came and went. This time Sido unloaded her heart. Why did Colette not stay at Rozven? Rozven where all was so nice, so secure, so supportive? And Sido deplored, "You have given yourself a master!! Poor thing."[3] A master! All her life Sido had remained as free as she could; her first husband — rich, sick, and drunk — was anything but a master; Captain Colette, who loved her so passionately and who depended on her, was never her master. Now Colette, who had made a life of her own, had chosen to give up the privilege Sido cherished above all, her freedom. As if that were not enough to upset her, Sido had learned piece by piece that Jouvenel had left an angry mistress, Countess de Comminges, who was seeking revenge. She urged Colette to tell her if she had received death threats. But even that did not seem enough to explain Colette's stubborn absence and her ambiguous letters. Was she pregnant or sick? Sido was ready for all the turmoil of Colette's life; however, she could not say that all this left her indifferent.

In August Colette countered by sending Sido a picture of the medieval castle belonging to the Jouvenels, counting on the impressive turrets to charm her mother. Sido agreed that it looked like a castle from a fairy tale, but could not help asking if Rozven, which had been described as such a dream house by Colette, had now been discarded as a useless toy.

In an attempt to win Sido's approval, Colette sent her Jouvenel's photograph. Sido remarked that he looked extremely healthy and added nastily that she hoped the journalists of Le Matin were not going to ask Colette to extend the same magic cure to them. Sido was not won over; she was afraid that Colette would be the loser, and repeated her pathetic request: when would Colette come for a while? She wondered how one could care so much for sensuous delights. She remembered a time when she, too, was fatally attracted to a man but, quoting Molière, she bantered: "The sinfulness was wiped out by marriage." This was precisely Colette's secret goal. She wanted the aristocratic title and the standing it would give her in society. She wanted to be baronne de Jouvenel, comtesse des Ursins. She had been shunned by some of Missy's titled friends for whom she was only a courtesan and had felt humiliated.

Colette knew Sido's weakness for chess. Jouvenel was eager to challenge her to a game of chess. Finally Sido expressed some interest. In November Colette asked her mother if she would come to Rue Cortambert; Sido told her to set a date as soon as possible before the weather turned too cold. She discreetly mentioned that she was old. The same stubborn question came up like a ticking clock, "When are you going to tell me when I can come to see you? When?" Colette was impervious to her mother's ill health. At last she asked Sido to take the train and come to Paris. Very gently, Sido told her that she had not left her room for two weeks and would not be able to travel all winter.

Jouvenel sent her a charming letter asking her to call him by his nickname Sidi, so Sido wrote to "Sidi" that Willy, who preceded him, had been a terrible fool, since he had been unable to keep Colette — wonderful Colette, who could speak when she was eight months old, could sing when she was one year old. And again the pathetic request came at the end of the letter intended for Jouvenel, but mailed to Colette, "Do at least write!"

A few days later Sido received a letter; before opening it she felt tears on her cheeks. She knew what she was about to read; Colette was not coming. And so it was. This time Colette had bronchitis. It was a threadbare excuse. Colette was totally engulfed in her incandescent love affair with Jouvenel. Sido could only answer that she should stay in bed, insisting that show business was too much for her and so was her "husband," who was too young for her.

After Christmas Sido complained that Colette was ignoring her illness and her fits of suffocation, so terrible that sometimes she would rather die than suffer another. She knew Colette would not come, since she had signed a contract to dance in Brussels. Achille was upset by his sister's attitude; he wrote that their mother could live provided she was spared emotional turmoil. He insisted, "Do come, you may bring your dog."[4] On January 12, 1912, Sido was hopeful: "At last! You are coming! I will see you!" but it was March before Colette came for a few hours and left in a hurry. An unexpected parcel arrived for Sido, a framed picture; it was an enlarged photograph of Colette at age five, sitting gingerly on a chair. Sido had given the photograph to Willy many years ago. Willy, who had learned that Sido was seriously ill, had it mailed by the photographer without a word. It was an anonymous, discreet gift. Sido was touched.

At the end of August Colette came for a day and two nights, which she spent writing letters to friends; she told Christiane Mendelys that Jouvenel thought forty-eight hours at Châtillon was plenty, which made her exceedingly happy because it proved he needed her. As for Sido, Colette wrote that "she could last," and that was all she needed from her mother. To Wague she wrote that her "dear saintly mother" was "insufferable," that she was not gravely ill, but having a fit of "I want to see my daughter"; again she rejoiced that Jouvenel had granted her only a three-day leave. It occurred to her that Wague might disapprove. "I don't want you to look at me with your penetrating, critical, and disillusioned gaze . . . I know better than you do that I am a f—— bitch."[5]

Sido had urged her once again to marry Hériot, since with him she would be financially free to write great works; if not, her talent would be squandered on journalistic endeavours. On the twenty-fifth of September Sido died in Châtillon. Two days later Colette wrote to Léon Hamel that her mother had died and she was not going to the funeral. She would tell no one and wear no mourning. The only thing that annoyed her was that she could no longer write to Sido and felt sorry for Achille. She went on playing in *L'Oiseau de Nuit* and living as usual. Colette would write in *My Mother's House (La Maison de Claudine)* that, years before she died, Sido had forbidden her to wear mourning because she liked Gabri only in pink or in certain shades of blue.

On October 7 Colette and Jouvenel drove to Castel Novel, having been formally invited by Madame de Jouvenel, Henry's mother, whom he already called "your mother-in-law." Mamita was not an ordinary woman; she smoked cigars and drank brandy by the full glass. After a flamboyant love affair with Monsieur Chevandier de Valdrome and an illegitimate daughter, she came back with her daughter to resume her life with Baron Léon de Jouvenel. Edith was in her teens when Colette visited that autumn.

Henry de Jouvenel's younger brother Robert, a political journalist, was putting the final touches to his book *La République des Camarades*. The Republic's heroic times were over; now politics were governed by special-interest groups, which he summed up in a popular phrase: "Give me your rhubarb, I'll give you my senna." His analysis of the changing tides of French politics was widely read. Colette felt a true friendship for Robert; she admired this man, who was said to be even more brilliant than his flashy brother. He had just bought "an old ruin of a castle, Curemonte, which needed one hundred thousand francs for basic repair."[6] It was a happy time for Colette. She took long walks in the early morning while Mamita was playing tennis and Henry and Robert were supervising the farm.

October 22 Colette and Jouvenel drove back to Paris. When she boarded the train on October 28 to go to Geneva, where she was to perform *L'Oiseau de Nuit* at the Apollo theater with Wague and Kerf, Colette knew she was pregnant. In a letter to Hamel dated October 30 she told him she was curtailing a visit to "an incandescent Swiss woman" giving "the child as an excuse."[7] Instead of the visit, she boarded *The Bolivar* to tour the lake in "leisurely" fashion, which for Colette meant writing letters and constructing scenes in her mind for her next novel, *Recaptured (L'Entrave)*. Georges Wague recalled that after lunch on board, Colette fell asleep. A few days later, she wrote the most vivid account of the trip, "full of funny and very precise details that she had caught . . . without even looking."[8] The boat trip on Lake Leman is part of *Recaptured*.

During that week in Switzerland Colette corrected the proofs of *Prou, Poucette et Quelques Autres* brought by Paul Barlet, who came for twenty-four hours. She agreed to give a private show for Hamel's friend, Madame Dangenne, who was to be charged a stiff five hundred francs plus the orchestra fee.

A week before Christmas, at 4:30 in the afternoon, Colette and Jouvenel were married in Paris. Hamel was Colette's witness. For a week they celebrated the event: "We bounced from lunch to dinner, from dinner to supper, to a Christmas party which lasted until 7 AM and topped a week of excesses."[9] In a few days the new baronne de Jouvenel would turn forty.

# II

---

## BARONNE DE JOUVENEL

---

*"A frightful resentment is welling up in me against this bitchy character, who does not know how to feed or defend a woman"*
COLETTE, LETTER TO HAMEL

BARONNE DE JOUVENEL, still signing "Colette Willy," launched the year 1913 with an attack on women as she covered the presidential election in Versailles at the Hôtel des Réservoirs. The Congress had attracted a large crowd, and the galleries were overflowing with what appeared to Colette an unseemly number of women. She compared them to hens in a chicken coop: "What are they doing here?" She found their interest in politics grotesque, depriving them of that very feminine charm made of "incompetence, timidity, silence."[1] Antifeminism was strong at all levels of society. Colette openly and consistently condemned feminist political action and opposed civil rights for women; for a regular contributor to a leftist newspaper like *Le Matin*, it was peculiar. Henry de Jouvenel's field as an editor was unionism, which encompassed the fight of working women for economic equality. The integration of women into the trade unions and their right to have their own unions was a question hotly debated in parliament, with many senators defending the political rights of women. In 1907 the Council of the Seine Department lobbied for women to vote in local elections, a move meant to lead to the universal vote. In a referendum on women's right to vote conducted at the onset of World War I by *Le Journal*, an overwhelming number of readers — 505,972 — were in favor. The feminist newspaper *La Fronde* orchestrated several campaigns for the revision of the civil code, for the right to "voluntary maternity," for the vote for women, and against the prostitution laws, which penalized women only. The outspoken editor in chief, Marguerite Durand, thought the author of *The Vagabond (La Vagabonde)* the perfect standard-bearer for the feminist cause. Asked to join in a discussion, Colette answered that she had no talent for that. "I am a peaceful soul who shies away from pugilistics."[2] In an article about chorus girls, Colette had one of her characters exclaim: "I know my rights, yes I do!" which drew the comment, "her equalitarian rage appeals to no one."[3]

That same spring, in "Les Belles Ecouteuses," Colette caricatured women she observed during a lecture given by "charming, famous and witty" Henri Bergson. They hid their lack of understanding by nodding their heads to the rhythm of his words. The few who came prepared, having read Bergson's philosophical works, were pictured as "obnoxious."[4] Colette never questioned the feminine status quo. In *Chéri*, Madame Peloux, a courtesan-turned-businesswoman, is held responsible for her son's depressive state, her financial success depriving him of the manly desire to achieve. Deprived of what should have been his world, he finds love in an aging courtesan who understands the masculine world and Chéri's needs and frustrations.

The gargantuan wedding celebration and the enormous amount of work took their toll, and Colette came down with gastroenteritis: "Pretty soon I looked like a wilted flower." At the end of January Colette and Henry left for a "well-deserved vacation."[5] Colette would have liked to go to Le Crotoy, deserted during the winter; she asked Hamel to find out if one of the two hotels closed for the season would reopen for her, as she needed a hiatus of calm and solitude. Four days *en tête-à-tête* with Sidi on a deserted coast would recreate the magic moments by the Lake of Geneva. Henry preferred to go to the Riviera with the Polignacs. The marquis de Polignac, who had a large financial interest in champagne and cognac, was sponsoring (along with *Le Matin*) a national Convention on Tourism that was to last until October. Jouvenel participated in several meetings organized by local chambers of commerce and gave a speech at the closing ceremony attended by the French president.

The Riviera was at the height of the season; Colette complained half-jokingly that if they kept on "resting that way, they would be brought back on stretchers." They had to be everywhere at the same time and they crisscrossed the countryside in "the marquis de Polignac's very fast car." Colette marveled "at Sidi's youthful lust for life." He had gone without her to the Mardi Gras ball until 5 AM, "happy to have hugged ever so many anomymous derrieres."[6]

There was also more serious entertainment. They listened to Wagner's *Siegfried*, dined with Gunsbourg, director of the Monte Carlo Theater, and visited Prince Albert's Oceanographic Museum. Their schedule was so crowded that Colette gave up a week in Saint Raphaël she had set aside to work on her novel, a rare occurrence for Colette, who always kept a tight control on her activities (Wague had nicknamed her "what time is it?"). To put aside her novel reflected Colette's priority in 1913; she was enjoying her life with Sidi and her new status as the baronne de Jouvenel. Later she made fun of Jouvenel's title, but at first she loved it and signed her calling cards "Baronne de Jouvenel" or "Baronne de Jouvenel, Comtesse des Ursins." She persistently asked Jouvenel to prevent his first wife from using the title "which is rightfully mine."[7] She even signed letters to her old friends Hamel, Wague, and Christiane Mendelys "Colette de Jouvenel." Colette knew that her marriage was reopening a layer of society that had shunned her since her divorce. Marcel Proust was trying to find friendly journalists to promote *Du côté de chez Swann* and after long deliberation on the propriety of doing so, "now that she was famous, brilliantly married," he had his book sent to Colette through Count Louis de Robert and proclaimed, "As for Madame de Jouvenel . . . I have the greatest admiration for her . . . I find that she has an immense talent."[8]

Colette's infatuation with the music hall was never stronger than at the moment she was to leave the stage. "I felt exiled from a kingdom that was mine."[9] In Nice she gave a lecture, "Backstage at the Music Hall" at L'Artistique. A puzzled journalist reported in *Le Petit Niçois* that Colette Willy had told her audience that "the ambience of the music hall was a moral and hygienic world where one could live at peace . . . where young girls were safer than on the Champs Elysées, where men were all honest, women never evil-minded."[10] The music hall, according to Colette, was energy, vitality, innocence, friendship, and — above all — it brought out a professional dedication unmatched in other trades. In their quest for survival, she said, the artists did not have time for fake personalities; they were unadulterated human beings. On the stage Colette could set free her passion, unleash her soul, play out her frustrations, and let flow her pent-up energies. Literature was the opposite, being the art of understatement, a disquieting, veiled world. In March *Music-Hall Sidelights (L'Envers du Music-Hall),* a collection of chronicles published in *Le Matin* from 1910 to 1912, was released by Flammarion. Except in "La Fenice," a Neapolitan music hall she visited with Auguste Hériot, the chronicles in *Music-Hall Sidelights* were not autobiographical. "I exercise my right to remain silent about myself." The critics praised her for her empathy; Rachilde compared her to Dickens. The *N.R.F.,* the new journal of the literati, wrote, "Madame Colette Willy lays bare the misery of their lives . . . her eloquence is so powerful because she brightens it up with a smile and so much more striking because it seems unintentional."

Early in April Colette, six months pregnant, danced *L'Oiseau de Nuit* at the Apollo Theater in Geneva with Christiane Kerf and Wague. Her two old friends were pampering her. She performed twice on private stages. That spring she bade farewell to the music hall and her career as a mime and dancer. "Every night I was saying 'adieu' to one of the good times in my life. I knew perfectly well I would miss it."[11] She referred to her music-hall days as "those happy days," "a time which I called happy." She felt that she had lost what made her "special," "different," that she was giving up "that special brand of insolence that goes with the artist."[12]

Colette's pregnancy was not to interfere with her other activities; she rode her horse, walked her white bulldog in Le Bois de Boulogne, went on hunting for antiques, and played endless card games with Hamel. Charles Sauerwein told her, "Do you know what you are doing? You're reacting to the pregnancy like a man . . . a pregnancy should be more cheerful than that. Put on your hat and come and have a strawberry ice cream at Poirée-Blanche."[13] Colette could be feminine but never to the point of pretending that she enjoyed motherhood. She described herself as "a rat rolling away a stolen egg."[14] She was not conforming to the reclusive manners of French women, who would hide themselves "as in shame,"[15] wrote Colette, and stayed at home resting.

Colette was seen everywhere: at the opening night of Wague's pantomime *La Barbara*, at the tumultuous premiere of Stravinsky's *Le Sacre
du Printemps*, the thirty-five-minute ballet choreographed by Nijinsky
at the newly opened art-deco Théâtre des Champs Elysées. Since *Ubu
Roi*, Paris had not enjoyed such a scandal. The public did not like the
jagged rhythms and the dissonant sonorities any more than the stylized
choreography. When the dancers put their hands to their cheeks, some
people started to shout "a dentist! No, two dentists!" Catcalls, whistles,
jokes, insults, and obscenities never stopped. Fistfights broke out as the
music went on. To quiet the audience, Diaghilev kept turning the
lights on and off while Nijinsky, in the wings, was shouting the count
to the dancers. (It had taken him 130 rehearsals to create a choreography that matched the complex score. The show lasted for only four
performances. The Ballets Russes were in financial trouble. The Vienna
Opera Orchestra had refused to play Stravinsky's *Petrushka* for their
1913 New Year's Eve concert, calling it "dirty music.") The group of
supporters — Princess de Polignac, Misia Sert, Ravel, Debussy, and
Colette — were applauding wildly. "*Le Sacre du Printemps* is an extraordinary, ferocious thing," wrote Debussy. "You might say it's primitive
music with modern convenience."[16] A few weeks later, Colette was at
the opening night of Diaghilev's ballet *Jeux* on a score by Debussy.
*Jeux*, danced in modern dress, was a *pas de trois* with ambivalent sexual
overtones set to a revolutionary music that broke down the classical
harmonic hierarchies into independent blocks of sounds. The Cubist
masterpiece was coolly received.

She left for Corrèze to supervise the modernization of Castel Novel;
the lack of running water and toilets, still an urban luxury of the upper
class, was more than she could bear. Jouvenel's grand vision for the restoration of "that old ruin,"[17] mostly financed by Colette, was mentioned to
Hamel with restrained irony. Meanwhile Colette was still struggling with
her novel; advertised as a sequel of *The Vagabond (La Vagabonde)*, *Recaptured*
was not going well. "Only my novel is a problem . . .For God's sake, don't
talk to me about *Recaptured*! I do it day by day, with difficulties, I cannot
get ahead and I would like to see all my characters in one hundred feet
of . . ."[18] She was writing her novel in a hurry as it was being serialized.

Back in Paris, by mid-June she was still fuming. She had rewritten
the end three times and wrote to Paul Barlet, who edited her text, "Oh,
why don't you want 'impermeability'? 'Obscurity' would be my last

concession, all the other shades are too weak! I would even like 'impervious.' I am not going to proofread tonight. Bye-bye synonyms!"[19]

The serial was gaining on her, and in the contest between book and child, the child won. On July 3, after thirty hours of unremitting labor, Colette gave birth to a daughter, named Colette Renée — Colette for her paternal patronym and Renée after the heroine of *The Vagabond*. She called her child Bel-Gazou (pretty warbler), the nickname Captain Colette had given her. She marveled at her daughter, at "her nails resembling in their transparency the convex scale of a pink shrimp. The small sex, a barely incised almond, a bivalve precisely closed, lip to lip — " She found her "well shaped and pretty with slit eyes and a lot of hair."[20]

As soon as she could travel, Colette left for Castel Novel with a wet nurse, a cook, a maid, and a private nurse, supervised by Madame Pot, her midwife. The restoration was going at a very slow pace and the castle was littered with splintered wooden partitions, plaster, old curtains, and "the new toilet bowls. New, alas! and threatening to remain so for a long time,"[21] which did not prevent a stream of guests from visiting. By the end of spring, Missy was back in the fold. Madame La Fierté (the Proud One), as Colette nicknamed her, was again apprising Colette of her latest conquest, an actress from La Comédie Française.

A month after Bel-Gazou's birth, Colette's letters show a woman obsessed by her work rather than by her daughter. Her struggle to finish *Recaptured* revealed her determination not to allow motherhood to overtake her art. "My touch of virility saved me from the danger which turns a writer who becomes a parent into a mediocre author. . . ." She saw the writer in her as her masculine self, "a bachelor of forty" who rescued her need to write without too much difficulty because of, in Colette's own words, "the accidental characteristic of my pregnancy"[22] — accidental taken in the logician's sense: nonessential.

By September Colette had finished the last two chapters. The three last days she worked nonstop for eleven hours; the following day, still not satisfied with the end, she started all over again. "Hamel! Dear Hamel! Fructifying Hamel! Pleasant and discreet Hamel! I have finished *Recaptured*. I exult with relief but I vomit it and I despise it."[23] Colette never liked the conclusion of the novel, which she found constrained and artificial, a conclusion her heroes "did not believe in."[24] In this conclusion, Colette had written her much-quoted phrase, "I think that many women wander as I did before returning to their rightful place, which is within the boundaries set by man."[25]

The novel is a study of the complexities of love. The plot is slim. Renée, the Vagabond, has met Jean and his young mistress, May; she has fallen in love with Jean, and May is pushed aside. After many love's labors lost Jean and Renée end up together — but is it love, or only lust? Central to the story is Jean Masseau, whose model is Paul Masson.

In the early days of their friendship, Colette was overwhelmed by Masson, as is Renée by Masseau. Renée feels that Masseau has spiritually seduced her. Until they met, Renée had gone through life like a sleepwalker, defined only by others. It was good to have others to blame, others to thank. "How long," asks Renée, "would I have followed that half-dream?" Masseau teaches her to take charge of herself, to face her own contradictions, to be self-reliant. "Masseau helps with the savoir faire of a madman to bring curiosity back into my life, a taste for intrigues and adventures, the need to be wanted — there is room for all that in my life and for worse and even better."[26]

Masson was for Colette what Wilde had been for Gide, the guide who helped her define her ethics and her aesthetic. In *Recaptured*, Masseau/Masson is her past, and in resuming her dialogue with him, Colette continues to explore the possibilities of a definition of love. On one hand, there is little May and many other little Mays "who live only for the moment, defined and limited by their fluttering pleasures. The past . . . is Max/Missy — missed and feared — secure, without a flaw like a superb and impassable wall."[27] The present is Jean/Jouvenel and carnal love. "I have never known before," says Renée, "the intelligent joy of the flesh which immediately recognizes and adopts its master and for him becomes easy, docile, generous. . . This is so beautiful, so easy, this does not look like love."[28] Can sexual attraction between a man and a woman become love? Colette explores the topic in *Recaptured* and again in *Mitsou*. Masson had told her that like art, love is the sublime art of fakery.


Fourteen months after his mother's death, on the last day of 1913, Achille Robineau-Duclos died of cancer in Paris, where he had settled, unwilling to live in Châtillon once Sido was gone. Colette felt that the tall, handsome, brilliant brother, "the one without a rival" had often crowded her out of her mother's affections. He showed an emotional dependency on Sido all his life. Colette's last mention of Achille is his sadistic portrait in "Domino," the story of the marinated puppy, first published in 1944 in *Broderies Anciennes*, then again five years later in *Autres Bêtes*. "Domino" was Achille's bizarre eulogy. Colette did not attend her brother's funeral. It is generally assumed that Achille destroyed Colette's letters to Sido, maybe as many as two thousand. It seems more likely that his wife, Jane, burned the lot to protect her family and her daughters from future scandals. She was outraged by Colette's way of life, and deeply resented her husband's admiration for his notorious sister and his unfailing love for Sido who had a not-too-discreet involvement with a wood merchant. After Achille's death she severed all links with Colette and was so resentful of her in-laws that she stated in her will that she was not to be buried with either the Colettes or the Robineau-Ducloses.

## "Sigh No More, Ladies, Sigh No More"

Colette's second marriage was proving to be a repeat of the first; Henry de Jouvenel, whom she called Sidi, the Pasha, even the Sultana, was a compulsive seducer. Colette wrote to Marguerite Moréno, "Sidi is a sweet whore (puteau)."[29]

Colette kept the same group of friends; with Jouvenel she attended the rehearsals of Sacha Guitry's and Albert Hermant's plays, and she kept in touch with Judith Gautier — the beautiful Judith, who had become plump and placid, but who was still exploring Oriental music, inspiring Dukas, following the career of her godson Siegfried Wagner. As the only woman member of the Académie Goncourt since 1910, she was a literary power broker and Colette wanted badly the Prix Goncourt. She continued to exert her fascination over women: Meg Villars, Missy, Marguerite Moréno, and Natalie Barney, who after Renée Vivien's death had settled in the heart of literary Paris, at 20 Rue Jacob. The international set streamed into Natalie's salon on Fridays, mingling with Léon Barthou, Robert d'Humières, and baroness Deslandes. This was Colette's preferred circle of friends; she pointed out to Jouvenel "two lesbians from London who are worth the trip."[30]

Her marriage to Jouvenel had not changed her need for lesbian love. Now she was chasing Samuel Pozzi's daughter, the poetess Catherine

Pozzi, who had been passionately, if platonically, devoted to Georgie Raoul-Duval. Georgie had died in November, "killed by love, the powerful love which cannot be mentioned."[31] She had cultivated Catherine Pozzi, whose ambiguous charm fascinated her entourage. Marguerite Moréno, back from Argentina, "tried to find out if the little girl, who had excited her years ago, had become a more accessible woman."[32] Catherine relished the attention but remained aloof. She had just divorced the playwright Edouard Bourdet and was having a secret affair with Paul Valéry. Colette and Jouvenel both courted her: "Colette has fallen in love with me and pesters me; these triple arrangements to which Georgie had not converted me, tempt me less than ever. However, I remain ambiguous and nice, because Jouvenel is *Le Matin's* editor and phones me every bit of news."[33]

Colette became involved with the actress Musidora; born in 1884, she was sixteen when she read *Claudine at School (Claudine à l'Ecole)* and, like so many other girls fascinated by Claudine, she wrote Willy an admiring letter and visited his bachelor apartment. On learning that Colette was the author of the *Claudines*, Musidora transferred her fascination from Willy to his wife. Having seen Colette only from a distance, she sent her a letter: "Madame, I admire so much your talent as a writer, I would give my life if you would ask for it." She also told Willy he was wrong to betray such a beautiful wife and confessed she was completely overwhelmed by her feelings for her. Would he help draw Colette's attention to her letter? Willy, whom Musidora calls "My Protector" in her *Memoirs*, obliged, and Colette sent a reply. She had kept Musidora's drawings of Claudine, "even the drawing of Claudine naked and beautified, seated against an Indian blue background. Believe me, my child, I will not ask for your life or anything else. In spite of my way of life, I am a wise, quiet woman, I don't make friends easily, but I remain very true to my friends. I am not yet old, but my youth is leaving me. I do not try to hide that fact and will be glad to shake your hand."[34]

Early in February of 1914 Colette gave a lecture on Molière before a performance of *L'Ecole des Femmes* at the Théâtre Femina, shocking the audience by declaring she did not care for his verses, which were not "sonorous" enough for her taste, and confessed to Moréno how she really felt: "Merde for Molière," she wrote. Musidora, who attended the lecture, penned a hyperbolic review of Colette's performance and mailed it to her. Colette answered with an invitation to lunch. "From that day on I clung to her,"[35] wrote Musidora, who was fast becoming a movie star; she had signed the previous year with Gaumont and under the direction of Louis Feuillade, was filming a serial, *The Vampires,* which would turn her into an international celebrity. "Vamp" was becoming synonymous with "beautiful" and "sexy." The Vamp was stirring up a storm in Colette's life; it was the type of intricate situation on which she thrived. Nothing gave her greater pleasure than transforming her lovers into devoted beings who not only felt total submissiveness, but were addicted to it. As usual Colette multiplied her lovers. "I have neither the desire nor the right to belong to one single hero. . . ."[36]

Colette read some *Dialogues de Bêtes* in Tournai, followed by a two-week tour in Belgium with Musidora. In April the Jouvenels were seen at a preview of *La Revue Galante* at the Folies-Bergère. Musidora appeared in a skimpy costume in an adaptation of the novel *Paul et Virginie.* Colette's infatuation with Musidora was so intense that, according to the feminist journalist Louise Weiss, Henry de Jouvenel became violently jealous and had two guards posted outside the door of Musidora's dressing room to prevent Colette from entering.

Sidi too fell under Musidora's spell. Soon the Jouvenels and Musidora were an inseparable trio, an arrangement that did not go unnoticed. In July Colette spent two weeks with Musi at Rozven: "The beach was for us alone. The jade blue waters and the golden sand were like an immense Fra Angelico palette."[37] After two weeks of the submissive, adoring Musi, Colette was longing for Jouvenel. He came, enjoyed "life on the beach . . . swam in the nude, Pro Pudor! and rolled over in the sand."[38] Colette was supervising the modernization of Rozven, swimming, writing articles, and planning a new novel, which was to be *Chéri.* The gestation of a novel was a time of emotional instability for Colette; she needed a security blanket. Willy, Missy, and Hamel had provided moral support, a creative environment that boosted her self-confidence; at Rozven, she was unable to come to grips with her story. Since she had to be intellectually urged on, Henry de Jouvenel wrote out a detailed plan in twenty-two chapters, Cartesian, mathematical; when she saw it, Colette burst into tears. It was the end of an illusion. She was alone with herself, alone with her art. She realized that Henry, with his baccalaureat, had a superficial culture and would never be of any help.

World War I

Europe was teetering on the brink of war. On July 31, Jaurès, the socialist leader and founder of *L'Humanité,* who opposed the war, was
gunned down in the street by a nationalist. Violent reactions were expected. Jouvenel phoned Colette at Rozven to let her know that war
was likely to be declared and the situation in Paris was volatile. Colette
had her chauffeur drive her and Musidora to Saint-Malo to get the latest
news. As they arrived, posters announcing the mobilization were being
plastered all over town. Back at Rozven, Colette organized their departure. Nursie-Dear and Bel-Gazou were to stay at Rozven; all the male
servants were leaving for Paris to report to their units. The chauffeur
drove Colette and Musidora, speeding through Paris to Neuilly. Jouvenel
joined the 44ème Régiment d'Infanterie Territoriale as sergeant, and
was soon promoted to second lieutenant. On the eve of his departure,
Sacha Guitry gathered friends for a farewell dinner; Marguerite Moréno
was struck by Jouvenel's looks: "As soon as he put on his uniform he was
another man, removed from Colette. It is strange how a uniform can
change the way a man thinks and loves. . . ."[39]

The first months of the war were particularly bloody. France was totally disorganized. Paris became a dead city as trams, cabs, and buses
stopped running. The government left for Bordeaux. The enthusiasm of
the population was overwhelming; persuaded that the war would be over
in a few months, men went to fight eagerly for "France, Republic, and
Humanity." The French armies started on the offensive and lost battles on
the eastern and northern borders. In September a German plane flew over
Paris and dropped leaflets: "The German army is at your door, you have
no choice but surrender, signed Lieutenant Von Heidessen"; he dropped
three bombs, one of which killed an elderly lady. More planes followed;
Parisians shouldered their hunting guns and fired at them. Orders were
given to the armies to fight without looking to the rear: "If going forward
is impossible, keep your ground and die rather than retreat."[40]

With Jouvenel gone, Colette felt lonely. She could not stand silence
and solitude. The cook, the chauffeur, and the gardener had gone to war,
the female servants had returned to their provinces. She turned to the
protective fold of feminine friendships; soon a female clan organized
around Colette, who called it *le Phalanstère,* the Phalanx, a word and

notion straight out of Fourier's Utopia. The phalanx had four members. Musidora, the Vamp, "little Musi," "my child Musi," moved in with Colette but rented an elegant pied-à-terre a block away. Colette's "dear soul," Marguerite Moréno, whom she loved "extremely," her link with the past, lived on the Rue Jean de Boulogne in the vicinity; they were so attuned to each other that they believed they communicated through extrasensorial means. The fourth member of their group was Annie de Pène, "who left her husband to live maritally with Colette."[41]

Colette borrowed one hundred francs from Musidora, not out of necessity but as a security blanket. "The phalanx of the sixteenth district," as they named it, was meeting at her place, so "Colette would be relieved of domestic worries and could write with total peace of mind." Musidora, who came from a poor background, took over the chores, cooked the meals, and did the shopping. "We spent a few unusual evenings while I was doing the dishes, Marguerite Moréno dried them reciting *Andromaque* with her deep, magnificent voice."[42] During the war Annie de Pène became Colette's lover and confidante; in a way she replaced Missy. She lived in a big house a few blocks from Colette and, as a writer herself, provided her with an affectionate understanding. She had lambasted her contemporaries in *Modern Puppets (Pantins Modernes)* and expressed the difficulties of being a woman in *The Escapee (L'Evadée)*. She came from a distinguished family of journalists — her grandfather had founded the dailies *Le Gaulois* and *Paris-Journal*, and she was editor in chief of *l'Eclair*. Separated from her husband, with whom she had had a daughter, her present companion was Gustave Téry, the director of *L'Oeuvre*. Annie was an intelligent, organized woman whom Colette depended upon for everything from coils for her mattress to luxuries like truffles and fowl when food became scarce. A photograph taken at that period shows Colette seated in an armchair, Annie kneeling at her feet pretending to play the guitar. Catherine Pozzi was amused by the phalanx: "Tonight I have dinner at Colette's, she plays at Paris under siege with Musidora, a little whore from the Folies-Bergère — Colette always has a little whore at hand — they cook, hoard, and lead the life of savages preparing their daily food. They both live on biscuit, vegetables, and sardines, when nothing warrants it, they admire themselves as clever Robinson Crusoes. Moréno shares their dinners once in a while, dazzling them with satirical impromptus."[43]

High-society women organized hospitals and soup canteens for the

Belgian refugees who poured into Paris and for the wounded, who were slipped in during the night so the population would not be demoralized. All the boutiques on Rue de la Paix were closed except Léo Weil's, a jeweler, where courtesans decked out in pearls and diamonds made tricolor cockades that were sold to benefit the Red Cross. Misia Sert crisscrossed Paris to collect linens from the plush hotels in her Mercedes driven by designer Paul Iribe, dressed as a deep-sea diver, with Jean Cocteau in a male nurse's uniform (especially made for him by the couturier Paul Poiret) and the painter Sert, in large checkered knickerbockers, holding his Kodak camera.

Colette volunteered for a night watch at the Lycée Jeanson de Sailly, which had been turned into a hospital. "It is a terrible job . . . thirteen hours on the go, in the morning one is a little haggard."[44] She did not stay long, a few days, less than a week. Her name is not listed in the Jeanson de Sailly's roll of volunteers, but Colette's legend as a volunteer night nurse has endured. Given her innate repulsion for sickness and death, it was an act of courage — she was still little Gabri, panic-stricken whenever Sido asked her to bring a bunch of flowers to an elderly lady who had taken to bed.

She did not stop writing for *Le Matin* the first two years of the war. In August her column, "Le Journal de Colette by Colette Willy," was replaced by "Propos d'une Parisienne," and was not signed. It was a reportage on Paris during the war, a Paris that had mysteriously been purged of all the gangs of "Apaches" who used to terrorize Parisians at night, a Paris where the moon and the stars were shining bright now that all windows were blacked out, where during the day the streets were quiet and filled with elegant strollers. Elegance, thought Colette, was an act of courage. "I have never seen so many beautiful women!"[45] By the end of October the tone had changed. The opening sentence of her last "Propos" was, "There is suffering everywhere."

Theaters and music halls were officially closed, but illegal ones were attracting a public of young women, old men, and "good-humored foreigners." The forbidden shows took place in a "narrow, smoky room" where the sounds were muffled and people danced between the sketches. To appease the censors, Colette described in her article the heartbeat of the public as patriotic and optimistic. They only sang along with "songs from the past"[46] and rose to listen to the Belgian anthem, followed by *La Marseillaise*, the Russian anthem, and *God Save the King*.

"I love you," wrote Jouvenel from the front at the end of August. "She exults,"⁴⁷ noticed Moréno. For in spite of her anger at Henry de Jouvenel, whom she found weak, feminine, and profligate, Colette wanted to go beyond their attraction for one another to reach a lasting relationship.

Jouvenel's unit was stationed near Verdun, a garrison town in northeastern France; its fortress was the main protection for the road to Paris. The front was ten kilometers farther north. The garrison was a sort of independent enclave with its own command. Soon Verdun was filled with wives and mistresses; rentals were at a premium. Mistinguett, the music-hall star, rented a house and settled in with Maurice Chevalier. It was not difficult for Colette to get a visit permit as a journalist. Jouvenel had rented an apartment. The first thing Colette told him was "by the way, Annie is coming. Why? asked Jouvenel. To cook beef in red wine."⁴⁸

Even though Colette found Sidi "very much to [her] liking," "very handsome," looking like "a first-class pharmacist," and though he found her "not unattractive,"⁴⁹ she pursued her plan to bring Annie to Verdun, writing detailed instructions for the trip. Jouvenel felt that a ménage à trois was more than the military would allow and asked Annie not to come, warning her that the authorities were taking themselves even more seriously since they had nothing to do. "Verdun is the biggest flop of the war,"⁵⁰ wrote a disillusioned Jouvenel, who had hoped to be in the thick of things.

There was sporadic fighting, which Colette enjoyed. "What a fine cannonade, Annie! It is magnificent. The house shakes, the windows rattle." In this ambience, Colette thrived. Her letters to Annie are peppered with erotic allusions to her passionate nights with Sidi: "As Louis XIV used to say to Madame de Maintenon, I won't go into that in more detail." She added, "I am modest, I am not like such and such obscene guy, I do not brag, like a certain disgraceful officer at knowing how to play at 'up for Annie.'"

In another letter, Colette prepared a weird oral quiz that Annie was to give Jouvenel when he came on furlough:

> Annie: "What are you?"
> Jouvenel: "A darling girl."
> Annie: "And what else?"
> Jouvenel: "A sort of beauty, etc., etc. . . ."

And Colette concluded, "He is the perfect example of a darling girl."⁵¹

There was a good deal of irony in these erotic games, and the boundaries between masculine and feminine were imprecise, floating. Colette's games linked the erotic with an epicurean love for food, which Annie tried to satisfy by sending parcels full of delicacies. "Annie, the black pudding!!! . . . The black pudding and the butter." Or again, "I have yet to sing the posthumous praise of the truffles, those beautiful noble truffles."[52] Within the peculiar order she had organized, Colette was happy. There is not a single note of fear in her correspondence. From Verdun she anticipated her life in Paris, where she planned to take cooking lessons from Annie. "If you are willing, I will have hours of fascinating lessons with you. . . . I am already planning mad evenings at the cinema and incomparable hours at the Petit Casino."[53]

On December 2 Colette was at the citadel in Verdun, watching a battle that must have sounded to her like a Wagnerian opera. "The noise is magnificent and as varied as the noise of a storm, now close at hand, now at a distance, now sharp, now dull." She spent Christmas at the citadel.

On New Year's Day, with a group of officials, she went to Clermont-sur-Argonne, which had been reduced to rubble, as were all the villages they drove through. It was bitterly cold. There were wooden crosses here and there, machine guns under a few branches, a pack of mules under a thatch, a group of soldiers, a convoy, a church without windows where one could hear an "old carol from Burgundy" — in the eerie landscape of war, Colette heard a Christmas carol from her native province. Her chronicles in the war zone were idealized reality.

Her group was to distribute food and clothes, not to the soldiers, who had more than they needed — "they had ten thousand geese for Christmas, they had wine, oranges, chocolate" — but to the children of the stricken villages. Colette was surprised to see so many of them coming out of the ruins. "Where do they sleep, where do they eat?" She was invited to visit makeshift dining rooms and classrooms in cellars where the missing ceilings had been replaced by logs. In "Children in the Ruins" ("Les Enfants dans les ruines"), Colette stressed the thin line between the normal and the abnormal. She gives a surreal description of a meal: "A few officers . . . a very Parisian official, two pleasant and peaceful women in the midst of ruins, eating serenely and elegantly as if they were in Paris"[54] to the sound of the music provided by the constant firing of the guns.

Colette was learning to play chess with Sidi. "This is the only remaining pledge of love that I can give him and I am giving it to him."[55] She did not like the slow pace of chess, preferring to paint. She painted objects, idealized objects, saying that art could never be found in the simple rendition of reality, but demanded a reordering, a rethinking of reality. (Her paintings were destroyed in a fire in the World War II when the apartment where she stored them on Rue d'Anthouard was bombed.)

Early in January she left Verdun, but was back for a shorter visit in February. The war had entered a new phase. The Germans had launched their spring offensive in the Argonne, bombarded Reims and, in Flanders, used mustard gas. Colette was "terrified," but soon, contemplating the winter-bound country, the snowflakes and icicles on the train windows, she forgot the danger. "No difficulty in getting here, an indifferent gendarme, in short the best of journeys." The difficulties started with Jouvenel; they quarreled right away and "we exchanged such insults. . . . Rows between married couples are dreadful. . . ." What really appalled her was the feeling that her own life was blacked out. She rebelled and refused Jouvenel's advice to take shelter in a cellar on the pretext that "a cold is a lot more dangerous than gunfire." There was a claustrophobic strain in Colette that extended far beyond physical entrapment; any form of confinement, physical or emotional, triggered a rebellious reaction. She wrote to Annie, "After dark I have been granted the right to a short walk." She walked along the river Meuse. The sound of guns in the distance reassured her. To the eerie silence of her room she preferred any sign of human presence. In her letter, she talked again of the "reassuring beat"[56] of the guns.

Colette left after a few days, but came back a third time in early May after receiving a letter from a disheartened Jouvenel. "My dear love," he asked, "you are still there, aren't you? You love me still?"[57] After a grueling journey, Colette was back in Verdun. In the past three months the situation had changed; the town, no longer an independent district, lived under military rule. It was constantly bombed by German airplanes: the slow Tauben, later replaced by the more deadly Aviatik. Colette felt trapped again: "I am passionately in favor of life. Horror of horrors, I have to live behind shutters,"[58] which, of course, she did not do. She was covering the war for Le Matin; in "Verdun" she reported on the devastation wreaked by the new German planes. As she watched the bombing, she was told by a platoon to take cover under a bridge. When it was over, she and an officer's wife who was with her walked back to Verdun to find trees knocked down and children looking for shrapnel in a hole made by a bomb. The newspapers reported that a German submarine had sunk the *Lusitania* with twelve hundred people on board. The idea of death crossed her mind, and she claimed that if she were to die in war-torn Verdun, she would have no regret. "I am enjoying the calm that comes to people who have achieved their aim in life,"[59] wrote the forty-two-year-old Colette.

Having assessed the situation and where she stood with Sidi, she wrote to Annie, "and I do not need to talk about him, for you know he is the shining light of my life."[60] She lucidly described the tension between love and sexual attraction in *Mitsou, or How Girls Grow Wise (Mitsou ou comment l'esprit vient aux filles)*. Like Mitsou, a music-hall actress in love with a lieutenant, Colette felt that the immediate reward of physical love could lead to an idealized form of love: "My love I will try to become your illusion . . . let's start by the easiest . . . give me again the surprise of following you so easily into pleasure. . . ."[61] She returned to Paris. Her articles on Verdun were not published; their publication was probably overruled by the censors, who disapproved of female reporters in combat zones.

In June Colette was sent by *Le Matin* to Italy, which had just joined the Allied forces. Rome was a haven buzzing with diplomats, spies, and socialites. On arrival in the Italian capital, when she registered as baronne de Jouvenel at the Hotel Excelsior, she was denied a room and treated like an adventuress usurping a name. The confusion arose because Claire Boas, the divorced wife of Henry de Jouvenel, was still using her married name and had a suite at the Excelsior; she was a celebrity in Rome. Her political salon in her sumptuous apartment on Boulevard Saint-Germain in Paris had been the center of a diplomatic ploy to persuade Italy to join the Allies. Gabriele d'Annunzio, then at the height of his fame, and the socialist journalist Benito Mussolini wanted Italians to join the war. The first baronne de Jouvenel commissioned a huge Italian flag to be made, its staff engraved by a Parisian jeweler. She traveled to Italy with a party of journalists and d'Annunzio, who made rousing appeals to the people from Genoa to Rome. The crowds showered them with lilies of the valley. When Claire Boas and her bejeweled Italian flag reached Rome, she was acclaimed by the Italian press, which favored war. Colette was outraged by the incident at the Excelsior. "That may be too much for my forgiving nature," wrote

Colette to Léon Hamel. She wanted the exclusive use of a title "that is rightly mine"[62] and forcefully asked Jouvenel to remedy the situation. Nothing was done.

She settled at the Hotel Regina, on Via Veneto, in a suite next to Gabriele d'Annunzio. She wandered around Rome with the writer Sybille Aleramo; Count Primoli opened the doors of Roman palaces to her. At night with Gabriele d'Annunzio she visited the "osterias of the Trastevere." D'Annunzio gave her two volumes of *In Praise of the Sky, the Earth, the Sea and the Heavens,* inscribed "To my adored Ally, I give these foreboding *cantos ante lucem,* Rome, June 1915" and "To my sister in Saint Francis of the animal kingdom . . . I offer this book born from the Etruscan sea." Colette sent a thank-you note: "Mon cher Maître and new friend . . . I take along with me your poems and the Brummel liquor, the latter less tonic than the former."

In July she went back to Paris, spent some days in Rozven, dashed to Verdun, then returned to Rome early in August. Travel for civilians was difficult; trains were used to move troops. Nothing deterred Colette. Her reportage on Italy was published in *Le Matin* and part of it in *Le Flambeau.* Colette's difficulties with the censors grew with her interview of the Austrian prince of Hohenlohe in Lugano, where a large colony of Germans and Austrians lived, closely monitored by the Allies. The prince had told her that, were he younger, he would be fighting in the German army, but, at his age, his only dream was to live in a garret in Paris. Colette tried rather clumsily to circumvent the censors by insisting that it was a dream shared by many Germans. In 1915 only six of her articles were published in *Le Matin,* and from January to June in 1916 not a single article signed "Colette Willy" was printed by the Parisian press. Until the end of the war, *Le Matin* was off-limits for Colette, even though Jouvenel was still one of the editors in chief. She finally placed some articles in *L'Excelsior,* which had a limited readership; founded in 1910, it was the first magazine to make extensive use of photojournalism.

In the fall she was able to resume publication of "Le Journal de Colette" in *La Vie Parisienne* until the end of the year. In April a collection of her articles on animals was released under the title *Creatures Great and Small (La Paix chez les Bêtes),* which included texts published in *Prou, Poucette et Quelques Autres* and in *Les Vrilles de la Vigne.* She dedicated her book to "any unknown soldier . . . bloodthirsty, sweet and full of dreams like the First Man on the planet, stretched along his good gun, a blade of grass between his teeth, with a snake around his wrist and a docile wolf against his heels." The volume was published by a small press, Crès et Cie, and did not sell. Colette needed money. She wrote a pantomime about animals and performed it with Wague for a charity gala. It was probably not a success; with Musidora's help she turned to the movies.

Theaters, music halls, and dance halls reopened to cheer up the soldiers, who were given furloughs after a year of war. The Folies-Bergère staged *To the End!,* the vaudeville *Visions of Glory* with Marguerite Moréno, and the French sang *La Madelon, Rose of Picardy* or *Tipperary.* The great successes of the war movies were Judex, with Musidora, and *Les Mystères de New York.* Rome had become the movie center of Europe, and Musidora had settled in the Italian capital. So Colette left for Rome; she would commute back and forth between Italy and Paris until the end of the war.

In September of 1916 she left for Cernobbio on Lake Como and joined her brother-in-law Robert de Jouvenel and Zou, his mistress at the majestic Villa d'Este. Robert was editor in chief of *L'Oeuvre,* which claimed to be the only paper to give a true picture of the situation: "Idiots don't read *L'Oeuvre.*" By the end of September they were joined by Second Lieutenant Henry de Jouvenel, who had been assigned to a civilian post. The Jouvenel brothers thrived on the high life of the Villa d'Este, where "people changed three times a day and then changed again for the evening."[63] The women, noted Colette, were preoccupied only by their looks. Their weekly schedule did not vary: one hour for haute couture, one hour for lunch followed by the coffee hour, then teatime. Colette preferred to go rowing; always a perfectionist, she took lessons and crisscrossed the lake as "if it were a mere puddle,"[64] staying three hours at the oars. She was also busy negotiating the movie rights of *Claudine at School (Claudine à l'Ecole)* and *Claudine in Paris (Claudine à Paris)* with the Lombarde Cinematographic Society.

By the end of October Colette and Henry had gone back to Paris; Jouvenel had been appointed head of an information service. In November, the Jouvenels bought a *hôtel particulier* at 29 Boulevard Suchet; it was a house set in a large garden, with the fortifications and the Bois de Boulogne as a background. Colette, who had coveted that house for over a year, negotiated the purchase with its owner, the actress of *Les Variétés* — another of her old paramours, Eve Lavallière. She arranged a rendezvous in Auteuil on the old fortifications, a sort of wild ravine of dubious reputation, full of acacia and maple trees. Lavallière was wearing a light blue sweater, the latest fashion launched by the budding Coco Chanel. Pulling up her sweater, Lavallière showed Colette that she wore neither corset nor bra, "nothing disguised her girlish breasts."[65] Colette repeated her visits until Lavallière moved out to the Champs Elysées and baronne de Jouvenel moved into the house she wanted. Pretty soon she put Annie de Pène in charge of the remodeling.

In *Places (Trois-Six-Neuf)* Colette wrote that she lived there alone with her aging cat, "my man in the East and my child in the country,"[66] depicting a solitary woman opening the windows to save the panes from shattering during the shelling of Paris at night. That was literature; "her man" was not in the East, but in Paris busy with *Le Matin,* busy with politics and extramarital love affairs. By the end of 1915 it was evident that their marriage was under stress; in his *Journal Littéraire,* Paul Léautaud noted: "It seems that the couple Colette-Henry de Jouvenel is not doing too well. Jouvenel still has a genuine literary admiration for her but the passion is over and he has no qualms about finding some distraction elsewhere."[67]

Barely a few weeks after moving into Lavallière's *hôtel particulier,* the Jouvenels were back in Rome, where they spent Christmas. Jouvenel was showing Rome to French parliamentarians, "twenty-four of them. Rather him than me," exclaimed Colette, who refused to do more than what she deemed necessary. "I will not let myself be invaded."[68] All things considered, her life in Rome was much like life in Auteuil, "except for churches and museums."[69] In April she learned that Léon Hamel had died. Colette dreaded her return to Paris, where she would miss him more than she did now in Rome. Her trusted confidant had made handwritten copies of Colette's letters, which he had prudently edited. Jouvenel left for Paris; Colette stayed in Rome waiting for Musidora, who was to produce and play the lead in *The Vagabond,* directed by Eugenio Peregro.

## Cinema

The Colette-Musidora collaboration had started the previous year with *Minne,* the first movie produced by Musidora. Colette had written the screenplay, which was based on *The Innocent Libertine (L'Ingénue Libertine)*, and taken a keen interest in all aspects of moviemaking. She was there every day and saw the rushes. During the shooting one of Musidora's financial backers refused to put up any more money, so Colette advanced the funds. The film, to be released by Films Lumina Co., was advertised in *Le Film* in December: "*Minne*, a dramatic comedy (1250 m.), screenplay by Mme Colette (Colette Willy) from her novel *The Innocent Libertine* played by Musidora." The film, which cost thirty thousand francs, was never distributed. It was probably stopped by "Anastasia," the nickname given to censorship. The erotic dreams of a teenager were a risqué topic for the nascent art.

In Rome, Colette stayed on location during the filming of *The Vagabond*. She liked scriptwriting, which she dubbed "a manuscript by images." "I am quite proud to be one of the first writers who will have done — without any help — a movie image by image." She found the writing of a screenplay "astonishing gymnastics." Colette disagreed with the Italian directors and their conception of "truth, life, and bleeding reality."[70] She complained that in the scene where Renée Néré unlocked her husband's writing desk to find his love letters, the director wanted Musidora to pry open the drawer with a large carving knife, then he wanted her to wait for her husband with her forehead against the windowpane, lacerating the blinds with her nails and teeth. Notwithstanding its shortcomings, *The Vagabond* was a success in France; the critic of *L'Intransigeant* thought that Musidora "was excellent" but deplored the fact that Colette Willy's heroine had been "Italianized." Henri Diamant-Berger in *Le Cri* also thought that "the Italian director . . . had not understood the book with its sensibility so totally French."[71]

The success of the film gave Musidora the backing she needed to start her own movie company, La Société des Films Musidora. She commissioned an original screenplay from Colette, *The Hidden Flame (La Flamme Cachée)*, for ten thousand francs. Shot in Rome, the film was the story of a student, Annie Morin, who married a young millionaire but was in love with a poor student. To be able to marry him, she ruined her husband, hoping to drive him to suicide, but died in an explosion without reaching her goal, after having outraged and driven away the man she loved. The movie and the screenplay exist no more. Reading the press clippings of the day, it is obvious that *The Hidden Flame* was an avant-garde movie; all the exteriors were filmed on location and the interiors were carefully researched. Colette did not want a repeat of *The Vagabond*. Before the film was released in 1919, there was a spate of articles about the priceless set and the furniture, worth more than one hundred and sixty thousand francs.

Colette supervised the publicity; in *Le Figaro* she underlined what was new in her movie. "*The Hidden Flame* has very short subtitles. The audience will easily be able to follow 'the action, which is dramatic, romantic, and fantastic' by watching the animated scenes."[72] Colette again wanted to suppress words and rely entirely on mimodrama. Neither the critics nor the audience liked the movie, which lost forty-five thousand francs. Having lost money in the movie business, Colette would not work for the cinema again until the 1930s, when she wrote the script for Max Ophuls' *Divine,* then wrongly advertised as the first screenplay written directly for the screen by Colette.

She believed in the new art. As early as 1914 she reviewed films for *Le Matin* and for *L'Excelsior,* and from May 28 to July 21, 1917, she was the film critic for *Film,* the first publication entirely devoted to the cinema. When she left *Film* because "there was no money in it,"[73] the movie director Louis Delluc took over her column. He praised her for having contributed to the success of two groundbreaking movies: *The Scott Expedition to the South Pole* in 1914 (the first great documentary film, which opened up a whole new area) and two years later, Cecil B. de Mille's *The Cheat,* which had a deep effect on French movie directors from Louis Delluc to Jean Cocteau. "The French cinema between 1919 and 1924 rested entirely on *The Cheat.*"[74] Actors were asked to interiorize acting, departing from the earlier excesses of mimics and pantomimes. Colette understood the new dramatic language invented by Cecil B. de Mille. She was the first movie critic to say that the cinema had "to forge its own autonomy." She praised Sessue Hayakawa, the Japanese actor, and supported the avant-garde of an art in search of itself.

Her experience with the cinema in Italy during the shooting of *The Vagabond* prompted Colette to write "Short Manual for the Aspiring Screenwriter," first published in *Excelsior,* then reprinted in *Film* and in *Filma.* She denounced the clichés used in popular movies. A "sensational movie" is never based on actual events; it presents the principal actors in enormous close-ups, particularly the female character, always in "décolleté, often armed with a hypodermic needle or an ether bottle, she sinuously turns her serpent's neck toward the spectator, revealing enormously wide eyes and slowly bites her lower lip before disappearing in the mist of a fade-out." The lead is always a man of undetermined age, who is responsible, after three or four thousand feet of film, for the fate of a teenager, a widow, or a divorced woman. He needs "to be enormously proficient in horsemanship, swimming, jujitsu, boxing, marksmanship, and tightrope walking." He is either "the Avenger — or what amounts to the same thing — a Bandit, Mastermind of a secret association of criminals, he smokes Turkish cigarettes, which he discards with a wicked gesture." The female character is either a femme fatale or a socialite suffering from a brutal, jealous, alcoholic husband or from the consequences of a "youthful indiscretion." She is always dressed in black taffetas with a tiny hat. The script of a movie with a woman as its lead is always centered around a letter. Colette's main criticism was aimed at the directors who, instead of using "those Italian gardens with peerless porticos, statues and fountains, cascading roses and trailing wisteria . . ." endlessly recreate the same scene around a sofa where "it is easier to be assassinated, to embrace a mistress, to fall into a swoon or melt into tears."[75]

Written with a dose of irony, the "Short Manual for the Aspiring Screenwriter" advised directors not to cater to the least discriminating viewers and to avoid stereotypes, the abuse of close-ups, and studio artifice. She was aware of the possibilities of an art that most intellectuals despised as cheap entertainment. For her, cinema was an art.

## You See . . . Plus Ça Change

The *Claudine* movie rights and the Colette-Musidora partnership rekindled the feud between Colette and Willy. From Switzerland, where he had settled during the war, anonymous articles about the relationship between Colette and Musidora and their "dubious" financial deals were reprinted in the Parisian press. The Vamp, who had been Willy's mistress until 1911, when she swapped him for Colette, was described as "looking dazed and having rotten teeth."[76] The insult triggered a response in *Cinema*: "This impersonal but prolific author has tried by a belated scandal, fortunately averted, to annoy a splendid author, Mme. Colette, and an interesting artist, Mlle. Musidora. Suffice it to say that Mr. Willy gets royalties from the *Claudine* series, which are not his."[77] It was a reference not to the novels but to the musical. Colette felt that any movie rights for *Claudine* and its sequels were hers and hers alone. They were still bickering about the rights for the musical. In 1911, in *Comoedia Illustré,* Willy had painted a humoristic picture of the greed triggered by its success: "Well, we are so many to share the cake crumbs. . . . There is first, Mme. Colette, with whom I have signed the novels from which I have drawn the libretto. . . . The larger piece of the cake, and rightly so, belongs to the composer."[78] Fifty percent of his rights were to go to Colette after she had threatened Willy with a lawsuit. Colette did not want to share anymore royalties; with the help of Musidora, who, as a producer, knew the intricacies of the royalty laws, she circumvented Willy's claims. He answered with two vengeful romans-à-clef, *The Good Mistress (La Bonne Maîtresse)* and *Ginette, the Dreamer (Ginette, la Rêveuse).* In *Ginette, the Dreamer,* Musidora was derided as "a star of the suburban flick houses, Dora Musi — who seeing I paid her no more attention — had me insulted in the feminist reviews by Loquette Wely, the ex-dancer, now a zoophile novelist." In *Film* and in *Filma,* Musidora and Colette answered in kind.

This battle of egos was, for the most part, anonymous. In November 1917, in a byline article in *L'Excelsior,* "Those Men Before the War," signed "Colette Willy," she went one step further. The theme of the articles was "Have you ever known any Germans?" For the general readership, it was a patriotic piece done in a confidential mood. Colette confided that as a tourist, she had seen "the Germans eat and drink." After a paragraph on their way of life, she wrote, "It is not in Germany that — to astonish and charm the readers of *L'Excelsior* — I find my *Boche* (a demeaning term for Germans) but here in Paris." Then came a murderous portrait of the Viennese musician who had composed the score for *Claudine.* Colette accused him of using ghostwriters, so that when the musician, "who did not compose much and the author — excuse me for that word — of the libretto" met for the first rehearsal, they had no idea of what they were supposed to have written. This article à cléf was easy to decipher: the libretto writer was Willy, the musician Rudolphe Berger, who had come to Paris at the age of nine and made his career in the French capital. When the war broke out, Germans and Austrians living in France were rounded up and sent to concentration camps in Ardèche. Berger took refuge in Spain; unable to cope and depressed, he committed suicide. This prompted Colette to write, "this 'very Parisian' composer, really a Viennese, now — having killed himself a year ago — conducts in triple time, sad processions in purgatory.'"[79]

Colette's main target was Willy; beyond the usual leitmotif of "the author who cannot write" lay a more dangerous implication. In *L'Echo de Paris,* the fanatic academician Frédéric Masson had demanded that Willy and all the Wagnerians be executed as traitors. Willy, who still defended Wagner's music, asked, "If I like tea, does that make me a . . . Chinese?"[80] The war was whipping up nationalism and the hatred of anything German; Wagner was the symbol of the German soul. By recalling that Willy had collaborated with Berger, Colette was giving his enemies more ammunition.

Willy was now living in Geneva with Madeleine de Swarte. At the onset of war, he had fled Brussels when the Germans invaded Belgium. He was more famous than ever; his book *Siska's Friends (Les Amis de Siska),* written with Curnonsky, sold some two hundred and forty thousand copies; he was under contract with Albin Michel. For the third time, he had changed his looks; he now wore a bowler, a monocle, and a mustache. *L'Echo de Paris* gave him an advance of one thousand francs to write "objective articles" from neutral Switzerland, but only one was printed, his idea of objectivity differing from that of *L'Echo's* editors. He joined the staff of *La Suisse,* the francophone newspaper, and signed sketches and shows for the Swiss stage, thirty-seven titles in all — some were performed in Parisian cabarets. He did not refrain from Germanophobe jokes. When the Swiss authorities asked him to dispense with them, he translated the famous English musical, *The Geisha.* He befriended the surrealist poet Tristan Tzara and his friends, who proclaimed that there was "nothing, nothing, nothing." Willy did not share in their nihilism, but could not resist their love for mystification. He answered an ad placed by a Swiss widow looking for a husband; posing as the director of "an enriched guano factory, soon to be converted into inflammable materials,"[81] he told her that he had lost his wife, who had been decapitated in a train accident in a tunnel; only her torso was found. This surreal correspondence, which lasted several months, was published in his novel, *The End of Vice (La Fin du Vice),* in 1925.

His need for money was endless as he kept on gambling away all his earnings. He asked the Society of Authors for help and got none; but Guillaume Apollinaire, who until his death kept up a correspondence with Willy, came to his rescue in *Le Mercure de France.* He wrote about the difficulties encountered by writers trying to make a living in Paris — "That is why Willy, who is one of our best observers of Parisian milieux, had to take refuge in Geneva."[82] Difficulties or no, Colette and Willy did not stop lashing out at each other via the media. The production of the musical *Claudine* with Maud Lory in July 1918 provoked a few more sparks, but kept the names of Willy and Colette Willy in the public eye, to their mutual benefit.

Colette needed money; she sold her jewels and some of her manuscripts, enlisting her friends to find buyers. Annie de Pène found someone willing to pay three thousand francs for *The Innocent Libertine,* and Musidora arranged a meeting with Prince Sixte de Bourbon-Parme. "Do you agree with the sum?" asked Colette, cautiously. "Absolutely,"[83] said the prince, who left with the manuscript of one of the *Claudines.*

Life in Paris was getting harder; food was rationed and milk was only allotted to children under three and to old people. The population was getting restless; strikes broke out and battalions rioted, which did not keep Tout-Paris from the première of Jean Cocteau's *Parade* by the Ballets Russes at the Théâtre du Châtelet. *Parade* brought together Erik Satie's first stage music, Massine's first cubist choreography, and a poet's first attempt to express himself without words. For the program of *Parade,* Apollinaire invented a new word to describe poetic reality: Surrealism. The ballet stirred up a small scandal; it was deemed unpatriotic to stage such frivolous slapstick. Cocteau boasted to Colette that *Parade* was as great a scandal as *L'Après-Midi d'un Faune.* It was completely upstaged by the arrival in Paris of General Pershing and the American Expeditionary Corps.

Colette left for Castel Novel to see her daughter, now four, whom she had not seen since the war broke out. The child ran barefoot, spoke English to her nurse, and a heavily accented, provincial French to her mother. Bel-Gazou was exactly what Colette wanted her to be; she was "like those English children, radiant, free, intelligent. . . . "[84] Colette was seduced by the beauty of that "little Eros pushing a wheelbarrow." "My daughter is a darling, what a child movie star she would be!"[85]

During the second part of the year Colette wrote extensively. Henry de Jouvenel was now the private secretary of his friend Anatole de Monzie, newly appointed undersecretary of the navy. Colette published the novelette *Mitsou, How Wisdom Comes to Girls* in installments in *La Vie Parisienne* under the pseudonym "Marie," the name she gave to her imaginary alter ego when she was a little girl. The public did not like the story, a love affair between a lieutenant and a music-hall artist. *Mitsou* was pushed back to the "bad pages" of the *La Vie Parisienne,* the magazine the soldiers took to the trenches. Colette hastily put an end to it. Later she revised the book and signed it.

The money problems of the Jouvenels were overwhelming. The advance for *Les Heures Longues,* a selection of articles published in December, was paying off some furniture bought three years earlier. "You see, plus ça change . . ."[86] she wrote to Wague. Isabelle de Comminges was demanding that Jouvenel pay six thousand francs more per year to raise their illegitimate son Renaud, who was languishing in a boarding school; Jouvenel asked Colette to find a diplomatic way to refuse. She wrote to the former rival who had wanted to shoot her that she was no longer the Colette she had known six years earlier, but another Colette, already "far from the ruthlessness and pride of evil-minded youth."[87] This sobering feeling was made even more acute by the discovery of Jouvenel's young mistress, Germaine Patat. Colette felt threatened by forces she could not control. Jouvenel was to be reintegrated into the armed forces; he told Monzie, now the minister of transport, "If I am killed, you won't have much to say about me. You could write my love life, I give you the book's title, *From the Wandering Jewess to the Vagabond (De la Juive Errante à la Vagabonde)."*[88]

In a state of disarray, Colette lost a manuscript she was taking to a newspaper in the metro; she had no copy. "Well, I am tough, but that evening Sidi found me in bed, shivering . . . by 90°F outside."[89] The last day of the year, Second Lieutenant Jouvenel left to join his unit. As soon as they were apart, they found the words to express their feelings.

The war was in its last months but the population had lost all hope. Jouvenel's unit was fighting in the Oise region; he was with the headquarters as the regimental color bearer. One day he saw a German patrol and, thinking they wanted to surrender, he walked toward them. He got a citation from his unit for this act of bravery and a five-day furlough. Colette was exhilarated by Sidi's citation, which was printed *in extenso* in *Le Matin.* She wrote to all her friends, telling them that Sidi had been "in the thickest of the battle." She asked Wague to find a way to let Missy know about Jouvenel, for she "loves acts of courage."[90] Colette needed to prove to Missy, and maybe to herself, that the choice she had made in marrying Jouvenel had been the right one.

In the fall, just before the armistice, an epidemic of Spanish flu rav-
aged Paris. Thousands died and were buried amid growing indifference;
four years of war and millions of deaths had increased tolerance for suffering. Apollinaire was one of the first to go; he had been an acquaintance from the old days, but having sided with Willy, had disappeared
from Colette's pantheon. The epidemic struck closer when Annie de
Pène died in October. "That such a warm and lively creature can disappear. It is maddening, like a stupidity. I think egoistically, that I will not
hear her voice in our daily telephone conversations, that she will laugh
no more her high-pitched laughter . . . how long am I going to miss it?"[91]

At the flea market, where they hunted for antiques, Colette had
bought Annie an 1830 calendar, bound in blue silk with a painted porcelain cover. For each day of the week, Colette had written, "Monday, go
and visit Annie," "Tuesday, go and visit Annie," and so on. On the last
page she added, "and until the end of my days, it is my only wish"; but
Colette shed no tears for that dear friend. Her behavior during the wake
shocked Liane de Pougy, an unfriendly observer, who noted with dismay
that Colette believed "neither in God nor in the Devil." She was
"dancing and gorging herself" next to the room where "the body of the
woman she loved the day before lay on her deathbed . . . she was clam-
oring 'we shall all go the same way! The dead should not sadden the
living!'. . . Poor Colette," added Liane, "ballooned with blurb, bursting
with resentment, envy, ambition! And it is well known that she wants
the Legion of Honor."[92] Colette went on an eating binge, saying that the
dead were always wrong, and took Annie's daughter Germaine
Beaumont to a restaurant to eat oysters, telling her that food was the
best cure for grief. She turned away from the unavoidable termination
of life to concentrate on its promises. This was a deliberate stance;
"Death does not interest me — not even mine." Dawn was her spiritual
hour, not dusk.

For Colette, her friends never died; she continued to hold conversations with them in her mind, sometimes with the help of a medium. She
went to tarot readers, palm readers, and fortune-tellers. Aware of the ambivalent position of her readers vis-à-vis spiritualism, she warned them
"Don't expect a profession of faith of any kind from me nor any passion
in my visits to the privileged people who fluently read the invisible. It is
curiosity that drives me. . . . Without curiosity I exist no more."

At the onset of war the government forbade any form of palm

reading; thousands of women were being ripped off in their pathetic desire to know if their loved ones were still alive. An underground network of seers soon sprouted; Colette, informed through the grapevine, went to Rue Caulaincourt to "the sleeping medium, whose emaciated face and body frightened the faint of heart." Not being one of the faint, Colette often came to listen to "indiscreet truths." At one seance, the medium told her that she saw a man Colette identified as Captain Colette and assured her that he was looking after her. "Why now?" "Because you are what he would have liked to be, but couldn't."

Efforts to recall Sido failed; instead, Achille appeared. "I have never seen so sad a dead man," exclaimed the medium. Colette felt "vaguely jealous,"[93] for she imagined her mother taking care of her brother or busy somewhere else. In the great beyond Sido kept on pursuing her own life, too independent, too elusive to be captured by any medium.

These seances gave Colette "something to dream about, something to touch my heart." Although Sido was convinced that there was nothing after death, no coming back, and that Colette "should not wait for the slightest sign," Colette never shared that belief entirely. She reported the conversation with Captain Colette to Claude Farrère, who also believed in some form of afterlife, "I am so overcome with joy that your seer saw him standing behind you, so proud of you who have become what he wanted so much for himself."[94] Colette never went as far as some members of Lorrain's *Petite Classe,* like Jeanne de la Vaudère. The priestess of the spiritual beyond, author of *Mortal Embrace, The Half-Sexes,* and *The Androgynes,* Jeanne had retired and lived in her château of Parigné-l'Evêque where, it was rumored, she communicated by torchlight with her parents, whose glass coffins lay in the cellar.

A newcomer in Colette's entourage, Francis Carco, was at the beginning of a very successful literary career. He had caused some ripples with the release of his first book of poems, *Instincts.* He gathered a group of friends and journalists, whose names read like an intellectual Gotha Almanac (the *Who's Who* of the aristocracy), under the gaslight in the narrow, medieval Rue Visconti. Most came in top hat and tails; Carco, his pale, chubby face hidden by a fringe of black hair, wearing an undersized dinner jacket and an oversized, overstarched shirt, read his poetry in the street. Colette had met him at *L'Eclair* in Annie de Pène's office;

he had just published a well-received first novel, *Jésus la Caille,* set in the Montmartre underworld. Colette raised her two arms in a familiar gesture. "So you are Carco, and Jésus la Caille, where is he?" "But . . . he is downstairs, hustling." "Oh, my Colette," exclaimed a glamorous socialite who was with her, "Did you hear that? Hustling!"[95]

Colette struck up an instant friendship with the rotund young man, born François Marie Alexandre Carcopino-Tusoli, whose father, like Captain Colette, had been a civil servant in French Guiana. Carco was the black sheep in a family of career diplomats and historians. He barely finished high school and moved to Montmartre to write and paint. To eat, he stole bread and milk delivered at dawn to the steps of bourgeois buildings and, being well dressed, never attracted the attention of the concierges. He tried out a singing career in provincial music halls under the name "Jacques d'Ayguières," did some ghostwriting, and was part of the camarilla of young writers who surrounded Willy in Paris or Brussels. Carco collaborated on two Willy novels, but came to share Colette's hatred for Willy, who had painted him in *Siska's Friends* as a drag queen. "I opted for Colette. . . . I knew from Willy that Colette was not easy to live with."[96]

She liked Carco. "I have adopted you, Carco. There is no adoption without — at least — the illusion of protection."[97] Carco received the ultimate present from Colette, a ream of crisp, blue paper, the gentlest to the writer's eyes. She thought they were kindred spirits: "I have the feeling that we think in the same language." She was intrigued by his depiction of Montmartre, "A beautiful closed world, somber and simple, where three hundred words of argot are enough to express everything." She saw in this sobriety of expression the main virtue of slang, for it "almost suppresses conversation, allowing that closed society to stay true to itself,"[98] a notion extremely appealing to Colette, a minimalist idiom supplemented by an involved body language. She liked "the strange bureaucracy of the prostitutes' existence, their austere way of life, with no laughter," the tragic dimension of the underworld. "You are the master of that type of literature. . . ," and piece by piece, she analyzed Carco's books with the patience and modesty of a disciple. She arranged to have one of his books published in *L'Oeuvre.* She paid him the ultimate compliment: "If Jean Lorrain were still alive, he would be kneeling in awe."[99] With Carco Colette would again explore the fringes of society. He was heavily addicted to opium and occasionally entered a clinic to be detoxified.

The war over, the old dance halls, which had fallen into oblivion, were enjoying a revival; the nightlife and intellectual center moved from Montmartre to Montparnasse. France danced to the tunes of the tango, the foxtrot, and the new "Negro dances," led by foreign soldiers noisily celebrating the Victory. The halls from the Rue de Lappe to the Rue des Anglais, made famous by Lorrain, had reopened. It was the heyday of Le Père Lunette and Mimile Vacher's dance hall on Rue Monge, where a long narrow hallway, with room for only one customer at a time, led to a packed dance hall. One evening in a bal musette (a dance hall that featured accordion music) on Rue de Lappe that belonged to Rodilon Albaret, Marcel Proust's ex-manservant and chauffeur, the crowd became rowdy and the police made "a brutal entrance" and pummeled the patrons with their rolled capes, weighted with lead in the seams. Standing on a table, Colette cried out, "At last some poetry!"[100]

Carco, Colette, and her lover, an unnamed, glamorous socialite Colette described as "appetizing," went to cafés that "bowled Colette over." She had seen many disreputable, yet to a certain extent fashionable, places; Carco showed her the seamy side. "We rambled from street to street from the Place d'Italie to the Gobelins," and they stopped at a dilapidated caf'conc to listen to amateur vaudevillists and aging singers in red sequined dresses — "the place was not safe . . ."[101] They often went for tea to L'Etincelle, a homosexual meeting place.

Carco befriended painters struggling to make a living — Picasso and his friends, and Modigliani, whose works were traded in the Montmartre cafés; Carco was dealing in paintings. Colette asked him to put a collection together; her tastes were classical. She did not like cubism, which ignored perspective, "that mysterious thing somehow divine."[102] She was attracted by Turner and the mists of Corot; she liked some Claude Monet. She said she would sell all the cubists and art-deco artists for a sculpture of a panther by Fritz Behn, famous for his statues of Nijinsky and Caruso. Carco advised her to buy several Modiglianis he had in store, but she refused, preferring to invest in watercolors by Chas Laborde, Charmy, and Dignimont.

Colette entrusted Carco to the woman who had become her most constant companion, the poet Hélène Picard, who wrote intense sensual verses. Her first book of poems, L'Instant Eternel, won the Académie Française poetry award in 1903; the following year the jury of the Prix Fémina awarded her the title of Poet Laureate for a poem on George

Sand. She had been part of Colette's entourage since 1915, when she separated from her husband, a civil servant, to settle in Paris and live close to Colette. The poet fascinated Colette. Born in 1873, the same year as Colette, she had been raised in a garrison town and had lived not far from the red-light district. Her tales about "the boarders were so weird that they were hard to believe."[103] Hélène collaborated with Colette at *Le Matin;* she became her "benevolent secretary" and was entrusted with Colette's professional and private affairs.

Colette and Henry de Jouvenel were both attracted by the beautiful, frail, blonde Germaine Patat, a fashion designer and a remarkable businesswoman who made a fortune exporting her creations to South and North America. Hers was the first company founded by a woman to be traded on the French stock exchange. In their trio, Germaine was the strong, equanimous, understanding force. Colette's correspondence with her covers sixteen years; like all her lovers she called Germaine "my child" and turned to her whenever she needed advice, money, or had messages for Jouvenel. She also entrusted Germaine with the education of her daughter, Bel-Gazou. Their friendship became the theme of Colette's novel *The Other One (La Seconde),* published in 1929.

New friends did not replace old ones, however; Colette kept in touch with Missy, Princess Ghika, José Maria and Misia Sert, Barthou, minister of education, and Georges Wague, who had been appointed professor of mime at Le Conservatoire National d'Art Dramatique (thanks to Colette), where he taught a new generation of actors from Jean-Louis Barrault to Marcel Marceau. In June 1919 Colette gave a lecture at the Trianon Lyrique on "Wague and Pantomime," reiterating her love for this wordless form of art. Sacha Guitry had become the favorite playwright and actor of the *théâtre du boulevard.* Musidora, at the zenith of her career as an actress-director, kept in touch with her "dear godmother" when not "dear mother." And Colette answered, "of your old and saintly mother, my dear child, anyone can say what they want but not that she produced a mediocre child."[104] Colette had learned from Sido how animals push their brood out of the nest for the next litter. Musi was set free to be replaced by Germaine Beaumont, Annie de Pène's daughter, a writer and poet who became Colette's secretary at *Le Matin.*

In 1919 Meg Villars returned from the United States and landed at

Boulevard Suchet; she had yet to divorce Willy, which she did the following year. She soon became Henry de Jouvenel's mistress in an occasional ménage à trois. She was the Parisian correspondent for *The Tatler;* for twenty-five years she wrote an entertainment and society column signed "Priscilla."

The first summer of peace was spent at Rozven with Meg Villars, Germaine Beaumont, Hélène Picard, Germaine Patat, Jeanne Diris, Jeanne Landre, (one of Willy's recent collaborators), Bel-Gazou, and Sidi, who deserved the nickname "Pasha" more than ever. Carco and Colette's future collaborator, the playwright Léopold Marchand, the son of the owners of the Folies Bergère and L'Olympia, were often invited.

Carco recalled that one morning at breakfast, Colette greeted Hélène Picard "with such a concupiscent look." Keeping her gaze on the poet, she went to get a pair of long scissors and, without a word, slowly walked up to Hélène and cut her hair. Hélène uttered in a doleful and childish voice, "Oh my Colette! My Colette!" "You look much better. And now breakfast! Sit where you like, my children!"[105]

Carco became the focus of their erotic games. Hélène Picard took very "indecent" photographs of him; "Without knowing it, I was the object of a feminine conspiracy." Colette was never more interested than when she could observe the doings and undoings of relationships within her charmed circle. Carco wrote of Colette, "the fox knew how to defend herself; she did not refuse to mingle with men, but it was to have them at her discretion."[106] She declared that in Rozven she wanted "neither to read, nor write nor think," a pronouncement usually indicative of an imminent intense creative phase, preceded by strenuous physical activities. She swam three times a day; she went crabbing, and seining for prawns. During the full moon she spent most of the night fishing for flatfish. It was not enough to clear her mind; she plunged into her woods "to clear the forest slope of the old underbrush, to cut a stairway in the hill, to exhume a small pine wood, which had been buried for years, from a coppice of brambles and thorns."[107] Germaine Beaumont felt she was watching a primitive ceremony, with Colette a sort of druidess, scratching the soil with her bare hands, cutting and pulling in a frenzy. Colette was getting ready for her next novel, *Chéri.*

—◊◊◊—

By 1919 France, who had lost ten and a half percent of her productive male population and had over one million permanently disabled, wanted only to forget, and books about the war held little appeal. Colette's *The Longest Hour (Les Heures Longues)* and *In the Crowd (Dans la Foule)* did not sell, despite the usual good reviews.

Paris was alive; a vast number of foreigners thronged the city and European royalty brought glamour to the capital. There was a gala ball for the queen of Belgium, whose courage during the German invasion had won the admiration of the French, there was a ball at the British Embassy, where Tout-Paris bowed and curtsied before the royal couple. Elsa Maxwell, the American journalist, socialized on a shoestring. During the peace conference, politicians and statesmen descended on the capital; suffragettes like Christabel Pankhurst lobbied intensively for women's rights.

Colette and Jouvenel were back at *Le Matin,* which still kept two alternating editors in chief who took turns every fortnight. This had, "among other advantages, that of creating a little cat-and-dog fight between . . . Stéphane Lauzanne and Henry de Jouvenel."[108] But Jouvenel, by controlling every detail and by caring for his staff members "with the best part of his earnings," was building up a following. Colette rejoined the paper as a reporter-at-large; in June she became literary editor, in December drama critic. By the end of 1919 Colette and Henry de Jouvenel were overseeing *Le Matin,* he the political pages, she the literary and entertainment news. Colette attended opening nights armed with a pair of black opera glasses; in 1920 she reviewed over fifty plays. She contributed reviews to *L'Eclair, La Revue de Paris, Le Journal,* and *Le Petit Parisien.*

Her work as a drama critic was striking and totally new: she had firsthand knowledge of the stage's professional aspects and was not only interested in the text, the set, the actors, and the directors, but also in the audience as a part of the show. She reviewed with equal thoroughness every variety of show business: the circus and La Comédie Française, tragedies and modern drama, Ibsen, Shakespeare, children's theater, Les Folies Bergère or Le Casino Paris, Maurice Chevalier, Joséphine Baker, and Mistinguett.

At six in the evening, almost daily, Colette arrived at *Le Matin,* a building painted dark red. She dressed in a strictly tailored suit and wore tight boots and a tiny hat covered in a short veil with large velvet dots that made her eyes look larger and even more fiery. In winter she warmed her hands in a muff of otter fur. She went straight to Henry de Jouvenel's sumptuous suite of offices to discuss the business of the day before repairing to her office by a small staircase to meet with her secretaries. She put on "her magnificent tortoiseshell glasses, which made her look like a young doctor"[109] and expedited the daily report. Her enormous and regular workload as a journalist would have been overwhelming had she not learned from Willy — and that master journalist, Saglio — how to delegate. Hélène Picard, Claude Chauvière, and Germaine Beaumont did some of the work, went to opening nights, and took notes.

How did she manage to work so intensely? She slept seven hours a night and often catnapped a few minutes as she sat at her desk. She ate enormously; not only did she have a box of chocolate handy, but Arthème Fayard (the slim, appetiteless publisher) was astonished to see Colette enjoy a snack of hearty wine and cheese as she worked at her desk cluttered with papers, proofs, and books. Her office looked like an actress's dressing room; it was filled with bouquets and the walls were covered with photographs, caricatures, and sketches. On her sleek American desk she kept a photograph of Gabriele d'Annunzio wearing the Arditi uniform, inscribed, "To Colette in remembrance of Rome, Fiume, September 1920." After the war, d'Annunzio, who felt that Italy had been treated unfairly by the Allies, gathered a thousand volunteers and captured the town of Fiume. The d'Annunzio expedition was denounced by the French Government. But Colette liked his baroque *grandezza:* "Not bad at all . . . Hurray for the theatrics. He took Fiume, he is quite a man. This is how I understand politics, pure opera!"[110]

Colette's office was in stark contrast with Henry de Jouvenel's offices on the second floor, where liveried ushers guided visitors up the great staircase or handed over papers and mail to Jouvenel in grand style. She was intellectually unpretentious and unassuming; an assistant editor could send her text back, indicating what he wanted her to modify, and she would do it. One day someone crossed out "pregnant woman"; Colette asked what word he wanted her to substitute for the proper term. She was patient, even humble when it came to improving her trade. Sapène, the commercial director of *Le Matin,* had shown her how to extract "the maximum of juice from the minimum of words," and how to review a play in twenty lines. She was grateful to Sapène for having taught her that a journalist should always, at any cost, be in the thick of things. He had once rolled himself and his camera in a carpet to be in the conference room where diplomats were to meet. She credited Sapène for her scoop with Queen Marie of Rumania. At six o'clock on a gray morning on March 5, 1919, Colette waited for the royal train at a small provincial station. Hopping aboard with an armful of orchids, she was led into the royal compartment at quarter to eight and granted an exclusive interview. In Paris Colette stepped off the train with her story ready; all the other reporters were preparing to board it to interview the queen.

She helped many hopeful writers who came to submit stories to her by analyzing their work. She told Georges Simenon, "You're too literary. Cut out all the literature and it will work. . . ." "That was the most useful advice I ever had in my life,"[111] asserted the master of suspense.

She told Renée Hamon to follow her first impression, to avoid rare words, and never to lie, because lying develops the imagination and "imagination is death to the reporter," to guard herself against the temptation of lyricism, and never to write the report on the spot. "One does not write a love story while one is making love."[112]

Her advice to the aspiring novelist Germaine Beaumont was not to be "too concise."[113] To condense too much frustrates the reader who has to make too much of an intellectual effort and soon loses interest. Colette told her to use her senses for descriptions: first the eye, then the nose, and only then, the ear. She said she should always interrupt her work by taking a walk or drinking a cup of tea. Reading was extremely important, she averred, even if some books were boring; without it, one ended up with a cramped style and lost all lucidity and sense of criticism. Writing was an exercise that required as much discipline as any athletics.

She told Claude Chauvière never to settle down, to always be on the move, to avoid becoming old. She believed in sport and "mental sport," a constant alertness, a constant, ever changing curiosity. Debauchery, meaning excess whether in work or pleasure, profited only by accident and harmed daily work; if you were drunk or exhausted, you could write a short story or a novella, but that was the limit. "I have never believed in debauchery, I think I was right."[114]

She was no less demanding when it came to her own writing. Well aware of the value of her work, she was one of the best-paid journalists in France; the director of *Les Nouvelles Littéraires* was appalled by the sum she quoted for a paper. "But André Gide asks a quarter of your price!"

Colette answered coolly, "Gide is wrong. If we the famous ones ask a low price, what will the others get?"[115]

In 1918 Rachilde had predicted that Colette would become one of the great journalists. She created her own genre, writing a journal-like text filled with impressions of people and things, lyrical pages on nature, and thoughtful pages on daily events. She wrote about a soldier dreaming of the carpet he would have at home when the war was over, about the workman who ate a piece of bread on the steps of the metro, about the joy of the barber who spent Sunday in the fields, about her three-year-old daughter ruling the chicken coop at Castel Novel, about the dogs trained to find wounded soldiers. She reported on a boxing championship, a parliamentary session, the peace talks at Versailles, the tour de France, murder trials, car accidents. She described passersby watching street pavers, and chickadees making love in her garden. She wrote about the pain of animals tortured by humans: the little goat carried to market by its tied legs, blinded by its own blood; the humble rabbit with an eye torn out; the birds raised for food and killed by crushing their beaks. Nothing was ever indifferent in her columns; the slightest incident exploded with meaning. When she wrote about captive animals in the zoo, she touched on their right to happiness and freedom in such a disturbing manner that the reader felt guilty.

## The Genius Who Wrote *Chéri*

The year 1920 started with the serialization of *Chéri*, a story of the love of a nineteen-year-old boy for a forty-nine-year-old courtesan. Colette had written a short story for *Le Matin* in August 1911 about a young man called Clouk, because of the slight click or "clouk" made by his nostril with every breath. He was rich, weak, and had an older, tyrannical mistress. Clouk alternated with the character named Chéri, also rich and weak, with a tyrannical, older mistress. But Chéri's main feature was his beauty. In 1912 Colette wrote four stories about Chéri in *Le Matin* and four about Clouk. The elaboration of *Chéri* was arduous; Colette complained it was hard to write, that writing was a sort of curse; she thought at the time that *Chéri* was the best of her works. She was so eager to have Proust's opinion that she sent him the galleys before proofreading them, explaining that *Chéri* was a kind of novel she had never written before; the others she had written "once or twice." She meant that *The Innocent Libertine, The Vagabonde,* and *Recaptured* were variations on a theme, a repetition "of some vague Claudine."[116] *Chéri* was different; she had written it without clinging to anyone for emotional support. "It was the first time in my life that I felt entirely sure to have written a novel about which I would neither blush nor have doubt. . . ."[117] In intellectual circles *Chéri* was extremely well received. Proust called Colette "the genius who wrote *Chéri*."[118] André Gide rapturously congratulated Colette for her daring and her understanding of the least admitted secrets of the flesh. Anna de Noailles memorized some of Colette's pages. Montherlant wrote that he could not hold back exclamations of admiration. Georges Duhamel said, "We are all small fry compared to you."[119]

Colette's standing in literary milieux remained ambiguous; paradoxically, she was never published by a major literary press. She was generally considered a writer who expressed female sensibility; she had been ignored by the *Nouvelle Revue Française,* which had replaced the aging *Mercure de France* in setting new literary trends. Now the *N.R.F.* praised *Chéri* and called Colette a writer reborn. However, there were some powerful discordant voices: Souday in *Le Temps* deplored that Colette had abandoned naturalism and in so doing, her true voice. She should leave objective psychological studies to men, "for women only know how to write, even in novels, about their personal perceptions."[120] Jean de Pierrefeu criticized Colette for letting the unconscious take over her characters, thus appealing to the lowest levels of society; he felt that her art, which rejected culture and aesthetic refinement, turned humans into animals: "No one has more genius than Colette, but she has too much genius to go on degrading it."[121] Colette sent a letter to Pierrefeu asking why he thought her novel degrading when she had never written anything as moral as *Chéri,* wondering how the study of sufferings could be vile.

From January to the fifth of June, *Chéri* appeared in installments in *La Vie Parisienne.* It was then published by Charles Saglio, who did not pay the promised sum for the novel soon enough; Colette, always in need of money, flew into a rage and refused to dine with him, accusing him of trying to exploit her. She declared that she would remain Lucie Saglio's friend, but was dropping Charles out of her life. To win her back, Lucie gave her a rare ebony tree to plant in her garden; Charles promptly sent a cup of blue crystal filled with chocolate. Colette's wrath melted only when Lucie wrote that she had wept reading *Chéri*. When Colette received a sumptuous pineapple decked with grapes and apples from Charles in January of 1924, she reminded him affectionately how many times they had quarreled and made up over the years and thanked the Saglios for their unwavering friendship.

Henry de Jouvenel had come back from the front with a sense of frustration. He used *Le Matin* to vent his anger, "It never occurred to us that soldiers were a minority in France, that the home front saw beauty in the war, that governing had never been easier than during these four years and that victory would not remove the men in place."[122] Veterans agreed with him; Jouvenel founded the Federal Union of Veterans, and *Le Matin* organized an enormously successful National Convention of Veterans.

It became obvious that if Jouvenel wanted to play a decisive role in postwar politics, he had to run for office. "On his own initiative, he would never run for election," said Anatole de Monzie, "but I was ambitious for him."[123] In the summer of 1919 Sidi was at Castel Novel campaigning for a seat in the chamber of deputies; the radical party of Corrèze preferred a long-standing, dues-paying member. Jouvenel conceded the point and ran the following year as an independent candidate. During that year he led a stirring campaign in *Le Matin* for the burial of the Unknown Soldier beneath the Arc de Triomphe. He also managed to bring together the leaders of several unions of intellectuals — a political masterstroke. A survey conducted by *Le Matin* had revealed the lack of solidarity and the appalling economic status of French intellectuals: the teachers, scientists, engineers, musicians, actors, writers, and journalists. Henry de Jouvenel cajoled each of their representatives into a meeting, where he had the floor to himself. After a couple of hours, he managed to federate them under the "neutral auspices" of *Le Matin*. The Confederation of Intellectual Workers was the first of its kind; it grew to some fifteen thousand members and was imitated in twelve countries. Three years later, in the Sorbonne's grand amphitheater, *Le Matin* convened an international meeting of intellectual workers. Henry de Jouvenel solemnly confederated them.

In January of 1921 he was elected to the senate for nine years. He registered with the Radicals, then with the Radical-Socialist

Democratic Left; at times, he changed his status to "unaffiliated," to finally settle on "Independent Leftist." In two years Senator Jouvenel made twenty speeches on topics ranging from physical education to the Bank of China; his admirers said they "were equally meaningful and thoughtful," while his detractors said Jouvenel expressed his bafflements so articulately that at times they resembled convictions. But they all agreed with Paul Valéry, that "he conceived easily and had a natural relish for ideas."[124]

At *Le Matin* Jouvenel's trademark was to open his columns to contradictory opinions, to play host to "the happy diversity of minds.... Many hypotheses are needed to make a science and many discussions to achieve an average of truth. Constant polemics make headlines."[125] But he realized that polemics were often based on false news, so he proposed an international agreement to punish certain forms of misinformation, including tendentious reports, incorrect headlines, and even omissions. International watch groups would report any infraction to an international tribunal of the media. "Do we not, O journalists, see the blood, strength, and faith that are left in this country flow out of the hundred wounds our polemics inflict every day?"

Jouvenel's political notions were based on the same concept; he saw a nation tired "of parliamentary groups and of local politicians . . . a nation more and more eager for a policy . . . that would guarantee man the right to live, the right to work and the right to progress and would guarantee the country the right to pride and the right to glory." This vision was the platform of Jouvenel's "Unknown Party." He set himself up as the Republic's censor, but he also "became its prodigal errand boy, carrying out for it an extraordinary number of missions abroad." Jouvenel was the hero, yet never the leader, and in refusing to accept the politicization of his ideas, Jouvenel found himself without a following and without a coherent program. In *A Great Experiment: The League of Nations,* Lord Robert Cecil gave this assessment: "Henry, with all his brains, was not prepared to take enough trouble to achieve success." He was a brilliant dilettante and a *jouisseur.*

Lordly and gracious, Senator Jouvenel used every means at his disposal to modernize the Corrèze region: paved roads, electricity, and even an airport near tiny Varetz, which became the only village of three hundred inhabitants with such a modern feature. In the summer, Baron and Baronne de Jouvenel arrived in their chauffeur-driven limousine with the cook, the maid, Gamelle the dog, and their Persian cat. On Sundays, they hosted the people of Varetz; sometimes in the evening, they gave "cultural soirees" where only the local dialect was spoken. Colette supported Jouvenel's political career, attending meetings whenever her presence could help her husband, giving dinners; her prewar public image had to be modified and she was aware of it. Her new position at *Le Matin* sent the right signal; Colette was now totally focused on her literary career, becoming the *grande dame* of French letters.

This transformation would have been easier without Willy, who never forgave Colette for having spread rumors that he never wrote a line. His brother, killed blowing up the dreaded Grosse Bertha, the cannon that bombarded Paris, was a war hero, while Willy, hounded by creditors, could not even go back to chair the family business. In his self-derogatory style, he described himself as rejected and ruined, and in his book *Ginette the Dreamer (Ginette la Rêveuse),* manipulated by a woman writer, obviously Colette. In a facetious and mean preface, Willy explained that the book was the counterpart of *Claudine at School.* This time it was not the diary of an adolescent but the confession written by a woman on her deathbed. He said that he could not publish the weird confessions in full and had to rewrite them entirely. First he had to cut out whole chapters full of lesbian scenes that the author (read Colette) had plagiarized from Pierre Louÿis's *Chansons de Bilitis,* or Renée Vivien's *A Woman Came to Me.* He had to delete entire paragraphs lifted from Rachilde, even from his own *Lélie, fumeuse d'opium.* "Was it stupid kleptomania . . . ,"[126] asked Willy, or was it to hurt him? He ridiculed Colette's descriptions, saying that she put the wrong trees in the wrong climate such as cypresses and olive trees in Burgundy. He was referring to the blunder in *A Clean Little Old Man,* a novel signed "Willy". Colette, at his request, had written a description of a Mediterranean landscape, but had then decided to transfer the plot to Burgundy. The text was not edited, leaving the hero spitting from his window in Burgundy into the waves of the Mediterranean sea five hundred miles away. Colette in turn attributed this blunder to Willy in *My Apprenticeships (Mes Apprentissages).* This preface, which held no meaning for readers, was transparent to their entourage. Willy's characters reminded them of Sido, Captain Colette, and Achille. Playing on Colette's dread of illness he made his heroine die of syphillis, which she had caught by going to bed with an old poet. In his novels Willy kept making innuendos about Colette and mocked her in

*Mademoiselle Thulette's Virginity (La Virginité de Mademoiselle Thulette).* Willy was under contract with Albin Michel, the well-established Parisian publisher. His books were extensively reviewed, his name constantly in the press. *Ginette the Dreamer* could not and did not go unnoticed.

Nobody infuriated Colette more than Willy. She was so perturbed by his attacks that she could not stop raging about him at a dinner attended by Princess Ghika, who noted in her diary, "April 4, 1920 . . . I dined at Madame Gillou's with Colette, who rules the whole literary section of *Le Matin*. She started to vilify Willy horribly. We were embarrassed." In the course of the evening she attacked Willy relentlessly, swearing that he had never written a line of his novels and had exploited her as a ghostwriter. Willy was being sued by a Belgian ghostwriter for nonpayment of royalties and was arguing that it was his publisher's responsibility, not his. To make her point, Colette pulled out "revealing papers from her purse. . . . It was painful," said Princess Ghika, who thought her stupid not to see that this defamation and hatred were odious, even ridiculous. "Maybe she is still in love with Willy who was her first victim and whose sad situation excites her resentment." She noted that Colette was not happy with Henry de Jouvenel, whom "she stole" from Isabelle de Comminges, that she felt "betrayed, rejected, treated badly."[127]

Jouvenel had never asked his first wife not to use the title "baronne de Jouvenel." The situation was demeaning for Colette, as the influential first baronne was immersed in international politics, and the peace conference filled her salon with foreign diplomats. Claire Boas, baronne de Jouvenel, was committed to the idea of an independent Czechoslovakia; she put the Czech Eduard Benes in touch with Aristide Briand, the French premier. Czechoslovakia was an idea conceived in her salon, which prevailed when the peace treaty was discussed. To receive the delegates who came to Paris, she organized La Bienvenue Française and Le Club Interallié. Foreign politics were not Claire's only interest: Marie Curie's friend, she launched *La Journée Pasteur* to raise money for scientific research and created exchange scholarships and welfare funds. She found some relaxation in writing and published maxims and fairy tales under the name "Ariel" in several newspapers, including *Le Matin*. Claire's wealth and influence made her a most visible baronne de Jouvenel, creating embarrassing moments; even the presidential Palais de l'Elysée did not know how to handle the situation. When Henry de Jouvenel received an invitation to an official dinner addressed to him alone, he replied, "Every evening I dine with Colette, baronne de Jouvenel." President Poincaré sent an excuse and an amended invitation.

Under Colette's growing pressure, Jouvenel finally asked Claire to stop using his name, but she was set on keeping it. A subtle diplomat, she sent her son Bertrand de Jouvenel, sixteen, with a bunch of flowers, on a mission to appease Colette. In February of 1920 an embarrassed and unhappy teenager arrived at Boulevard Suchet to meet his father's second wife. He was led into the drawing room, where he retreated behind the piano in the darkest part of the room. The door was thrown open. Colette walked in briskly, saw no one, and said to herself, "But where can the child be?"[128] She spotted Bertrand and marched up to him promptly, a short, stocky, swift, and powerful woman. He was taller than she, and as she approached she raised her head and her curly hair slipped across her forehead. Years later he would describe "the majesty" of her forehead, the beauty of her eyebrows, the perfect triangular shape of her nostrils. Her eyes were heavily made up with kohl and she wore a thick coat of lipstick, yet her mouth was shaped with a fine, curving line. Bertrand was struck by Colette; he felt she had a strange, overwhelming power. Later he noticed that she walked by throwing her leg from the hip without bending her knees — a swift gait, reminiscent of the marquise de Morny's. At first glance there was a flash of attraction between them. He easily obtained the permission Claire Boas requested; for his sake there would be two baronnes de Jouvenel.

Bertrand's visit was followed by Colette's to Claire Boas; it took only twenty minutes for them to become "old friends."[129] She invited Claire to come to Castel Novel for Easter to join the whole family; although Claire was tempted, she decided to remain in Paris, entrusting Bertrand to Colette. Jouvenel was delighted; Colette could sense in him the serenity of a pasha happy with his peaceful harem. She wrote to her "dear soul," Marguerite Moréno, that Bertrand was charming, very tall, very slim, a passionate reader of history, politics, and economics, and an athlete who practiced running and boxing. He had lived the charmed life of a protected heir between his paternal grandfather, set on making him an old-time gentleman, and his doting maternal grandmother. He often stayed at her estate in Montmorency. She was very refined; with her delicate fingers she would play endlessly with rose petals, which she always kept in a precious bowl on a table next to her chair. Bertrand loved the civil, slow-paced ambience, the arbor covered with creeping vines, the pond covered with water lilies. Money was never mentioned. Bertrand heard for the first time that his family was extremely wealthy when a fellow student mentioned it to him.

Bertrand's paternal grandfather, Léon de Jouvenel, was an archconservative who resented Henry's position at *Le Matin* and his political commitment to the radical-socialist left. His reaction was to make a conservative of Bertrand. At Castel Novel, Bertrand was awed to discover that Mamita, his paternal grandmother, had had an affair and that his aunt Edith was illegitimate. In that wealthy and sophisticated milieu, illegitimacy was more easily accepted than divorce, which Bertrand found out very early in life. He was playing in a park when a lady he did not know said, "You must not play with my daughter, because your mother is a divorcée."[130] He had seldom seen his father, and never his half brother Renaud, known as "le petit Comminges" (for he did not bear the name of his illegitimate father).

Bertrand spent the summer with Colette and the ever present Germaine Beaumont, Germaine Patat, and Hélène Picard. Colette gave Bertrand books she loved, books written by her friends when she was a young woman: Marcel Schwob, Jean de Tinan, Marcel Proust. *Chéri* had just been published. She inscribed a copy for him, which read "A mon fils *Chéri* [To my *Darling* son] Bertrand de Jouvenel."

Bertrand noticed that the three women looked at him, whispered, and laughed a lot. One evening Colette talked to Bertrand privately and asked him which of the three women he found the most attractive; he did not understand the question and gallantly answered that they were all equally charming. Colette added that he should become a man; Bertrand still did not understand the meaning of her words. Another evening as she said goodnight to him, she kissed him on the lips. Bertrand almost dropped the oil lamp he was carrying, but Colette said simply, "Hold the lamp steady."[131]

Germaine Beaumont, at thirty-eight the youngest of the three women, was put in charge of educating Bertrand, and invited him to her room; he left in the middle of the night, defeated and weeping. Colette opened her door and called him in. This licentious interlude turned into a love affair. The Greeks deemed such a fatal attraction a curse of the gods and made it the stuff of tragedy, but there was nothing tragic in this romance, which lasted five years. She was forty-seven; he was sixteen.

Having adopted Bertrand, Colette also adopted Renaud. His mother, Isabelle de Comminges, constantly reminded him that his maternal ancestors went back to the Crusades, while his father's nobility was, at best, recent. In 1920 Renaud was in an English boarding school, neglected by both parents, who forgot to pay his board and tuition. The forlorn twelve-year-old was subjected to psychological abuse and begged his father to pay, since his mother would not, and added sheepishly that he would like to see him. He never met Isabelle de Comminges's three legimate children by her husband, Count Pillet-Will. She was terribly cold: "I don't wish a mother like that to anyone. It's enough to traumatize a child for life." His judgment on his father was no less uninviting — "he made himself feared."[132]

Colette found Renaud "terribly fascinating, charming, wild, destructive." At Rozven she discovered new joys: "If you could only see . . . Sidi-Neptune surrounded by his little tritons, Bertrand, Renaud, Colette II and his stout triton, me. . . ."[133]

Renaud was a deeply frustrated child, a nuisance to his mother and a burden to his father. His role model as a child had been Auguste Hériot, his mother's lover for two years after Colette had left him for Jouvenel. By a strange twist of fate, Colette gave Renaud his first taste of family life; she took him in, giving him a room decorated with Chinese artifacts and a sofa bed upholstered in black velvet. When he was sent to a French boarding school, he felt exiled again, but Colette wrote him long, affectionate letters explaining that Bel-Gazou was also going to a boarding school. Colette expressed her feelings better on paper for, according to Renaud, Colette saw children as a burden and was excessively demanding. He and Bel-Gazou were constantly reminded that they were not behaving properly; he felt they were treated with less affection than the dogs. He teamed up with his half sister — "My Caulette . . . was closer to me than anyone, so much that for years she was my shadow."[134]

Colette had little patience with the two children; when her daughter was stung by a wasp at the dinner table, she scolded Bel-Gazou for having excited an insect that meant no harm. Following Sido's principles, she was teaching them to respect animal life. She had a young black puma named Bâtou and a Brazilian squirrel that jumped on people's shoulders and startled Jouvenel, who was not crazy about wildlife. There could be worse; one could find a garden snake winding innocently among the plates on the dinner table. Colette advocated teaching two-year-olds to read and to work. She argued that children do not differentiate between acquired knowledge and games, and that it was a waste of time and intelligence to let them wander freely in the limited realm of a child's consciousness (the hazy domain of imagination) rather than teach them to read, write, and feed their intelligences the way Sido and the captain had once fed hers. Colette had no tolerance for sloth; she came to resent her daughter when it became obvious that Colette II would not follow in her tracks. She used a whip to train her dogs; she did the same to Bel-Gazou. Léo Marchand once snatched her whip away just as she was about to strike her daughter.

The fall of 1920 was a happy time for forty-seven-year-old Colette. On September 21 she received the Legion of Honor; Renaud and Colette II tied red ribbons around her fountain pens and decorated her desk and stationary with red bows and bunting. They counted every letter and telegram: four hundred letters, telegrams from President Poincaré, Sarah Bernhardt, Marquise de Morny, and Princess Ghika.

Marcel Proust and Anna de Noailles were also awarded the Legion of Honor that year; gallant Proust wrote that the red ribbon meant even more to him since he received it at the same time as Colette. This honor meant a lot to her, but had not come easily. The March issue of *Fémina* carried an editorial asking why actresses received the cross of Chevalier de la Légion d'Honneur, while women writers were constantly by-passed? *Fémina* put out a feature article, "The End of a Nonsense," arguing that Colette's red ribbon had been won thanks to the insistence of the press, which had put on pressure, organized petitions, and even a plebiscite. All the literary establishment had been up in arms to obtain this distinction.

On November 11 Paris celebrated the anniversary of the Victory lavishly; the Jouvenels were in the presidential box in the grandstand to witness the burial of an unknown soldier under the Arc de Triomphe and the lighting of the Eternal Flame. Jouvenel's vision had prevailed.

Colette had her first face-lift in 1921. (Tout-Hollywood was coming to Paris for cosmetic surgery in the private clinic of Doctor Dufourmentel.) She also decided to lose weight; she had daily massages.

Colette explained to Léo Marchand that she had set her mind on slimming down, but God was playing tricks on her. It was raining every day, so she drank to comfort herself and ate to forget the weather.

In her quest for the fountain of youth, she tried blood transfusions, checking into a private clinic for a treatment that lasted five days; every day she received a transfusion from an adolescent girl, who was lying next to her. The young blood did not attain the desired result; Colette suddenly had fainting spells and high fever. Yet she declared that her eyesight had improved and that she could breathe better. She never stopped looking for new cures. In 1941 she gave a lecture on the work of Dr. Jaworski, who was injecting his newly found serum of youth into animals in the zoo; old females regained enough youth to be fertile again and give birth to cubs. Colette — then sixty-eight — told her audience that since she could not bring an animal from the zoo, she was presenting "another kind of animal, who had benefited from the same treatment, myself."[135] Over the years she experimented with injections of bird serum, had a second face-lift, and checked in to Swiss clinics for the latest cures.

Colette had a visceral repulsion for physical degradation; even pets had to be healthy. When Annie de Pène's cat was ill, Colette told her to put the cat to sleep promptly, not to prolong its agony or her own pain. Paul Léautaud, the writer who spent his royalties sheltering abandoned and mistreated animals in his home, was shocked to learn that Colette had simply thrown her cat's dead body into the ditch surrounding the fortifications of Paris. After that, he saw Colette as a born lion-tamer, with very little compassion. Carco and Cocteau saw her kill a bird with her own hands, when it became obvious it had no chance of surviving. For her, it was an act of mercy, for them, pure savagery.

Claude Chauvière, who loved Colette enough to leave her husband, attempted to describe her hard-to-fathom personality: she was repulsed by people who were poor, sad, ugly, sick, mentally ill, or unlucky. However, when they came across her path she would help them. Colette had her own way with people, animals, and even plants; she would deprive a bunch of violets of water to force them to give up all their fragrance, admitting that it was cruel, but necessary for what she wanted from them. She behaved the same with people.

She hid a lot of untamed impulses behind good manners. Yet she would suddenly say, of someone who had angered her, that she could pop out his eyeballs with her thumb, her hand slowly mimicking her words. Once she infuriated someone so much that he lunged at her; she knocked him out with a stick. When she saw the fellow unconscious on the floor, she innocently asked her friends what to do with the body. Claude Chauvière said that those who had never been scratched by the claws of "feline Colette" called her cruelty "refreshing" and spoke of her "catlike caress." But there was always a threat in that caress; Colette took, caught, retained, and owned without encountering any resistance from her entourage, which seemed hypnotized by her. If she noticed a spot on a friend's scarf, with a strange animal reflex she would smell it, even lick it with the tip of her tongue, and identify it as greasy or sweet or salty, then pick up a bottle of spot remover immediately and rub off the spot with energy. Some of her tamer friends thought she would fit beautifully in a jungle and said that she preferred animals to people; Colette commented that animals preferred her to any human she knew. In "Assassins," she mused, "I believe that civilized beings cannot charm an animal," that only people with a murderer's instincts attract and tame wild beasts. When she reported on the trial of the mass murderer Landru for *Le Matin,* she commented on "the pleasure of killing," which she described as "the charity of giving death like a caress and blending it with erotic games."[136] She remarked that cats and tigers hug their prey and lick it before they kill it.

Bonmariage, who depicted Colette as cruel, insensitive, and self-centered, added that her redeeming factor was her commitment to hard work. She overtaxed herself to make a living, never helped anyone whom she did not dominate or even own, and inspired the devotion of a cult leader. She was her own universe with its time, space, light, and darkness. She had her own parameters, her own inner laws, and no sense of guilt. She was extremely lucid, "Biographers have a tendency to believe that it is easy to be a 'monster'; that it is as easy as to be a saint. Not so, for the vocation of sainthood demands a certain degree of passivity rather helpful."[137]

She was unapproachable when she worked. She scribbled, tore up, declared she would drop the whole business, and yet went on writing on her blue paper. Devoid of self-complacency, she was a very demanding critic, and "honored her work"[138] with all she could demand of herself. A worker and craftsman, she referred to her books as objects made in pain, with extreme care, with a relentless search for perfection. In her library she kept the *Manuels Roret,* which described every step in every craft, giving the technical vocabulary of the cabinetmaker, the glassblower, the weaver, the pottery maker. The unfolding of the story was of great concern to her. She proceeded page by page, rather than by whole sections, working like a journalist. Since all her novels were first serialized, she adopted the format of the short stories published in *Le Matin:* twelve pages in her handwriting. Dissatisfied, she would begin a new page rather than make corrections. She regularly worked in the afternoon from three to six, wrapped in a blanket, ready to snap or growl at anyone present. She would shout, "Get out!" at her friend-secretary, who promptly vanished; then she would suddenly throw the door open to ask, "You will come back later, won't you?"[139] To relax, Colette played or composed for herself on the piano in her drawing room, or she painted a branch of fuchsia, or a sketch of herself in pastels or watercolors.

In an interview with Frédéric Lefèvre, she repeated that she had never had an urge to write and was never influenced by anybody. She had no passion for what she called "my trade," but did not treat it lightly. She could neither dictate nor type. "I conceive slowly and since I cannot conceive without writing, or write without conceiving . . ."[140]

If one considers that her works fill fifteen volumes (discounting adaptations for the theater, dialogues for films, and countless lectures), if one adds in her enormous correspondence (she wrote five or six letters a day), it is impossible not to speak of an exceptional facility, of a talent flowing with incredible ease. Her constant complaints to her friends and her statements to journalists were a way to diffuse any attempt to discuss her work; she systematically dodged any question. Paul Valéry was the only one with whom Colette could talk shop, in a dialogue they kept to themselves.

The writer who hated to write said she wrote because it was a way of having the luxuries she craved, her *hôtel privé* in Paris, her estate in Brittany, some acres of woods, a rare book, a painting, something that would bring her joy. Colette loved to buy, but did not like to pay; her rapport with money puzzled her friends. To the question, "Do you like money?" she would answer, "I hate it, that is why I put it in jail in my drawer and lock up as much of it as I can."[141]

A lawyer who knew her well said, "Colette is wealthy, but where is the money? Her books are constantly reprinted, she gives well-paid lectures, she writes for several newspapers, not counting *Le Matin.* She must

hoard fortunes." Her manuscripts were selling for "the price of plat-
inum." But Colette's bank account could suddenly go flat; she was interested in ventures like the stock market or movies.

She liked precious stones and was very knowledgeable about them;
she could state their origin, value, and history. She knew who owned
certain famous jewels, that a string of black pearls the size of walnuts was
a gift from the emperor of Japan; that a diamond necklace had once belonged to Marie-Antoinette, then had been given to Empress Eugénie
by Napoleon III before Vanderbilt gave it to Otéro. She was an inquisi-
tive shopper, always learning the words of the trade, the origins of the
goods. At the Palais Royal, in a little store selling needlework, crewel,
and related items, the owner still remembers her conversations with
Colette, who could spend an hour comparing the hue of the threads she
would use. In her favorite stores the salespeople crowded around her
and unrolled their finest material; she felt and studied velvets, satins, and
silks with her fingers. She was known for her buying sprees. At her couturier's, while she tried on a dress, a jeweler would come with gems, or
someone else with expensive handbags, and she would be tempted and
buy. At her milliner's she would put a hat on her fist, turn it about, discuss it, and modify its shape. She loved perfumes and sprayed each room
in her homes with a different fragrance to complement its style.

She took a whole day of relaxation at her hairdresser's and fell asleep
in a cotton gown while someone dyed, curled, and dried her hair, and
gave her a manicure and a pedicure. At noon her hairdresser locked the
door and he and his wife served Colette a tasty lunch of veal and french
fries with a light wine from the south of France and oranges shipped
straight from Spain; seated in her chair, swathed in towels, she enjoyed
the well-seasoned lunch and her coiffeur's conversation. Descriptions of
food, in her letters as in her works, are hymns to gourmandise in which
she let her lyricism flow. Banquets at Castel Novel, dinners at 69
Boulevard Suchet, feasts at Rozven, the discovery of small gourmet
shops here and there, snacks on her desk at *Le Matin* — this constant
gratification had its consequences. Colette ballooned to one hundred
and seventy-eight pounds and started to wear loose dresses. Gone was
the slim, lithe Colette Willy with a tight belt around her tiny waist, gone
the muscular, beautifully proportioned Faun, the seductress of *The Flesh
(La Chair)* with her sculptural breast. Yet Colette was extremely attractive in a vital way; she was in her triumphant maturity, a force of nature.

Her Arab friend, the Pasha El Gabour ben Gabrit, once exclaimed at the end of a dinner, "What a grand woman, what a great woman you are!"[142] He said that there should be an exception for her and that she should be allowed to have a harem of men. Facetiously, as an ultimate compliment, he added that he would be happy to be one of her husbands.

## The Perversity of Gratifying an Adolescent Lover
## Does Not Devastate a Woman, Quite to the Contrary

Colette had spent the major part of the spring outside Paris, crisscrossing France in her limousine driven by Jean, her chauffeur. In March she was in Nice with Carco and his wife; Sidi, no less addicted than she to motoring, came for "a day, discounting the night."[143] At the end of May she was at Castel Novel with Léo Marchand, adapting *Chéri* for the stage. Back in Paris she attended the opening of *Caducée* by her friend André Pascal (Henri de Rothschild) and the yearly ritual of the awards ceremony at Le Conservatoire, which marked the end of the theater season. It was overshadowed by the boxing match of the century, between Georges Carpentier and Jack Dempsey. *Le Matin* had installed large screens outside its building to relay the match. A new culture was rolling in with the Roaring Twenties; the treaties of Trianon and Saint-Germain had ratified the new map of Europe. But an undercurrent of nostalgia was setting in, Le Mercure de France released a new edition of *Claudine Married (Claudine en Ménage)*, and Polaire played Claudine in *Claudine in Paris* for three weeks before leaving on tour.

On July 12 Colette left for Rozven "with a motley family of Jouvenel children, a daughter of my own, two sons who came to me from elsewhere, but are charming."[144] Germaine Patat, Robert de Jouvenel, and his mistress Zou were the first group of vacationers. Meg Villars, now divorced from Willy, arrived with her fox terrier; the kids managed to teach it to climb a tree by fixing sticks to the trunk. Meg came to Rozven several summers in a row. Léo Marchand arrived for a working vacation; he was writing the stage version of *The Vagabond*.

In an explicit letter to Moréno, Colette wrote, "There is also Bertrand de Jouvenel, whom his mother entrusted to me for his health and misfortune."[145] After some hesitation, their interlude of the previous summer had resumed; Colette was stuffing him with food and rubbing him with sand. When he left for four days, Colette asked Hélène Picard to look after her "wolf cub," carefully keeping up the facade of the caring and concerned stepmother of a frail adolescent. Bertrand was anything but frail; he was a slim and trim sportsman. Colette mothered him, declaring she was saving the life of her husband's ailing son, that nobody knew how to take care of him. Bertrand called her "Ma Mère Chérie" (My Darling Mother); Renaud, reserved and lonely, called her "Tante Colette" (Aunt Colette) or "Madame."

Bertrand, the bookish young teenager, learned "that bread had a taste, that the wax myrtle had fragrance, that poppies had color."[146] He followed her everywhere; they hunted for teapots in antiques shops in Saint Malo, for shrimps in a puddle of water. In those days, his consciousness had become like "a parasite" of hers. Later he added, "It is impossible to express how much I owe her for having nourished me in such a way."[147] Colette was amused and moved; she wrote to Marguerite Moréno that Bertrand followed her "like a puppy." She also gave her some advice, for Moréno had fallen in love with a young girl, her Mélisande-des-Fortifs (Mélisande of the slums) and had asked Colette if she should get involved; Colette urged her to indulge in any passing temptation and to satisfy her craving: "What are we sure of, except of what we hold in our arms, while we hold it?" She added wistfully that seldom do we have a chance of owning anything, and she reminded Moréno, "I still love you."[148]

Colette was reigning over her extended family. Her well-being triggered past memories, and she talked to Bertrand about her childhood and her native village. He thought her stories were so enchanting that she should write a book to recapture the spell. In the fall she took him to visit Saint-Sauveur, where she had not set foot since writing *Claudine at School* almost thirty years earlier.

The first text of *My Mother's House (La Maison de Claudine)* was published on October 15. *Le Matin* announced on its front page, "From now on, every Saturday, Colette, the Literary and Drama Editor of *Le Matin,* will be publishing a series of short stories." They were released in book form the following year. Colette's title was *La Maison de Colette.* Her editor, Ferenczi, argued that *Claudine* was better for publicity. This was the book that was to mold the definitive image of Colette. Looking backward, she recreated her native Saint-Sauveur, turning it into the nostalgic picture of a small, tightly knit family and a rustic dream that has haunted humankind from Theocritus and Virgil to the Flower Children. Bertrand believed he had contributed to Colette's return to her roots, but more probably it was Proust's *Remembrance of Things Past* that launched the creative process. *My Mother's House*, a book of recollections made up of seemingly unconnected short stories, was written in eight months. Colette was in an intense period of creativity; not once did she complain that a page "made her sweat blood."[149] In her impatience to see the short stories in print, she published some of them in *La Revue de Paris* and one in *La Nouvelle Revue Française*. Over the years Colette reviewed and reshuffled the order of her stories; the definitive edition was published in 1930. By then the emphasis had shifted — in the first edition Gabri had held the story line, and the two opening stories were all about the rites of passage from adolescence to womanhood. Then Colette refocused the book on her mother, Sido's two marriages, and her interactions with her children and with the villagers. She was an allegorical figure set in a realistic background: the village, its inhabitants, the woods, and the gardens. The critics ignored Sido's nonconformism and the unconventional education she imparted to her children. They also ignored that Sido was an atheist, that she spoke proudly of her wealthy quadroon father, pointedly reminded Colette of her African ancestors. They either saw an unsophisticated story — "No artifices to mislead us" — or "some sort of prose poems," "marvelous stories of childhood," "a Claudine without vice."[150] They found that Colette had succumbed to a writer's temptation to write about her childhood. The book did moderately well at first, then steadily became a best-seller; readers related to the life of a provincial town. Mireille Havel in *Les Nouvelles Littéraires* summed it up: "We join up with our heart, with our memories, which are similar to hers."[151] Some stories were reproduced in anthologies and school manuals, and they became the favorite choice of the ministry of education, which administered the national examinations. It made Colette a household word, but totally distorted her image.

Colette went back to Castel Novel in mid-September with the children and Bertrand — "How magnificent it is. Why go to Switzerland . . . ?"[152] Nursie-Dear, "the terrible nurse," was overlooking everything, allotting only six cloves of garlic a meal for Colette, who found "the lack of well-schooled domestics"[153] relaxing. A cyclone wrecked the region and created more excitement than she cared for. Jouvenel visited the stricken areas and came home exhausted and feverish. They were invited to dinners and races organized by a famous breeder in Pompadour. Colette crammed in as many working hours as she could, lamenting the intrusion of the outside world in her country retreat. Back in Paris, she finished the adaptation of *Chéri* for the stage and contributed to *La Revue de Paris*. In November the publisher Crès issued the first anthology of texts by Colette in his collection for young readers, *La Bibliothèque de l'Adolescence*. Two volumes of collected articles, *La Chambre Eclairée* and *Celle qui en revient, suivi de quelques dialogues de bêtes*, had been released earlier. In November, exhausted, Colette checked into the Hôtel de France et d'Angleterre in Fontainebleau for a few days of rest and solitude.

She returned to Paris to cover the sensational trial of Landru. This serial killer had slaughtered several women, dismembered them, and burned their remains in his kitchen stove. He was sentenced to death, but before leaving the courtroom, he asked Colette for an autograph.

*Chéri* opened at Le Théâtre Michel; Lucien Lelong had designed the costumes. When the curtain came down, everybody looked for Colette, who was finishing her dinner in the restaurant next to the theater, seated at a small table, serenely eating a melon. The public had wept, the acclaim was overwhelming. "It is worthy of Colette, this is the ultimate praise."[154] In an interview, Colette explained that her characters had first come alive in dialogues. She had started *Chéri* as a play and written the last act, but the first and second refused to materialize, so she decided to leave it as a one-act play. (The director of Le Théâtre du Gymnase thought the subject was wasted as a one-act play and refused to produce it.) Then her characters had slipped into a novel. Colette had asked Léo Marchand to collaborate on the stage version. Colette addressed Léo with the affectionate "tu," while he always used the respectful "vous." She called him "my child," a name she gave generously to her young friends and lovers. In December of 1921 she announced that they were adapting *The Vagabond*.

Poincaré formed a new government and Colette's friends were appointed to key ministries: Barthou was minister of justice, André Maginot minister of war, Léon Bérart minister of education, and

Jouvenel was on the short list for a cabinet post. Colette began eradicating her past. She instructed Claude Chauvière to destroy entire correspondences: "When I was her secretary . . . my main assignment was to tear up letters!" Colette asked her friends to get rid of evidence of her indiscretions and to stop any mention of her previous entanglements — "Now I have a husband, a position, a family."[155]

In 1921 *Le Petit Bleu,* a conservative daily, published some innuendos about Colette's mores; she believed the source of the damaging information was Aline de B., an actress who was a regular contributor to the newspaper. Aline's mother had been janitor of a building on the Rue Marbeuf, where Colette and the marquise de Morny had shared an apartment to which they invited teenage girls; Aline and two of her friends had spent long hours in the pied-à-terre. Colette had given the fifteen-year-old Aline her first expensive hat and arranged for her to enter the Conservatoire d'Art Dramatique in the class of Georges Berr. She sponsored her debut in a play by Willy at the Comédie Royale just before the war. Currently Aline was in a play by Bonmariage at the Théâtre Impérial, which belonged to the owner of *Le Petit Bleu.*

Colette arranged a meeting with Bonmariage, whom she had not seen since the beginning of the war, to ask if he could help. She told him that she had a file on Aline, who was kept by an industrial plutocrat, but Aline's secret lover was the marquis Adhémar de Montgon, editor of *Le Petit Bleu.* Could Bonmariage stop the leaks, which only Aline could document?

Count Bonmariage was a respectable front for certain private circles; he was known to organize nude dinners, and was addicted to opium. He wrote plays and short stories and was director of several short-lived political newspapers, which he described as a pool of bribes and influence peddling. Two days after meeting Colette, he let her know she had nothing to fear anymore. "Now you know too much! You have the upper hand,"[156] was Colette's cynical remark. To thank Bonmariage, she offered to publish one of his short stories every month. He was instructed to bypass her assistant, who discarded half the manuscripts submitted to her; he brought his first short story directly to Colette. Not even a deal could bring Colette to lower her standards — Bonmariage had to rework his tale. Colette herself went to pick up the finished manuscript, but Bonmariage was not at home. His newly wed wife was trying to find an excuse for his absence — it was raining, he could not find a cab. "I have known your husband for a long time, he must be with a mistress," quipped Colette, laughing. To her dismay, the young wife burst into tears. "It was only a joke," said Colette, "Men are all the same, they don't deserve our tears."

The Bonmariages and Colette had dinner at Le Petit Durand, after which she invited them to her home. They were alone. Jouvenel was giving a lecture in Rouen, and Colette had given her private maid, Adna, leave until midnight. The house was dark, and Colette led Bonmariage and his wife directly into her room. The bed was not made, clothes and linen were thrown around, there were piles of books, manuscripts, and fountain pens everywhere, as well as bottles of perfume and a collection of boxes of face powder. Colette threw off her raincoat and hat and went to get "Henry's special Armagnac" and three glasses. She kept the couple until two in the morning, playfully alluding to the count's secret past. As they left, she remarked that they were lucky to go home to bed together, "It is the only thing that counts in life."[157] Bonmariage blamed this encounter with Colette for the first rift in his marriage. As soon as they left Boulevard Suchet, Madame Bonmariage, shocked by the evening, made a violent scene. Colette, obsessed with the fear of blackmail, had manipulated the situation to regain the upper hand.

On February 26, among the popping of flashbulbs, Colette was back on stage for the one-hundredth performance of *Chéri* playing Léa, the aging courtesan. She had just finished *Journey for Myself (Le Voyage Egoïste),* again using unrelated vignettes and meandering through her past while reflecting on the present. The book was written for Bertrand. "I lead you tenderly because you are a pretty Parisian child. . . . I lead you religiously toward my house of other days. . . . I still have to conquer you, my garden." "Dimanche," the opening vignette, is a love poem as delicate and beautiful as the text written long ago for Missy; while the narrator visits her past, her lover falls asleep: "I am somewhat jealous, because it seems to me . . . that you remained over there in a very old garden and that your hand was holding the rough hand of a child who looks like me."[158]

*Journey for Myself* was released by the art publisher Edouard Pelleton, while Colette set sail for Algeria on a four-week trip with Bertrand. First they stayed with Pierre de Polignac in his villa; two years earlier he had married Charlotte Grimaldi, crown princess of Monaco, and Colette was the couple's close friend. Then Colette and Bertrand moved to Algiers. Their arrival coincided with President Millerand's state visit to Algeria;

ministers and secretaries swarmed all over her hotel. President Millerand, learning that the baronne de Jouvenel was in Algiers, invited her to be his guest. In a scenario worthy of a slapstick comedy, Colette, now on the list of official guests, had to attend tea parties and the *fantasia* — a traditional equestrian show — in honor of the president, while Bertrand waited in hiding. They returned to France, Bertrand still incognito (and seasick), and arrived at Castel Novel to find Jouvenel ready to leave for Paris. He commanded: "Take a bath, I'll give you a ride." Two days and a thousand kilometers later, Colette had equipped Bel-Gazou for boarding school and seen her doctor. "You are suffering from a series of phenomena of castration,"[159] was his quaint diagnosis.

On her way to *Le Matin,* a truck hit Colette's car, which was thrown against a pile of construction beams; she and her chauffeur were pulled out of the wreck unhurt. Undaunted, Colette met with Moréno and the film producer Diamant-Berger to discuss an adaptation of *Chéri.* She also discussed the movie project with Caroll-Kelly, a female producer from America.

### Colette, Parisian Hostess

By 1923, 69 Boulevard Suchet had become "one of the ten focal points of literary and political Paris," always crowded with "an endless parade of Japanese, Americans, Greeks, autograph seekers, managers, writers, painters, musicians."[160] Colette had redecorated her *hôtel particulier,* covering the walls with silk and velvet. In the main salon there was a grand piano and above it hung a painting by Colette. Her rooms housed a growing private collection; she had rare tapestries in a small drawing room, and, on several tables, a collection of crystal paperweights. She had collected them with Annie de Pène during the war and had started a fad — she often gave her visitors a white rose embedded in glass. Truman Capote, who visited her in 1948 on Natalie Barney's recommendation, was gratified with one, as was his friend, P.B.

The French doors opened on the garden Colette had designed herself, a carefully planned disorder of climbing plants, rustic herbs, and bulbs brought by friends from everywhere. She selected only plants on which insects and butterflies thrived.

Colette worked on the second floor in her boudoir, next to her very large bedroom; the walls were covered in pink toile de Jouy with rustic prints, a material handmade according to century-old patterns. The bed, which had been made to her specifications, was, according to Renaud, the largest in the world. Jouvenel's bedroom was a smaller one; its walls were covered in a pale green material printed with La Fontaine's fables. Colette's boudoir was decorated in brown and blue, and rows of blue Guyanan butterflies in glass boxes hung on the walls. The windows opened on the trees of the Bois de Boulogne. She worked while chain-smoking at a small desk cluttered with pens, blue paper, and manuscripts; after a while, she would throw a shawl on her lap, then one on her shoulders, then another one, so that after a long session she seemed lost in a cocoon. As soon as she put the cap on her fountain pen, Patipati, her dog, knew that work was over and rushed barking to her; they walked down a narrow staircase to the dining room, tiled in black and white slabs, for a cup of tea. Bertrand thought Colette's means and taste did not measure up to his mother's elegant and sumptuous apartment; Renaud found that whatever Colette's homes lacked in luxury was compensated for by refined strangeness.

Colette's group of *habitués* included the couturiers Chanel, Poiret, and Patat, Princess Edmond de Polignac and her niece Armande, Anna de Noailles "in a tailored suit and silver shoes," Princess Ghika, Marguerite Moréno, Louise Hervieu, "the blind writer who kept her hat on, even for breakfast and kissed her horse on the mouth," Hélène Picard, "that witch of genius," "the mysterious, melancholy and smiling Carco,"[161] Léo Marchand and Henri Bernstein, both playwrights, the academician Pierre Benoît, and the Spanish infante Don Luis Ferdinand, "drunk on drugs" and escorted by his homosexual friends. Jouvenel was the candidate of the rich and intellectual leftists, who also found their way to Colette's salon: Louis Aragon, the elegant surrealist turned communist, several patrons of the arts, such as "the exquisite" Monsieur Rodier, the textile manufacturer, designer, and creator of a light knit material favored by Coco Chanel and Germaine Patat. The other Maecenas, a regular at Colette's gatherings, was Francis Ducharne, a silk manufacturer; as soon as *My Mother's House* was published, he bought the house in Saint-Sauveur from Achille's daughters, who had inherited it and put it up for sale. Ducharne had a plaque set on the facade that read "Ici est née Colette" (Colette was born here). The Ducharnes gave Colette the use of the house for as long as she lived; she rented it out. Her correspondence with the local attorney reveals a vigilant businesswoman, keeping a close watch on rents and tenants. After decades of paying for repairs and taxes, the Ducharnes asked Colette's permission to sell the house to her tenant, a local lawyer. In a typically Colettian way, she wrote in her memoirs that an admirer she had barely seen twice presented her with the Saint-Sauveur house.

At a dinner in June Colette met a Parisian personality, the Abbé Mugnier, "a witty, rosy-faced little man with forget-me-not blue eyes behind a pince-nez, a tuft of gray, smoke-colored hair, which he would twirl with his finger when puzzled and an expression of harassed benignity."[162] He had a passion for literature and an enormous dose of skepticism. Asked if he believed in hell, he replied that he did, since it was a dogma of the church, but that he did not believe there was anyone there. He kept up an enormous correspondence with writers and intellectuals, among them Bergson, Proust, Cocteau, Montesquiou, and Barrés. He also kept a diary full of lively portraits of the celebrities of the first half of the twentieth century, in which he tried to go beyond the public image and to understand the mystery of creativity and human behavior. "I think," he noted in 1916, "that the sexual instinct is the explanation of everything since everything comes from it. . . . But who is going to thoroughly investigate our origins? A stupid modesty or a stupid sexual indulgence prevent any serious study."[163]

The Abbé had come "to meet Colette (ex–Colette Willy)"; he told her he had prepared himself for the meeting by reading "The Nightingale" in *The Vine's Tendrils (Les Vrilles de la Vigne)*. She answered rather sharply, "For my part, I made no preparation at all"; he thought her harsh. Colette, dressed in a white Moroccan crêpe creation by Germaine Patat, "looked like a child" who had received no education, did not know how to behave, knew no restraint, and was nevertheless amusing and even good natured. She addressed her husband as "mon chéri," which was not done. She spoke about what caught her eye, the food, a flower, a piece of furniture, the wine in her glass. She invited the Abbé to christen her nine-year-old daughter. After dinner, as Colette was talking to Madame Bernstein, the abbé noticed she squeezed the lady's breasts several times as she congratulated her on her good health. He thought her strange and that if her husband cared for decorum, he was to be pitied.

Ten days later the Abbé had lunch at Colette's with André Maginot, the minister of war and creator of the Maginot Line, and Princess Marthe Bibesco, the Abbé's spiritual ward. The lunch was abundant and so were the wines. The table was decorated with delicate bouquets of sweet peas. Maginot was seated at Colette's right, the dog Patipati on a chair to her left and next to the dog, the Abbé. After lunch Colette took the Abbé and Princess Bibesco on a tour of her garden, where she plucked and pressed flowers to bring their fragrance out: roses, tuberoses, gardenias, narcissi, mint, geranium, and absinthe. He noticed that Colette wore makeup on her lashes, had gray-green eyes and something rough and hard in her expression; as for Monsieur de Jouvenel, he looked concerned and sad.

Slowly the Abbé fell under the writer's spell. "What poetry! Colette is the divine wasp who has tasted the sweetness of the cake."[164] He admired her for not having deprived herself of the joy of feeling, touching, and seeing.

The dysfunctional family was showing signs of strain. At Castel Novel, sixteen-year-old Pauline Vérine, who had been Bel-Gazou's maid for three years, refused to look after her anymore; she was unmanageable. Fourteen-year-old Renaud had a crush on Colette, the only person who had shown some interest in him; the lonely boy took one of her rings, as he would have taken a glove or a handkerchief. The school principal called Jouvenel to inform him that his son wore an expensive woman's ring and refused to say where it came from. Apprised of the incident, Colette said that the ring was hers, that she thought she had lost it; angry, she asked that Renaud be punished. Jouvenel flew into one of the flaming rages for which he was famous and arranged with the Public Works Department for Renaud to spend a few months working on the roads, breaking stones with a sledgehammer. For centuries this had been the task allotted to gangs of convicts in chains; it was no longer so, but the connotation remained. Renaud saw himself as a convicted criminal sentenced to hard labor. Bertrand, horrified by this demeaning and harsh punishment, begged his father to spare Renaud from such a humiliation, but in vain, as Isabelle de Comminges sided with Jouvenel. In the fall, Renaud was sent to a boarding school in England. Bel-Gazou was sent to a boarding school in Saint-Germain. Later she would also be sent to a boarding school in England. Renaud and Bel-Gazou felt rejected and neglected by their famous parents and this brought them closer.

Turning her life into literature, Colette was writing *The Ripening Seed (Le Blé en Herbe),* inspired by her relationship with Bertrand. Colette's situation had radically changed. Henry de Jouvenel had all but disappeared, spending less and less time at 69 Boulevard Suchet, briefly stopping by between trips; Colette was relying emotionally on Bertrand. Their encounter, like her life with Missy, proved to be a source of literary renewal. Possessive Colette convinced herself that Claire Boas de Jouvenel was not only her rival in Bertrand's affection, but was her son's nemesis.

Whenever Bertrand spent a few days with his mother, Colette complained of the harm done to his health. In February he was sick; "I think he suffers from a chronic *emmerdité* caught from his mother."[165] Claire imposed five hours of tennis and five hours of ballroom dancing on him weekly, and Colette complained that "the child" arrived at Rozven exhausted, burnt-out, and running a high fever. But — thanks to her — the next morning he was almost back to normal, wolfing down fresh cream and lobster. This concern for Bertrand's health was merely a pretext; Colette needed some justification for the care she lavished on her stepson. She sent detailed health bulletins to Germaine Patat, to be passed on to Jouvenel.

Colette and her stepson met in Rue d'Alleray, a gloomy street in a shabby part of Paris. Blindly devoted Hélène Picard had rented the apartment in her own name, referring to Bertrand as the "co-renter"; she was in charge of looking after his welfare when Colette was away. In *The Ripening Seed,* Colette gave the name of this street to Madame Dalleray, the woman dressed in white (in the early twenties, Colette often wore white in the evening) who seduces the adolescent Phil. The corollary story of the love between Phil and Vinca was also inspired in part by real facts. Colette encouraged a flirtation between Bertrand and his friend Pamela Paramythioti; the office at *Le Matin* was their mailbox, where Colette also received Bertrand's letters. Was it pure thrill or total thoughtlessness? Absent for a few days, it occurred to Colette that the letters would be opened by her secretary. She dispatched a tactical letter to Marguerite Moréno, who was to go to *Le Matin* — carefully avoiding the second floor where Jouvenel had his suite of offices — proceed discreetly to the office of a trusted copy editor, and instruct him to make sure that not a single letter addressed to Colette would be opened.

Colette could always count on Moréno, although it is hard to imagine how Marguerite, by now a movie star, could walk without being recognized past the liveried ushers stationed on the staircase. This episode was not part of *The Ripening Seed*. In the book Phil, having discovered sex with Madame Dalleray, shares his newfound knowledge with Vinca under the stars. Bertrand would later say that it was the only episode not true to life; Pamela wanted to go to the pied-à-terre on Rue d'Alleray, but on the way, in a gentlemanly manner, he persuaded her to turn back.

Colette worked with Léopold Marchand on the stage version of *The Vagabond*, which proved long and difficult, as "I am too unsure of what I am doing."[166] The director suggested a scene with amusing dialogues and one final crisis between the two lovers; Colette preferred to bring out the vagabond's "true personality ... the egotistical fear of suffering."[167]

In January Colette gave a lecture, "Man in the Animal Kingdom," at the Théâtre Athénée and signed up for a lecture tour on the Riviera in March. A few days later, on February 3, *The Vagabond* opened at the Théâtre de la Renaissance and ran until the end of March. But the publication of *The Threshold (Le Seuil,* the first title of *Le Blé en Herbe)* in *Le Matin* was controversial; outraged letters flooded in from readers who found the situation amoral. The editors had already prevailed on Colette to modify the fourteenth installment, so that Phil did not make love to Madame Dalleray. Nevertheless, the reactions were violent and publication was stopped at the fifteenth installment.

This scandal came at the least opportune moment; Senator Henry de Jouvenel was climbing the political ladder, which, according to some observers, could take him to the presidency. Drieu La Rochelle thought that Jouvenel had the makings of a president, but could anyone imagine Colette at the Elysée? She was perceived as the stumbling block in her husband's career. When it was rumored that Jouvenel was to be appointed to the French embassy in Berlin, a photograph of Colette in a skimpy costume was published in a German daily with the caption, "The next French ambassador's wife?" The sharp-eyed abbé Mugnier noted, "He (Jouvenel) would like Foreign Affairs. But would Colette be accepted? Colette has a long past (men, women), she was on the music-hall stage. . . . If Jouvenel cannot succeed in rehabilitating Colette, he could divorce her. She is in fact afraid that he will."[168]

Colette's rehabilitation campaign was three-pronged. First she tried to crack the most conservative of French institutions by having a play included in the repertoire of the Comédie Française; this attempt failed. Her second effort was directed at L'Académie Française; in February an article on the front page of *L'Eclair* announced that Jean Richepin had persuaded Colette to be a candidate for a seat at L'Académie Française — "Will she run?" This meant visits to amenable academicians and garnering support from powerful individuals or groups, like the Société des Auteurs. Sarah Bernhardt sent Colette an invitation and brewed her a cup of coffee herself among her Gothic bric-à-brac; they reminisced about Catulle Mendès and Marcel Schwob. The Polignacs, powerful patrons of the arts, supported her, but the opposition of the all-male academy could not be overcome. Her third move was to have a promotion in the Legion of Honor, where there was also formidable opposition. She made some calls on political salons. After World War I literary salons were *passé,* while political salons were "in." She went to visit Claire Boas de Jouvenel, Isabelle de Comminges, and Germaine Patat, "who had real literary, artistic, and political salons with the celebrities of the day." Colette "charmed us by her wit," recalled Boris Eliacheff, "she was interested in the events in the USSR, asking a lot of questions about Stalin. . . . Is it the rise of a new star or just a flying comet?" Then she mused, "I really should study those new Cossacks and write something about them."[169]

While Colette was campaigning, forming alliances with Claire, Isabelle, and Germaine, Henry was womanizing, constantly seduced by women who stalked him as consenting prey. His loyal friend and cousin Kerguézec used to say, "he is a woman," that he was as "coquettish as a whore."[170] Colette's marriage was stormy, but she was still charmed by his lyrical eloquence and style. After a violent discussion in which they accused each other of being unfaithful, Jouvenel shut himself up in the bathroom. Colette opened the door to find Henry prostrate on the floor. Afraid that he had had a stroke, she was about to rush to him, but stopped when she noticed his suit, shirt, and tie neatly folded on a chair.

There was a principal new woman in Henry's life, the Rumanian princess Marthe Bibesco, described by Colette as a woman "with the bones of a horse and a novelist who wrote novels in two volumes."[171] Considered one of the beauties of European aristocracy, she was part of a group of French-speaking Rumanians who chose to write in French before World War I. At the turn of the century a fairly large number of foreigners — Rumanians, Poles, Russians, and Americans —

participated in and influenced French intellectual life. They wrote novels, plays, essays, and memoirs, and achieved literary recognition. None were more celebrated than Countess Anna de Noailles and her cousin, Princess Marthe Bibesco.

Born into a family that included many dignitaries in the Balkan states during the rule of the Ottoman Empire, she was engaged at fourteen and married two years later to young Prince Bibesco. This title came from an ancestor who had occupied the throne of Rumania from 1842 to 1848, during the revolutions that swept through Europe. Once in Paris, the princess soon realized that she was shunned because Prince Bibesco's mother, a French aristocrat, had created an enormous scandal by becoming a citizen of a German state for the sole purpose of getting a divorce, then forbidden in France. Soon Prince Bibesco began taking low-class mistresses. Eighteen-year-old Marthe, who had just given birth to a daughter, sought refuge in literature. Her life was guided by a burning passion for literary recognition and political power, and a constant need of money. She was said to have been the German Kronprinz's mistress, and their affair was lampooned by the Allied press during World War I. In her memoirs, she turned her first encounter with Kronprinz into a historical moment, one in which she held "the destiny of the world in her hands."[172] In the twenties she had love affairs with the king of Spain, Prince Beauvau, Lord Carrington, Ramsay MacDonald, and Henry de Jouvenel. For over fifty years Marthe Bibesco, convinced that she was the heart and soul of Europe, wrote novels and memoirs about the royal families of Rumania and Great Britain, as well as other luminaries — Tsar Nicolas II, Churchill, Gorki, Mussolini, Goering, Ramsay MacDonald, and others — turning literature into a dream of power.

In 1923 the thirty-four-year-old princess was free, having reached a friendly agreement with her husband. They never divorced and enjoyed a supportive friendship to the end. That year she published her international best-seller, *Isvor: The Land of the Willows*. In Bucharest the book was ill-received partly because it was written in French at a time when Rumania was asserting its nationalism, but mainly because she described the country's medieval conditions. *Isvor* depicted a cruel world in which it was common to have picnics in cemeteries and people believed in vampires. They thrust a stake into the heart of any dead person suspected of vampirism during his life, then burned his heart on charcoal. When a girl had been seduced, in this land of willows, her parents married her to a willow tree, so that she could cover her hair with a kerchief like married women.

Princess Bibesco had met Jouvenel at several social gatherings. Early in 1923 Jouvenel suddenly declared his love. Throughout the spring he courted her, asking her to teach him English or to grant him a consultation on political problems in the Balkans. One day after a dinner at her home, Jouvenel left with the other guests, then came back, fell on his knees, and kissed her feet with theatrical devotion. Flowers, letters, and telegrams flooded her home and Princess Bibesco was charmed by this professional charmer.

## I Am Divorcing

In June Colette was at Castel Novel to finish *The Threshold;* she complained that her work was "a torment" and grumbled that the last page had deprived her of an entire day. The novel was published in July under its new title, *The Ripening Seed,* and Colette's new signature: "Colette." However, "Colette Willy" had not ceased to exist; several new editions of *Claudine Married* kept the name alive.

She had invited Claire Boas and Germaine Patat to Castel Novel; Henry came, but left immediately after receiving a telegram from Marthe Bibesco. She was convinced that he was the political genius whom she had dreamed of to "shape history." She defined her passion for Jouvenel in historical terms: "Your idea of what you can do for the History of France sends me into rapture. . . . You know that I have a deep understanding of historical voluptuousness. . . . Become everything you can be. Let me see the French miracle arise through you. Let me witness this mutation of a man into a God. The fact that you have chosen me to share your divinity is enough for me to die of sheer bliss."[173] Such lust for power made a theatrical storm of their love affair; it suited them both.

Colette settled at Rozven, where she stayed throughout September, watching from afar Jouvenel's liaison, which had the support of her mother-in-law. Mamita was the princess's best ally; she saw her as the perfect match for a future president. At Rozven Hélène Picard, Germaine Patat, Léopold Marchand, and Bertrand waited and watched. In July, as the French delegate to the League of Nations, Jouvenel was in Rumania with Princess Bibesco on an official mission. Then he left for Geneva to lead the French delegation on the Disarmament Commission. He asked Marthe to come, but she refused, afraid of meeting Isabelle de Comminges, who was also very much involved in politics. Colette had also refused to go with her husband, afraid that her presence would do more harm than good. His proposals for disarmament and reparations were unanimously approved by the delegates of forty-four countries. When Colette learned about his impressive success in Geneva, she quipped that all that remained was to proclaim Jouvenel king of France.

In November Colette went on a lecture tour in the south; Bertrand joined her in Avignon. Jouvenel and Claire Boas agreed that the love affair between Colette and her stepson should be put to an end; it was becoming a matter of gossip all over Paris. The publication of *The Ripening Seed* had only confirmed what Tout-Paris knew; Colette, with her thoughtless bravado, was seen with Bertrand everywhere. Several times a week he was her escort at some première or gala. The incestuous relationship between stepmother and stepson was affecting Jouvenel's career. Since Bertrand was interested in economics and politics, Jouvenel seized the occasion of a dinner at 69 Boulevard Suchet (on a rare evening alone with Colette and Bertrand), to tell his son that he had been invited to Prague by the statesman-professor Eduard Benes, minister of foreign affairs and later, president of Czechoslovakia. Colette declared abruptly that Bertrand would not go; her decision was final. Upset, Jouvenel left the table and the house, while Bertrand stayed. Colette then went on another lecture tour; her topic was "The Theater Seen from Both Sides of the Curtain." When she came back, Jouvenel had moved out.

Colette felt that she was being manipulated, the target of a plot to lead her against her will onto a path where everything was carefully planned against her. She was seeing treason everywhere. Meg Villars had become very close to Mamita — why? asked Colette. She wrote to Christiane Mendelys that Sidi had left during her lecture tour and she had not heard from him in a month; she added, with no further comment, "I am divorcing."[174] Sidi was taken by surprise, for he had no intention of marrying Princess Bibesco; his enduring love was Germaine Patat. She, too, had been affected by his latest affair and had lost so many pounds that Colette was worried for her health and begged her to come to Rozven, for she longed to hug her elegant little body. As for Jouvenel, she said she had endured all she could — he was not even paying his daughter's boarding school fees.

One day as she was walking her dog in the Bois de Boulogne, she was approached by a political friend of Jouvenel's, who spoke diplomatically of her husband's talents and future. How could she divorce such a man? "I have my reasons," replied Colette. "Are they good ones?" "He is too expensive,"[175] was her terse answer.

Her decision now irrevocable, Colette decided to go on a two-week vacation. Before leaving she worked at a harrowing pace, writing a screenplay, several articles for *Le Matin,* discussing with Armand Colin a project for a children's book, the terms of her collaboration with *Le Quotidien;* signing a contract for a monthly paper with the director of *Vogue.* Colette was also editing novels for *The Colette Collection (La Collection Colette),* to be published by Ferenczi; her contract called for one novel a month. She convinced Ferenczi to increase her output, and two titles came out in February, after which the novels of *The Colette Collection* — twenty titles altogether — came out sporadically.

Having pocketed a large advance from Flammarion for a collection of short stories, and with a new wardrobe in her luggage, she headed for the Swiss Alps with Bertrand. They spent two months at the exclusive Royal Hotel and Winter Palace in Gstaad. Her physical energy took over; the first day she took a ski lesson, then practiced ice skating. She had not skated since the days of the Palais de Glace and Polaire. She went tobogganing, but finding the toboggan too slow, she teamed up with the young marquis de Gallifet and bobsleighed on steeper slopes, delighted to discover that winter could mean a scorching sun and a violently blue sky. She wrote to Moréno that she would come back to Paris broke, in high spirits, and with a sunburn on her nose. In February she dashed back to Paris to give a lecture on "The Theater Seen from Both Sides of the Curtain" at the Université des Annales.

She was considering an offer from *Le Journal* — an annual salary of thirty-six thousand francs for a weekly byline on the front page and the serialization of her next novel; she made a counteroffer of forty thousand francs. *Le Journal* was *Le Matin's* direct competitor. Appalled, Henry de Jouvenel asked her to reconsider; but she could not, said she, afford a financial disaster on top of her personal disappointment. Anatole de Monzie was using his diplomatic skills to arrange the quietest possible separation; Colette turned to him. Should she accept the offer from *Le Journal,* she could not, for reasons of professonal ethics, join its staff for three months, which meant a lack of income. She asked Monzie to prevail upon Jouvenel to help her financially during that period — and what about his repeated promise to give her a car? She resigned from *Le Matin,* dismissed her chauffeur, sold a painting for eight thousand francs to a buyer sent by Francis Carco, and immediately returned to the snow of Les Avants, a ski resort near Montreux where Bertrand was waiting for her. He had spent the previous week at Megève with his mother, who pressured him to ask Colette to postpone her trip. Colette was in no mood to compromise. During the long train trip to Montreux, Colette, alone with no one to see her, broke down; she was sick all the time, "poisoned by my problems."[176]

She spent a month with Bertrand, forcing him to adopt her regular schedule. This was easier than in Gstaad, since there were no tourists and only two pairs of journalists. Colette was editing some of her previously published short stories for Flammarion. If there is a common theme in this collection, *The Hidden Woman (La Femme Cachée),* it is the ill-defined zone between sanity and madness, the tricks played by perception on the senses. "The Hidden Woman," the first short story in this slim volume, is about the metamorphosis of a faithful wife during a masquerade at the opera; hidden by her costume, she tastes "the monstrous pleasure of being alone, free . . . ," governed only by her senses. The volume was coolly received; it disconcerted the critics, who found that Colette had wandered too far from her usual topics. They saw in Colette's collections of short stories hastily assembled volumes; but after *The Ripening Seed,* Colette took great care to regroup her short stories along thematic lines, which fitted into a larger project *à la* Proust or *à la* Balzac in the study of human passions.

Painstakingly, Colette was working on a new novel — not the one she had planned to work on when she left Paris — "of course, another one," she confided to Francis Carco, "and it is awful to think, as I do every time I start a book, that I have no talent left, that I never had any talent."[177] She was toying with the idea of a business association with Germaine Patat; she felt she would be a good partner since she was motivated by that old bourgeois drive, the quest for success. From Switzerland she contacted Monzie again; she had no money, her daughter's tuition had gone up, and Jouvenel should do something.

Monzie's noncommittal answer was that Colette II would always be welcomed at Castel Novel.

Colette had a meeting to arrange a settlement with Henry, now minister of education, in Anatole de Monzie's office; she relinquished all claim to Castel Novel, and in exchange got the house on Boulevard Suchet and the promised car. She did not lose a moment: the day after the meeting she placed an order for a red Renault and signed up for driving lessons. But she was disturbed by a call from Henry, who icily declared that from now on they had nothing to say to each other. Bitter and regretful, she failed to understand his attitude, since they had allowed each other so much leeway in their marriage. Her philosophy of expanding relationships, in which bonds naturally evolve from friendship into love, from love into friendship, was once again put to the test.

But Colette's friends were rallying around her. Winaretta, the princess de Polignac, gave her a car, since Jouvenel was not yet paying for the Renault. In April Colette gave a lecture on fashion in the haute couture salon of Lucien Lelong; from then on she would regularly report on the world of haute couture.

Her main preoccupation was Rozven, her castle by the sea, threatened by a pharmacist who had bought a small, adjacent piece of land and built a wooden shack on it so that his children could enjoy the beach. Colette bought all the land at a premium price, encircling the pharmacist. Her next goal was to buy him off. To pay for the deal, she turned to Germaine Patat, who mailed her a check. As if compensating for the divorce, Colette was building a new addition to Rozven, putting on a new roof in Paris, buying sixty meters of a rare material in Saint-Malo for the Rozven staircase, and redecorating the boudoir in her *hôtel particulier* with a material bought in Marseilles for four thousand francs. At the end of the year she had an outstanding bill for eighteen thousand, seven hundred francs; if Germaine Patat could not help again, she was ready to sell off her emeralds. She kept her jewels.

Bertrand moved brazenly to Boulevard Suchet, explaining that he felt responsible for the split between his father and Colette and that she needed to be protected — for it was too risky to live without a man in the house. But in mid-April, he went to Prague for three months as an assistant to Eduard Benes. He was active in student political groups and made speeches with ease. He was acting like a born politician, waving to the crowds and enjoying himself tremendously, remarked a saddened Colette.

The deal with *Le Journal* did not go through; Colette signed on with *Le Figaro,* whose literary director was Robert de Flers, an acquaintance since the turn of the century. *Le Figaro* announced that every Sunday, beginning in October, Colette would write a column titled "A Woman's Opinion" ("Opinion de Femme"); in the meantime, she would publish four articles a month. The first dealt with Eleonora Duse and Sarah Bernhardt; she was turning back to her favorite topic, the theater.

Colette's activities did not diminish; she took part in the deliberations for the literary Prix de la Renaissance, but not in the same fighting spirit as in the previous year, when she had imposed her own candidate. She reviewed a play by Sacha Guitry and went to the Conservatoire for the final competitive examinations; she obtained a position for Bertrand at *L'Oeuvre,* launching his career as a journalist.

Political France was in turmoil; hyperinflation sent the franc tumbling and, in its wake, the government; Jouvenel was replaced at the ministry of education after two months. On July 2 Robert, Henry de Jouvenel's brother, died. The night before, Colette had been awakened by a scream, "not a very loud scream,"[178] but it sounded like the voice of Henry calling next to her; the impression was so strong that she turned on the light, drank some water and looked at her watch — it was two o'clock. Colette, shaking and obsessed, called the clinic because she *felt* (her code word with Moréno to describe a state of awareness beyond normal perception). Robert had died at two that morning. Colette thought that Robert was the only person Henry had ever loved; she sent him a letter, knowing he would not open it, since it was his practice to leave unwelcome letters unopened. In spite of this hostility, she expected to be at the funeral; but she was not invited and felt deeply hurt to be so shunned by the family. Bertrand came back from the funeral in turmoil because his father had told him that his health came first and he did not want him to be unhappy. Bertrand translated these ambiguous words as meaning that Henry accepted his son's love affair with Colette.

In fact, there was another concerted effort underway to take Bertrand away from Colette. Claire and Mamita drove Bertrand to Doctor Trognon for a check-up. Once at the office, the meeting took a less-than-medical turn. Doctor Trognon, who had been briefed beforehand, told Bertrand that he was suffering dangerously from exhaustion and that he should go on a cruise. There was a friendly yacht ready for him. Bertrand was taken by surprise. He was twenty-one; it was his first love affair, and his family had known all along about his relationship with his stepmother. He did not know how to react — nothing precise had been said, except that he was tired; then Doctor Trognon pressed the issue and mentioned Colette. Bertrand, who had been raised in a tradition of discretion, felt it was a breach of etiquette. Without a word, he bowed to his grandmother, kissed her hand, and said nothing to his mother as he bowed politely to her and stepped out. Totally indifferent to accepted morals, Colette felt that Claire's efforts to sever Bertrand from her were horrible and cruel. She told Germaine that "the child's health" was again in jeopardy; she would have to do her utmost to soothe, feed, watch, and nurse the boy upset by his family. In a maniacal way, she constantly maintained that Bertrand's health was very bad, and the doctors, whom she obliged him to consult, always recommended rest. They left together for Rozven.

In August Bertrand went to Geneva to preside over the International Students' Union meeting, where he was offered the position of first secretary to the the League of Nations. He was also invited to go on a lecture tour in America. Colette expressed her disgust for such activities; she knew that politics were Bertrand's siren song. To counter her anger she swam a lot and went fishing on the rocks, but could not work. She made plans to play the part of Léa in a production of *Chéri* in December in Monte Carlo; she convinced Léo Marchand to play the part of Patron, the boxer. If the play worked, they would go on tour. Once again, theater would be her catharsis.

She arranged for a rendezvous with Bertrand at Mont Saint-Michel; the high tide was about to peak and completely surround the medieval abbey-fortress during the full moon. Bertrand arrived at three o'clock in the morning in a borrowed car — he had overturned once and his tires had blown out seven times. The hotel was closed, but he slipped in through a side door, found his room in the unlit passages, and joined Colette. She liked the youthful aspect of the adventure, being lost on an island with Bertrand. Meanwhile, Marguerite Moréno was writing to Colette for some counseling on her own love affair, strangely similar to Colette's: her nephew Pierre wanted to share her life, but she was still hesitant. Colette's words of wisdom amounted to gather ye rosebuds while ye may.

She spent the first week of September in Paris, meeting with publishers and newspaper directors and proceeding with her plans for a return to the stage. The daily *Le Quotidien* offered her the position of literary editor in chief; she asked for sixty thousand francs but accepted forty-two thousand against a promise of a raise, plus two thousand francs each month for her entertainment reviews. She would be assigned some *grands reportages* (feature articles) for an undetermined amount. *Le Quotidien*, with a circulation of three hundred and twenty thousand, had become the most influential political paper; its fortune rose and fell with the political interests it represented, *le Cartel des Gauches* (the leftwing group). One of its leaders was Léon Blum, whose friendship with Colette went back thirty years. The other was Prime Minister Edouard Herriot, rough-looking but refined and a brilliant conversationalist. It was rumored that Colette was his mistress, and that when he died his wife burned all her letters to him.

However, Colette did not stop negotiating with *Le Journal*. "I am using my diplomatic skills with Letellier, I dine and visit with a patience which, as you may guess, only conceals my stubbornness."[179] *Le Journal* was part of *Les Cinq Grands* (the Five Big Ones): *Le Petit Parisien, Le Journal, Le Matin, Le Petit Journal,* and *L'Echo de Paris,* which had signed a collective agreement with the advertising agency Havas, giving them a monopoly on advertising. Colette was aware that "advertising was a newspaper's blood" and had probably not forgotten that her uncle Landoy had founded the first newspaper entirely financed by advertising. Unhappy with Colette's move to *Le Quotidien,* the conservative *Le Figaro* cut her production to two articles a month. She resigned.

Meanwhile, she was making the most of her relationship with the prime minister; she pleaded with him for the infante Don Luis Ferdinand, in trouble with the French authorities and under threat of deportation. Herriot could not grant Colette's request, but she obtained a subsidy for Moréno to whom she wrote: "I have two thousand francs in my drawer for you. He would be happy if you accepted them, he could not have been more cordial and gentle. I gave him two manuscripts of *My Mother's House,* which he likes."[180] To help Moréno, whose South American tour had fallen through, Colette included her and her nephew-lover Pierre Moréno in the cast of *Chéri,* now in rehearsals; Léo Marchand and Germaine Beaumont were also part of "the literary cast."

The winter of 1924–1925 was hard for Colette; by putting enormous pressure on Bertrand, his mother managed to obtain his consent to marry an heiress. Jouvenel formally asked for the hand of Mademoiselle de

Ricqlès for his son and set the date for the official engagement dinner. Before the fateful dinner, Bertrand went to see Colette, who asked why should he go, since he was less than enthusiatic about this marriage. She saw him waver and suggested, "Don't go!" But Bertrand felt he had an obligation to go; *fiançailles* were a legal contract. As he ran down the stairs into the yard, Colette's window opened, and a paper fluttered to his feet. He picked it up and read, "I love you"; [181] it was the first time she had ever said these words. He ran back upstairs and did not appear at the official dinner. The scandal was enormous, as was the loss of face for the Jouvenels; the two families never managed to overcome the insult. Claire Boas was adamant; Bertrand must be taken away from Colette.

Colette and Bertrand spent four days in Marseilles, then resumed their life at Boulevard Suchet. But Bertrand was often gone, giving speeches and attending meetings in Geneva, headquarters of the League of Nations, while Colette was pouring out her soul and, according to her, her guts in a sequel to *Chéri*. In *The Last of Chéri (La Fin de Chéri)*, the darkest of her novels, the handsome, weak Chéri succumbs to despair and commits suicide because time robs him of Léa by turning her into an elderly woman. The 1914–1918 war has taken away life as he knew it and given an alien meaning to all things around him. Colette never went deeper into the analysis of love, the complex interplay of senses and emotions, and the doomed struggle between love and time. Anticipating the loss of sexual drive, Colette's aging Léa feels love burning lower, while Chéri clings to love's eternity. To recapture his past, he spends his days in the apartment of *la Copine,* an ex-*cocotte,* now old and poor, smoking and talking endlessly about Léa, whom she idolized. She has a whole wall covered with photographs of Léa. When *la Copine* leaves for a week, Chéri locks himself up in her apartment, lies down on the sofa, looks at Léa's photographs and, in quiet despair, knowing that Léa is no longer Léa, shoots himself.

*The Last of Chéri*, a meditation on fleeting time, which robs us of everything and finally of ourselves, is as poignant as Goethe's *Faust,* whose protagonist also lusts for timeless youth and timeless love. The critic Fernand Vanderem wrote that never had Colette's genius been so obvious as when she painted the tormented soul of a man of thirty, back from the war, who finds out that there is nothing left for him to live for.

Colette was now once more on stage; for three weeks, she played in *Chéri* at the Théâtre Daunou. As an actress, Colette was herself; the novelist Gérard d'Houville (Marie de Régnier) wrote that whoever had not seen Colette as Léa could understand neither the novel nor the play. She had many detractors, actors as well as critics; her naturalistic style was disconcerting to actors who had been trained in drama schools. She was always shunned by the theater establishment, but no one denied that Colette had charisma. The playwright Henri Bernstein talked about her extraordinary concentration and her hard-to-define, subtle irony and "yet massive strength"[182] in her portrayal of Léa.

*Chéri* was a success and reopened at the Théâtre de la Renaissance in April. It was pure coincidence that Colette's return to the stage occurred as Willy settled back in Paris. Madeleine de Swarte insisted on his staying in Paris, where she felt that he was much better off than in Monte Carlo, far from the gambling tables and close to his friends. As soon as he arrived, he was interviewed by Léon Treich for *L'Eclair*. Still yearning to clear his reputation as a writer, Willy spoke about his collaborators, giving their names and the titles of the novels written with them. The old feud flared up. A few days later in *Le Journal Littéraire*, Edouard Keyser signed a series of articles, documented by Colette, in which Willy was portrayed as a writer who did not write, but exploited the talent of others, namely Colette and Curnonsky. On December 13 *Le Journal Littéraire* published an answer by Curnonsky; he felt it was up to him to set things straight. His article was a long and precise review of Mr. Keyser's "erroneous assertions." Keyser had stated that *Un Petit Vieux bien propre* was written by Curnonsky alone; "Not true," replied Curnonsky, "I wrote it with Willy, he never denied my collaboration, neither did I." But fifteen years ago, Willy's name sold a book, "mine did not; besides, there is between Willy and myself an affection that no one and nothing could ever break up."[183] Curnonsky added that aside from a mutual friendship, Willy and he also shared certain secrets, which they would disclose whenever they felt they had to. It was a direct threat to Colette.

Léo Paillet interviewed Colette and asked her how she wrote *Les Dialogues de Bêtes (Creatures Great and Small)*. "Alone," she replied, and added, "I could show you something very curious, for instance, the manuscripts of the *Claudines*, entirely handwritten by myself. Only a few notes of a pornographic nature are due to the hand of my 'collaborator.' But let us not insist."[184]

A year later the manuscripts made their first appearance. On March 27, 1925, *Les Nouvelles Littéraires* published an interview by Frédéric

Lefèvre. Colette had showed him twenty-eight notebooks — the kind used by schoolchildren — filled with her handwriting, with but a few words crossed out or corrected, with only a few remarks by Willy here and there. The manuscripts, she said, had been retrieved from Willy by Paul Barlet to prevent Willy from destroying them.

On April 3, *Les Nouvelles Littéraires* published Willy's answer. He wrote with restraint, saying that he preferred the first *Claudine* to *The Last of Chéri,* which he regarded, nevertheless, as a masterpiece; he called Colette a genius. He stated again that he had collaborated with Colette, even more than the public was aware of; he had even written articles signed "Colette Willy." He recalled that their quarrels had kept a playful tone for years; he used to call Colette "the last of the lyrics" and blame her for being too much like a man — to which she answered by telling him that he was too much like a woman and that his style was too fussy. He did not mention the manuscripts of the *Claudines;* later he described Paul Barlet as a draft dodger whom he had rescued and fed, only to be robbed by "this ungrateful footpad."[185]

The vicissitudes of the manuscripts of the *Claudines* remain a mystery. Colette had those of *Claudine Married* and *Claudine and Annie,* and there were persistent rumors that the manuscripts of *Claudine at School* were in Belgium. There is a theory that the manuscripts were fabricated after the unexpected Claudine craze; it is based on the fact that before 1900, several witnesses and Colette herself talked about *les feuillets,* the loose pages on which the manuscript was written. In 1936 in *My Apprenticeships,* she said that she had bought some notebooks like the ones she used at school to write her first novel. But in an interview on *Retreat from Love (La Retraite Sentimentale)* in 1949, Colette, when asked if she had written it like the other Claudines, "always on your famous notebooks *Le Calligraphe,*"[186] unexpectedly answered that before her famous notebooks, she had used others *(avant j'en ai eu d'autres).* She was already very choosy and could write only on a rare American paper with blue lines; she added that she had owned the first fountain pen in Paris.

As for Willy, none of his manuscripts remain; he destroyed them all. Willy had his own way of establishing the final text of the novels he signed: each draft was typed, and when the new version was ready with the additions from several "collaborators," the old one was destroyed. By the time the last typed copy reached the publisher, the alternative versions of the work in progress had all been destroyed. This was a departure from the accepted practice of sending a handwritten manuscript to the publisher.

The glittering season on the Riviera opened with the creation of Maurice Ravel's *The Boy and the Magic (L'Enfant et les Sortilèges),* libretto by Colette, at the Monte Carlo Theater. Colette, who was playing in *Chéri,* could not attend the event. She arrived in early April.

Claire Boas's agenda was still to marry off Bertrand; he was sent to Cannes for the Easter holidays. In the hotel next to his was Claire's hand-picked candidate, Marcelle Prat, a writer and Maeterlinck's niece. She was attractive, intelligent, interested in arts, and sophisticated; Bertrand gave in. Aware of the plot, Colette met the situation head-on. She telephoned Bertrand and invited him to lunch at Cap d'Aïl, where she was staying with Marguerite Moréno, her nephew-lover, Pierre Moréno, and their friends Monsieur and Madame Bloch-Levallois and Maurice Goudeket, who was Madame Bloch-Levallois' lover. Colette nicknamed her "the Chihuahua."

After lunch Colette asked Bertrand to come to her room. Throughout the night they had a long, serious discussion. Although he was ready to spend his life with her, in the end he finally agreed that it was impossible for them to remain lovers. At daybreak Bertrand left.

Colette prepared to return to Paris; Moréno's friend Goudeket was in a hurry and planned to take the night train, so he offered Colette his car and chauffeur. Chance had it that no seat was available on the night train, so Goudeket drove back with Colette, who sent a postcard to Hélène Picard, announcing that she was coming home, "a magnificent return by car," adding, "what a constant turmoil in my life."[187]

# III

---

## FOURIERIST COLETTE

---

*"Oh gods, how lovable he is!"*
COLETTE, LM, P. 116

𝒥N MAY 1925 COLETTE was booked for two weeks at the Opéra Music Hall on the Champs Elysées. The two-part program began with a lecture by Colette followed by *Chonchette,* a play by de Flers and Caillavet — a formula very much in fashion. Colette's topic was her music-hall days, but she also read "two exquisite literary pastiches, Poum and La Chienne trop Petite."¹ Her eyesight was becoming weak, but she refused to wear glasses in public. Her lectures were written with oversized letters, but she quickly had all the pages mixed up and ended up improvising, at which she was very good. When she read she had a tendency to lower her voice, and some of her words were lost.

After the performance she dined with the "gracious Chihuahua" and her husband at Maurice Goudeket's elegant "but cold" apartment. She was seeing a lot of Moréno's friends, complaining that they made her drink too much. She also told Marguerite that she had had with Maurice "one of those conversations, which start at ten before midnight and end at eleven twenty-five in the morning."² With Maurice she was having those long literary discussions she used to have with Marcel Schwob. She enjoyed these nightly conversations more and more amid "an orgy" of

cigarettes, Vittel water, oranges, and grapefruit, for Maurice was a physical fitness addict. Colette's new partner understood "with his antennae,"
and she felt as if some beautiful weather had suddenly burst over Paris, a
long blue day. During the three-day trip to Paris Colette had been impressed by Goudeket's erudition and hedonism. She always needed
someone with whom to discuss her ideas and to reassure her, for Colette
never lost her intellectual inferiority complex, which went back to her
mother's praise of the Landoys. Jouvenel was not the supportive presence she longed for, as he was more inclined to criticize her work
without taking the time to understand it. She was deeply hurt when he
found the topics of her novels too narrow: forty years later she was still
wondering if there were some truth in his criticism or if he was totally
blind to her purpose. Jouvenel never publicly acknowledged Colette's
talent. With Willy and his friends she had been surrounded by very stim-
ulating literati. Willy, who was still making fun of "Vivette's lesbianism"
or "Claudine Educator" in humoristic newspapers, nevertheless constantly called her a literary genius. With Maurice Goudeket, Colette was
finding the same intellectual support without the downside for, unlike
her two ex-husbands, Maurice had no literary ambition. A man of the
world, he admired Colette and understood her. He helped her to clarify
her philosophy and encouraged her to write the best of her novels and
essays. Their friendship began on a note of profound understanding and
exaltation and continued with the same enlivened intensity to the end.
For thirty years their dialogue never stopped. The worries of the past
were melting away as she was expecting the daily visit of the young man
she called, "my nightly storyteller." Her life had become pure poetry:
"Acacias, acacias, more acacias and roses, fast-flowing waters and hours
flowing even faster." In June they drove to Saint-Sauveur — an eerie,
unreal drive in one-hundred-degree temperatures — to attend the official unveiling of the pink marble plate bearing the inscription, "Colette
was born here." Anatole de Monzie, who remained Colette's and
Jouvenel's friend despite the divorce, presided over the ceremony, representing the government. With Maurice "at the wheel" Colette had only
seen roses, honeysuckle, and the ancient wisteria on the fence of her
house in Saint-Sauveur, where she had refused to step. She led Goudeket
to believe that the house had been auctioned off when she was fifteen
because of her family's ruin. After Colette's death, he would repeat the
tale in his lectures about her.

Everything had become so gentle in her life that she had the dream-like feeling of someone falling from a steeple and floating in magic comfort in midair; she let herself roll along like a planet in the sky, no longer in control of her destiny — she felt bewitched. Again and again she called Maurice a "dark Satan," such "a dark, dark, dark boy," insisting on the concealed side of his personality. Maurice's mistress, the Chihuahua, whom Colette now called "that unfortunate woman," had realized what was happening; she started stalking Maurice and Colette everywhere. She telephoned day and night, questioned Colette's maid, her secretary, even Léo Marchand and his wife. So Maurice decided to tell her the truth; but Colette, always ready to take things into her own hands, took Chihuahua aside for fifteen minutes before the four of them — she, Goudeket, and the Bloch-Levalloises — were to dine together. She told her that she "was a charming person," but that friendship and inquisition were incompatible. She forced the stunned Chihuahua to promise that she would no longer make phone calls but would wait for Colette to call her first, would never turn a dinner into a tragedy or an evening into a sequestration. Neither of them pronounced Maurice's name. The whole affair looked like a comedy between well-bred and discreet people; all was settled with understatements and decorous smiles.

Chihuahua said she would relinquish all claims on Maurice and asked Colette to let her know if she was truly happy. Colette snapped back, "I will leave the place of my happiness and run to send you a telegram." She explained to Moréno that the conflict had lasted six days, but was over now; she called the Chihuahua a spoiled child who needed only a stern dressing-down to be good. She was now as tame as a kitten. Her advice to Moréno, who was attracted to Chihuahua, was "with a cudgel, you will do with her whatever you wish." Colette, unaware of her cruelty, congratulated herself on having shown so much patience, but "the boy was worth it. . . . He is exquisite."

Then, on June 21, a cry of joy: "*Ah! la, la et encore la, la*! and never enough la, la! . . . Oh the satanism of quiet people! So you want to know who that guy Maurice really is? A scoundrel and this and that and even a good guy, and his skin is pure satin." She experienced that rare human luxury, friendship with love, and could hardly believe it. She spent all her weekends with her "companion who looks like the classical Satan,"[3] who is in French imagery the irresistible charmer who snares his fascinated prey, tempting them with what they most desire.

In July she wrote to Marguerite, "Do not think I am crazy or wild! My dear Soul, it is much more serious." Peace had come into Colette's life; as she wrote she watched her "very dear companion, a tanned and sleeping body" in the shade of a blue curtain. "Oh gods, how lovable he is!"[4] She loved his silence, she loved his talk, she loved his nonchalant ways, she loved to watch him rest in the evening. She found the "dark boy," as she liked to call him, so subtle that she felt clumsy next to him.

### Maurice Goudeket

The man who had come into Colette's life was quite different from Henry de Jouvenel, the brilliant political orator, very different from Henry Gauthier-Villars, the dazzling *boulevardier*. Maurice was thirty-five, not as young as Bertrand de Jouvenel and less handsome. He was not a multimillionaire like Auguste Hériot, yet she found him the perfect companion; she soon referred to him as her best friend. She confessed to Moréno that she loved him passionately; after ten years, this lover became her third husband. He remained her lover, husband, best friend, partner, financial counselor, and manager for the rest of her life. In her will, written in 1948, Colette made him her sole literary executor.

Maurice Goudeket was born in Paris on August 3, 1889, the year Paris celebrated the first centennial of the French Revolution by erecting the Eiffel tower; he called himself the *Tour Eiffel's* twin. He was from a wealthy, middle-class Jewish family. His father, a dealer in diamonds, was Dutch, his mother French. Maurice was raised to fear the outdoors; his father refused to take him and his elder brother to the Bois de Boulogne, because it had been scientifically proven that trees absorb all the oxygen from the air. As a reaction against that deprivation, Maurice sported a tan most of his life.

Maurice's mother was a strong, domineering woman, a nagging wife who quarreled for the sake of quarreling. Her husband, a quiet and peaceful man, was dragged into loud arguments in spite of himself. Maurice and his brother were terrified as her voice rose and the quarrels reached dramatic proportions. Maurice was even more upset when she abused the servants. She would emerge from the kitchen or the pantry red in the face and pleased with herself, and he felt she was enjoying her power over helpless people. The servants lived in garrets under the roof where they froze in winter and suffocated in summer; they began their chores at seven in the morning and worked till midnight. When she dismissed them, Madame Goudeket never failed to search their battered suitcases to check if they had concealed any stolen object. This final humiliation revolted Maurice.

Madame Goudeket dealt with her sons capriciously, punishing them without any clear cause. She had a way of humiliating them to assert her power; she not only slapped their cheeks, but commanded them to keep their arms by their sides and to raise their faces to meet the blow. Maurice saw this not as a punishment but as an insult. Years later he still felt uneasy when he remembered his mother and envied the lucky ones for whom the word "mother sounds exquisitely."[5] Maurice's love for Colette, his unwavering devotion as she became an invalid, may have stemmed from this nostalgic feeling — regret at not having been able to love his mother. He felt closer to his father, but not close enough to talk to him about his own problems, for Monsieur Goudeket wanted only one thing from his children: marks of respect. When they met him on the street, they never addressed him without taking off their hats and holding them until he gave them permission to put them back on. Whenever he left on his many business trips, Maurice and his brother escorted him to the railroad station. Monsieur Goudeket never used slang and always remained polite and aloof.

Maurice went to the Lycée Condorcet and was in the same class as Jean Cocteau. An avid reader, he was drawn to philosophy and read Plato, Locke, Condillac, Spencer, Spinoza, Kant, Hegel, Fichte, the Bhavagad-Gita, and various esoteric works; he tempered his philosophical flights by studying Montaigne, who interested him in human nature and psychology. The well-known poet Gustave Kahn was his mother's cousin, and Maurice grew up dreaming that he would also be a poet. Kahn, an advocate of free verse, had cofounded the reviews *La Vogue* and *Le Décadent* with Jean Moréas. He did not encourage Maurice's vocation, who reached adolescence in a society in which sons meekly followed in the steps of their fathers. So he introverted his dreams and decided his destiny was to live for one great platonic love: he would be Dante for a Beatrice. He felt his body protesting against these dreams and went through a period of deep emotional turmoil. The highly sexed but chaste adolescent could not chase lewd pictures from his mind; the bosom of a maid, the calf of a woman going up a step, a bare neck were enough to torture him. The long gloves and button boots women wore at the turn of the century became erotic objects, fetishes; the rustle of a silk skirt gave him a lump in his throat. He woke up three or four times every night and in the dead of winter in his unheated bedroom he could not bear a blanket. In despair he turned to his brother, got only dirty jokes for an answer. Later, Maurice deplored that neither teachers nor parents talked to him when he was obviously distraught and failing at school.

Maurice became a successful businessman, an international dealer in pearls and precious stones. The two Goudeket brothers were typical playboys, always seen in the company of pretty girls from the Champs Elysées to Montmartre. They went barhopping, ending the night at Les Halles. They no longer went to the slaughterhouses in La Villette for a glass of red wine blended with fresh blood from the butchered cattle; the pre–World War I playboys went to the Pré-Catalan farms at daybreak and drank a glass of fresh milk straight from the udder. Maurice described *la Noce* as a sort of bureaucratic need to have fun every night in the same bars with the same people. He slipped away from any involvement, but kept a *poule de luxe,* one of the new-era courtesans dressed by Coco Chanel or Lucien Lelong. Every evening, in dinner jacket and black tie and wearing a monocle, he dined in chic restaurants, leaving extravagant tips.

At twenty-one he made a decision that would change his life. Born in Paris of a Dutch father, he had the option of choosing his nationality. French citizenship meant eighteen months of military service, which was not required of Dutch citizens. To avoid the draft Maurice opted for the latter; but in 1914, as soon as war was declared, he enlisted in the First Regiment of the Foreign Legion, like many foreigners born in France. Fighting in the trenches, Maurice was wounded and assigned for the rest of the war as interpreter to a British battalion. He wrote a few poems, which he published later.

During the long hours spent in the cold, wet, muddy trenches, Maurice devised his own philosophical system: life was to be cherished, and the search for happiness was a duty. But happiness did not mean egotism, selfishness, the joy of success, or sensuous pleasures — it was the joy of being alive savored thankfully, day by day, minute by minute. Happiness was to be preserved at all costs when hardship struck. Happiness should be as normal as breathing. In the trenches he started to practice deep breathing and repeated his mantra, "I am breathing therefore I am happy." He never abandoned his Stoical-Epicurean system.

Maurice Goudeket left two books, *Close to Colette (Près de Colette)* and *The Joy of Growing Old (La Douceur de Vieillir)*, in which, at the age of seventy-five, he still spoke of his "impatience to live" that pulled him out of bed at the crack of dawn. Each night as he fell asleep he was eager for tomorrow. He loved everything a new day brought him: his first cup of coffee, which had a new taste every morning, the daily newspapers heralding in the world, the mail perhaps informing him that someone had left him a few billion. This reasoned approach to each minute, his philosophical sense of joy, this unfaltering curiosity created a genteel environment. He was interested in art and theater; a knowledgeable bibliophile, he built a large collection of extremely rare books.

At thirty-five he was short, slim, elegant, soft-spoken, and reserved. He was part of a wealthy social group with connections to the artistic world.

Colette, barely out of love, was in love again. According to Paul Léautaud, she was not only pretty at fifty-two, she radiated physical pleasure, love, passion, and sensuality.

Colette's friends wondered who the new man in her life was; gossip had fed on her love affairs since the days of Willy. An irresistible curiosity drove the socialite poet Anna de Noailles to find out firsthand. The butler announced the countess. As Colette greeted her, Anna looked at Maurice as if she intended to turn him to dust, saying, "Monsieur, I am the most intelligent person of the century." With poise he retorted, "I am glad to hear that, until this moment I thought it was I."[6] Anna was absolutely charmed and called him "dear Maurice" on the spot. She described him as "that symmetrical creature with a well-centered nose." During the visit Colette vanished into the garden and brought back some fragrant flowers.

"What is this?" inquired Anna.

"Melissa," answered Colette.

"There it is at last! This is the melissa I have so often mentioned in my poems!" exclaimed a jubilant Anna. Maurice wondered how a poet could use a word that had no objective meaning and was nothing but a sound. "It is a poet's privilege," said Colette. "Everything I have to learn, she is able to invent."[7]

Colette thought it only natural that Anna de Noailles was "crazy about Maurice," that the princess de Polignac "kept inviting him, that Hélène de Chimay quotes his witticisms." Realizing her friends' infatuation with him, she commented, "I grabbed him first" *(j'ai été vite).*[8] But to most people his presence in her life remained incomprehensible. Paul Valéry made dirty jokes about him, calling him "Mr. Good-tail." Even those who liked his affable manners kept wondering what attracted such a woman to such a man.

In July Colette and Maurice left for the south of France to spend a few days in La Bergerie, a villa he rented from Armand Citroën. The trendsetters were moving away from Nice and the Riviera, away from the grand estates, to settle in more modest dwellings with rustic names like "The Sheepfold" or "The White Shed" in the hills around tiny fishing villages. On the spur of the moment, Colette decided to sell Rozven and buy a house in Saint-Tropez.

In August she went on tour playing Léa with the Tournées Baret, a grand tour of the casino towns: Royat, Toulouse, Foix, Cauterets, la Bourboule, Saint Jean de Luz, Deauville, and Monte Carlo. As Colette and Maurice rode in his magnificent car everyone stopped to look at her. The couple would drive a hundred miles to have dinner at some inn, and Colette would arrive fifteen minutes before the curtain went up. She had no time to put on her makeup, and walked straight onto the stage. Harry Krimer, who played Chéri, wondered: "She is not properly dressed, she has no makeup, she does not look right."[9] Then, three minutes later, the miracle happened; everyone was captured by her magic, audience as well as actors. There was a sort of melancholy charm in her eyes, in her voice. Harry Krimer could not explain why he was so deeply moved every evening as he listened to her. The audience who came to see Madame Colette left with the impression of having witnessed an emotional happening, of having been privy to her life. The actors could always count on her whatever went wrong. At Cauterets, for example, the only available bell was a sheep bell. When Léa was supposed to hear a doorbell, the sheep bell's typical clang was heard and the audience burst out laughing. "They have let the sheep in," said Colette, and they cheered her. In another town, when Léa's telephone rang, no telephone was to be found; suddenly a hand thrust one through the canvas. "God's hand,"[10] commented Colette to the public's applause.

Colette returned to Paris determined to turn over a new page.

Rozven, which she had called her necessity a few months earlier, was put up for sale. As soon as she had reached a decision, Colette wanted it implemented immediately, but her divorce settlement had been dragging on since April. In the fall she found out that Henry de Jouvenel had not paid in full for the house on Boulevard Suchet; there were still twenty thousand francs in balance due and the owner had started proceedings against her. Until that matter was settled, the divorce could not be finalized. Colette could neither sign a mortgage, nor sell Rozven, nor buy the house in the south of France, nor even finalize the agreement with Monsieur Ducharne for the house in Saint-Sauveur; she was still legally married and needed Jouvenel's signature for everything. She turned to Germaine Patat, who could help by pressuring Jouvenel, who now seemed in no hurry to divorce; Colette had heard that he was wondering why he had disorganized his life.

After yet another political upheaval, Jouvenel's political mentors were back in power: Anatole de Monzie as minister of the treasury, then of education; Aristide Briand as minister of foreign affairs. Briand appointed Henry de Jouvenel high commissioner in Syria, with viceregal powers; Henry arrived there on December 1. That same day Princess Bibesco left Bucharest, where she had attended the marriage of her only daughter, to join him in the Middle East. Now she considered herself free to divorce and wrote to Jouvenel that his shoulders were broad enough to carry an empire, hinting that she was ready to assist him in the task. She landed in Palestine to find a cool Jouvenel. Her trip to Syria was disappointing and painful. On her way back to Rumania she had a car accident and her chauffeur was killed. The Parisian press reported the accident, but Jouvenel did not send a note. Back in Paris, she met Mamita and also a deceitful Jouvenel, who claimed to have written her many letters; to this transparent lie Marthe ironically replied, "And I have received them all." The next day she received a cold letter, in which she was addressed as "Madame," concluding with the words "peace and solitude."[11] The following year Jouvenel married the multimillionaire widow of Charles Louis Dreyfus. In *Julie de Carneilhan,* Colette drew a stunning *portrait à cléf* of Henry de Jouvenel under the thinly masked character, Count d'Espivant, an unethical and manipulative man.

Princess Bibesco turned for comfort to Lord Carrington, the new viceroy of India. The day he left to take office, the man who had said, "that disease that some call love and I call Marthe" died when the dirigible he was traveling in exploded over the French coast. Marthe found solace with Ramsay MacDonald — "Delicious joy to live with a man who wields such power." [12]

Bertrand de Jouvenel married Marcelle Prat, to his mother's great satisfaction, in December 1925. On that occasion Colette wrote him a long letter, which was intercepted by his bride. Years later Marcelle recited Colette's beautiful letter to Bertrand, who was amazed that she had kept it to herself and memorized it. He never lost touch with Colette; he wrote to her whenever he needed support. He felt nostalgia for the wonder years he had spent with her, when she shared with him some of her magic understanding of the world.

### The Writer-Actress

Colette was booked for two weeks at the Théâtre du Parc in Brussels. She coached Tréville, the new Chéri, before rehearsals, but could not make him feel the part; he was "too young, too dry." [13] Colette was acclaimed in Brussels; she got a standing ovation every night and was received by the queen, who loved literature. She was just back from an official trip to India where, displeased that the official functions did not include a visit to Rabindranath Tagore, she had slipped away from the royal party and traveled incognita to meet the poet. She shared with Colette a love for music and nature; both could name the wildflowers they saw. Elizabeth's esteem for Colette grew with the years.

Colette ended her run in Brussels with an attack of bronchitis and was barely able to last to the end of the show, "after . . . a horrible night, syncope, despair not to be able to leave . . ." [14] for Maurice was waiting for her in Paris, where he had only come for a weekend. "Providential" Alba Crosbie took charge of Colette and shepherded her back to Paris. Sweet, blond, devoted, discreet Alba Crosbie was Colette's new companion. Irish by birth, she was part of an Anglo-American group who had settled in the dilapidated Palais-Royal, renovating it.

In December 1925 Colette played Léa in Marseilles with Marguerite Moréno, "a tragedian turned comedian by Colette's decree," [15] and the brilliant, upcoming Pierre Fresnay as Chéri; Colette, who had never liked Harry Krimer, had closely followed negotiations to book Fresnay.

She was in an upbeat mood, having finally finished *The Last of Chéri,* a novel she began in March 1924, with a cry of deliverance: "Let that one die."[16] She rushed back to Paris to correct the proofs of *The Last of Chéri* before leaving in January on another tour. Fifty minutes before the train's departure, she was still working on the proofs.

The cast was a new one, Maurice Lagrenée, who created the part of Chéri, was back; Colette felt so comfortable with him on stage that she kept changing or adding lines. "I can add anything," said Colette during an interview, "for I am also the author."[17] The remark did not convey what Colette was really doing. She improvised whenever she felt it could improve a scene and played on her audience's emotions. Lucie Delarue-Mardrus noted that Colette was particularly impressive when she remained silent, mesmerising her audience, sensing how long she could hold them. The critic Albert Flamant compared her to a luscious Renoir. Georges Wague said she should never have left the stage, and recalled that he had never given Colette her salary all at once, because she would immediately spend it on trinkets, such as pens with little inserts of glass through which one could see, magnified, the local cathedral. The playwright Henri Bernstein and Coco Chanel came to see her, both shockingly dressed in identical "evening pajamas" — Coco's latest creation. He declared, "Is Colette a great actress? I don't know. I only know that this is a bantering, haunting, disdainful, cruel, subtle and massive, formidable performance."[18]

In Nice Colette settled at the Hôtel Plaza with her "little companion Alba." Nice was at the height of the winter season: "Everybody from Paris whom I care never to see is here."[19] Claire Boas de Jouvenel gave lavish soirees at Le Négresco; a journalist from the *Chicago Tribune,* thinking she was Colette, came to interview her but immediately left when he found out she was not the writer-actress. Colette was amused by this reversal of fortune.

She bought a pair of parakeets and set them free in her suite, but at night put them back in a cage; as she locked up the female she was attacked by the male, "who thought I was mistreating his mate." Parted for barely ten minutes, they went "wild with despair. It was really beautiful,"[20] as a mirror of Maurice's love for her. From London and Paris, where he was on business, he was writing letters "full of youthful love, ... magnificent love letters." In a flash of candor, Colette acknowledged, "To accept his love, what cannibalism on my part."[21]

Still sick from her annual bout with bronchitis, Colette, coddled by Alba, came back to Paris to play Léa at Le Théâtre Michel; again she directed the rehearsals, insisting on true-to-life acting. Meanwhile at the Opéra Comique, *The Boy and the Magic,* which had been such a success in Monte Carlo, was a flop. The French critics found the opera-ballet childish and disorganized. It was the story of a child punished by his mother, but comforted by objects and animals: a Wedgewood teapot, a Chinese cup, a squirrel, cats, dragonflies, owls, a book of fairy tales. Ravel, who had taken ten years to finish the score, had integrated modern trends: the teapot danced ragtime and two cats meowed a duet.

Colette, haunted by her usual money worries, yet living, according to Claude Chauvière, "sumptuously," was producing highly paid advertising texts for the furrier MAX and for La Maison de Blanc as well as writing the texts for an album by the painter Mathurin Méheut, *Look (Regarde).* She was exhausted. *The Last of Chéri* was released by Flammarion in March; a thirty-two-page chapter was missing. When she found out, the first edition of thirty-five thousand copies was already in the bookstores; there was no way to recall the books. Colette had worked a year and a half on her novel; she had corrected the proofs between rehearsals, on tour, through her divorce, without checking the continuity of the chapters; the printer was not responsible, she was. The mishap deeply upset Colette. The second printing comprised two hundred and seventy-eight pages instead of two hundred and forty-six.

Publicity had been extensive: *Aux Ecoutes* had drummed up the readers' expectations. There would be revelations "since Madame Colette always put her life in her books and her plays." The tabloid leaked that Colette was fuming against Jouvenel because he had contrived to make her resign from *Le Matin,* pretending that he had already sent his own resignation to the board of directors.

"Are you going to stay?" he was reputed to have asked casually.

"Well, no, if you are leaving."

She then wrote her letter of resignation, which he took and gave himself to the director and having achieved his goal, remained at *Le Matin.* Madame Colette's close friends hoped that this story would be in *The Last of Chéri.*[22]

If this was meant to start of a media war with Henry de Jouvenel, it fizzled out; by March the divorce settlement had been honored, and Colette, "crazy and divided as usual,"[23] left for Saint Moritz with Alba

Crosbie. She then went to Morocco, where she spent three weeks in April with her "charming companion," Maurice Goudeket. They were the guests of El Glaoui, pasha of Marrakesh. In Rabat they attended the festivities marking the end of Ramadan and marveled at the quantities of gifts the Moroccans gave their sultan. In Meknès they were greeted by children in local costumes, but Fez stole their heart. They spent a few days alone in El Glaoui's palace, set in gardens trilling with nightingales and planted with the rarest kinds of trees, where "the wind and the night blend disquieting perfumes." They were attended by a retinue of slaves. Colette loved Fez, "a prison of flowers and fountains," the whinnying stallions running in the Arab cemetery, the storks on the coppery city walls so much that she reserved a room for a week in the Palais Jamaï, the old vizier's palace, to unwind, to think, and to "spew out some notes on paper."[24] She did not use the resulting works immediately; two years later *Vogue* published one article, "Déjeuner marocain." "Notes Marocaines" would be integrated in the definitive edition of *Prisons et Paradis* in 1935.

The event of the spring was Princess Paley's benefit gala, which took place in the salons of her husband, the couturier Lucien Lelong, at 16 Avenue Matignon; for this occasion Colette wrote and directed a sketch for three popular stars. It was "a little inferno," for the three actors tried to upstage each other. The international set, who had paid one thousand francs each for the evening, crowded the garden roof, lit by luminescent fountains and moving colored rays of changing lights to listen to Colette's sketch, dance to the music of a jazz band perched between chimneys, and dine "in grand ducal style."[25]

Colette's life continued to be as crowded as ever. Maurice's former mistress, the Chihuahua, complained that Colette was neglecting her, although she was now Moréno's friend. Colette, always afraid of losing someone's affection, was begging Marguerite, "Do love me again." She instructed her to spread the word that she was "virtue itself."[26] She sent flowers and letters to Meg Villars, who had undergone an operation, and took charge of Germaine Patat. Henry de Jouvenel had broken up with Germaine, who was wasting away. Colette prescribed a red-meat diet and took her to the restaurant Dagorneau at La Villette slaughterhouse. She also took care of the chronically sick Hélène Picard, who was in dire need of money, having lost her job when Colette left *Le Matin*. Colette promoted her work, asking editors to publish her articles and writing to inquire why they did not. She urged Hélène to get a settlement from her estranged husband and sent over her own lawyer. She booked Hélène in a bed-and-breakfast in the country, where she could pick her own vegetables. The place was recommended by Katia Barjansky, a sculptor Colette had met in Rome during the war and for whom she had written a preface for her exhibition catalog. Barjansky made a bust of Colette, who gave it to d'Annunzio. "Thanks to that sorceress Katarina, I have today your beautiful lively bust on my table, but I would like to know the secret of your prose. I kiss your hands remembering Rome in 1913,"[27] read the poet's thank-you telegram.

Colette's successful return to the stage had not put a damper on her journalistic ambition; she dined with François Coty, the beauty-product maverick owner of *Le Figaro,* and coaxed the management of *Le Quotidien,* but to no avail.

Suddenly, Colette abandoned journalism. It would be a seven-year hiatus during which she wrote her most creative works. Before settling at her writing desk, she rearranged her priorities. She disposed of her properties; Rozven was sold. Over Maurice's objections (for he was afraid of decisions made on the spur of the moment), she rented her *hôtel* on Boulevard Suchet to a couple of American expatriates and charged Bernard Bloch-Levallois, the Chihuahua's husband, with finding her an apartment: "I am looking for a new boat in which I can steer better. . . . He [Maurice] does not know how some creatures . . . profit every time they can move out of their country, out of their house, out of their skin, if they can take with them . . . the essentials, *their* essentials."[28]

Colette needed an anchor point. She had chosen a peasant house on two and a half acres near Saint-Tropez: four rooms, a kitchen, a terrace, and a few steps leading to a secluded beach. There was a small vineyard, a vegetable garden, some fig trees, some mimosa trees, a small pinewood, and a well of clear water. A vine of muscat grapes grew around the well, so Colette renamed her new lodging La Treille Muscate. In a week she had organized a shipment of part of her Rozven furniture to the south and zoomed through France to await the movers, who took four weeks to show up. Impatient to move into her own home, she bought a broom, two gasoline hot plates, three pans, and two spring-beds and mattresses. Colette felt like "a Tahitian"; at night she dragged her mattress onto the terrace and slept under the stars. Maurice was commuting between Paris and Saint-Tropez. Alba, "that clean little soul *really,*"[29] drove Colette around in her ten-horsepower Citroën.

In September Colette was back on the stage in Bordeaux with Marguerite and Pierre Moréno. In November she was on a lecture tour in Switzerland, speaking about her experiences in the music halls, again focusing on the theater as seen from both sides of the footlights. Life went on.

Throughout the fall Colette and Léo Marchand reworked the stage adaptation of *The Vagabond*. In this production Colette was Renée, and Pierre Renoir (Auguste Renoir's son, who was to become a remarkable movie director), was making his debut as Maxime Dufferein-Chautel, while Paul Poiret played Brague. Colette directed the rehearsals in Poiret's salons. The couturier Poiret was more talented as a designer than as an actor; he never learned his lines and she had to prompt him every night. However, he played in a natural way, which was exactly what Colette wanted from the cast. He also made her nervous by arriving for the show barely on time. He felt no need to rehearse, but was very pleased with the thousand francs he received for each performance. Her irritation grew "at having to deal with such a megalomaniac as Poiret."[30] On stage they were a strange couple, for he looked like Buddha, but together they generated an enormous amount of publicity.

The front page of the program read like an advertising billboard. "Colette's couturier on stage and in town is Lucien Lelong . . . . " Her hat (Marthe Régnier), her shoes (Pérugia), the carpet (Carahékian), the chandelier (Boin-Moeyersoen) — nothing was omitted.

The play opened at the Théâtre du Parc. Tout-Bruxelles was at the premiere, led by the Prince de Ligne. The king and queen, who were on a trip, missed "a brilliant performance by Madame Colette, the author-actress," according to the *Luxemburger Zeitung*. The tour went on to Switzerland and arrived on the Riviera for the Christmas season; the last performance was at the Monte Carlo theater. "Great success," reported Colette. In Paris *The Vagabond* played at Le Théâtre de l'Avenue throughout January. The stage version focused on Renée Néré, victim of a philandering husband. Abandoned, without money, she has to work and becomes a music-hall artist. The critics of the Roaring Twenties saw a "psychological mystery" in the refusal of the "vagabond" to marry Maxime and rejoin her social class. *The Vagabond* was not a feminist play. "It is not the protest of a woman who feels she has been denied her rights";[31] it is only the story of a woman who has loved too much and suffered too much to attempt another marriage. Colette was not con-

vincing in the part. Natalie Barney summarized the general feeling: "A
Vagabond indeed, a walking pedestal topped with a tiny triangle of a
face, compactly plump, with an octoroon complexion and the air of an
owl in broad daylight."[32]

In fact, this tour of The Vagabond put an end to Colette's career as an
actress, even if she did not realize it at the time. A year later Moréno
wanted to produce Chéri in South America, but did not ask Colette to
join the cast. Colette was hurt. She asked Léo Marchand to find out if
the project was taking off, for she would jump at the chance to go on
tour in Argentina and make a great deal of money. The project did not
materialize. She was hoping to go to Germany; her German publisher
was ready to finance a performance of The Vagabond and one of Chéri,
and Colette would give a lecture. This did not materialize, either.

Then she turned to the movies. She hoped for a partnership with
a producer, Monsieur Broissat or with Germaine Dulac, a producer-
director since 1915, a successful pioneer who had produced forty
movies between 1918 and 1930 and who, in 1930, became artistic director for Gaumont and created France-Actualités. They met but
nothing came of it. She complained that she was not tough enough
when it came to business.

### I Am Heading for My Empty House
### Brimming with Promises and Ambition

Colette loved La Treille Muscate as she had loved Rozven; she immediately began to improve and make additions: first a room, then a terrace, a
patio, another room, an outside staircase, and a garage with a room on
top for a caretaker. Saint-Tropez, as yet undiscovered, was picturesque
and quiet, the hiding place of a small group of Montmartre painters.
Colette's neighbors were the painters Dunoyer de Segonzac and Jean-
Luc Moreau, and the musician Hélène Jourdan-Morhange, who became
her close friends. La Treille Muscate never stopped expanding like a
living thing; Maurice soberly remarked that the house was never beautiful or comfortable, because of the constant presence of workers noisily
finishing some part of the building. In July of 1927 the house was still
not functional: the bathroom was still missing, the "w.c." was not in

working order, the shutters were leaning against the wall, the furniture was heaped in the space called "the bathroom." Colette took over the management of the remodeling, organizing the teams and driving the workers "like a warden"[33] while the frustrated cook was weeping over the soup she was preparing on top of a small stove in the garage.

On August 28 electricity was installed; Colette invited the neighbors over to see her new gadget, a refrigerator. She designed the garden and flowers spread, vines crept up the walls, birds drank in hanging crystal troughs; sunflowers kept goldfinches around the house. She fed nine cats, four dogs, one magpie, and a turtle. She loved semicamping in the balmy climate of the Mediterranean and created the illusion that La Treille Muscate was a paradise. Colette was not the only one to see it as a magic dwelling; the caretaker referred to the garden as "The Park," while the little grove was called "The Forest."

Colette rose before daybreak; she went into the garden and greeted the cats, who played around her as she walked through the vineyard and back. Then it was the dogs' turn; they walked along the shore on a narrow path filled with the fragrance of wild thyme, mint, and rosemary, while all the aroma of the hills of Provence rose with the breeze. Colette came back to breakfast with Maurice on the terrace. Then she worked in her garden with such energy that Maurice retreated. She kneeled or sat on the ground, pulling up weeds, scratching the soil with her bare hands, planting until she decided it was time to go for her one-kilometer swim followed by a lunch of fish and salads, accompanied by a large supply of wine. Colette picked out a crust of freshly baked bread, dipped it in olive oil, rubbed it generously with garlic, and sprinkled coarse sea salt on top; throughout the meal, she ate raw garlic cloves as if they were almonds. Then all the shutters were closed for a short siesta. When Colette got up, she sat at her small desk, set in a corner facing blank walls so she would not be distracted, and started to work.

Maurice was not a man of the woods, the fields, or even the gardens, but he was a cat lover. He used to pick up strays when he was a young playboy and treat them to a bowl of milk as he went barhopping. He and Colette bought a prize-winning blue-gray chartreux cat at a feline show; Colette also bought Souci, a female bulldog who had won first prize at a dog show. To pay for "the marvel," she put the construction of a wall to hide the vineyard from the road on hold.

Having "divorced from a lot of luxury" and distanced herself from the Jouvenels, father and son, Colette was also practically separated from her daughter, who was raised by Germaine Patat. Colette II, expelled from a boarding school in Saint-Germain, was sent to another one in England to learn "equality from the British and that necessary hypocrisy that is the hallmark of her personality and that of her father."[34] Bel-Gazou, raised by everyone and no one, was a problem teenager; Colette, her grandmother Mamita, and her ever traveling father gave her too much money and the free use of their cars. Bel-Gazou had only to call one of their chauffeurs whenever she wanted to leave school to go home or shopping. She was dressed by Germaine Patat, who designed boyish clothes for her that Colette liked, as well as very feminine dresses. Colette entrusted Bel-Gazou to Germaine with the feeling that her daughter was in better hands, frankly admitting her own need to feel free. She thought the age gap between her daughter and herself was too great and her lifestyle too particular for Bel-Gazou to adapt to, and told Germaine Patat that she was happy with Maurice Goudeket, that Bel-Gazou was not an essential part of her life. However, Colette was shocked by Colette II's grade reports and by her teachers' comments that she was arrogant, lazy, weak, vain, and deceptive. She deplored the fact that Colette II never made any effort as a student; this she could neither understand nor accept. She spoke about work with a sort of passion; she was committed to her work; she worshiped work in general. She wondered what Bel-Gazou would become and why a child who had everything, who was taken to concerts, museums, plays, the opera, and sent to the best schools could remain ignorant and indifferent to all.

Remembering the little girl so full of promise, Colette wished Bel-Gazou would stop being known as Henry de Jouvenel's and Colette's daughter. She was convinced that having two famous parents was enough to annihilate Bel-Gazou's innate qualities. When Bel-Gazou was punished and grounded for a week, Colette sent her a letter full of wisdom, explaining that her punishment was the result of her attitude, that she was treating her teachers and fellow students too loftily, and warned her that arrogance leads to failure, which is always one's fault. Then Colette sweetened her comments by telling Bel-Gazou that she too could have become arrogant growing up in Saint-Sauveur, a small village full of peasant girls who were slow to learn, to grasp things. Yet she had never allowed herself to behave as if she were superior to them.

Bel-Gazou was wrong to think "it is good enough"; she did not want her daughter to settle for mediocrity.

When Colette found out that Bel-Gazou smoked in secret, she gently reasoned with her. She had seen men devastated by the tyranny of a habit. She had seen cocaine addicts and morphine addicts; they were not different from nicotine addicts. She tried to convince Bel-Gazou that one took out insurance against trouble by remaining free from any addiction. Colette hammered at this idea, repeating that habit made one a coward and a liar. To smoke a cigarette after dinner was of little importance; to smoke alone, to drink alone could take one very far down the road. Bel-Gazou should fight; it could be hard, but it gave a lot of satisfaction. She warned her daughter not to forget that certain tobaccos were washed in opium and highly addictive.

Deeply worried, Colette called Germaine to the rescue and asked her to insist that Jouvenel call the family doctor and tell him to give Bel-Gazou a serious warning. Colette, who feared no excess, no experience — provided she remained able to cut it off at will — was afraid her daughter was already hooked on tobacco. She felt a genuine concern for Bel-Gazou's welfare and a deep disappointment of having a child without ambition. But she was proud of Bel-Gazou's good looks; she seemed to be carried away by her physical perfection. She raved about her graceful arms, her lovely shoulders, her sturdy legs, her round face with dimples. As far as her education was concerned, she finally resigned herself to be happy when her daughter passed a typing exam.

Whenever Colette was shocked by her daughter's behavior, she turned to Germaine, once urging her to ask Bel-Gazou not to drop her clothes everywhere for the maids to pick up. Colette was annoyed that she never bothered to empty her tub or flush the toilet and told Germaine that it showed a lack of dignity. Colette felt that the educational system was at fault, that Bel-Gazou had not been taught to do anything practical: she could not sew and had no idea how an iron was used or how an oil lamp was lit. Over and over, Colette repeated that Jouvenel should take more care of their daughter.

When Bel-Gazou was fifteen, Colette became upset because her daughter never wrote to her, alleging she could not write a "witty" letter. Colette rejected this as an excuse for her laziness. Bel-Gazou was not only lazy, she was putting on weight. Colette convinced herself that her daughter's shortcomings were due to a kidney deficiency; no doctor was ever able to find one, but Colette was sure of her own diagnosis — she had seen ripples on Bel-Gazou's skin, which indicated water retention.

Discreetly and generously, Germaine Patat raised Bel-Gazou. She tried to give her a job in her haute couture business, but Bel-Gazou did not persevere. She inherited half a million francs from her aunt Edith, who died at twenty-two, built her own house in Saint-Tropez, bought an apartment in Paris, and became even more independent.

Whatever the problem, Colette relied on Germaine Patat. She put her in charge when Hélène Picard fell ill, asking Germaine to find an apartment and a nurse to watch over Hélène as she grew more and more disabled. Colette called Germaine "my child," referring to Bel-Gazou as her little sister. She also named Germaine "the keystone," because she held so many people together.

## As a Writer Colette Is Still to Be Discovered

For all her newfound fascination with Saint-Tropez, Colette's life was in Paris. She needed a place to work and the support of Maurice's invigorating dialogues for the book — half essay, half memoirs — she had in mind. She needed Alba's devoted attention. Only Colette's close circle of friends knew of her relationship with Goudeket, who was extremely discreet even in Saint-Tropez. The German writer Kurt Rossner, who spent several summers at the seaside resort and knew Colette well, was surprised to learn of Maurice's existence. He thought that Colette, whom he always saw surrounded by beautiful women, had only lesbian affairs. In Paris Colette and Goudeket kept separate apartments.

In January of 1927 Colette moved into a mezzanine apartment in the historic Palais Royal, across from the Louvre. The apartment was a sort of long tunnel she rented from Alba Crosbie, who lived above on the "noble" floor in the same block. It was airless and dark; the arched window opened onto the gallery and the lamps had to be turned on all day. Colette had the apartment lined with cretonne, including the ceiling, so low she could reach it with her hand. She bought some dark Spanish furniture, encrusted with mother-of-pearl, and filled the apartment with flowers and rococo trinkets. The first impression was that of a pretty box, the second, of warmth and coziness; she called it "a drawer." For three years it would be her home. Colette had willfully locked herself out of social life, like Balzac and Proust in their cork-lined rooms; she, who loved fresh air and sunshine, retired into her "drawer," putting an end to Colette the Parisian hostess. She dismissed her staff, keeping only Pauline. The rectangular garden of the Palais, lined with a double row of lime trees, with well-trimmed rosebushes around the fountain — the opposite of what she liked in a garden — did not bother her.

Colette began writing *The Break of Day (La Naissance du Jour)*, literally "the birth of day," a novel as different as it could be from the despairing story of *Chéri*. It was "bathed in poetry and of unequaled density,"[35] thought Maurice Goudeket, who witnessed the novel unfold page by page. In May Colette felt the need to visit her house in Saint-Sauveur. "Thirty-three years, imagine, thirty-three years that I had neither seen the interior of the house, nor the garden! Emotion so powerful, impression of abolished time!"[36]

In a letter to Léo Marchand in the summer of 1927, she said she was progressing with enormous difficulty; she had written eighteen pages blindly without knowing where the story was going. She complained to Christiane Mendelys that she could not answer her letters because she was working so slowly; she was growing desperate. On August 3 she wrote to Moréno that she worked with unbelievable disgust and dogged resolve. To justify the painful creative process, she again persuaded herself that she wrote to pay the bills. She told Moréno that she never possessed much money and probably never would; for her, to be rich meant being loved by Maurice and a few friends, to have a small piece of real estate, a car in good condition, health, and "the freedom not to work when I don't want to work or cannot work." Three weeks later she announced that she had written twenty-seven pages and on September 14 she had a total of "thirty-five pages and despair."[37] She interrupted her novel to give two lectures in Belgium in Ostende and Brussels. In January she was working with a discipline that allowed her "to keep some self-respect."[38] She had rewritten a scene between herself and "a man" eight times and was so frustrated she could not sleep. Since December she had managed to write thirty-five pages, but felt she had overcome a stumbling block; by mid-January she thought that the novel was progressing. She moved to Saint-Tropez.

There she became upset because Maurice had to leave on business and her work suffered when he was gone too long. La Chatte the cat and Souci the dog were despondent; they sat on the doorstep waiting for Maurice: "They have no decency in their grief." The three of them took refuge in Maurice's office, where Colette picked up his yellow paper and wrote that the summers spent with him "were becoming more precious, more poignant."[39] For the first time she expressed some anguish, some fear of losing him; would he still be her friend next spring? For she felt she was robbing him of any plans he had made for his own future. For years Colette feared that her relationship with Maurice was doomed. She imagined that he could only be part of her life temporarily, while he thought that he was privileged to be loved by Colette and that it could not last. Neither of them spoke of permanence and kept their anxiety to themselves. Some critics saw Colette exorcising her fears of losing her young lover in *The Break of Day*. She projected herself as an aging woman who had lost her sexual drive and renounced love, accepting the peace brought to her senses by the coming of age. She was fifty-five and Maurice forty. The theme was not new; Léa had expressed the same fear and the same growing serenity. Maurice denied that this renunciation was true, for these were the halcyon days of their passion. Maurice warned against taking Colette's writing as being autobiographical. Yet everything seemed true to life: La Treille Muscate, the garden, the vineyard, the sea, the pets. Colette is the main character and she describes herself "in minute detail." But she warns her readers, "Perhaps you imagine I am drawing my own portrait? Patience: it is only my model."[40] She had first used a quotation from Proust: "This I which is myself and yet perhaps not myself." She reshuffled facts, dimmed some details, enlarged some memories. Sido and the Captain are part of the cast of characters, so are Dunoyer de Segonzac, Hélène Jourdan-Morhange, and Francis Carco; only Henry de Jouvenel is never named, being referred to as "my second husband" or "one of my husbands" or "Monsieur x." In this long meditation Colette describes the mellowing of love. Only in autumn does one gather grapes to make wine, and the grape harvest became the metaphor for love as she experienced it in her years of maturity. But, beyond that theme *The Break of Day* is a meditation on good and evil. It is a journey into the discovery of self, into the process of creating Colette.

In 1927, after going through Sido's papers, Colette, with a pang of recognition, brought her mother into the limelight and proclaimed her debt. Colette had not been aware of their resemblance, while Sido had known it all along and wrote, "Whom should I talk to about my states of mind, if not to you, to you my beloved self, who knows me and loves me."[41] Colette's obsession with her mother grew so strong that she felt "pushed out" of herself. She credited Sido with her values, her revolutionary ethics. "I imitated her ways, I still imitate her."[42] Until now the mother figure in Colette's novels had been either nonexistent — Claudine is an orphan — or a castrating presence like Chéri's or Phil's mothers.

As it became more evident that Sido was another self, Colette sifted with growing eagerness through her memories, recalling the past, conjuring up a scene, a conversation, addressing Sido as a living presence, "You to whom I turn constantly" or "You who accompany me."[43] It is hardly surprising that in the spring of 1928, as she visited the garden of her childhood, Colette felt the presence of her mother: "There I did see her again for one fleeting moment."[44] She felt that Sido's blame or indulgence, both "equally seductive," sank into her consciousness over the years and "surge[d] now" in her writings. She was so eager to pay back her debt to Sido that she partially quoted, partially rewrote her mother's letters, turning them into short masterpieces, and came up with a surprising conclusion: "Who of us is the better writer? Is it not obvious that it is she?"[45] With such humility that it hints of guilt, Colette acknowledged that Sido's mental domain was out of common reach and asked herself, "Won't I ever catch up with her?" "It is high time that I present her otherwise, not through my own professed taste for chores without urgency or significance, to go beyond what we — disrespectful children — used to call the cult of the little blue saucepan."[46]

Colette adopted Sido's didactic method and like her never conveyed her beliefs directly, but through anecdotes, recollections, and dialogues. In *The Break of Day* she uses Sido's letters as points of light in her reflection on love, nature, and the nurturing role of woman. "I am her impure survivor, her rough image, her faithful servant . . . she gave me life and the mission to carry out what she herself had seized and abandoned like a true poet."[47]

In *The Break of Day* Colette, who shared with Sido a predilection for the break of day, stepped into a new light, a new vision of things and beings, including herself. Sido's unorthodox remarks, her nonconformist behavior, her views on love and marriage, her understanding of Colette's homosexual as well as heterosexual affairs came into focus. Colette never named Fourier, but she left clues in her texts: an anecdote about Victor Considérant here, phrases taken from Fourier there. *The Break of Day* opens Colette's Fourierist cycle. In 1929 she wrote *The Other One*, a Fourierist approach to the triangle of the husband, wife, and mistress, followed in 1930 by *Sido*, the exploration of Sido's personality and ideas. This in turn was followed in 1932 by *The Pure and the Impure*, Colette's essay on love.

Fourier's radical sexology, *Le Nouveaux Monde Amoureux*, remained unpublished until 1967, mainly because his disciple, Victor Considérant, thought it too shocking for his contemporaries and centered his efforts instead on Fourier's economic reforms. But the unpublished material was pivotal to Fourier's Utopia, which revolves around passional attraction, and was discussed by his disciples. Among Sido's papers Colette must have found either notes taken by her mother or a copy of *Le Nouveaux Monde Amoureux*, for at times Colette uses expressions taken almost verbatim from Fourier's essay.

Fourier's reform of the economy was based on a social minimum, or entitlements to health care, food, shelter, and work for all. His sociological reforms were centered around a *sexual minimum*, the right to erotic satisfaction for all, in total freedom, with some absolute restrictions: no coercion, either physical, mental, or emotional; no harassment of any kind; no constraint; no restraint; and no sexual activity before the age of fifteen and a half, which could be achieved by promoting sports. Fourier rejected all previous philosophical theories and called his theory *l'écart absolu*, the absolute divergence. He was inspired by the astronomer Kepler's *Harmonices Mundi*, the harmonies of the worlds. Kepler described the motion of the universe as a divine concert, in which aberrations in the course of some heavenly bodies, far from unsettling the general harmony, introduce diversity into the perfect ensemble. Fourier applied this idea of a cosmic orchestra to his social utopia: passions, any passions, even Christianity's deadly sins — with the one exception of sloth — have a function in society. Fourier's goal was to reach happiness for all through a total gratification of the senses. Heteroerotic and homoerotic satisfaction were on the same scale. Polygamy, by creating bonds among benevolent *harmonians*, was viewed with favor as an expansion of friendly relationships. He believed that by legitimizing proscribed customs, "like polygamy," his code would require people to do in the open what they already did in secrecy, thus turning sexual attraction to good use. He advocated the repeal of established moral standards: "All these philosophical whims, called duties, have nothing to do with nature — duty is man's creation; attraction comes from God. In order to understand God's design, one must study sexual attraction . . . without taking duty into account, since its definition varies in each century and in each country, whereas the nature of passion has been and will remain invariable for all."[48] Colette concurs, "There is nothing that the human creature strives to perform with such stubborn resolve as an imaginary duty."[49]

In *The Break of Day* Colette expounds Sido's ethics: "I celebrate that primal clarity which dimmed and often put out the small lights painfully lit by the contact of what she called 'the common mortals.'"[50] Addressing her mother, Colette writes, "You used to flee the pestilential austerity of virtue. . . . You detected with disgust charity capable of more than one crime." She marvels at Sido's ability to probe "with the same delight good and evil," and stresses Sido's insight in "rebaptizing according to [her] own code, old poisonous virtues and poor sins, who have been waiting for centuries for their share of paradise."[51] Colette yearns for "a time long gone when good and evil were mixed like two beverages, blended into a single one,"[52] and claims that "to abstain or to consummate, the sin is no heavier one way or another for 'great lovers' of her kind — of our kind."[53] When she wrote about love in its least accepted forms, Colette wondered, "Am I once more imitating my mother, whose particular candor inclined her to deny the existence of evil, while her inquisitiveness searched for it and she contemplated it, entwined with good, with a gaze full of wonder."[54]

Fifteen years after Sido's death, Colette reconstructed her portrait stroke by stroke. "Now that I know her better, I can interpret certain fleeting expressions," a flash of "merry frenzy, a universal scorn, a dancing contempt, which trampled me with all the rest, happily." She could explain these sudden flares by Sido's need "to escape from everything and from all, to soar toward a law written by herself for herself." She depicted her in one of those moments "standing passionately still under a cherry tree, her face lifted toward the sky from which she banished all human religions."[55]

For a long time Colette was mystified by her mother's interpretation of love. In a letter quoted in *The Break of Day*, Sido writes about her husband, "What a pity that he loved me so much! It is his love for me that annihilated one by one his beautiful talents, which would have driven him to literature, to science." But Captain Colette had renounced all ambitions and made Sido the center of his world. "That is what I found devoid of any excuse. Such a great love! How reckless!"[56] For years Colette was unable to solve the riddle posed by her mother. "Free and soaring high, she calls constant, exclusive love 'reckless,' then doesn't condescend to explain herself. It is up to me to understand. I do what I can." Sido's judgment on the captain's devotion is central to Fourier's appraisal of love: "Nature conceived love in order to multiply infinitely man's social bonds."[57] Monogamy is restrictive, antisocial; a monogamous passion is counterproductive. Any exclusive passion ends in failure and even death. According to Sido, Captain Colette committed intellectual suicide; in Colette's novels, Chéri's passion for Léa drives him to suicide, as does Michel's love for his wife in *Duo*.

Colette, too, viewed marriage with reservations. "Love has nothing to do with life together — to the contrary, most of the time it dies from it." The state of matrimony reveals itself to every couple "in all its preposterous coarseness."[58] In *The Vagabond* Colette defined marriage as "domesticity that turns so many wives into a sort of nurse."[59] In *Landscapes and Portraits (Paysages et Portraits)* Colette recalled the little sermon delivered by Sido on the eve of her marriage to Willy. She did not like to see her daughter "going away with a man. . . . It is revolting that such things are permissible" — Sido had been married twice and was not proud of it. She conceded that she always said "outrageous things, but truly one should marry one's own brother, if one wanted to know what one is getting into! And even so!"[60] She had explained, "It is not divorce, it is marriage that I blame. Anything would be better than marriage."[61]

So thought Fourier, who deplored that "the Convention, which in 1792 trampled all prejudices, did not destroy the only one that had to be destroyed, the institution of marriage."[62] He was convinced that once emancipated from "conjugal slavery," women would surpass men in their dedication to work, dependability, and nobility of character in all functions of the mind and body, which do not entail only physical strength. Fourier believed that monogamy had no potential for social harmony. He disparaged both law and religion for allowing only one kind of union, "enslaved monogamy," and censured them both for requiring "that the union be consummated physically," forbidding purely sentimental relationships.

Colette consistently deprecated marriage, "This jail that one calls life together."[63] She flouted "this school of demoralization constituted by the impeccable life, divided into voluntary chores." She assumed that "the inexorable repetition of the same daily virtues" lead to disorder and even to crime. She shuddered at the thought of what it would have been like "to be confined to one single man,"[64] to be one of those women who believed in total monogamy; they were, in her opinion, no more than old maids. Like Fourier, she had little respect for those he called *monogynes*. He saw, in his utopian society, multiple lovers as a network of "partners" to be trusted and relied upon. Colette had the same approach; she kept up bonds with lovers turned comrades and friends. Colette wrote in *Recaptured*, "It was fatal that the fundamental, the old normal instinct of polygamy would arise in Jean."[65] In her novels and in her life, Colette never blamed what she called "the normal instinct" and never felt any guilt about it.

In *Claudine and Annie,* Claudine chides Annie, a neglected, dutiful wife, "A love, even a forbidden love would have made you bloom." She adds, "when one loves in a certain manner . . . betrayals become unimportant."[66] Claudine decides to correct Annie's unhappy situation by acting as a go-between. She traps her homosexual stepson, Marcel, between two doors — calling the boxlike trap "the confessional" — and whispers in his ear that she wants him to make love to Annie. He refuses, but she bargains and wins. She shuts the door of "the confessional" and justifies herself entirely. "I did the right thing . . . I wanted that, behind closed curtains, [Annie] could leisurely enjoy a pretty doll." She felt she was "a generous soul in love with love, the soul of a selfless go-between."[67] Colette made Claudine act like a Fourierist confessor; "the art of the sympathist, which is unknown in our civilization, provides instant matching of personalities . . . anywhere and under any circumstances. . . . The task of arranging sympathetic relationships" belongs to "confessors," and "women will excel more than men in this sort of work."[68] A guiltless Claudine leads the reluctant couple to Annie's bedroom and remarks, "I went to my own bed full of joy, high on a noble fever, which was not in the least impure. Positively not."[69]

Colette professed that love could become "a bureaucracy without diversion," except when a new combination "pushes the old man toward the teenager and Chéri toward Léa."[70] In this she adopts Fourier's order of things: "Boys love mature women, girls mature men. . . . A woman between forty-five and fifty ... will easily seduce an adolescent sixteen to seventeen years old. A sixteen-year-old girl will be passionately attracted to a handsome forty-five-year-old man. Since the choice is free, there will be relatively few lads who become passionately attached to lasses of their own age. Nature loves contrasts and readily links people of disparate age."[71] Colette spoke with zest of "the season for sensuous devotion" and celebrated it as a truce in "the monotony of encounters between equals." Alluding to her own experience, she explained "the perversity of gratifying an adolescent lover does not devastate a woman, quite the opposite."[72] She cherished the memory of "the adolescent's tears of delight"; she spoke of "a spoliatory genius ... an enchanting and hypocritical pedagogy."[73]

With candid self-justification, Colette expounded what she saw as a law of nature: "a sixteen-and-a-half-year-old child does not know that an unfathomable order places on his way ... beautiful missionaries";[74] their mission is to allow the young mind to rest happily, while the young body reaches maturity in their care. At fifty-five Colette defined her role as that of a "missionary," the ultimate function in Fourier's gynaecocracy.

In *The Evening Star (L'Etoile Vesper)*, Colette, who was then seventy-three, wrote that she had learned from Sido that even as hair turns white, "love carries on with the priceless pain of loving." Sexual pleasure is a right "as long as one has enough strength and intelligence to partake in love."[75] In the silent ongoing dialogue Colette kept up with Sido, her mother's voice rings light and vibrant: "Is it really necessary to renounce being young? I don't see the need or even the decency."[76] From Sido she inherited "the gift of shaking off her years like an apple tree shedding its blossoms." Sido had warned her that "to the grave, one constantly forgets old age."[77]

In *The Break of Day*, after reminding her readers that in our culture a mature man is entirely free to love teenage girls, Colette proclaims that mature women should be free to love teenage boys, and repeats that "this nonsense,"[78] the age gap, does not bother her. In *Chéri* Colette chose to paint this type of love, scorned by society. Chéri is nineteen, Léa forty-nine; it is Chéri who takes the initiative to turn their long affectionate relationship into a sexual involvement. It is he who, with tears in his eyes, whispers the first words of love and "begs never to separate." Colette concluded with a profoundly Fourierist remark: "... by losing, you, your old mistress, me, my scandalous young lover, we lost the most honorable of our possessions on earth."[79] She was convinced that, as Fourier noted, "when love is gone, man can only vegetate and seek distractions to hide the emptiness of his soul." For her, love justified everything, love was beneficial, love was indeed the divine passion.

The age gap is a recurrent theme. In *Claudine in Paris* Claudine is in love with Renaud, a man twice her age. Minne offers herself to the aging Maugis. In *The Ripening Seed* Phil is sixteen, Madame Dalleray thirty-two. In "The Cap," ("Le Képi") Marco, a mature woman, has a love affair with a man in his twenties. In "The Tender Shoot" ("Le Tendron"), the girl is not quite sixteen, the man forty-nine, and it is Louisette who seeks physical gratification, cautiously, but enough to make him feel a love object: "I wondered sometimes if Louisette did not use me as a rake would use a consenting girl."[80] In "The Prime of Life" ("La Fleur de l'Age") Madame Vasco is, at sixty, a healthy, vibrant, indomitable socialite, beautified and made-up; her husband, at thirty, dreams of a peaceful, cozy life, and is happy when he can avoid his wife's social merry-go-round and sit by the fireplace or tend the flowerbeds of their elegant home. "Another old man!" is her disillusioned remark as she leaves alone for the next ball. Gigi is fifteen and Gaston thirty-three when they fall in love in *Gigi,* and Colette reminds her readers that this was her own case. In "The Tender Shoot" the narrator interrupts the story to ask Colette, "Were you not sixteen when you declared that you were in love with a bald man, who at forty looked twice his age?"[81] In *The Pure and the Impure* she comments, "Youth is not the time to seduce but to be seduced."[82]

Colette made a point of illustrating Fourier's subversive sexology, not only in her novels but in her life. She approved of Marguerite Moréno's liaison with her nephew Pierre Moréno: "I am glad that you are there, so far, so comfortable, so locked up in a love that is your landscape."[83] Marguerite was living on her estate with Pierre, managing the vineyard and the winemaking. Marguerite compared him to Dionysus — "this kid is an emanation of Nature."[84] Both Colette and Marguerite saw nature's order in love, any love, every love.

In *The Break of Day* the dawn of Colette's new awareness also shed a sweeping light on her empathy with animals, as she was becoming more and more suspect to her own kind. "But if they were my kind, they would not hold me in suspicion." She agreed that the human "who sides with the humans has good reasons to step back from the creature who chooses to side with the animals." She conceded that from a strictly human point of view it is "by the alliance with the beast that monstrosity starts."[85] Again Colette reaffirmed her difference with the world around her, which judged monstrous what she saw as the natural order.

In Sido's papers Colette found the fountainhead of her own vocation, the call she heard with her "mental ear," the message aimed at her. Attraction being the force that bonds all creatures, Colette felt related to the creation as a whole and acted as its medium, its passionate interpreter.

## I Like to Look At People At the Precise Moment When They Signify Something

In Paris, Colette and Maurice kept separate quarters. He lived in a large apartment at 34 Avenue du Président Wilson; she lived at 9 Rue du Beaujolais. Maurice provided her with a supportive love, even during periods when they scarcely saw each other for weeks on end. He provided her with a stability that enabled her to feel emotionally sheltered. As soon as her divorce from Jouvenel was finalized and Bertrand married, old friends who had seen her only occasionally regrouped. Colette returned to the musical salon of Princess de Polignac, who was known to her close friends as "Winnie" and who supported modern music. She had launched Le Groupe des Six: Darius Milhaud, Poulenc, Germaine Tailleferre, Arthur Honegger, Louis Durey, and Georges Auric. She was devoted to Diaghilev, and paid for the production of Stravinsky's opera buffa, Mavra, based on a story by Pushkin. She also financed Eric Satie's group, L'Ecole d'Arcueil. In 1925 a penniless Satie was dying of cirrhosis of the liver. The princess had him admitted to a private hospital, where he spent his last days surrounded by a small group of friends, drinking champagne and opium-laced medicine.

As a patron of the arts and sciences she was matchless, financing laboratories at the Collège de France and archeological expeditions in Greece, giving money to help restore the Hagia Sophia in Istanbul and creating the Musée Gauguin in Tahiti. She presented the Institut Océanographique with a floating laboratory, "The Winnaretta Singer," for underwater studies. She financed the cost of a six-year study of coral reefs in New Caledonia, as well as studies of hormones and hallucinogenic mushrooms. The Fondation Singer-Polignac financed Salvation Army hostels in Paris, the Society for the Preservation and Rehabilitation of Young Girls, and buildings for workers. The princess bequeathed an extensive collection of paintings and objets d'art to the Louvres.

Winnie was fond of Colette and admired her work. She gave her a car after her divorce, as well as an antique table so she could write in bed and a diamond necklace hidden in a bunch of flowers. Both were naturally witty and had a down-to-earth attitude. In public they enjoyed bantering, making the most of their distinctive accents: Winnie's Americanized French, dry, precise, spoken through clenched teeth; Colette's softly rolling *r*s. They exchanged memories about sapphic friendships that went back to pre-*Claudine* days: Baronne Zuylen de Nyvelt, Missy, Princess Murat, Olive Eleonor Custance (married to Lord Alfred Douglas), Elizabeth de Grammont, separated from her husband to live openly with lesbian lovers. The princess would come to Colette's apartment for a snack of mulled wine and cheese, looking very comfortable, whereas in her own home, she often had the appearance of a slightly embarrassed guest. She would tell Colette of her longing for "a Walden-like simple life,"[86] a rustic simplicity that Colette found in Saint-Tropez and Winnie in her small weekend retreat at Jouy-en-Josas.

The princess's inner circle was discreetly homosexual: Cole Porter, Jean Cocteau, Clara Haskie, Rosamond Lehmann, Renata Borgatti, Dame Ethel Smith, and Violet Trefusis. It created an Anacreontic ambience where everybody felt at ease; there was an unwritten set of rules that guarded all guests from any gaffe.

Being homosexual did not guarantee acceptance; Gertrude Stein, for instance, was never part of Winnie's group, being too masculine, too bohemian. Virgil Thomson, a close friend of Stein's, could never arrange an invitation, and Elsa Maxwell's repeated efforts and Cocteau's pleading on her behalf yielded nothing. The implicit rule was that scandal should be avoided. In that respect Colette could be trusted absolutely — gone were the days of "Toby-Dog Speaks Up" ("Toby-Chien Parle"). Friends used to make jokes about the secrecy: "You are homosexual, aren't you? Then let's talk about music."[87] The high-society lesbians were self-protective, cautious, and discriminating. After the scandal created by her love affair with Vita Sackville-West, Violet Trefusis settled in Paris and was shielded by Winnie, who mothered her until they pursued other affections.

Masked balls allowed cross-dressing; at a ball in 1928 the princess and the marchesa Luisa Casati came dressed as Tristan Bernard and his wife. Colette came as Léa, escorted by Poulenc as a convincing Chéri. At a ball given by Daisy Fellowes, Princess de Polignac's niece, the theme was Parisian personalities — Winnie and Elsa Maxwell *both* dressed as Aristide Briand, *both* sporting a musketeer's mustache. Colette came once again as Léa, with the prince of Monaco as Chéri. She suggested that Maurice impersonate Marguerite Moréno because his hips were so narrow, asking Germaine Patat to design a dress for him and adding that he could then put on his stationery, "dressed by Germaine Patat." Colette, attracted by any hint of androgyny, spoke in her letters of Maurice's slim figure, his skin "smooth as satin." On a picture taken in Sainte-Maxime he looked, she said, like a newlywed bride in her veils. Unfriendly people nicknamed Maurice Peau de Satin (Satin Skin). But Colette's true friends were all fond of Maurice.

Their closest friends were a couple of artists who had a summer home near Saint-Tropez. Luc-Albert Moreau was a painter, a lithographer who illustrated *The Break of Day*. Colette first called him "Saint Luc," then settled for the tender, childish nickname, "Toutounet." His companion was the musician Hélène Jourdan-Morhange, whose nickname was "Moune"; she was fifteen years younger than Colette and her husband had been killed in the war. Colette and Moune exchanged an almost daily correspondence, starting in 1929 and ending with Colette's death.

Moune had been a wonderchild. She was ten years old when she won the Conservatoire National de Musique's first prize as a violinist. Maurice Ravel considered her his best interpreter; she seemed destined to become a great soloist, but suffered from "the violinist's cramp," which put an end to a promising career. Colette helped her to become a music critic. Her articles appeared in a variety of respected periodicals such as *La Revue de Paris* and *Les Lettres Françaises;* her books on Ravel and Le Groupe des Six were considered definitive works.

Luc-Albert Moreau and Hélène Jourdan-Morhange lived at Les Mesnils in the forest of Rambouillet; on Sundays they invited groups of painters and musicians like Ravel, Auric, Poulenc, and Germaine Tailleferre as well as architects, writers, doctors, and scientists, such as Professor Mondor and Pasteur Valéry-Radot. Rustic simplicity was no longer just for Saint-Tropez; it became a *must* for Parisian weekends. On Sundays Goudeket's chauffeur, Guy, drove Colette to the Place de la Madeleine, where she would have long technical discussions with the grocer about the ripening point of different cheeses before putting them in the car, which was soon permeated by an aroma delicious to the true connoisseur. The next stop was at a butcher's, selected by Colette for his meat and his picturesque slang. When they arrived at Les Mesnils Colette and Luc-Albert dismissed everyone and broiled the steaks. Barbecued steaks had appeared on the French menus of avant-garde gourmets with the arrival of ragtime and the Charleston. This, of course, started a culinary reaction spearheaded by Curnonsky, elected Prince des Gastronomes, who was collecting nineteenth-century recipes of French traditional cuisine. "Minute steaks" were one of Colette's triumphs; the other came on "truffle day." In season, she had these culinary delicacies shipped from Périgord and prepared them herself, pouring a bottle of champagne into a skillet with bits of bacon, salt and pepper, then throwing in the expensive fungus. When the truffles were done, she had them served on plates and the sauce poured hot into port glasses. The afternoons at Les Mesnils were devoted to music.

Colette's friends had little to do with café society. She was taken with Violet Trefusis, admiring her intelligence and patronizing her in literary Paris. The first time she met Violet, she glanced at the rosy-cheeked beauty and breathed "Violet? *Mais non!* Geranium!" Parisian Anglophiles wooed this daughter of Mrs. Keppel, Edward VII's mistress. Violet's tumultuous passion for Vita Sackville-West added spice to the spoiled enfant terrible. She settled in Paris because there she was free to say and do what she pleased. But to ward off any possibility of scandal, Mrs. Keppel chaperoned Violet whenever socially necessary and "cast a protective veil over her daughter's amours." Her inner circle comprised Colette, Princess de Polignac, Marie Laurencin, Lucie Delarue-Mardrus, Misia Sert, Jean Cocteau, Max Jacob and his lover Maurice Sachs, and Francis Poulenc, nicknamed Prince "Thurn-und-Taxis" because he had an impassioned crush on a taxi driver.

Violet bought Saint-Loup, an abbey described to her by Marcel Proust, who had given its name to one of his characters. Colette, struck by the Gothic aspect of the ruin, which reminded her of Debussy's opera *Pelléas et Mélisande,* renamed it La Mélisandière and felt a kinship with the place. In *Don't Look Around* Violet Trefusis drew a portrait of Colette in her fifties: "To use a word that must astonish those who do not know Colette, she was 'cozy.'. . . She adored comfort and disdained luxury. She had many phobias: any kind of snob, social, literary, political.

Especially she disliked women whose conversation was as skimpy as their diet."[88] Dieting was becoming a fad, but Violet and Colette liked food. Like all her aristocratic friends, Violet was mesmerized by Colette, "la grande gourmande," who turned a dinner into a lyrical hymn to food. How daring this was in a society bred never to mention the food on the plate! Literature, arts, and travel were dinner-table topics, not what was concocted in the kitchen. Colette, who never forsook her part as the *Huronne,* broke that high-society taboo, and made converts. She gave Violet Trefusis a recipe that stunned her cook: "the seven-hour leg of mutton." It had to simmer overnight with a pig's shank and herbs in an earthenware casserole. The next day the mutton would be tender enough to be eaten with a spoon.

This established Colette's image as "a whiz-cook," although Princess Ghika proclaimed she was a great writer but no cook at all. The Abbé Mugnier, who recorded the idiosyncracies of Parisian society, watched Colette at dinner. She greeted the mushrooms in cream sauce with an exclamation that no one understood. "I was told," noted the Abbé, "that it came from the salesmen's slang."[89] She awed everyone by identifying the ingredients of every dish, like a culinary Sherlock Holmes. She explained that her eyes were very weak but that her taste buds and olfactory organs were outstanding. (Her sense of hearing was so keen that she could hear a mushroom emerging from the soil and pushing aside a leaf. She once heard an iris bud opening its petals.) At table she never engaged in literary discussion, and her dissertations on food were her clever way out. At a dinner at the art dealer Bernstein's home, Colette launched into a Fourierist digression on gourmandise. It was a way of knowing, of tasting, of appreciating not only food but all things of the senses. Colette explained that there was a gourmandise related to cuisine and a gourmandise related to voluptuous, sensuous pleasures; she insisted several times that the quest for purity was just a temptation like any other, no more noble. Nobody understood her. So when the abbé asked her if she would ever write a novel that he — a priest — could read, she answered that she would write a book "that would be a debauchery, an orgy of virtue."[90]

Still Colette continued enjoying places where the lowest strata of society gathered: Rue Sainte Apolline, Rue de Lappe, or Rue de la Gaîté. Francis Carco was her guide to the secret dens of Montparnasse, where cocaine was openly sold; he had given Goudeket "a friendly welcome from the first day." They went to *bals musette* and to brothels, "watching and chatting with the naked girls when they were not 'on duty.'"[91] Colette found in the dregs of society what she had liked in the chorus line of the music hall: people who were struggling to survive. She was looking for raw human nature in the back alleys of Montmartre; her quest was so systematic that Goudeket found it "bureaucratic."

Colette never described the places where the smart set met, yet she kept up with them. She showed up at Josephine Baker's Chez Joséphine in the Rue Fontaine, where the star arrived after her show at the Folies Bergère, cloaked in white furs and followed by her maid, her chauffeur, and a white Eskimo dog. Colette reviewed several of Josephine Baker's shows, praising her progress and her dedication to her art. She celebrated Baker's perfect body and her dances, which "will teach discretion to the Parisian nude dancers."[92] Colette admired the child of nature in Baker; she belonged like herself in the Fourierist paradise. From her music-hall days, Colette had kept a professional tone; she addressed Baker, Chevalier, Sorel, and Mistinguett with the familiar "tu," never losing her love for "the strange world of actors, a world of magnificent, corporate solidarity and of individuals no less magnificent."[93]

Following the success of La Revue Nègre, American dances became the rage. Two unlikely associates, Elsa Maxwell and the British designer Edward Molyneux, opened a nightclub on Rue des Acacias; everybody went there to dance the "pony dance," created by the Dolly Sisters, who along with Clifton Webb were the main performers. Few Parisians patronized nightclubs or boîtes, which were packed instead with the international set. During the twenties thirty to fifty thousand Americans had elected to settle in Paris, from the Ritz to the Montparnasse stables-turned-studios. Colette always kept a step ahead of the crowd. Since her days with Willy, she had always been with the avant-garde.

At the end of March 1929 Colette was once more El Glaoui's guest. She traveled with Maurice; her plan was to cross Spain to be in Seville for the Holy Week and then spend some days in Tangiers. Her aversion to museums and monuments found fertile ground in Spain; "Finally it is over," she sighed happily. She did not like El Greco — "The crooked noses of all El Grecos, chalky boned noses . . . " She found the Seville "cathedral intolerable," the priests hateful, "one, ten, a hundred of them who perorated and paced the pavement on their heavy soles; it is obvious that God is their household carpet."[94] Having finished off her cultural duties, she visited the country her own way, spending the evenings at

some Caf' Conc' to watch Rosa Casa, who danced like "a prudish bour-
geoise" and dancers trussed in their corsets, whose silhouettes reminded
her of Toulouse-Lautrec. Never tired of crowded places, she drank beer in
an overflowing tavern with "a staircase packed with soldiers,"[95] where no
señora had ever set foot, in a country that enforced sexual apartheid.

Colette was disappointed by Spain. She had loved the Spanish colony
in Paris, its excesses and panache. Spain was Moréno, Raquel Meller,
José-Maria Sert, la Belle Otéro, and Louis Ferdinand, the Spanish infante, who came to a ball naked, his body painted blue. But she found
the Spaniards in Spain punctilious, hated the dry Castilian landscape, and
could not bring herself to write to Moréno, who had the devotion of an
exile for the country of her ancestors.

It was with a sense of relief that Colette and Maurice landed in
Tangiers at the pasha of Marrakesh's Villa de France. To Hélène Picard she
wrote that it was the Garden of Eden; she described to Misz Marchand
orange blossoms as big as sunflowers, so fragrant that it would make one
die if the wind did not blow away some of the fragrance. The estate had
been landscaped by an American architect; the beds came from Germany,
the furniture from England, and the mattresses were "made of one hundred thousand francs worth of Moroccan wool."[96] There were bathrooms
everywhere but, as the pasha was away, no water and no electricity. So
they retreated to a new hotel that smelled of fresh paint.

In Gibraltar they dined on board the *Eros*. Henri de Rothschild's
new yacht was on her maiden trip, and he invited them for a cruise on
his boat whose name was a statement.


During these intense years of writing, Colette became more and more
interested in supernatural phenomena. Joseph Delteil, who knew of her
fancy for it, put her in touch with the strange Count Carlos de Lagerme,
a poet versed in astrology and the symbolics of stones and colors. He
sent her a book of poems that fascinated her: "How I love things I only
half understand. They are even more beautiful glimpsed through the
regular lattice of beautiful verses." She asked the count to chart her as-
trological map, which he sent her along with the symbolic chart of
colors. She was exhilarated: "Now I know why I need blue stones, blue
glass, blue paper and sapphires," and she promised to send him a copy of
*The Break of Day*, where he would find "a hundred times the word 'blue,'

for I can't help using it." She surprised an interviewer "who had a certain distrust of mystery," when she assured him that her watch, which was there a minute ago, had again taken a trip "and people still swear that objects don't live."[97]

At La Treille Muscate she discovered that she was a dowser; a neighbor, who found underground water by holding a forked twig in her hands, showed Colette how to do it. Colette cut a Y-shaped twig of mimosa, and the small branch turned fifteen or twenty times, hurting her palms. Maurice found her barefoot, a small forked branch held with both hands, stepping like a priestess accomplishing a sacred rite. She loved the mystery of the twig pulled by a force from below, and when Sextia Aude, who had revealed her power to Colette, tried to give it a rational explanation, Colette refused to listen, fearing the mystery would become less mysterious. She would repeat, "How beautiful is that which we do not understand"[98] and rejected all explanations. Maurice asked her if she really believed in the supernatural; her reply was that whether she believed in it made no difference to her. She deplored that "the French theater cares so little for the supernatural, even for that blend of reality and unreality that is the hallmark of the English theater, Shakespeare, Shaw . . . to name only those two, we know how they take us from the real to the unreal by the flying bridge of humor." The supernatural was the realm of poetry; it had its roots "before life on earth began"; the poet "does not invent but remembers." A poet, Colette explained in her portrait of Jean Cocteau, is "a being who has kept the branchiae that the still amphibious human has before birth and that disappear with the first breath of the newborn."[99]

Colette told Maurice she communicated with animals. In 1926 they were living in a hotel on the Saint-Tropez harbor, when in the middle of a quiet night, Colette jumped out of bed. Maurice asked if she were not feeling well, but she did not answer — she was listening intently to something. Maurice listened and heard nothing. "He is drowning," she said. "A man?" asked Maurice. "No, a dog."[100] She was gone; Maurice looked through the window to see Colette in her nightgown running to the water. In slippers and robe he ran after her, but she was already coming back. She had caught a drowning fox terrier by the nape of the neck and pulled him to safety. She was angry — the dog had been swimming for a long time and was exhausted; someone must have thrown him into the water.

Once in a house she visited with a friend, she was met by a cat abandoned by the previous renters. The cat took her from room to room, begging, "asking her questions with demented words"; Colette held back her tears. When she was with animals "she became of the same species, of the same essence; she was able to foresee their reactions, to understand the nuances of their language."[101]

Throughout 1928 Colette had been writing *The Other One* with enormous difficulties. In the spring Colette complained to Marguerite Moréno that she had written eighty pages, but had had to tear up forty. In the summer she wrote to Goudeket that she had torn up thirty pages; she had promised her novel to Ferenczi by mid-June, so she decided to forego her summer in Saint-Tropez and lock herself up in a remote, expensive, almost deserted hotel, Le Château d'Ardennes, near Brussels.

*The Other One* was the transparent transposition of the relationship between Colette, Germaine Patat, and Henry de Jouvenel. However, when it was published Patat asserted that Meg Villars was the model for Jane, not herself. In *The Evening Star* Colette, alluding to the novel, wrote, "Novel called à *clé*, how you tempt us! How you challenge our pen not to harm but to tell the truth . . ."[102] It dealt with the commonplace situation of a man, a wife, and a mistress, but the originality of *The Other One* lies in its unconventional resolution of the crisis. In a Fourierist approach, a new bond is created; peace and comfort come out of a situation that traditionally festers with hatred, rivalry, and misery for all concerned. Disloyalty, betrayal, anger, and guilt are all washed away, the love triangle is turned upside down, and the relationships are evaluated and reorganized in a healing and beneficial new order. The wife and the mistress find out that their relationship is more precious than their relationship with Farou, the philandering husband. They recognize the special bond that unites them, acknowledging the need they have for each other and the happiness that emerges from their alliance.

When *The Other One* was published in 1929 by Ferenczi after being serialized in *Les Annales,* Colette told André Billy that she was worried; the philosophy of the last pages was not understood by the critics, although most saw that the whole story was written with the conclusion in mind. The novel was "profound" according to Edmond Jaloux in his *Nouvelles Littéraires.* In *Le Figaro,* Henri de Régnier missed the point, noting that it was the perfect ending for the husband — two women meekly accepting his unfaithfulness. Benjamin Crémieux, disappointed by what he called "this return to the harem," blamed Colette for being "conservative" and cynically noted, "anything rather than destroy a household!" Vuillermoz saw the novel as a study of the feelings of the mature women, who choose "to eliminate all the elements of discomfort and favor all the happiness-producing armistices."[103]

In an interview Colette explained that her novel was "based on the solidarity that can exist between two rival women . . . the one who has betrayed can only think of the woman she deceives. Her true sentimental concern will be with the woman whose place she has unduly taken."[104] In the manuscript at the Bibliothèque Nationale, a line adds a dimension to Fanny and Jane's peaceful understanding: "in their pride and their pleasure, taste the newness . . ." The sentence remains unfinished. The "newness" of a situation that creates peace and happiness is the focus of this novel. After confessing her betrayal, Jane takes Fanny's hand and Fanny cannot reject a hand "she was waiting for." She thinks that if Jane goes away, Farou will soon reestablish with some other woman this "haremlike type of happiness," and says to herself, "I will not replace her."[105]

The situation seemed to flow straight from Fourier's speculations — "in *harmony*, supplementary loves will be honored and they will not be a source of deception. They will be all the more readily accepted in that both men and women will be linked by bonds of friendships with members of their own sex." Fourier's "amicable bonds" erase all hostility because of the earnest wish to create happiness for all. He conceded that what he named "amicable love" was usually considered "one of the greatest sins . . . when a man or a woman has concurrent relationships . . . each partner must consent to the pleasure of the other and the friendship among all three is doubled as a result. . . . Such relationships," concluded Fourier, "rely on homosexual love."[106] All prejudice set aside, in *The Other One* Colette created an epilogue worthy of *harmony:* Fanny, the wife, turns to "the help that could only come from feminine solidarity, even a little shaky, a little treacherous, a feminine solidarity constantly disengaged by man, constantly reengaged in spite of man." Jane, the mistress, appraises Farou and Fanny and the scale tips toward the woman: "You Fanny, you are much better as a woman than Farou as a man. Much, much better . . ."[107]

With her three husbands, Colette practiced the "triple harmony." She believed that "in a voluptuous trio, one is always betrayed, often two. . . ."

Most of the time it is "the closeted patriarch, the clandestine Mormon," since man is the "traditional instigator." Man only seeks pleasure, "his snare is crude," he offers "no sentimental bond, no caring, no love." Man's concept of the trio is impure because he seeks only an egotistical pleasure. On the contrary, the friendship between wife and mistress is nurturing. When one of the two women has some strength of character, as was the case with Colette, the weaker woman "normally yields, blossoms, demands a tender, total possession." With Meg, with Germaine Patat, with Musidora, with Lily de Rème, the trios unraveled and Colette remained victoriously the pivotal love of the woman who could only beg, "possess me for I have nothing to hide from you. I feel pure, I am your ally, no longer your prey."[108] The sensuous trio turned into a loving duo, the man who brought them together being expelled.

Two years later, in 1931, Colette was again analyzing the trio. The manuscript of *The Pure and the Impure* at the Bibliothèque Nationale shows that Colette corrected and rewrote the last two pages of her essay, dealing with what she calls *l'harmonie ternaire de l'amour*, using a Fourierist expression. One crossed-out sentence reads: "Everything discourages in our climates those shocking polygamies . . . their best chance is to be born with the summer and die with it." The open spaces, the beaches, the leisure give the trios "some of the oriental serenity . . . but misleads them as far as the true capacity of the heart is concerned. . . ."[109]

In May Colette gave a lecture at the Université des Annales. The Swiss publisher Gonin asked her to write a text for *The Earthly Paradise (Paradis Terrestre)*, an album illustrated by Paul Jouve. She liked the chance to describe wild animals, so in June she went to the famous Antwerp Zoo to look at tigers, lions, and panthers. She came back depressed at having seen so many wild animals behind bars. She found comfort in Brittany with Misz and Léo Marchand, who had bought the Château de Costaérès. There she was in her favorite element: the ocean, the rocks, the sand, fishing at dawn. Like any other fisherman, she boasted about her daily catch: the very first day she caught eight spider crabs, two lobsters weighing two pounds each, and countless fish. She felt dizzy with excitement. In ten days she caught twenty-four lobsters, nineteen spider crabs "larger than a human skull," and countless pounds of shrimp. But she missed Maurice, who was in Paris. As soon as he was free, they left for La Treille Muscate. There Colette wondered how she could find the strength to sit at her desk, when everything drew her out of the house: her zinnias, "large as side tables," her grapes of such perfect oval shape.

In September Colette was asked to be the drama critic for *La Revue de Paris*. She accepted because of *La Revue's* international readership, although it would be a lot of work for little money; two months later she resigned. It was taking too much of her time. She spent December at La Treille Muscate with Maurice; Saint-Tropez was quiet, so she wrote steadily. Back in Paris she moved to the Hôtel Beaujolais, because the owner of her "drawer" was considering legal action against Alba, who had sublet the apartment to Colette without his consent. Her doctor had also blamed Colette's recurrent bronchitis on the poor ventilation of her apartment. Maurice decided to remedy the situation discreetly; he bought La Gerbière near Montfort-l'Amaury so Colette could have a peaceful haven to write. The estate thrust forward like the prow of a ship above a steep slope; the house was small enough to satisfy Colette's taste for dwellings "cut to a normal man's measure" as well as "her need for large airy spaces."[110] She immediately built houses for the birds and had long conversations with the old gardener. Maurice could never get accustomed to seeing her use her hands to pull up roots, scratch and turn over lumps of earth, always in too much of a hurry to fetch a tool. But he had been right; during her stay in La Gerbière Colette announced to Moréno, "I have written forty-one pages! . . . everything is rather beautiful."[111]

In February of 1930 Colette was back in Berlin, where the previous October she had been the guest of honor of the Franco-German Society. Otto Grautoff, its president, organized a large-scale welcome, with cameramen waiting for Colette at the station. For four days she gave lectures, opened the book fair of deluxe editions, signed her books, and was invited to soirees and to a lunch with the French ambassador. Colette was a celebrity in Germany, which prompted Sarrasini, owner of the famous circus, to invite the author of *Dialogues de Bêtes* to plead his case. Sarrasini wanted to move five hundred animals from his zoo to France, but French circus owners were putting up strong opposition; by enrolling Colette and some powerful French journalists, Sarrasini thought he could win his case in the French press and sway the authorities. He gave his sixty guests a lavish dinner, served by clowns, jugglers, and acrobats under the big top, and followed it with a private performance. At the time nobody understood his urge to leave Berlin. In 1935 he was ordered by Hitler to get rid of the Jews, Africans, and Yugoslav Gypsies in his company; he tried to leave Germany for South America. The night before embarking at Antwerp, the tent housing his elephants was set on fire, and the elephants died in the blaze.

In July Colette and Maurice went on a cruise in Henri de Rothschild's yacht, *Eros*. Colette had accepted because it would only be a small party, including Misz and Léo Marchand, who were soon to leave for Hollywood, and the movie producer Philippe de Rothschild, Baron Henri's son. Baron Henri was a playwright who wrote under the name "André Pascal." A multimillionaire with many interests, he had at one time studied medicine; not long ago he had built a theater. He had spent twenty-nine million francs on his boat, but was shocked when Colette and Maurice told him that during their recent trip through Spain they had rented a taxi to drive them from Madrid to Algeciras. He could not believe such wastefulness and kept referring to that "crazy taxi ride."[112]

The *Eros* was sailing to Norway. For thirty hours they were tossed by a storm and took refuge at Kiel, a motorboat took them in to shore to see Marlène Dietrich in Joseph Von Sternberg's *Blue Angel,* which had just been released. Colette found the ambiguous Marlène striking, her androgyny befitting the essay she had begun. She was also taking notes on the trip as she did every time she traveled; they would be part of *En Pays Connu.*

It was midsummer in Norway; there was almost no night. Colette was having trouble with the sun, since "it is never in the place where it should be."[113] She needed to know from which direction the wind was blowing; she checked this every day wherever she was. She did not like the easterly winds and told Maurice, who felt especially well when they blew, that "he was like all cats . . . when the wind is from the east, they dance."[114] But she was like a plant; she loved humidity, it suited her temperament. She advised her readers and radio listeners to find out which weather was best for them and to move to a climate where they would prosper — a sensible, if impractical piece of advice.

On August 9 the *Eros* moored at Le Havre, and Colette and Maurice drove to Saint-Tropez, which was becoming an outpost of the Ritz. Parisians were pouring into the little fishermen's harbor; rows of Hispanos and Bugattis were blocking access to the port, where elegant women were photographed for *Vogue.* As Colette came out of the little store that sold newpapers, she would find thirty people clustered at the door watching her. Colette had only herself to blame, for she had written enthusiastic letters about the joy of southern living, saying she felt like a "salamander" in the hundred-degree heat, among pine trees bleeding their fragrant sap, near a sea of "fierce blue."[115] She invited Anna de Noailles to join her in drinking white wine at the fishermen's ball and enjoying watching the handsome boys dance with each other. Soon her friends were trickling down to Saint-Tropez. Natalie Barney had a house in the hills, while Lucien Lelong bought a residence next to La Treille Muscate — he arrived with three cars, two chauffeurs, and a powerboat. But Colette perceived the first serious signs of an invasion when she met a group of habitués of Le Boeuf sur le Toit hovering nearby, "two and a half kilometers" from La Treille Muscate, noted Colette, as if marking the rise of a flood. Le Boeuf sur le Toit was the stronghold of Parisian snobbery; it was noisy, flashy, and outrageous, the epitome of the new chic. After World War I it was chic to wear Coco Chanel's pajamas, chic to smoke opium, chic to howl at Dadaist demonstrations, chic to be invited to Count de Beaumont's fancy balls, chic to be part of the New Left, chic to be seen at Le Boeuf.

Snobbery had changed; society was less interested in discussing literature, art, and music than in the sheer phenomenon of celebrity. Clothes became the measure of economic success or failure. Social prejudices had changed; before the war homosexuals met at places off the beaten track, like Colette's Semiramis Bar or Proust's male bordellos, while they put on a pretense of acceptable normality at Larue's or the Ritz. But at Le Boeuf sur le Toit, sexual ambiguity was chic. On any given day one could see Louise Balthy, Colette's old flame, with Romaine Brooks; the princess Marie Murat openly dallying with women; the Duchess d'Uzès smoking her clay pipe; Chanel and Misia Sert on the lookout for artists to launch; Cocteau and his clique. The phenomenal success of Le Boeuf sur le Toit was due to its owner, Louis Moysès, who knew everything about everybody and let his restaurant be used as a mailbox. The decor was art nouveau, which had come of age; above the bar hung Picabia's *Oeil Cacodylate,* covered with habitués' signatures. The centerpiece was a bizarre musical instrument, L'Orphéal; except for the two pianists Wiener and Doucet, no one could operate its keyboard. Wiener, the musician-composer, was well known to Colette; his father owned the patent for the polyhymnal instrument and sold eighty Orphéals, ending up with eighty lawsuits. Wiener and Doucet began their long association on the concert stage at Le Boeuf, where they mainly played American music.

The Le Boeuf crowd was converging on Saint-Tropez. "Tout-Paris and Tout-Montparnasse are on the harbor, Mme. de Cl(ermont)-Tonn(erre) in pajamas, Mlle Lefranc as a deck boy, Madame Walter in overalls, Daniel Dreyfus in shorts . . . etc. etc. . . . The 1890 fancy hat ball is replaced by 'the noodles ball' with everything, necklaces, belts, head-dresses, made of coloured bits of macaroni, noodles . . ."[116] complained Colette. She was intrigued by Léon-Paul Fargue's tales of swaps and bac-chanalia, which she summarized as "my wife for your elder son." The poet Paul Géraldy commented that this was Arcadia.

It was not Colette's concept of Arcadia; she branded it the snobbery of vice. It was vice for vice's sake. "What a narrow domain obscenity is! One suffocates at once, and one gets bored," she wrote of "that poor, in-fantile, excited author of *Lady what's her name's Lover*. It is so terribly adolescent and sophomoric."[117] Colette found D. H. Lawrence boring.

Colette had an inherent mistrust of intellectual snobbery, but her cu-riosity compelled her to find out about it. Léon-Paul Fargue, the poet laureate of the eccentric fringe of Tout-Paris, was Colette's friend. He took her to private Dadaist meetings at the estate of Madame de la Hire, whose husband had been Colette's and Willy's first biographer. One night a Dada group hypnotized itself en masse and Renée Crevel, the surrealist poet, persuaded six sleepwalkers to hang themselves on a coat-rack, which collapsed under their weight. Poulenc and Satie were at the piano, while Cocteau blew an automobile horn and played the castanets. *L'Acte Gratuit* had no meaning for Colette; she blasted Antonin Artaud's *Théâtre de la Cruauté* and his play, *Les Cenci:* "I am afraid that murder, rape, and scalping will bring disappointment to M. Artaud." Cruelty for cruelty's sake made no sense. "There are not thirty-six ways to eat a heart or dismember a child. Artaud's is the theater of vehemence, not the theater of cruelty or terror."[118]

Crude violence, raw eroticism, and a generation who "enjoyed watching" Lilian Gish being tortured in *Broken Lily (Lys Brisé)*, played and refused to work, was incomprehensible to Colette, whose definition of work was broad enough to encompass the demimonde. Sloth re-mained the cardinal sin. To Pauline, who asked her when she was run-ning a high fever why she was writing instead of resting, Colette replied, "Because it is my job."

Colette was worried about Colette II, who loved fast cars and parties, who always dragged along with her a phonograph and twenty-four
pounds of records. "What to do with her?" The Patat Company, hurt by
the Depression, was on the brink of bankruptcy; to save her business
Germaine was considering selling Mondésir, Bel-Gazou's haven for so
long. In August Solange Bussy filmed a remake of *The Vagabond;* the
part previously played by Musidora was given to Marcelle Chantal.
Colette II, who had no talent for haute couture or business, was hired as
an assistant.

Renaud de Jouvenel came to Saint-Tropez; two years earlier Henry
de Jouvenel had legally declared him his son. Colette was happy to see
him. He told her he wanted to be a writer but Colette felt it was only
because of her. She encouraged him to be himself: "I hate to see anyone
trying to be like someone else, even like Napoleon." Renaud was unsure
of his literary calling; he was wavering, discouraged, and talked of suicide. Colette explained that she had never felt that she was "called" to be
a writer, but always had to push herself: "I work with a silent hate. How
can there be anyone with a calling for literature! . . . I have often had to
resurrect myself. To hear discouraged words from a twenty-year-old! It
may be natural at twenty to leave life easily, but *merde* for such negative
people, don't be one of them."[119] Renaud and Bel-Gazou left for Castel
Novel to meet their father's new wife and her two daughters by her previous marriage. With his wife's fortune, Jouvenel was modernizing the
crumbling Castel Novel and had bought a villa on the Riviera as well
as the historic mansion in Paris of the legendary French diplomat
Talleyrand, one of the marquise de Morny's ancestors. Jouvenel could
now indulge in his love for art and luxury; he gave sumptuous receptions and had his cigars made specially for him in Cuba. Colette wrote
to Germaine Patat, with some irony, that she would never know such
wealth — anyhow, she had renounced much of life's luxury.

With Maurice at her side, Colette followed the stoic part of her nature more and more. She stopped smoking abruptly, fearing the devastating effect of any addiction after Jean Cocteau had been found in a
vegetative state at L'Hôtel du Port et des Négociants in Toulon, so sick it
was feared he would not survive. Francis Carco had had to sell his
Cubist paintings and enter a private clinic; Pierre Louÿs had died in
1925, poor and destitute, living off a small pension from *Le Secours des
Beaux-Arts* — thanks to Anatole de Monzie, his burial was paid for by

the ministry of education. *Aux Ecoutes* wondered who would get his royalties, "a suspicious male lover or a drug dealer?"[120]

## The Last of Willy

In January Willy died, plagued by debts. Over the years friends had tried to reconcile Willy and Colette. The last time they met Willy was promoting *Ça Finit par un Mariage,* a lively book equal to the best prewar Willys. A whole chapter dealt with the latest trends: Dadaism in poetry, Cubism in painting. His interest in new literature was as keen as ever; he was the first to be interested in Raymond Roussel's surrealistic, spooflike books. Colette had just published *The Ripening Seed,* signed "Colette," having forever discarded "Colette Willy." They happened to meet at a literary dinner; Willy wrote to Curnonsky that she now had a rear end as big as a stagecoach, "which must make her very unhappy, but me very happy."[121] Colette left before the end of the meal, without a word.

Willy suffered from headaches and had been sinking into a deep depression. Before his death he wrote rambling letters, asking Yvette Guilbert and Polaire for help. Rachilde, upset by Willy's financial woes, wrote an article in *Le Mercure de France,* reminding Willy's Parisian friends of his generosity, of how he had always been ready to help anyone in need. She spoke discreetly of Colette as someone "much stronger than he, and so much more cruel."[122] The *Nouvelle Revue Française* published *L'Esprit de Willy,* an essay portraying him as one of the best French humorists.

Twice — in 1927 and 1928 — Willy was hit by a taxi; he remained partially paralyzed. He spent his days sitting by a window, listening to music. He complained to Rachilde that Colette called him an "imbecile" in public. Henriette Charasson, a writer who had done work for both of them, asked Colette to visit him and to make up because he had no hard feelings at all and felt persecuted by her. She answered "You are much too nice, you cannot understand."[123]

His friends decided to launch a subscription and place the proceeds in a bank account, but not under his name, so as to keep his creditors from seizing it. Curnonsky and other friends asked Colette to participate, but she refused. The subscription brought in four thousand francs.

On January 12, 1931, at seventy-two, Willy died after receiving last rites. La Société des Gens de Lettres took care of the funeral expenses; there was a solemn mass on January 15 at the Church of Saint François Xavier. Three thousand people followed the hearse to the Montparnasse cemetery. Present were the minister Léon Barthou; René Doumic, representing the Académie Française; a delegation from the Académie Goncourt; and others from La Société des Auteurs Dramatiques and La Société des Gens de Lettres. The editorial staff of *Le Mercure de France* was there with Alfred Valette and Rachilde. The tribute paid to Willy by journalists and writers was impressive. With Willy, an entire era had vanished: the time of the *boulevardier*, of the gentleman of leisure, of cafés and salons, of duels, of conversation as one of the fine arts — a time when wit was the epitome of all social graces.

Ten days after Willy's funeral the magazine *Sur la Riviera* published an article, "Willyana," followed by a second on February 1; they were long excerpts taken from pages Willy had written ten years earlier at the request of Jules Marchand, publisher of the small magazine. They were comments on the four *Claudines,* written directly on Jules Marchand's copies of the novels. Supposedly, the notes were intended for him alone; had Marchand some ax to grind against Colette? The excerpts were chosen to support Willy's claim to shared authorship of the *Claudines;* Colette felt that Willy had had the last word and reacted with anger. Her answer came with *My Apprenticeships* in 1935. (Willy's *Indiscrétions et Commentaires sur les Claudines* were published in their entirety in 1962, a limited run of fifty copies for a group of bibliophiles.)

Colette had not obliterated Willy from her work. In *The Other One,* Farou has some of his characteristics — he is a playwright who makes witticisms in Latin; his plays are performed at Les Bouffes du Nord (which closed in 1904) and at the Scala. There is a description of the never-forgotten Monts-Boucons and of their long-gone friends, Maeterlinck, Porto-Riche, and Bataille. He remained her obsession and the shadow behind the last of her male characters. In *Gigi* he is the model for the wealthy *boulevardier* named Gaston, the very pseudonym Henry used as a journalist when Colette was reading *Lucrèce* on the sly, wearing the very same dress as Gigi. Colette was then sixty-nine and still had not forgotten Willy.

## The Pure and the Impure

Expelled from her "drawer" but determined to come back to the Palais Royal, Colette enlisted her friend Jeanne Mauduit, who lived there, to look out for a store with a mezzanine; she would turn it into a pleasant apartment. But she needed an immediate solution and moved to the Hôtel Claridge on the Champs Elysées. This temporary arrangement lasted four years. "Maybe," wrote Colette in 1942, "if the Hôtel Claridge had not gone under financially, I would still be living there."[124] Her apartment was on the sixth floor and had two rooms with balconies and a sweeping view of Paris, a bathroom, and a kitchenette in a closet. Pauline had her own room. Colette had her suite hung with wallpaper shipped from London; it had a dark background, barely visible under bright flowers and birds. She replaced the furniture with her own, using the balcony filled with geraniums to dine with her friends, and even to sleep under the stars in warm weather. A pillow, a blanket to roll herself in, and she was happy to enjoy the fresh air she always craved. She called the place "my turret" or "my dovecote." Maurice continued to live in his own apartment. The Claridge clientele was cosmopolitan: princes from India, British aristocrats, and famous entertainers. Colette described a quiet week as one with only three invitations, but she could instruct the porter to say that she was out when she needed to be alone. "A writer works well in a hotel."[125]

"Seduced by my aerial peace, friends came to settle under the same roof. . . ." They were of three kinds, "the restless, the dissolute, the hard-working." What she liked in a hotel was the guests' discretion. Never shy of contradictions, Colette praised the silence of her suite, but also spoke of doors "so thin" that after five o'clock she could smell the "felt-like fragrance"[126] of whisky and, later in the night, the potent aroma of opium. Her "dovecote" on the sixth floor became a gathering place. Adrien Fauchier-Magnan, a historian famous for his princely way of life, had been a friend since World War I; he and his wife belonged to a set of art-loving millionaires. In Morocco they had been the guests of El Glaoui, who, dressed in flowing white robes, had spoken with them through an interpreter; they were astonished to meet him in Colette's apartment dressed in Western clothes and speaking flawless French. The Claridge was El Glaoui's pied-à-terre in Paris and Colette shared his circle of Parisian friends. Simone Berriau, his mistress and lifelong friend, became one of Colette's favorites, as she was attracted to her unorthodox personality.

At seventeen Simone had eloped, dressed as a boy, and run away to Morocco with a lieutenant. The disguise was not convincing enough. The military authorities discovered the truth and Colonel Berriau, the colonel in charge of the case, placed the lieutenant under arrest and ruled that the minor be shipped back to France by the first boat. Simone was not shipped back, because the colonel fell madly in love and married her. She was about to give birth to their child when Colonel Berriau died suddenly of an ear infection. So Simone returned to France, where Albert Wolff, the well-known composer and conductor of the Opéra Comique, discovered that she had a ravishing voice. Simone took lessons, dazzled the right people, and was soon singing the leading parts in *Carmen* and *Pelléas et Mélisande.* At the top of her singing career, as she was celebrating at Maxim's with friends — including El Glaoui and Colette — Simone swallowed a peppercorn, which landed on her vocal chords and caused an inflammation. When it was over, she had lost her voice. She became a movie actress (Colette wrote the screenplay of *Divine* for her) but essentially Simone turned to business; she launched a chic restaurant and a fashionable beach resort on the Riviera, sold her own brand of wine, and later bought the Théâtre Antoine.

She managed her vineyard with the same *maestria* as her theater in Paris. She produced Sartre's play *The Red Gloves (Les Mains Sales),* which was an uproarious success, for every evening a group of communists came to protest and scream. After the show Simone threw elegant parties, drowning any political differences in champagne. She relaxed by competing in car races and by collecting paintings and brilliant lovers. Her boundless energy astonished even Colette, who would stay in her southern estate, Mauvannes, when she was tired of being confined to her apartment. Simone was a dark beauty with fiery eyes, splendid teeth, and a cascade of silky black hair; she always wore a tiny hat, a sort of jockey cap with a strap under her chin. Everybody was puzzled by this choice, yet for some unknown reason she fancied this small headgear and was buried with it.

Maurice moved into his own apartment at the Claridge after his luxury dealership in pearls collapsed following the 1929 crash. Pearls, once the symbol of success, lost their appeal when Coco Chanel made costume jewelry fashionable and started using cultured pearls from Japan. Maurice gave up his large apartment on Avenue President Wilson; in February he sold La Gerbière to Coco Chanel — it was only coincidental that the couturier who contributed to his ruin came to his rescue. Maurice and Colette had known Coco for many years; at one time Colette had been dressed by Chanel. Later she wore Germaine Patat's or Lucien Lelong's creations exclusively.

The marquise de Morny also moved to the Claridge. Adrien Fauchier-Magnan, who met her for the first time at Colette's, was astonished by her tiny feet and masculine attire. One day as they waited for the elevator, the marquise asked him not to call her "Madame" when they walked out into the lobby, since the staff was accustomed to call her "Monsieur le Marquis." Colette and Missy had kept in touch only occasionally, but when Colette performed in *The Vagabond,* the marquise went to congratulate her: "You were magnificent, My Colette . . . Tonight as you said the same words, you had the same looks."[127] The friendship resumed. Missy's "sons" had regrouped: Sacha Guitry ruled unchallenged over the théâtre de Boulevard and still called Colette "Collerette." Prince and Princess Ghika, tormented by their common love for young Manon, went through the pangs of a ménage à trois until George and Manon eloped; eventually Liane divorced, then remarried the prince. They had stopped seeing Missy for a while because Missy smoked cigars, which gave Liane migraine headaches. Missy said that her migraines were boring, and Liane took offense. However, when her marriage crumbled, she sent a letter addressed to "Father" (since she had married Ghika, whom Missy called her "son"). Missy arrived in her shining red car with her chauffeur and accompanied by her chambermaid — her usual retinue. The media had lost interest in the emperor's niece, who went on with her life. She went cruising on Henri de Rothschild's *Eros,* and was seen in Venice and in London, in high-society lesbian circles; she was still investing in theater and movie productions. She was a difficult guest, sweetly but firmly refusing to eat eggs, fish, green peas, lima beans, tomatoes, veal, pork, cheese, cakes, strawberries, and apricots. That was not the end of her list of dislikes. She only ate the central stalk of lettuce leaves and the stems of cauliflowers, and cucumbers had to be freshly cut. If chicken was served, she only ate the drumsticks; if hare, only the thighs. She had an exquisite manner of stating her preferences, which never offended but drove the hostess to distraction and the cook to despair. She liked to concoct all kinds of weird but apparently effective remedies and practical devices: she made an ointment that suppressed pain in Liane's big toe when she had a fit of gout; she had a lotion for shiny nails, some magic cream to clean copper, and plans for a rolling ladder for a library. She boasted of having invented tanks before anyone built them. Concerned with the writer's comfort, Missy brought Colette a new gadget, a lamp that could be clamped anywhere and then adjusted; Colette was never without that lamp, which would become *The Blue Lantern (Le Fanal Bleu).*

Colette wrote to Hélène Picard that her book was progressing slowly, was stirring up memories of old loves, and had to do with physical atttraction and unisexual love. It still had no title; should it be *Eddy (Remous)*, or would Hélène prefer *Foam (Ecume)?* The manuscript had a tentative title, *The Deceiver (Le Fourbe).* Finally Colette gave her essay a title culled from *The Ripening Seed, Ces Plaisirs.* The whole sentence reads, "These pleasures so thoughtlessly called physical,"[128] implying that they involve body and mind. Ten years later, in the 1941 edition, *Ces Plaisirs* became *The Pure and the Impure,* its definitive title, when she revised "this book by which I hope to add a personal contribution to the sum total of our knowledge of the senses."[129]

In this essay Colette examined the sensual attractions that drive human nature. Using dialogues, confessions, and "more or less disguised memories of herself,"[130] Colette presented heterosexual and homosexual case studies to illustrate her philosophy of love, echoing Fourier, who wrote: "My theory is limited to utilizing the passions just as nature gives them and without changing anything.... Misled by political and moral systems, let us begin by seeking a more dependable guiding light than the so-called reason that has led us astray.... Which of our passions bears some mark of the divine spirit? Can we find any trace of that spirit in our frenzies of ambition, in our perfidious administrative and commercial affairs, in the inconstancy of our friendships, in the discords of our families? No, greed, deceit, and envy betray the absence of the divine spirit. But there is one passion which retains its original nobility, which keeps the divine fire burning in mortal men, which gives them a share in the attributes of the Deity. This passion is love. Love is a divine flame, the true spirit of God who is love.... Love is the most powerful agent of passional rapprochement even between antipathetic characters."[131]

Love was the panacea for curing the ills of civilization. With typical Fourierist equanimity, Colette claims that "there is only one love, that everywhere its language and its motions are the same,"[132] be it heterosexual or homosexual, and that the senses are a better guiding light than the heart. "What is the heart? . . . It is worth less than its reputation . . . the body, that's something else!"[133] In an article published in 1937, "My Ideas on the Novel" Colette speaks of her writing "as a regular, obstinate work, which derives its joys exclusively from Nature and Love."[134] Later, looking backward, she wrote: "Love, food of my pen and of my life."[135] Never did Colette renounce her investigation of passions, never did she write about anything but love. She mentioned with a touch of irony that the unfaithful, sensuous Henry de Jouvenel had chided her, "But can't you write a book that is not all about love, adultery, half-incestuous liaisons, breaking up? Isn't there anything else in life?" Colette retorted that "in a novel and outside of a novel"[136] nothing could fill the place of love.

The Pure and the Impure is Colette's most revealing book; "It will, perhaps, be recognized one day as my best work." She was in her seventies when she said to her friend Glenway Wescott, "I happened to read it the other day and I took pride in it."[137] Goudeket remarked, "If Ces Plaisirs had been written in a didactic mode, no doubt it would have been praised to the skies; it would have been said that the problem of the senses had been treated for the first time in a true philosophical spirit."[138]

Colette was an imperturbable moralist, amoralist, or immoralist, according to her critics. Few caught, through revealing flashes, the carefully guarded secret of a strong, manipulative writer who denied systematically that she had any "general ideas." Colette, who always concealed her large forehead under a screen of frothy curls for fear of exposing her true self, hid her intelligence under a pretense of simplicity and an apparently materialistic approach to life. She carefully played the part of a woman who wrote but did not "think," dismissing the idea that her work had any philosophical undercurrent. She quipped in an interview with Frédéric Lefèvre, "I have to warn you that I am not in the habit of saying definitive things,"[139] and she stopped another reporter who wanted to discuss her ideas with "I write, must I also think?"[140] However, Edmond Jaloux felt that the beauty of Colette's style "was not only the result of a felicitous assemblage of words . . . this woman with no claims to philosophy, with no claims of any kind, is one of the most beautiful cosmic minds that I know."[141]

Colette's lasting literary passion was Balzac; in her works she mentioned twenty-three titles and fifty-five characters from Balzac's *La
Comédie Humaine*. Colette knew that Balzac admired his contemporary,
Charles Fourier. Like him, Balzac, in his *Comédie Humaine*, gave passions
a paramount importance, tracking them down in their disguises and
identifying them under every cover — under the fallacies of assumed
motives and justifications, half-smothered by hypocrisy, righteousness,
greed, ambition, and fear. "Fourier was certainly correct in considering
passions as impulses that guide man and societies," wrote Balzac. "The
passions are indeed the movements of the soul; thus they are not bad in
themselves. In taking this position Fourier had, like all the great innova-
tors, like Jesus, broken with all the world's past. According to him, it is
only the social milieu in which the passions move that renders them
subversive. He has conceived the colossal task of adapting the milieu to
the passions, of destroying the obstacles, of preventing the conflicts. But
to regulate the play of the passions, to harness them to the wagon of society, is not to give rein to the brutal appetites. Is it not to promote intelligence rather than sensuality?"[142]

"I have a long-lasting habit of taking Balzac at his word," said Colette,
"to go with him anywhere it pleases him to lead me."[143] Balzac nurtured
Colette the writer, Sido nurtured Colette the woman. Both led in the
same direction, questioning the accepted definitions of good and evil, especially "if one gives to carnal intercourse its ancient name of evil."[144]
Colette's most successful literary conceit was to make her mother the
herald of her own radical beliefs and to veil with daughterly devotion the
most unconventional ideas. In *Sido*, as in *My Mother's House*, she wrote
from the point of view of a child who can see no wrong in her mother
and accepts outrageous statements as the marks of a superior personality.
By this device Colette conjures for her reader the child he or she was,
who listened to and accepted a superior wisdom. Colette marveled at
Sido's tactful ways as she moved through life immune to blame: "I don't
have, my dearest, your light steps to cross certain paths. I remember that
when it rained you had almost no mud on your shoes."[145] By placing herself under her mother's aegis, Colette took shelter: My mother did ... my
mother said ... this was my mother's way ...

Well aware that George Sand was treated with condescension whenever she added philosophical implications to her love stories and that
Madame de Staël was branded a *femme savante* when *femmes savantes* were

traditionally ridiculed as bluestockings, Colette denied any ideological commitment with a disarming sense of humor; "No more than my charming, crazy mother am I attempting to change whatever exists."[146] Yet she could be "pitifully in earnest" and at times wavered between turning into "an argumentative Colette" with "the hairdo of a Russian student," lecturing for "free love," or a "forty-year-old Colette, consumed by a young love, ripe and soft under her makeup . . ." She searched between these two possibilities "for a narrow sheltered path, guided by a friendly hand."[147]

Catherine Pozzi, who had known Colette since 1903 — when both were under Georgie Raoul Duval's spell — noted that Colette *created* her public persona, an image carefully crafted for the public at large: "Everything is fake in Colette . . . she makes herself into a certain person . . . she constantly touches up the image, she rearranges it and checks it in human mirrors. Her cuisine, her sensuous gastronomy? She can't cook a cutlet right."[148] Paul Géraldy thought that everything in Colette was a matter of attitude. "At lunch she is busy with the melon, with the anchovy pie, 'she made the dough herself,' pretense? Without any doubt. Her trips to the kitchen have helped the cook less than she claims. But what pretense is not better than literary pretense?"[149] At seventy-three, Colette summed up her attitude toward reporters: "They think that I have sweeping theories. It is not up to me to reveal them . . . I made my choice a long time ago — or, to be more truthful, I advertised my choice."[150] She did create her image, and at the last it bothered her to have become "an old stereotype,"[151] a country girl from a small village, a candid pagan corrupted by an old husband who exploited her talent.

Beyond the stereotype, and from the start, there was the Fourierist Colette. "To dare . . . What more could I dare? I have been told often enough that living according to love, then according to the absence of love was the worst kind of presumptuousness."[152] Already, in *Claudine Married,* Claudine elucidated for Renaud what was and was not vice. To have lovers did not imply that one was depraved: "I take a lover without love . . . that is vice . . . I take a lover whom I love or simply desire . . . I consider myself as the most honest of all creatures . . . I sum it up: vice is evil done without pleasure."[153] In *Paysages et Portraits* Colette created Valentine, who thinks in clichés, is narrow-minded, prudish, and bigoted. Colette would like to hit her on the head "to shake out all the prejudices, the bits of ideas, the rubble of principles, which make such an immoral din."[154]

Colette called "immoral" impure, what Fourier branded as contrary to the Creator's design. "If it is absurd not to believe in God, it is no less absurd to believe in him halfway, to think that he has neglected to provide for our most urgent needs with a social order that would ensure our happiness." Fourier asserted that a "social code" analogous to the plan that regulates the movements of the stars did exist, but that humans have been unable, as yet, to recognize it. "Passional attraction is the drive given us by Nature, prior to any reflection and it persists despite the opposition of reason, duty, prejudice, etc. . . ."[155] Colette thought, like Fourier, that all sexual preferences were normal. In a long letter to Radcliffe Hall she criticized her for having implied in *The Well of Loneliness* that her lesbian characters felt abnormal. She explained her own belief to her "dear John" (Radcliffe Hall's name among her lesbian friends): "I feel that if a so-called 'abnormal person' feels abnormal, it is really not so. Wait. I'll put it more clearly: an 'abnormal' man or woman must never have the feeling that he or she is abnormal. Just to the contrary." Nothing was abnormal in love.

Colette opens *The Pure and the Impure* with a Socratic dialogue between herself and Charlotte, a woman in her forties, in an opium den. Charlotte has a twenty-two-year-old lover, whom she brings to the den "as a reward" after he has taken good care of his health for some time. Colette hears them make love on the upper level of the dark studio and thinks that Charlotte grants "an almost public pleasure" to her young lover, giving him "the highest idea a man can conceive about himself." But Charlotte tells Colette that it would be "too good, such a young man's love," if she were not obliged to lie, to pretend, to deceive by faking sexual pleasure. She loves him, "But what is the heart, Madame . . . it is not demanding!" The heart "always ends up loving." Countering the famous Pascalian axiom that the heart is unpredictable, Colette asserted that it was not the heart, but the body that was unpredictable, "unintelligible." She called sexual attraction the Inexorable, wondering why it is always referred to as the senses — "Why not the Sense?"[156] The Inexorable, along with the five senses, gives us the awareness, the exhilaration that allows us to experience life in its fullness. She calls passion "the imperious, savage, and secret love, which binds me to the earth and to all that surges from its womb."[157]

The need for sexual gratification is no different than the demands of the other senses, and she finds it "strange" that "an act forbidden by no law, punished by no sanction"[158] is not acceptable to many women if not blessed by some religion. Women who abstain from physical love live in a vague, guilty sadness, which has no moral value and no justification for Colette. This priority of the sensual over the sentimental derives from Fourier, who believed that in attempting to proscribe physical love and praise the sentimental, both were sacrificed. Sentimental love should come only after, not before, the physical impulses have been satisfied. Fourier defined sentimental love as "half love" and because women are more likely than men to fall prey to sentimental illusions, he warned women to resist its entrapments, since "when all the amorous needs of a woman are provided for, when she has had all the physical lovers, orgies, and bacchanalia (both simple and compound) that she wishes, then there will be ample room in her soul for sentimental illusions." Yet in spite of his emphasis on physical love, Fourier called sentiment "the noble side of love."[159] Only in antiquity was some account taken of men's natural desires, if not women's; but "since Cato's time" a system of repression has been justified by the Christian fear of mortal sin and a danger "much worse than mortal sin": the upsurge of venereal diseases "which dates only from the past three centuries."[160] He admitted that, in that respect, sexual repression made sense.

Colette's Charlotte is the perfect example of that philosophy. She loves her young lover without being attracted to him physically. She does not look for a selfish sensual gratification; she has reached the stage when she can indulge in the luxury of sentimental love. In Colette's pantheon, Charlotte is "that heroine,"[161] for she has mastered the Inexorable.

After the heroine, Colette presents the case of a misuse of the senses, the sapphic poet Renée Vivien. "The ephemeral, the melting creature" was so addicted to alcohol and drugs that she could barely taste food; she had a fascination with darkness and death, which Colette considered the most "misplaced" curiosity. She noted that, having destroyed her senses, Vivien had "an immodest regard for [them] and for the techniques of physical gratification." Colette concluded, "I am hostile to those who burn themselves out."[162]

Don Juan was her next example. Colette had been toying with the idea of a play on Don Juan for years. She discussed her project with "a successful playwright," who told her to forget it. "Why?" she asked. "Your concept of Don Juan, dear friend . . . What could it add to the other concepts of Don Juan? . . . Don Juan is a hackneyed type, whom no one has understood." In spite of this unflattering opinion, Colette persisted. For the part of Don Juan she had in mind the aging Edouard de Max.

"Edouard, what do you think of it?"

"I am too old, my dear."

"Precisely — in my play, I need someone your age."[163]

But de Max died and Colette gave up the play. However, she included her concept of Don Juan — whom she called Damien — in *The Pure and the Impure*. Colette's Don Juan "spoke little and disparagingly of women" and summed up his philosophy in four words: "Give nothing, accept nothing." Colette blamed the perpetrator of "a thousand and three" infidelities, not for running from woman to woman as did the traditional Don Juan, but for a specific flaw, which is only a flaw in the framework of Fourier's philosophy. Whenever Damien decides to leave a woman she vanishes from his life as definitely "as if he had dropped her into a well." Colette qualified this as "his useless task,"[164] and could not accept that Damien did not keep any sort of affection for the women he had loved. Damien represents the vicious side of inconstancy. According to Fourier, "This is truly a shameful aspect of civilized people, nothing is more odious than their almost universal custom of completely forgetting the very people they have idolized."[165] Damien's lovemaking is evil since it does not turn into lasting relationships. The true polygamist, on the other hand, is virtuous, for he or she practices "composed fidelity" and turns loves into lasting bonds. Colette practiced "virtuous inconstancy" or what Fourier called "the precious property of conserving friendship after love." She was the virtuous Don Juan extolled by Fourier, for she had the capacity of creating "one or several pivotal loves." "Pivotal love is truly transcendent faithfulness . . . neither men nor women are jealous of the unfaithfulness of their pivotal object, they are (his or her) confidant."[166] This notion was taken up by Jean-Paul Sartre and Simone de Beauvoir, who practiced two categories of love — the essential love, and the contingent ones.

In an extensive interview the journalist Parinaud mentioned Colette's Don Juan, as "a great guy." She lashed out that she had failed if she had given the impression that Don Juan was a "great guy."

In *The Pure and the Impure* the androgyne is the perfect being. "I have the fortune of being only halfway a woman,"[167] wrote Colette, who opened her study of homosexuality by asserting that true androgyny did exist. "I am aiming at the authentic hermaphroditism that burdens certain highly endowed beings."[168] There was a time in her life when she wanted to shed her ambiguity for the love of a man, to offer him "an honest female body and the, maybe fallacious, vocation of a servant." He was not deceived; he saw a virile streak in Colette, which she could not identify herself. He was attracted but fled nevertheless, and "then he would come back reproachful and mistrustful." She remembered that in those days one of her male friends had exclaimed, "You a woman! You wish you were." She had then turned to Marguerite Moréno, who advised her to put an end to her vain attempts at seduction and resign herself to the fact "that for certain men, certain women represent the threat of homosexuality." Moréno pointed out that many men have something feminine about them but it is only mental, they are not physically homosexual. Colette thought that she could discern these hidden characteristics in people when they slept. Certain men have a feminine gracefulness, and "sleep sweeps countless numbers of women toward the sex they would have chosen without doubt," had they been aware "of their true self."[169]

Colette faced her own androgyny and thought it praiseworthy to do so, for it takes a lot of courage to face in oneself what "stumbles and slips from the official sex into the clandestine one."[170] However, androgyny, the equilibrium between masculine and feminine, is rarely found. Most of the time a being wavers between his or her sexual definition. Colette thought that she and Moréno were examples of these "highly endowed beings."

Many of Colette's characters incorporate traits of the opposite sex that make them more attractive to their lovers. "The sound of Léa's voice, almost male, voluptuous"; and Madame Dalleray has "a virile smile, which often made her look like a handsome boy." Her young lover thinks of her as his "mistress" and sometimes his "master."[171] To Colette "the seduction of a being whose gender is uncertain . . . is powerful."[172]

Another type of superior being is Missy, whom she calls la Chevalière. Surrounded by a court of passionate and tremulous women, la Chevalière searches for a peaceful, sentimental haven; her natural platonism is always disappointed by the sensuous demands of the women attracted to her. Colette wanted to make her the archetype of the unisexual. One

evening over a game of cards, "Uncle Max" made a surprising confession in her soft, monotonous voice: in her teens she had had two lovers.
The first was her cousin Alexis Orlof, who was madly in love and
threatened to kill himself if she resisted. The second was Lord Hume, a
very handsome young man who adored her and begged her to marry
him. Not sure if she wanted to and a little bored by his insistence, she
told him to give it a try. For ten days she was his mistress; then she made
up her mind and refused to marry him. She was eighteen when she was
pressured into a marriage with the marquis de Belbeuf, which soon
ended in separation. To Colette she is the platonic androgyne forever
seeking her counterpart, who, not finding it, remains unfulfilled. In his
sexology Fourier did not reject heterosexual or unisexual platonic love,
"the great mistake of the sophisticated world . . . is its failure to recognize that genuine sentimental ties can only be formed by a few highly
refined individuals."[173] Colette called Missy "the most notorious, the
most misunderstood" androgyne, avoided by men and not understood
by women. She is "mainly left with the right, even the duty of never
being happy."[174]

While she was writing *The Pure and the Impure,* Colette read the
diary of Lady Eleanor Butler, published in *The Hamwood Papers* under
the title "Journal of E.B. and S.P., Inhabitants of a Cottage in the Vale of
Llangollen." Una Troubridge had drawn her attention to the text.
Colette integrated "The Ladies of Llangollen" into her study of lesbianism as the perfect example of a passionate and sentimental lesbian
love, one that endured for fifty-three years. In 1778 the couple had fled
to a Welsh village, where they spent a blissful existence together in a secluded cottage, never pretending to be a heterosexual-like pseudo-
couple, but simply two women sharing their lives with each other in
absolute trust and exclusive love. Colette wrote romantically about "the
magic that reduced the Welsh villagers to a state of devotion for the two
ladies."[175] Anticipating some ironic comments, Colette accused of per-
version any reader "who would have it that these two faithful maidens
fell short of purity." Then she questioned the meaning of the word "purity" in a society in which patting a cheek is proper, "but if the cupped
hand presses and lightly weighs a breast as rosy as a peach . . . there is
cause for blushes. . . . How hard it is to believe in innocence."[176]

In order to disarm her critics, Colette criticized herself, placing the
blame in the mouth of her straitlaced fictional friend, Valentine: "All that

is fine; when you want to exonerate yourself from something, you dress it up as literature."[177] Valentine reminded Colette that she used to go to the notorious Semiramis Bar, not to a Welsh cottage. Colette retorted that the lesbian owner-cook of the Semiramis was a warm, kind woman, a surrogate mother for homosexuals, showgirls out of work, young drug addicts, prostitutes, and lost dogs. Besides, "as I eat my dinner I enjoy watching entwined young girls dancing together for their own pleasure. ... I find it prettier than a ballet." She dismissed Valentine, saying, "There is no hope to bring me back to virtue" — with this sweet irony, Colette accepted being "charged with all the sins."[178]

After the platonic androgyne, Colette examined the case of another type of unisexual, featuring Amalia, a music-hall artist who gave her a lesson in successful lesbian love. "Mark this, a relationship between women can last a long time and be happy, but if one of the women assumes the character of a pseudoman"[179] it puts an end to the happiness of the couple. A woman is a total being with her own characteristics, not a pseudoman. By behaving like a pseudoman, a lesbian becomes a pseudoindividual, falling into the worst trap of the masculine stereotype: Don Juanism. Sapphic philandering is totally "unacceptable" because it is totally uncalled for. The delight of a constant presence, which stifles heterosexual love, "excuses Sapphic fidelity . . . two women absorbed by each other do not fear or imagine separation, nor could they bear it."[180]

As she was writing about "female unisexuals," she requested Marguerite's opinion, saying: "Of course, one could treat the chapter like this:

> The female unisexuals.
> A single chapter.
> There are no female unisexuals."[181]

She wrote that attempts by Gomorrah to measure up to Sodom did not succeed because Gomorrah was unable to forge its own autonomy. Its most visible group, the high-class lesbians she knew, was disappearing. In the thirties social changes were destroying the privileged group of idle women who "claimed individual freedom and posed as an equal of the imperturbable, solid male homosexuality."[182] She denounced the timidity and lack of power in Gomorrah. She saw it as an insecure, unassertive, wavering group. She implied that, until it found its own means of promoting social bonds and building on mutual attraction,

Gomorrha was of little consequence. She denied that it existed as an autonomous entity. Lesbians were unable to organize supportive groups to forge their own identity, so they kept on imitating men. She reproached herself for having cross-dressed when she was young, before knowing how to assume her own self.

In July of 1921 Marcel Proust had sent her *Sodome et Gomorrhe*. She was dazzled from the very first pages: "*No one in the world* has written pages like that about the homosexuals, no one!" She told Proust that she had wanted to write an essay on the same subject for a long time, but was "unable and too lazy to produce it." Proust had written precisely what she had in mind; "Once and for all, I swear that after you, no one except yourself will be able to add anything to what you have already written . . . everything is magnificent. . . . How I admire you!" She wished him good health, then retracted the wish — "would health dull such finely tuned senses? I feel that for you, I can reach the most murderous selfishness."[183] Maurice Goudeket recalled that whenever a new volume of Proust was published she left whatever she was doing and "without losing a minute, began to read with brooding attention"; every two years or so, she gave herself up to Proust "as to a wave." She used to say, "I go in at one end and come out at the other."[184]

However, she denied that he understood female homosexuality. "Since Marcel Proust has shed light on Sodom, we respect what he wrote," but when he depicts a clique of "inscrutable and perverse young girls" and calls it "Gomorrha," she failed to see "the striking truth that guided us through Sodom." She made her point strongly, "with all due respect to Marcel Proust's imagination or his error, there is no Gomorrha."[185]

She enumerated the possible nurseries of female homosexuality: "puberty, colleges, solitude, jails, aberrations, snobishness," but found them petty, as opposed to the powerful entity of male homosexuality, "Intact, enormous, eternal, Sodom looks down on its puny counterfeit."[186]

Colette called Sodom "pure," saying, "It is in my nature to see in homosexuality a kind of legitimacy and to acknowledge its eternal character,"[187] stating that "a woman betrayed for a man, knows that all is lost."[188] It is different when a woman betrays a man with a woman. "He, a mocking spectator," is sure to recapture her and usually does. Men have used Lesbos to their own advantage. The duke of Morny, Missy's father, a discriminating womanizer, "deemed that — diamond polishes diamond — a woman refines a woman." The duke would seek out a woman for an erotic collaboration, "I hand over to you an incomplete marvel . . . see to her perfection and hand her back to me."[189]

Colette's discourse on Sodom is a eulogy. She always felt at ease in "the atmosphere that excluded women." She called it "an oasis" where men "came from the dawn of time." In Sodom she found the only true unisexuals, "the existence of a category of males . . . which is reserved for males." She thought of her lasting friendships with homosexuals. "Did any woman observe them as long as I did?"[190] In *harmony* Colette would have been classified as an *omnigyne*, like Fourier, who wrote: "I discover that I loved lesbians . . . every male *omnigyne* is necessarily a Sapphinist or a protector of lesbians, just as every female *omnigyne* is necessarily a *pederastile* or protector of pederasts." *Omnigynes* have a "pivotal" quality, a philanthropic urge to please the opposite sex "in both the ambiguous and the direct modes."[191]

Later, in *The Black Opera Glasses (La Jumelle Noire)*, Colette keenly analyzed a play dealing with the passionate friendship between two men; one dies, the other attempts suicide, remains blind, and forever mourns the love that was his absolute. "Nothing can ever pacify those who have touched the brink of that precipice into which moral values crumble." She talked of "the fragile boundary that separates the pure from the impure" and quoted Balzac: "nothing can console us for having lost what we deem the infinite."[192]

In *Bella Vista* she treated the same theme. The story "Rendezvous" takes place in Morocco. Bernard is in love with and about to marry Rose, the sister-in-law of his powerful associate; Bernard's attraction to Rose is a combination of lust and ambition. They agree to meet secretly at night in a grassy cove. It is their first rendezvous. When they reach their love retreat, Bernard's torchlight reveals a bleeding youth lying on the ground; he recognizes Ahmed, their seventeen-year-old Arab guide. A sudden kinship, a warm sense of caring sweeps over Bernard; he asks Rose to help him to carry the wounded boy to their hotel, but she protests that it would destroy her reputation and runs back to the safety of her room. Bernard spends the rest of the night nursing Ahmed. As he waits for daybreak, he feels an exhilaration "as new as love." Rose loses all importance, all women seem suddenly interchangeable, "But one does not easily find a child in the shape of a man . . . precious enough to be worth the sacrifice . . . of a night of love." Rose "was my female, but this one is my equal"; only an equal can make him feel proud of himself. "With a woman, one is so easily a little ashamed of her or of oneself."[193] With this revelation Bernard discovers his true nature.

Colette concurs with Proust — "Personally, I found it absolutely indifferent from a moral standpoint, whether one found one's pleasures with a man or a woman and most natural and human that one would seek it where one could find it."[194] In her manuscript, several crossed-out sentences add revealing nuances to the published text: "Having reached a phase in life when the increasing peacefulness of my behavior smiles at the fading scruples of the mind, I hold that the thirst for 'the pure' is as common as the one that precedes it . . . which suits another age, and was the thirst for the impure." "The word pure arouses in me nothing but the need to savor it, or its opposite, which is no less worthy."[195]

Colette's candor as an exponent of the multiplicity of the modes of love is unmatched except in Fourier's culture-shattering sexology, in which he states it is "Nature's wish to excite us to pleasures of all degrees, to the simple, the composed, the polygamous, the omnigamous and the ambiguous."[196] Colette was in tune with nature and free of the guilts of Western civilization. She saw "no inconvenience" in making her own experience the core of her works, giving herself as an exemplary heroine. "Why should I halt the progress of my hand on this paper, which has gathered for so many years what I know, what I try to hide, what I invent and what I guess about myself."[197] Goudeket summed up the impression of many critics when he tried to explain Colette's ethic: "To Colette, it did not seem so easy to distinguish between good and evil. . . . It has been thought she loved scandal. . . . It was merely that she had personal ideas about what was scandalous. . . . She was amoral, if you like, insofar as morality is a code that is taught."[198]

# IV

---

## MADAME MAURICE GOUDEKET

---

*"To change is to live."*
COLETTE

COLETTE WAS WORRIED. Maurice's financial situation was going from bad to worse; in the general depression, the luxury business had been the first to be hurt. Germaine Patat had to give up the direction of her maison de couture. Colette tried to soothe her anxiety by telling her that things ripened and fell off in a natural sort of way, that we are always inclined to think we are the cause of the events in our life, but that it is not so — when an event is ripe, it happens; it matures and falls like a peach, like an apple, like a child from the womb. However, she plunged into a frenzy of work for fear of finding herself in the same predicament.

In February and March Colette gave a series of lectures in Paris, Austria, and Rumania; in April she was in Tunisia and Algeria. Everywhere she was met by journalists and cameramen. In Vienna she was greeted by a high-ranking diplomat at the railroad station, then attended a party organized for her, followed by a concert. The next day there was a reception in her honor at the French Embassy and a lunch with thirty guests. After her lecture she was whisked off to another party. The last day she had lunch with the press; a crowd had been waiting for her in the hotel lobby since nine in the morning. A royal reception awaited her in Rumania, where she was treated as an ambassador of the French literary establishment. The subversiveness of her life and views were lost; on November 6, 1928, she had been promoted to the rank of Officer of the Legion of Honor.

Summer was spent at La Treille Muscate, but on September 5 Colette fell into a ditch on a dirt road and broke her leg. The doctor diagnosed a fracture of the fibula. It was healing well when at the end of September Colette decided to return to Paris. She found her thick plaster so uncomfortable that she convinced the local doctor to remove it, which according to her he did with a hunting knife and pruning shears. He pulled on one side, Pauline on the other, as if they were opening a large oyster. Colette, determined to have her way, said she felt no pain at all.

The situation in France was worsening; Maurice was unable to start a new business. Colette confessed to Léo Marchand that they were going through a terrible period and she was looking for a way out. Lunching with André Maginot, she spoke of their financial woes. Maginot was an imaginative man, twice minister of defense and inventor of the Maginot line; he asked if Goudeket was planning to go back into the "luxury trade." Goudeket said no, the luxury trade was too depressed. Maginot convincingly argued that it was precisely the right time to go into that kind of business, since recovery was about to begin, and suggested that Colette should start her own business — in a sweeping gesture he drew a big sign in the air and said, "My name is Colette and I sell perfume."¹ Colette sprang into action immediately. Maurice tried to dissuade her, saying that her fame as a writer would suffer, but she laughed at him; she remembered the enormous financial success of the *Claudine* name. He tried to make her realize that she would be competing with well-established firms and that she would have to find a laboratory and give demonstrations of her cosmetics by making up her clients in public, but this proved a temptation, not a deterrent. Colette loved to change her friends' hairstyles, boldly cutting their hair. She relished the prospect of using creams and colors to bring out her future clients' true personalities. Maurice knew that Colette would get over it quickly if the venture failed, but never forgive herself if she did not give it a try. Colette was ready to do anything for her venture, even industrial espionage; she enrolled a willing Moréno, "My Dear soul, I would like — since you so

Musidora. Courtesy of Roger-Viollet.

Marguerite Moréno. Courtesy of
Roger-Viollet.

Polaire. Courtesy of Roger-Viollet

Colette's stepson, Bertrand de
Jouvenal. Courtesy of Roger-Violet.

Colette at the opening of her Institut de beauté in 1932.

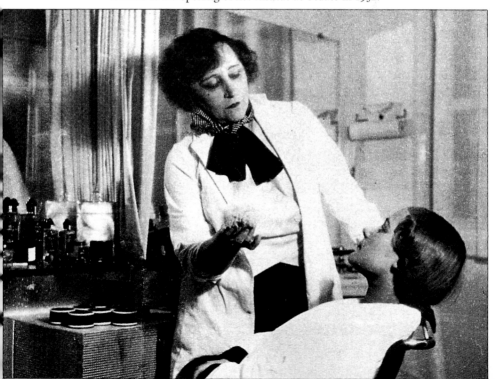

Le baron et la baronne de Jouvenel with their daughter at Castel-Novel..
Courtesy of Roger-Viollet.

Colette and her cats in 1939.
Courtesy of Roger-Violet.

Colette and Maurice Gaudeket
circa 1950.

Grand-Officier of the Légion d'honneur, présidente de l'Académie Goncourt,
Colette at her eightieth birthday party.

Colette at eighty.
Courtesy of Corbis.

The state funeral of Colette.

kindly offered to do it — I would like you to steal some Max Factor for me: their number 23 for the face and their brown one."²

At first the people she contacted were reluctant to invest money. Colette had a chain of cosmetics stores in mind, an idea that scared off her prospective sponsors. Finally the princess de Polignac; El Glaoui, the pasha of Marrakesh; Daniel Dreyfus, a Parisian banker and art collector; Léon Bailby, owner of several newspapers; and Simone Berriau financed the venture — each one investing two hundred thousand francs. Colette spent days in a laboratory choosing, tasting, sniffing, and examining test tubes; she decided on the shapes and colors of the boxes, the bottles, and the packaging. She wrote the flyers and drew her own portrait for the cover of the powder boxes. La Société Colette for the manufacture of beauty products was officially established on March 2, 1932; Colette rented a store at 6 Rue de Miromesnil and supervised the remodeling of the interior and the sign over the door herself. The news that Colette was going to have her own line of cosmetics was carefully leaked to the press; the journalists made it such an event that, according to her, they gave her fifty thousand francs' worth of free publicity.

On December 4 *Gringoire* started to serialize *Ces Plaisirs;* the readers of this conservative weekly protested and some canceled their subscriptions. After eleven weeks Horace Carbuccia, the director, sent Colette a telegram telling her that, under pressure from his readership, he had had to halt publication. In fact, he put *Fin (The End)* in the middle of a sentence. Colette was hurt and outraged; she considered this essay her best book and was ready to sue for breach of contract. She turned to Anatole de Monzie for advice. After consulting with him, she decided to do nothing — *Gringoire* had a circulation of eight hundred thousand — and use the incident as advertising when Ferenczi released *Ces Plaisirs* in one volume.

She found some solace when Dussane, an actress from La Comédie Française, who was famous as a lecturer, asked Colette to participate in her series of lectures on French folk songs. Colette sang five songs Mélie had taught her, in her rich mezzo-soprano voice. The following day she gave a lecture at the University of Les Annales, titled "Confidences d'auteur. Le Roman et nous. Mes Souvenirs" ("A writer's secrets. The novel and us. Remembrance"). Shocked by the violent reaction to her essay, exhausted by tension and the fear of failure of her boutique, Colette came down with an acute case of shingles; she had blisters all over the left side of her body down to her foot. The shingles lasted sixteen agonizing days. She was also suffering from her broken leg and she had an acute case of conjunctivitis. Still, she agreed to write the dialogues for the French version of the German film *Mädchen in Uniform.*

As soon as she could leave her bed Colette sent out invitations: "I inaugurate my beauty products boutique Wednesday, June 1 — I will be happy, Madame, to welcome you myself, 6 Rue de Miromesnil, and guide you in your choice of the most becoming makeup for the stage, or for the town."[3] The opening of Colette's boutique was a stunning success. In her store gleaming with chrome and glass, Colette, in a black-and-white suit, welcomed mobs of journalists, friends, photographers, autograph seekers, and admirers of all sorts. Princess Ghika walked in and was greeted by Colette, who exclaimed, "My fortune is made, Liane de Pougy is here."[4] Colette herself made up Cecile Sorel, a famous actress and old friend; Natalie Barney noted that Colette changed her method between one eye and the other, and the result was an asymmetry that made the actress look older. Natalie also commented that Bel-Gazou, on whose pretty face Colette practiced her art, had lost her healthy, tanned look and reminded her of a prostitute with heavy purple and pink makeup, ill distributed and glaring. Bringing out her clients' true personalities was not proving a success — Colette's reluctance to wear glasses in public led to a few mishaps. Among Colette's clients was Isabelle de Comminges; the former rival was now a friend. In August, after two months spent in her boutique, Colette left for La Treille Muscate. For two months she had remained on her feet five days a week, four hours at a stretch. She told Hélène Picard that she would not relax her obstinate will to succeed. She wasted no time in Saint-Tropez, opening a small outlet on the harbor for the "Produits Colette."

She did not stop writing during this period; *The Earthly Paradise* was published by Gonin in Lausanne and *Prisons et Paradis* by Ferenczi. *La Treille Muscate,* an album illustrated by Dunoyer de Segonzac, was also released in the summer. She began a new novel, *The Cat (La Chatte),* inspired by her blue-gray Chartreux cat, and in August she went on a promotional tour (chauffered by Maurice) to the southwestern resort towns from Pau to Biarritz before heading north to Luxembourg and Belgium. In October and November she gave two series of lectures as well as presentations of her cosmetics in France, Belgium, and Switzerland. She and Maurice took along the cat and the dog; Chatte kept "thanking them"[5] for having taken her along and learned to sit daintily in the dining room, just like the dog. Colette wanted her cat with her, as she was working on *The Cat*. Women rushed to see Colette, to hear Colette, to have Colette line their eyes, color their cheeks, paint their lips, and listen to their problems. In Tours the hair salon in which she was operating had to close its doors and refuse eager customers.

Exhausted by her tour and back in Paris, Colette fought a flu that was affecting her lungs. She was also suffering from an inflammation of the knee. She *had* to be cured within seven days, for on January 7 she was to lecture and promote her cosmetics in Amiens, and then again in Brussels; she was also booked in Toulon and Cannes. She spent eight days in bed applying poultices, turning her attention to her family problem. Colette II was refusing to go to Rome with Henry de Jouvenel, who had been appointed ambassador — she did not want to spend her time in evening dress, serving tea at the ambassador's receptions. An angry Jouvenel left for Rome without providing any financial support for Bel-Gazou, who needed her father's signature to draw on her bank account. Colette intervened and arranged matters between father and daughter.

Colette believed in the future of her cosmetics venture, and to finance it agreed to give thirty lectures. To make good use of her days in bed, she wrote French subtitles for the American film *No Greater Love* by Lewis Seiler, which was distributed in France as *Papa Cohen*. She found the work tedious, "quasi mathematical."[6] Maurice did his utmost to share the burden; he became the agent for an American company, selling washing machines and an instrument meant to unclog drains and lavatories, which Colette named "the weasel." She managed to get the director of the Claridge to reduce their respective rent by one thousand francs. In her letters she gives the impression that she was hard up for money, but in 1932 she was taxed on royalties that amounted to 285,751 francs, and in 1933, 299,684; this does not include earnings from her lecture tours.

So on January 20 at five in the morning, a sick Colette was on the road again. One night she thought she was about to die while she was giving a lecture in a bitterly cold theater. A doctor had boosted her with some shots and her chest was black-and-blue from cupping. She almost called Maurice for help, but resisted bravely and went on; as she talked she kept herself from coughing "the way one keeps from vomiting."[7] She was reaching the breaking point — she felt worn out by the long trip to Grenoble; the train was late; it was snowing; the dinner was horrible. She

wished it were all over. "All what? All over, simply all." Even her enormous success at the following stopover at Lyons did not cheer her up:
"Who is consoled by success? Not me."[8]

Back in Paris Colette spent a day promoting her cosmetics at the
Galeries Lafayette. While the director was displaying the Produits Colette
in a window, she autographed six hundred and fifty books in three and a
half hours, her "record."[9] In April *The Cat* was serialized in the weekly
*Marianne;* in September it was released by Grasset. Colette had spent
nights finishing it, working eleven hours at a stretch until daybreak.

*The Cat* is a subtle novel told on several levels. On the surface it is a
simple tale of a mismatch; a young couple separates after three months
of a failed marriage. Alain, the husband, at twenty-four still cannot free
himself from a nostalgic wish to remain a free adolescent — Saha, his
cat, incarnates this secret dream. In a fit of jealousy, his wife Camille
pushes Saha from the ninth floor. The cat survives, but Alain guesses that
Camille is the would-be murderer. Alain's craving for his past and
former solitude clashes with Camille's love for cars, bars, beaches, and
friends. He leaves her to return to his world: his mother, his garden, and
his only true love, the cat Saha. The dominant theme of *The Cat* is the
dream of an eternal childhood, of pure kinship with a cat as perfect as "a
little soul, as dainty as a fairy." It is a tale of purity, of Colette's own nostalgia for her childhood home, of her brother Leo's inability to grow up,
of her brother Achille's distaste for society.

Colette agreed to adapt Vicki Baum's novel, *Lac aux Dames,* for a film
to be produced by Philippe de Rothschild. He put together a promising
crew. Françoise Giroud, the script girl, would later become a journalist
and the first minister of women's affairs; Marc Allegret, the film director,
was André Gide's protégé; Dominique Drouin was Gide's nephew; and
Georges Auric was in charge of the musical score. Philippe de Rothschild
rented a whole floor, first at the Claridge to facilitate work for Colette,
then at the Château de Madrid in Neuilly, where the crew could work
together in luxury.

Colette wrote the dialogues nonstop, working from ten to thirteen
hours a day. The film crew came to her suite — some in pajamas, just
barely awake, others in bathrobes straight from the shower. Discussions
were always intense, decisions slowly made. When the crew left, Colette
rewrote the dialogue, then tore up a page, and yet another page, and finally started all over again in her compulsive quest for the right word,

the most musical phrase. She called them all back and the scene was re-peated. Suddenly she would feel the need for refreshments and Allegret would call for a bottle of champagne. Twenty minutes were sacrificed for dinner, after which work resumed until 2:30 in the morning. By then the crew was spread out on the carpet and sofa, and Colette had to send them to bed because she could work no more. The following morning they were all back, asking for another change in the dialogue. By the end of July Colette had finished and was ready to leave. She had her check plus a five-thousand-franc bonus for her "exceptional work";[10] what she thought exceptional was that she had had such patience and had remained cool all the time.

After the first months of intense publicity, the Produits Colette were not doing very well; a new injection of money was needed. Maurice fired the manager and took over; Colette felt sure things would be better now that he was supervising her venture. She had another cause to rejoice; Anatole de Monzie told her that he would obtain for her a promotion in the Légion d'Honneur. But when the promotions were published, Colette's name was not on the list. The council of the order had frowned upon her cosmetics business and Lépine, the former préfet de police who had overseen the scandal of the Moulin Rouge, was part of the Grande Chancellerie: "I remember a time when Colette wore around her neck not the red *cravate* of the Légion but a choker, where one could clearly read, 'I belong to Madame de Morny.'"[11] Next it was announced in the press that she was to succeed Georges Courteline at L'Académie Goncourt, but she was bypassed once more.

Colette presided over the Prix de la Renaissance and was a member of the latest literary award, Le Prix des Portiques, sponsored by the conservative weekly *Gringoire*. The specialized press of the music hall elected her honorary president. In a "referendum on princesses" organized by the journal *Minerve,* she was elected princess of letters, Marie Curie princess of sciences, Cécile Sorel princess of the stage, and Anna de Noailles princess of poets. Anna de Noailles had died on April 30 at the age of fifty-six. During her frequent ill-nesses Colette had spent many hours in Anna's room while the poet reclined on a chaise longue, never silent, feverish and restless. Colette and Anna were to-tally antithetic. Anna was attracted by Colette's sensuous approach to life; she credited her with having rediscovered ambrosia and went around Paris asserting that only Colette knew the secret of the Greek gods' drink (which was simply hot Beaujolais, cinnamon, lemon, and sugar). Colette was touched by Anna's hyperboles but disliked her way of discussing her poetry in public. According to Violet Trefusis, "Colette on these occasions would behave like a somewhat grumpy gardener, who had been dragged away from his work." But Colette admired Anna because she never gave up. She would gather enough strength during the day to be whisked off to a dinner party, where she would dominate the conversation until, having used up her energy, she was rushed home. "It was comforting to know that she died all day and dined all night," commented Violet Trefusis.[12]

Disappointed, Colette had left for Saint-Tropez. As soon as she arrived Marc Allégret appeared, soon followed by the actors and the crew. He wanted her to rewrite again the screenplay, which she did. At La Treille Muscate she felt reborn; she swam over a kilometer without fatigue and in a burst of optimism said she was entering her fifth or seventh youth. She was seen strolling along the harbor with Maurice in tow, surrounded by beautiful starlets. She would have loved to be able to afford the relaxing life at La Treille Muscate all year round — wearing a faded bathing suit or an old jacket, eating garlic. "To live without writing! Oh the marvelous life!"[13] Dining at the countess Thérèse Murat's, she declared she was not made to write — she was made to do nothing, to ride her horse, swim, and bask in the sun. Having exorcised her demons, Colette accepted the position of drama critic at Le Journal (circulation of nine hundred thousand). As soon as she had signed the contract, she regretted it, "as usual."[14]

In December Maurice made his debut in journalism in La République. At last the clouds seemed to show a silver lining, but in January Colette suffered from a severe attack of arthritis and was treated with x-rays without result. She ate enormously to cure her pain.

Maurice was liquidating the cosmetics business while Colette was "scribbling" a "little novel," Duo. In June her articles as a drama critic were released in a single volume, under the title The Black Opera Glasses. In the fall Duo was serialized in the weekly Marianne and published in November by Ferenczi. Duo seemed adaptable to the stage; she asked Léo Marchand if he would collaborate with her again, but he was too busy. The following summer, Paul Géraldy asked Colette if he could adapt her novel. "I would like you to succeed where I have failed,"[15] answered a disheartened Colette. Two more years went by and the project seemed forgotten, when in the summer of 1937 Paul Géraldy came to La Treille Muscate one evening with the play; he read it to Colette throughout the night, and when the sun rose, Colette knew the play was a winner. It opened at the Théâtre Saint Georges on October 10, 1938.

Rather than a *Duo,* the book is a *duel* between husband and wife — between Alice, the Fourierist, and Michel, the spokesman for traditional male values. While Michel is on a four-week business trip, Alice has a brief affair with Ambrogio, his business partner. When Michel comes back, Alice and Ambrogio revert to their previous friendly relationship. Inadvertently, Michel opens Alice's folder and a letter flutters to the ground; it is Ambrogio's grateful love letter. Michel is smitten by the proof that Alice has betrayed him and by the fact that she has no feelings of guilt. To Michel, who calls her betrayal "ignominious," she replies indignantly, "If because I had sex, once in my life, with another man, you must poison both of our lives, I prefer to go away now!" Michel hears only the word "once": "Once? You said once? Only once?"

For him, the only logical explanation is that Alice has been overpowered by her sexuality. But she explains that it is not so, it happened neither by chance nor by surprise. She was convalescing from the flu, and Ambrogio offered to take over the work she had to do in Michel's absence. He proved helpful, efficient, caring, and pleasant, and Alice found out that they had a lot in common.

Michel, "offended because Alice behaved as if she were innocent, screams that she was driven only by lust. Alice retorts in anger that she will have none of his clichés: "Are you going to oblige me to explain up to the last detail how surrender is the conclusion of a very long conversation, . . . the proof . . . of a trust, of a friendship that has just been granted and would feel scruples not to be even more prodigal?"[16] Alice sees her lovemaking with Ambrogio as the normal extension of an amicable bond that takes nothing away from her relationship with Michel. She begs him to understand. Colette emphasizes Alice's extreme difficulty in expressing why she feels innocent, and her infratext comes from Fourier's sexology, "When sentiment is denied the support of the physical, it becomes as uninteresting as a meal consisting of nothing but spices . . . if they were served with an excellent meal, they would be a precious complement."[17]

Unable to communicate what she feels, Alice confronts Michel, saying, "It is shameful what you are doing, shameful, and it leads nowhere, it mends nothing." She cries out in anger, "If you imagine that in the depth of my heart, I will be able to forgive you for this . . ." She gazes through the window — outside is a harmonious world, a spring night full of fragrances, of birdsongs, of moonlight that brings tears to her eyes as she thinks: "This is too stupid. . . . A night like this! To spoil a night like this!" She cherishes her love for her husband and wants to save it, unable to understand why it should be lost. She does not comprehend what he means when he says, "You haven't told me much except for the worst." Because of Alice's obvious inability to grasp what Michel considers "the worst," he makes his point: "The worst. You don't understand that the worst is precisely this friendship you gave this guy, those hours you spent talking together before going to bed together. You have even pronounced the word 'Trust.'" And Michel gives Alice a lecture on a man's notion of betrayal: "A surprise . . . a dizzy moment . . . a dirty hot spell . . . we men know what it is . . . let him cast the first stone he . . . who . . . you will never understand that a man forgives, almost forgets a brief sexual experience, a surprise of the senses."

These macho clichés seem so ridiculous to Alice that she cannot help laughing discreetly while Michel walks back and forth. As he speaks, Michel regains his dominant position as "the husband"; in a grand gesture, he seizes his wife by her elbows and calls her "my poor child," explaining that had she confessed that she had lost control briefly, he would have forgiven her. Alice tears herself free and threatens to throw the teapot at his head if he calls her "my poor child" once more. For Alice, her affair with Ambrogio demands no excuse; she cannot fathom the reason Michel is taking it in such a tragic mood. Their life should go on.

"If only I could tell myself that it was only an urge of the senses," repeats Michel. At last, to placate him, Alice falls into the trap and lies, "All right, I had sex with Ambrogio because I desired him! And I ceased having sex with him because I did not want him anymore."[18] She hopes that at last Michel will forgive and forget. Overcome by a jealousy that brings back in graphic detail visions of his own lovemaking with Alice — so beautiful, so in love — and Ambrogio's explicit words in his letter, Michel, after a night of physical torment, walks to the river and drowns himself.

## He Has a Charming Way of Asking: Do You Need Me?

The year 1935 started with another disappointment. Emile Fabre, administrator of the French National Theater, informed Colette that her play *Chéri* had been rejected by the committee because the language of the courtesans would offend the Comédie Française's conservative public. Had her play been less risqué, he would have been happy to produce it.

But news came from Belgium that compensated for this snub: Colette had been elected to the chair left vacant by Anna de Noailles's death in the Académie Royale de Langue et de Littérature Française. The official ceremony was postponed until the following year. Meanwhile, she presided happily over a lunch for the Paris media under the big top of the Amar Circus. With the band playing and flashbulbs popping, Colette baptized a newborn tiger with champagne. A reporter came to the Claridge to film her manuscripts, her hands, and her cat. On February 15 *Les Nouvelles Littéraires* announced the creation of Les Amis de Colette. Tristan Bernard, Pierre Brisson, Francis Carco, Jean Giraudoux, Edouard Herriot, François Mauriac, and Paul Morand were the board members of the association, which was to publish Colette's notes, drafts, and diaries. "Few are the writers, even the greatest, who had the privilege of being recognized and rewarded during their lifetime . . . Montaigne, Pascal, Chateaubriand, Huysmans, Loti, Zola . . . and some others who have today dedicated Amis, would have been happy to be so honored before their death. We have only one reservation . . . instead of being published in a modest bulletin available to everybody, Colette's unpublished manuscripts will only be available in limited and very expensive editions." The first subscriber was the French president, Albert Lebrun.

Colette had to move once more; the Claridge faced bankruptcy. She settled for the top floor of a new building, the Marignan, at 33 Avenue des Champs Elysées. Colette was enthusiastic about this hybrid between a hotel and an apartment building, with a concierge and a private restaurant; everything was included in the three-thousand-franc rent. Colette told Germaine Patat she should also rent an apartment. Isabelle de Comminges had already moved in, and Maurice had the suite next to Colette's — they modified the floor plan, opening a communicating door but keeping two separate entrances and two telephones. It was a lot of trouble and extra expense; for the sake of propriety Maurice thought it would be much more practical to be married.

There was another reason for their marriage. Colette was to report for *Le Journal* on the maiden voyage of the *Normandie,* due to sail to New York on May 29. Unmarried couples could not share the same room in an American hotel. "If we were married, there would be no problem," bantered Maurice. "Colette looked at me and suddenly I understood what our relationship meant to her."[19] To avoid the media, Maurice asked permission to omit the publication of the banns, which could only be done to avoid scandal. Therefore, Maurice declared that since people thought they had been married for a long time, the banns would inform them that this was untrue, and would be a matter for scandal. This byzantine excuse satisfied the civil servant in charge.

The marriage took place in Paris on April 3, 1935. Maurice was forty-six, Colette sixty-two; their witnesses were Luc-Albert Moreau and Julio Van der Henst, their neighbor in Saint-Tropez. Colette announced her marriage casually. She reassured Marie-Thérèse Montaudy, a friend for the past five years, that it was nothing more than a formality, and sent her a necklace she had made with beads from Saint-Sauveur, assuring her that it was a special gift. She asked her to take the marriage sensibly, without emotional displays, but the passionate Marie-Thérèse sent her three hundred and eighty tulips and two thousand lilies of the valley. Colette casually mentioned her marriage to Hélène Picard, joking about the seventeen-minute ceremony and the fact that in ten years they had never found a moment to formalize their relationship.

Colette and Maurice drove with their witnesses to Vaux-de-Cernay for a country meal of *omelette à la crème* and pork prepared according to a local recipe. April in Paris can be capricious; the sun was shining as they drove home, but suddenly snowflakes began to fall. Colette asked Maurice to stop the car, and she got out to feel the large, fluffy snowflakes on her face. It was a brief interlude — the sun swiftly came out of the cloud — but Colette never forgot the spring snow on that day.

On May 29 they set sail for New York. Colette had an expense account of one thousand francs a day and a credit for ten dresses and ten coats by Lucien Lelong. The *Normandie* was the biggest ocean liner ever built. For months all the French newspapers had described it as the flagship of French industry, heralding the prestige of the label "Made in France." A special train had been reserved for the journalists and, although the cuisine that awaited the guests on the *Normandie* had been announced as the ultimate in excellence, Colette (to maintain her public image as a country girl) arrived at the station with a wicker basket filled with homemade pâté, cold chicken, and some hard-boiled eggs. She made first item in the news and the journalists helped her empty the basket. Her sandals also made the news. "Colette turned up with bare legs and painted toenails. Of course, now it's the *dernier cri*."[20] The shoes were handmade for her in Saint-Tropez by a famous sandalmaker, who reproduced the pattern of ancient Roman sandals. They were not just any pair of sandals — the prince of Wales, not yet the duke of Windsor, also sported a pair of Saint-Tropez sandals.

Colette crossing the Atlantic in sandals caused a stir. They were better and healthier for a writer, explained Colette; she suffered from cold feet when she spent hours at her desk, and by discarding stockings and high heels she had set her feet free and restored her blood circulation. She declared a new life had begun the day she could spread out her toes.

There were three thousand Parisians on board the floating palace, the Tout-Paris of media, industry, and politics; among them was Bertrand de Jouvenel, now thirty-two years old, an internationally known economist. In the stateroom a gilded statue representing some allegory shuddered as the speed sent vibrations through the ship; Colette called it "The Statue of Terror." The dining room was the size of a cathedral; there were also theaters, restaurants, aviaries, game rooms, and boutiques overflowing with jewelry and haute couture fashion. Nothing like this had been seen since the *Titanic*.

Then came the "magnificent moment,"[21] the arrival in New York. The whole city seemed to have gathered on the quay. Everything that could float came to meet the *Normandie,* all the sirens blared, reporters boarded the liner, and there was a sudden rush of photographers toward Colette:

"Why do you go barefoot?"

"Because it is comfortable."

"How long does it take you to write a novel?"

"Not long enough."

"Have you written a novel during the crossing?"

"No," said Colette, "but I should have."[22]

Then things took a painful turn. Customs had never dealt with so many travelers at one time and the confusion was incredible; after standing in line for several hours, Colette entrusted an agent to get her luggage to her room and left with Maurice for the Waldorf-Astoria. From the twenty-fourth floor they looked at New York as its lights came on; they were to spend only two and a half days in the city before the *Normandie* sailed back to France. That evening they were expected to go to a banquet for eight hundred guests, presided over by Madame Lebrun, the French president's wife, and Fiorello La Guardia, the mayor of New York. Colette's invitation bore number 799, Maurice's number 800; they had been assigned the last two places, no one having ever heard of "Mr. and Mrs. Goudeket." Colette resented it and thought it had been willfully done, maybe by Jouvenel; she made fun of it in a broadcast four years later. Colette and Maurice did not go to the banquet or to the formal dinner for the writers, and Colette declined an invitation to visit a private collection of paintings. They reminded each other that they were on their honeymoon, and visited the Empire State Building, where they had their picture taken, and went to Central Park, Harlem, and the Roxy, with its five thousand seats, to watch the girls. They saw a movie with Mae West and took a taxi to buy some Parker pens, because "these were fresher"[23] than those in the shop on the Rue de Rivoli. Colette discovered Woolworth's; there were no such stores in France and she was fascinated, spending three hours buying gadgets. She and Maurice plunged into another cinema, walked back to the Waldorf-Astoria along glittering Broadway, bought candies in every drugstore, and ate them sitting on the sidewalk while chatting with a stray cat that had come running to her mewing "At last! Someone who speaks French."[24] Colette wanted to be an ordinary tourist, eating popcorn and mint candies, wearing a ten-cent clip bought at Woolworth's. The article she sent by radio from the *Normandie* to *Le Journal* was enthusiastic, "Five thousand, they sent us five thousand boxes of flowers . . . ! And fruits also." Someone had "a small Woolworth's"[25] sent to her cabin.

Back in Paris, Max Ophuls was shooting *Divine;* Colette went on location in the Billancourt studio and followed the film crew to Simone Berriau's estate, Mauvannes, where the exteriors were to be filmed. *Divine,* based on Colette's novel *Music-Hall Sidelights,* was released in November at L'Ermitage on the Champs Elysées; it was wrongly announced as "Colette's first screenplay written directly for the screen."[26]

It seemed that Colette had finally found her way to financial security — she received one hundred thousand francs for *Divine;* she sold the rights to *Chéri* for eighty thousand francs; she invested in rental properties on the Avenue Rodin; and she sold the film rights for *Claudine at School* to Serge de Poligny for an undisclosed amount. Her average earnings in 1934, 1935, and 1936 came to 302,230 francs; however, her fear of lacking money never abated. Maurice was translating *The Royal Family* by George Kaufman and Moss Hart, a play about the Barrymores; Colette was to adapt Maurice's translation for the stage. However, the project fell through.

The event of the summer was Bel-Gazou's marriage to Doctor Dausse; "My daughter is about to get married. What day?"[27] Colette did not know. She had received a letter from Henry de Jouvenel thanking her for letting the marriage take place at Castel Novel. Colette did not attend. "*Un mariage d'opérette* [a musical comedy marriage],"[28] she commented when she saw the photographs of the wedding. Bel-Gazou's sudden marriage was a surprise for everyone. Renaud, for one, did not understand why she chose to marry Doctor Dausse. He suspected this tall, bearded man, who was neither handsome, nor brilliant, nor wealthy, of marrying Bel-Gazou because of her famous parents. Renaud found him not only obnoxious but ridiculous when he came to pay his respects to Colette and presented her with a small potted orange tree, saying, "it resembles your daughter." Bel-Gazou told her brother that she had married to *normalize* herself. Renaud had never discussed her private life — "I knew her girls, she knew mine, but we did not talk about them . . . she had always women friends like her mother."[29] Bel-Gazou led a free and, according to Renaud, rather wild life, but she was not indifferent to respectability. Her father had remarried, her brothers were married, and even her notoriously free mother had just become Madame Goudeket. In August the couple was honeymooning in Saint-Tropez and stopped for a visit at La Treille Muscate. They seemed to get along; they acted like a friendly old couple. Two months after her marriage Colette's daughter filed for divorce.

Colette sent a letter to Hélène Picard assigning Bel-Gazou's conjugal adventure to its right place. "My daughter got married on August 11, she is divorcing, her reason admits no argumentation: physical horror. One cannot discuss such a thing."[30] She added that her daughter was at Castel Novel "for the funeral." Henry de Jouvenel had died two days earlier.

The letter was as cool as if none of this concerned Colette. The main topic was Hélène's newly acquired blue parakeets. "You have parakeets!!! I am bursting with jealousy." She complained about a sudden fit of flu, then threw in that, not having seen Jouvenel in twelve years, she would not have known him had she met him on the street. Then she went back to the parakeets in a postscript, instructing Hélène to keep them warm because they were prone to pneumonia. She reminisced about Sido's green parakeets and concluded her letter with the promise of a large cage and an urgent question: "a nesting place? Do they have a nesting place?" A few days later she sent a nest, a birdbath, and a bag of millet. This parakeet celebration, untimely as it seemed, was the display of a sense of humor as sharp as a blade, which Hélène, who had witnessed the Jouvenel episode since its very beginning, could fully appreciate.

Henry de Jouvenel's sudden death was covered extensively. He had spent the afternoon with Bertrand, just back from the United States, discussing the conflict between Italy and Abyssinia and his new appointment as minister for foreign affairs. That evening he visited the Salon de l'Automobile, decided to walk home, and dismissed his chauffeur. A few minutes before midnight a policeman found him collapsed on the sidewalk. Another rumor at the time was that Jouvenel had died in the company of a streetwalker in the gardens of the Champs Elysées; Bel-Gazou, who idolized her father, suspected Colette of having spread the story. In a malicious mood, Colette obtained the sales catalog of the Castel Novel furniture to be auctioned and made fun of the list of mediocre paintings.

After her divorce Renaud gave his sister moral and financial support, paying off Doctor Dausse's unpaid bills for the flowers he had sent Bel-Gazou. When an angry Doctor Dausse asked Bel-Gazou to return her engagement ring because the diamond was a family heirloom, Renaud had the "wretched diamond" removed and sent back to the doctor, then had a new one set for his sister.

## But None of His Letters Ever Asked Me to Turn Back

Throughout this eventful year Colette, unperturbed, was working on a book that was to be the last shot aimed at Willy, a posthumous settlement to their feud. She called it *My Apprenticeships, or What Claudine Did*

*Not Tell (Mes Apprentissages, ou ce que Claudine n'a pas dit).* She wrote to Hélène that she was working slowly, cautiously, with circumspection; she could not visit her because a single hour of relaxation undid a whole day's work. If she allowed herself a little fun, she said, she could not go back to writing; she complained that even her articles were robbing her of her time.

The text, which was so demanding and which needed all her attention, was an indictment of Willy as a man, husband, and writer, and a vindication of herself. It was a revisionist version of *Claudine*, no longer the free, outspoken Huronne, the androgynous creature who was both physically and mentally a healthy and happy human being. She described her shyness, her gauche endeavours to join a snobbish clan: "How timorous I was, how feminine I was with my sacrificed hair when I was aping a boy."[31] She was crafting the image of an innocent country girl, corrupted by a lecherous old miser and forced to write under lock and key novels she was not allowed to sign, a helpless young wife betrayed by her husband, brought by him into a corrupt society and finally abandoned without a penny, with no option but the music hall, the only profession available for those who had none. She had written *My Mother's House* for Bertrand; she wrote *My Apprenticeships* for Maurice Goudeket.

By 1935 values had changed; the bejeweled courtesans and witty *boulevardiers* had all gone the way of the dinosaurs. Now there were new standards of behavior and misbehavior: sports and the healthy look were in, so Colette adopted a new way of life. She was, as she matured, purposely turning into an image of Mother Earth. Her love for nature, food, and animals was becoming part of a myth that placed her at the heart of an earthly paradise. She presented her past as the misfortune of a misguided adolescent, candid and gullible, keeping secretly to herself and going through every experience, be it opium or trio lovemaking, unscathed, never influenced by anyone. "I imitated neither the good nor the bad."[32] *My Apprenticeships* was written as an autobiography with footnoted quotes. The first chapter began with a declaration that set the tone for the rest of the book: "During my lifetime, I have seldom known men called great by other men. They showed no interest in me. As for me, I avoided them." So no celebrities were to be found in her book. Her second statement was that she preferred "sapid and obscure"[33] men and women; to make her point she recounted her friendship with la Belle Otéro. This famous courtesan could hardly qualify as "sapid and obscure." In 1935 she was living in Nice; when she had gambled away her fortune, the grateful Casino granted her a pension. (She died in 1965, at the age of ninety-seven.) She had published her memoirs in 1925; a year later *Aux Ecoutes* published the keys to the pseudonyms she used. "Lisbette" was Colette; "Diane de Chandel" was Liane de Pougy; "Sapho" was Balthy; "Marquise de Jolival" was the Marquise de Morny; "Van Biren de Vilten" was Baroness Van Zuylen; and "Lucette Norbert" was Yvette Guilbert. According to Otéro, she had been entrusted with the education of "Lisbette," still in her teens, and found her not very gifted. As Colette writes in *My Apprenticeships*, "My little one," said she (Otéro), "you are not very brazen."[34]

After this preamble Colette examined the Willy case: "A novel should be written about that man."[35] Willy-the-gambler was portrayed as a cautious man who gambled pennies and hoarded money secretly. Willy-the-writer was branded a literary crook. However, in a list of great journalists, she included Henry Gauthier-Villars. To decipher the personality of this man she "had known very little," Colette (as an amateur graphologist) analyzed Willy's writing, perceiving in it "aristocratic taste, critical sense, the ability to bounce back, the desire to please and the art of deceit." She diagnosed a neurosis: he suffered from "agoraphobia," "megalomania," and "chronic haste" — "he was a sick man."[36]

Almost unanimously, the critics noted what Colette had chosen not to say, qualifying *My Apprenticeships* as a book written "to glorify silence."[37] Neither Georgie Raoul-Duval nor Missy were mentioned; the scandal of the Moulin Rouge was omitted; Natalie Barney became a social acquaintance; and Lesbos was shrouded in oblivion. Colette's life was fictionalized; she had become a protagonist in a work of superb craftsmanship. The critics had another reservation: they deplored the fact that she had said nothing of the process that led her to becoming one of the greatest writers of her generation, never explained how the very first novel she wrote turned out to be a masterpiece and a best-seller. She posed as a writer who hated to write and never gave a clue as to why she became "vaguely" conscious of "a duty"[38] vis-à-vis herself, to write.

*My Apprenticeships* drew some unfavorable comments. Paul Léautaud noted in his *Journal* that Willy's friends were enraged with her because of the way she had "savagely" demeaned Willy, turning him into a scoundrel, a liar, and a crook. "It is vile, it is almost dirty," said Louis Carro, a journalist. Deffoux, an old friend of the couple who was seated next to Colette at a dinner, embarked on a defense of Willy. "That old drunkard, what did he ever create?" asked Colette. Deffoux promptly answered, "You, Madame."[39] At a lunch with Professor Valéry Radot and Doctor Paulette Gauthier-Villars (Willy's niece, with whom Colette had remained very close through the years) Paulette turned to Colette and said suddenly, "Aunt Colette, you have committed a bad deed." "My child, I know it,"[40] calmly answered Colette.

After one dinner Abbé Mugnier noted in his diary, "She does not want to continue her memoirs because she is afraid to hurt and admits of having hurt Willy in *My Apprenticeships*."[41] Colette had said that Willy was remembered only because his name was forever linked to hers. This comment drew fire from his friends, who petitioned — and kept petitioning for years — to have a street named after him. In fact, Willy's name was inseparable from Colette's. In 1942 Maurice Goudeket, hiding in the south of France, stopped in Saint-Tropez and asked the new owners of La Treille Muscate if they would let him visit the house. He introduced himself as Colette's husband and was greeted with a warm, "Come in, Monsieur Willy."[42]

*My Apprenticeships* established the image of Colette as an abused and exploited wife. In 1948 the journalist Parinaud recorded a two-hour interview with her for the radio. Two-thirds of the interview concerned her life with Willy and the writing of the *Claudines*. His line of questioning followed the general assumption that Colette had written them under lock and key, that she had not been free in her early creative works, and had been forced "to spice up" her novels. Asking Colette to elaborate on this aspect of her work, his first question was about how she had written *Claudine at School*. Colette answered, "In the lack of comfort of an apartment on Rue Jacob," and said she had had no desk, but wrote on the dining-room table. That was not what he wanted to know, so Parinaud tried to put her back on track. Was not the first *Claudine* written under Willy's orders? He reiterated the same question about *Retreat from Love*. Colette's answer was a firm *non* — "the word is too strong." The reporter insisted. Had not Willy ordered her to write the *Claudine* series? Why had she not refused to be a ghostwriter? "Ordered? Ordered? What a word!" lashed back Colette. She stated that without Willy she would never have written *Claudine at School* or anything else.

Parinaud probed throughout the interview about Willy's participation. What type of participation? inquired Colette. Was not Willy responsible for the inception of certain characters? *Oh! non! Oh! non!* was Colette's definite answer. Willy trusted her, she said; she could write whatever she wanted as long as she wrote. However, Maugis was Willy's idea. He also made some small additions, but only after she had finished the manuscript. He never imposed any plan, topic, or characters on her beforehand. Parinaud switched to the "spicing up" of the novels but, like Colette in *My Apprenticeships* he made no allusion to Rézi and asked no questions about *Claudine Married*. He alluded instead to the sensuous scene between Aimée Lanthenay and Claudine. It seemed to him that Claudine spoke more like a boy than a woman, and he conjectured that Willy had participated in the writing of that scene. Colette's answer was again *non* — Willy had added nothing to the scene; she asked why a girl should not have the same feelings as a boy. However, Willy did suggest a few things a little more risqué; "already at that time I refused to do it."

Then, commented Parinaud, if Willy had so little to do with her novels, why did she make so many cuts in the definitive edition of her work? Was it not because these pages were not hers? Again Colette answered, *non*. She had discarded them because she found them not good enough. She had suppressed Maugis's letters and any passages on musicography because "they were not Willy's" but were written by his assistants. Colette was less clear about Willy's ways of producing books. He was surrounded by musicologists and writers who wrote for "the headquarters." Asked if she could be more specific, she recalled that Eugène de Solnières was dispatched to Bonn to collect the documents for *Le Mariage de Louis XV*. She did not know if the ghostwriters came in with finished novels or if they were given a plan. What she clearly remembered was that they called their collective output *travailler aux ateliers* (to work in the workshop).

Surprised by Colette's lyrical descriptions of afternoons spent with a girlfriend in an English teahouse on the Rue d'Argenteuil, a place she liked because it had no French patrons, Parinaud asked: was it possible that Willy set her free to wander? Wasn't she locked up at Rue Jacob, writing? *Oh! non!* replied Colette, she was never under lock and key in Paris. If it did happen, it would have been in the country, where the call of the outdoors was so strong that she would disappear and it would be impossible to find her; there she did have to be a little restrained to work. This did not seem to affect her love story with the Monts-

Boucons, "a ravishing place," "an oasis, the word is not too strong." In those days she worked as she did now, "hoping for the recess." She never was like Léon, the writer in *Claudine and Annie,* forced to work four hours a day. Whenever she felt unable to work, she would say to herself, "I am tired"[43] and do something else, some carpentry or some gardening. She felt she had not been demanding enough with herself in her early years and that, whatever excuses she might have had, there were pages she should never have written.

Was she annoyed not to have her name on her books? asked Parinaud. Again Colette's unequivocal answer was *non.* The only time she felt aggravated, she said, was the day she found a fake page of a manuscript complete with deletions and small annotations in Willy's handwriting. It was a page of either *Claudine Married* or *Claudine and Annie.* Parinaud asked what her reaction had been. Colette's unexpected answer was that her protest, made in very moderate terms, had had everything to do with a poor imitation of her handwriting *(sur le côté plastique de cette écriture).* She was shrugging off the whole question.

Concerning her divorce, Colette was explicit — it had nothing to do with literature. It had been Willy's decision to leave her; she had not been seeking a separation. She refused to answer any other questions concerning her private life with Willy. When he left her, she said, she fought to sign alone *Retreat from Love* because she had to make a living. She could not go back to Châtillon "destitute," "as a person who had failed by her own fault."

In the last paragraph of *My Apprenticeships,* Colette described herself alone in her apartment on the Rue Villejust, receiving many letters from Willy. But in none of them did he ever ask her to turn back.

On January 21, 1936 Colette was promoted to the rank of Commandeur de la Légion d'Honneur and Princess de Polignac gave an intimate party in her honor. On February 6 she had a one-woman show at the A.B.C. music hall; her husky voice, her rolling *r*s, her faultless sense of music, her magnetic presence still worked wonders on the public. "An unforgettable evening, this premier of the most illustrious writer of our time alone on the stage of a music hall."[44] Colette spoke of her career as a mime, of her tours through the French provinces with Georges Wague and Christiane Kerf, of her dreams to tame tigers and lions or to become a chanteuse. Then she sang four folk songs and concluded, "All said and done, I am a failed music-hall artist."[45]

She retired to La Treille Muscate to write the speech she was to give at L'Académie Royale de Langue et de Littérature Française. Tradition decreed that the new academician's discourse be the predecessor's eulogy. Colette said little about Anna de Noailles's poetry, but painted a vivid portrait of her friend. Princess de Polignac and Maurice accompanied Colette to Brussels. When the train reached the border, the Belgian immigration officer checked their passports; Colette had not renewed hers and so could not enter Belgium. The princess, who was tall and impressive, clenched her teeth and, hardly moving her lips, addressed the officer with cold indignation: "Your Royal Academy," she said, "is expecting Madame Colette to speak at her own reception. The session cannot take place without her!"[46] The officer was adamant — the passport was not in order. Goudeket noticed with amazement an expression of hope on Colette's face; all day she had been suffering from stage fright, and now suddenly it seemed that she would not have to give her speech. But the party was given the green light; she would have to deliver her speech after all. That evening, while she sat in the front row during the welcoming speech, she was racked by anxiety; but when she stood at the podium in her long black evening dress, paper in hand, she spoke with her usual ease. It was an emotional moment. In his welcoming speech the Belgian academician Valère Gilles spoke of Sidonie Landoy, mentioning that she had been raised in Brussels by her two elder brothers. "Oh, how well we knew them! Especially Eugène Landoy, who signed 'Bertram.' He came from France and communicated his brilliance to the Belgian press. He became one of the founders of *L'Echo du Parlement,* editor in chief of *L'Office de Publicité.*"[47] Gilles's eulogy of the Landoys went on: Raphaël, the witty poet; Eugène II, founder of *Le Matin d'Anvers;* Jules, who became director of the Fine Arts Administration; and Georges Landoy, who founded L'Université du Cinéma.

Ten years younger than Colette, Georges had died in extraordinary circumstances. He was editor in chief of *Le Matin d'Anvers* and, like all the Landoys, had a passion for social justice. He wanted to help underprivileged children, handicapped from the start by their poor intellectual background, and he thought that documentary films could provide them with the knowledge they lacked. In 1926 he created a school, L'Université du Cinéma; ahead of his time, he already perceived what educational television could some day accomplish. He had enormous support: forty thousand people enrolled within months. This drew the attention of American filmmakers, and in 1929 he was invited to the United States by the Carnegie Foundation. With a group of nine European journalists, he was taken on a tour of America's landmarks. One day at Yellowstone Park, he was walking behind his colleagues, looking at the crevices of bubbling water and the geysers rising from the volcanic ground. Suddenly the others heard a scream — Georges had been caught in the unexpectedly erupting stream of Castle Geyser and thrown into the boiling cascade. When they reached him, Georges was emerging on his hands and knees. He was rushed to Mammoth Springs Hospital; when they took his clothes off, his skin stuck to the material. Georges was lucid; he dictated a letter to his mother and joked about his accident being bad publicity for *Le Matin d'Anvers*. He died two days later. His body was returned to Belgium; the government, the university, the artistic, scientific, and business establishments sent delegations to his funeral. Thousands of people and students from the Université du Cinéma lined the street all the way to the cemetery. Colette did not attend his funeral, as she had severed all links with the Landoys.[48]

After the welcoming ceremony the new academician went off to celebrate with her friends. As the press was prevented from entering the restaurant, a French journalist interviewed the doorman, whom he depicted in a state of shock: "This Colette, who has her picture in every newspaper, comes here with a crowd, barefoot, yes, in sandals! With nails lacquered in red!!! We cater to diplomats from all over Europe, we have the elite of Brussels and there she is, in sandals with hair like an urchin! And you know what she ordered? She ordered Krieken-Lambic! We only serve the very best French wines and she ordered a dozen bottles of Krieken-Lambic!!! The owner did not even object! He said, 'Yes, Madame' and sent to the Red Door District! The worst in Brussels! to buy Krieken-Lambic in a tavern and bring it back! This woman! This Colette!"

The whole issue of *Pourquoi Pas?,* a Belgian weekly, was devoted to Colette; the magazine's editorial tried to pinpoint the reasons for Colette's appeal, for the unprecedented rush to the academy to listen to her acceptance speech. Some guests and journalists had even been turned back. The article's author commented that certainly talent erases all, and it is extraordinary that in a country whose moral conformism is

so strong, the Royal Academy has opened its doors to a talent so far removed from conformism. . . . Colette has heaped scandal upon scandal,
literary scandals — her books are very daring, Parisian scandals — the
Willy-Colette-Polaire trio, the marquise de Morny, the Moulin Rouge
uproar still not forgotten, the divorce scandal, the more or less nude performances in music halls, the marriage to Henry de Jouvenel (which appeared as a temporary haven of respectability) followed by a second
divorce. Her recent works remain scandalous, they do not conform to
moral standards. . . . All this is well known. . . . Yet an academic ceremony
brings this nonconformist into the fold with an apothesis."[49]

In another article she was compared to George Sand, the only other
writer whose life of scandals led to glory, and who ended her life as the
"Good Lady from Nohan." The great difference between Sand and
Colette was that the former addressed society's ills and was carried away,
like all romantics, by metaphysical anxieties, while Colette suffered no
philosophical anguish whatsoever. This straightforward approach, pon-
dered *Pourquoi Pas?,* discouraged criticism — "how can one criticize a
natural force?" Moral discipline may not be for women of genius.

Willy still had faithful friends in Belgium, one of whom wrote
some acrimonious lines: "In a heartrending and unpleasant work, *My
Apprenticeships,* with the subtitle *What Claudine Has Not Told,* Colette has
attempted to write a justification of herself, if not an apology. It is a
heartbreaking book, because she brings back her childhood memories,
she implies that corruption came to her through her blasé husband,
Willy. The book is unpleasant because it overflows with old grudges and
because the accused man is no longer here to defend himself. . . . We
knew Willy when he was one of the Kings of Paris, we met him again
when he had lost his money and glory and was an exile in Brussels. At
the Café de la Scala, he used to be surrounded by parasites for whom he
bought glasses of beer. He was generous and stoic in his downfall. We
cannot recognize him in this cold-blooded corrupter, this harsh slave
driver, who locked up his young wife in front of a desk and a ream of
paper, then organized a scandalous promotion."

He concluded that probably, "like George Sand, Colette will drift toward conservative morals and proprieties. After all, Colette is married
for the third time and has just received the red *cravate* of Commandeur
de la Légion d'Honneur and here she is a member of the Belgian
Academy. A new future is opening for her, a career filled with honors

and respectability. She is so talented that no doubt she will know how to tread this new path with as much success as the one that meandered through scandals and independence. . . . Belgium will have opened the gates to the royal path of respectability for Colette."

Unperturbed, Colette kept on with her Fourierist investigation of attraction and repression. *Gringoire* published *Bella Vista* in installments. It was composed of four short stories about homosexuality, incest, attraction, and fear, about a poor music-hall performer who had an abortion to avoid losing her job and was discreetly helped by the generous music-hall artists.

An article in *Le Journal* published on July 19, "Nouvelles du pays — Colette en Provence," provides an insight into Colette's transmutation of reality into art; it is the description of a dramatic trip from Paris to Saint-Tropez with the dog, the cat, and Maurice. They drive through a monstrous storm; the animals are in a panic and torrents of water splash over the black car, which turns yellow with caked mud. In a letter to Misz Marchand, Colette told her not to worry — "Do not think the description of the car, the dog, or the cat are exact."[50] Out of a totally uneventful and pleasant trip, Colette had created an adventure; *Dichtung und Wahrheit,* poetry and truth, are two separate things.

Colette resumed her work as *Le Journal*'s drama critic. The fourth and last *Cahier de Colette* in limited edition was published at the end of August; Colette also wrote the text for an album of exotic butterflies, *Splendeur des Papillons,* then left for Saint-Tropez. Isabelle de Comminges was also in Saint-Tropez; "the Panther" was now on very friendly terms with Colette. She was intelligent, read widely, loved music, spoke English and German fluently, wrote novels in a vivid style, and had translated a play. Through the years she had retained her beauty; she had supported Colette's venture into cosmetics, but did not understand why the would-be beautician let herself become overweight. "She looks like a monstrous turd on wheels." She watched Colette do her daily shopping for antiques, "dragging young beauties along to the market, Maurice trotting behind them, slightly ironic."[51] Isabelle was sharp, cynical, and loved to gossip with Colette. She confirmed that the Jouvenels' title was of very recent origin, and that although there had been "Jouvenels" earlier, they were not Henry's forebears and he knew it. Colette remembered Isabelle's scorn in *Julie de Carneilhan.* Something drew Colette irresistibly to her husbands' or lovers' women, and invariably she took them as models for her characters; when *Julie de Carneilhan* was published in 1941, Isabelle, Claire Boas, and Jouvenel's third wife all thought they recognized themselves in the novel.

Another year, another bronchitis: Colette spent three weeks recuperating at the Hôtel Negresco in Nice with Hélène Jourdan-Morhange. On January 21 she was back in Paris to prepare the publication of the third volume of *La Jumelle Noire*. Her articles as a drama critic were dubbed "impressionistic criticism." By the time the fourth and last volume was published, she had created an all-inclusive panorama of show business in Paris in the thirties. In March the movie *Claudine at School* was released. Colette had had little to do with the production; the director did not bring out the satirical charm of the character, and the film was a flop. The French National Broadcasting Company signed Colette on for a weekly program in the afternoon; her first talk, on July 2, was about Sido, who had become Colette's most popular character.

Maurice Goudeket was busy launching a new enterprise. With Georges and Joseph Kessel he founded, directed, and edited a popular weekly named *Confessions*. Goudeket was by now a ubiquitous journalist. He was on the staff of the newly created *Marie-Claire* and a regular contributor to *Match* and *Paris-Soir*. He was known for his broad culture, and the *Club du livre français* turned to him for a critical edition of the *Lettres de la Princesse Palatine*. He translated and adapted foreign plays.

Like the aristocracy of the late-eighteenth century, who danced while the Revolution was about to explode, the European rich and famous were not disturbed by the distant thunder of guns. In July 1936 civil war erupted in Spain; on August 18 Federico Garcia Lorca was shot by Fascist troops near Granada. Hitler was at the head of the German Reich. Colette did not write about the tidal waves of political change; she said nothing about the Bolshevik revolution of 1917, nothing of the rise of Fascism in Italy or the Front Populaire in France, nothing of the civil war in Spain.

## Palais Royal

The Marignan building had become so noisy that Colette decided to move. It was a modern construction with thin partitions; the doors and elevators never stopped clattering and the terrace leaked. It was time to leave. A residence had to nurture its inhabitant — if it radiated no pleasure it had lost its main purpose. Colette treated each relocation as a celebration; she loved the physical activity of packing and unpacking, pushing around the furniture, hanging the pictures. With Pauline's help, she did it with amazing speed; and even when she was not moving into a new home, she enjoyed moving the furniture around, rearranging everything for the sheer pleasure of it. Sometimes when he came in Goudeket did not recognize the apartment, but the naughty look on Colette's face discouraged any attempt to criticize. The changes could be so drastic that once the cat, coming in from the garden, did not recognize its home and fled through the window in panic.

Colette found an apartment on the Place Vendôme, a showcase of seventeenth-century architecture where Napoleon had erected the column made from twelve hundred cannons captured at Austerlitz and topped with his own statue. The address was prestigious, with the Hôtel Ritz at number 15 and the Ministère de la Justice at numbers 11 and 12. Under the arcades were the boutiques of Schiaparelli, Elizabeth Arden, Van Cleef and Arpels; Chanel was only steps away on the Rue Cambon. The apartment was under the roof, half-hidden behind a pediment, but offering a view of the Place Vendôme.

Then something unexpected happened. Arnyvelde, a *Paris-Midi* journalist, had long been asking for an interview; finally she granted him one. Among other questions, he asked why she had moved so often; Colette exclaimed that she had moved only fourteen times, and always out of necessity. Ten years earlier, when she was living in her "drawer" in the Palais Royal, she said, she tried to rent the big, sunny apartment just over her dark mezzanine floor; had she succeeded, she would never have moved again. The interview was published on December 6, 1936. The next morning she received a letter.

> Madame,
> I read in *Paris-Midi* that you want the second floor of No 9, Rue de Beaujolais. I am most willing to let you have it immediately.[52]

The coveted apartment became part of her legend.

Colette loved the Palais Royal, its quadrangle of regular, stately facades with arcades enclosing a garden. She liked the silky sound made by dozens of pigeons as they winged across the garden; the children playing in the sandboxes; the people on benches, reading or having their lunch. Neighborhood pets were known by name, including Lilly the tortoise, who took her morning stroll in the company of Pierrot the cat. It was like a small provincial town; everyone knew everybody else. The Bibliothèque Nationale was only a few steps away and its director, Julien Cain, would often drop by for a chat. From her window Colette could see the windows of Jean Cocteau or the decorator Christian Berard. Artists and intellectuals coveted this secluded area in the heart of Paris, with the Comédie Française at its southwestern corner, the Théâtre du Palais Royal and the Vefour Restaurant, two centuries old and still famous, at the northwest corner of the quadrangle. It was stately, yet bohemian. John Howard Payne was living there when he composed "Home Sweet Home." Sylvia Beach of *Shakespeare and Company* and Margaret Anderson of *The Little Review* lived on Rue de Beaujolais, while Barbara Harrison of *Paris-Presse* lived on Rue de Montpensier.

Colette had just moved in when Renée Hamon came to visit. Twenty-four years younger than Colette, she had become her close friend and a privileged confidante. Renée Hamon was "possessed by the demon of adventure"[53] and appealed to Colette's craving for exoticism. (Colette collected all sorts of "symbols of evasion: a compass, astrolabes, planispheres, an atlas . . . seashells," and travelogues. She treasured sixty-eight volumes written by early-nineteenth-century travelers, innocent explorers such as Ida Pfeiffer, who went fearlessly around the world with no more than ten pounds of luggage.)

Renée Hamon was born in Brittany in 1897. Her grandfather was a militant freethinker, and she was not baptized. She had an unhappy childhood; her mother divorced, and Renée was raised by her grandmother. Married in 1917, she lost her only child and divorced in 1920. Then she sailed to the United States to join an American soldier she had met during the war; a year and a half later she was back in Brittany, disappointed and penniless. But she was discovered in a beauty contest by a journalist who took her to Paris where she modeled for photographers and painters and did a little painting herself. She tried the movies next without success. She wrote to Paul Poiret who, intrigued by her witty letter, went to see her in her garret on the seventh floor, under the roof, in Montmartre. She was making ragdolls for a living; he bought one and became her friend. In 1926, when he accepted the part of Brague in the revival of *The Vagabond,* he obtained a small part for Renée, but she fell ill and was unable to go on tour. Once introduced to Colette, she was struck by a passionate devotion for her. She sent her flowers, skipping three or four dinners to save enough money for them.

Two years later Renée married Harald Heyman, thirty years her senior, the Swedish translator of Samuel Johnson; both were born adventurers. In 1933 she went around the world on a bicycle; she was not seeking publicity and there is no trace of her voyage. The following year she decided to sail to Tahiti to gather information for a biography of Paul Gauguin. She learned Maori and discussed her plan with Petrus Borel — a poet, a fellow Breton, and an admirer of Gauguin. He recommended Renée to the director of *L'Intransigeant,* who hired her as a reporter; Borel gave her a walking stick that had belonged to Gauguin and booked her a berth on *La Recherche,* sailing to Tahiti. There Renée found Gauguin's wife, a fat, old, toothless woman, and his mentally retarded son; she also found one of Gauguin's daughters living in the Marquesas Islands. Renée's husband joined her in Tahiti, fell under the island's spell, and settled there. Returning to France via Asia, Renée brought back a film shot on the island and published *Gauguin: le Solitaire du Pacifique.* Colette encouraged her to write a book about her experience, wrote an introduction, and recommended it to Flammarion. *In the Islands of Light (Aux Iles de Lumière)* was well received and Renée was awarded a grant by the French government, but her plans were curtailed by the war. She wrote another book, *The Adventure Lovers (Les Amants de l'Aventure),* dedicated to Colette.

Renée had a special niche among Colette's friends. She was called "The Little Corsair" and had conquered Colette by sending her wildflowers named "daphnes," which grew only in Brittany and reminded Colette of Rozven. She kept sending them to her for years. Renée's love was so deep that the word "cult" did not seem too strong to Maurice. Renée was more than a protégée — "You are for Maurice and myself, a very dear little girl."[54] One day she confessed to Colette that she had fallen in love.

"Ah! With whom?" asked Colette.

"A woman."

"So what! Is she pleasant?"

This time it was serious; Renée said she was going to be faithful.

"Not true. You are no more faithful than I. You are monogamous like me."[55] Colette explained that she had always practiced "successive monogamy"; she would end an affair when desire led her to another. To be faithful was a commitment that did not suit her, so successive monogamy was her form of faithfulness.

Renée kept a diary, detailing what she saw in Colette's apartment: her favorite wallpaper, ordered from London; the ceiling wallpapered, so that, lying on her sofa, Colette could see it as a continuation of the walls instead of a crushing blank space; the high windows hung with white-and-green drapes. When Renée looked for an apartment in Paris, Colette volunteered some advice: first of all, don't have a bathtub, it is bad for the health and weakens the system. She showed Renée her own arrangement: a small tub, a circular showerhead she could wear as a collar around her neck, a long rubber hose fitted to the faucet, and a terrycloth towel-glove for a vigorous rub. A faucet was leaking; Colette called for hammer and pliers and undertook the repair while Pauline, Maurice, and Renée watched. At first there was a burst of water but a drenched Colette finally stopped the leak, made the faucet work perfectly, and adjusted a loose doorknob on her way out. She loved to work with her hands, sometimes recklessly; while repairing an electric outlet, she burned her left hand.

Renée noted in her diary that Colette always wore a robe or loose dress when she wrote, never anything that would bind her waist or shoulders. When writing an article, she would place the exact number of sheets on her desk according to the proposed length of the text. Before sitting down she would glance at the garden and sigh, then close the drapes, turn on the lights, and start writing.

In 1938 Colette was sixty-five and Maurice fifty; Renée wondered what kept that lively, slim, trim, and sensuous man totally committed to Colette. Colette told her that it was her virility, the masculine part of her personality that attracted Maurice; "Sometimes I shock him, but I am the only person with whom he can live." As far as his sexuality was concerned, he was drawn to feminine women and had his "chicks," "but he could not live with one."[56] Theirs was the perfect pivotal love with many contingent affairs.

Whenever possible, Colette and Maurice spent their evenings in blissful peace, reading under the blue lantern. She came to share his love for certain classics such as La Rochefoucault and Chateaubriand — he even succeeded, where Sido had failed, in making her read Saint-Simon. "The hours slipped by harmonious and delicious, silence is a touchstone between couples," wrote Maurice, "There must be a very deep feeling between two people, if they can absorb themselves in reading and still feel a flow of tenderness and trust between them, in absolute silence, knowing that they are together and sharing their happiness."[57] Maurice was aware that he was criticized and called "Monsieur Colette." He wrote that love must be very weak if pride is the stronger, and that only a mediocre person cannot recognize a superior one. He believed that his part as Colette's husband had no precedent; it was his choice to devote himself to her well-being and happiness. Colette would sometimes tell him that she felt sorry for him for having a wife so much older than he was, but Maurice said that their disparity in age worked in favor of their understanding.

Colette was once again writing advertisements for the plush quarterly magazine, *Fiat,* for L'Eau Perrier, for a brand of coffee, Lucky Strike cigarettes, or La Maison de Blanc, putting her style in a nutshell. She signed a contract with the innovative *Marie-Claire.* She carefully avoided expressions she thought might be too crude for the readership and telephoned the editor in chief several times to consult her; Colette's humility was extraordinary when it came to her work. Maurice noticed her inferiority complex with surprise; when he told her she was considered by everyone to be one of the greatest writers of the twentieth century, she answered gruffly, "If it were so, I would have known it."[58]

Colette's radio talks and articles in women's journals were turning her into a personal counselor; she was the image of a broad-minded, all-knowing matriarch, and she received an enormous number of letters. Michel del Castillo, echoing this growing worship with some irony, referred to her as the "the Palais Royal's Madonna," the "Magician," and even the "Ogress."[59] In May of 1938 Colette joined the staff of *Paris-Soir,* one of the most widely read dailies; her first article appeared on June 6. On June 12 she canceled her contract with *Le Journal* and left for La Treille Muscate.

The playwright Edouard Bourdet, her neighbor in Saint-Tropez, was the new administrator of the Comédie Française. He was trying to modernize the repertoire and planned to produce *Chéri,* which he considered a masterpiece. Colette discussed the project with him. He wanted to bring the play closer to the 1938 public; she agreed, and decided to make some profound changes — to suppress the part of Masseau and the part of Chéri's wife, and to end the play like the novel. She often came to dine at Bourdet's Villa Blanche. As she climbed the flight of stairs to the terrace, stopping to catch her breath, she would sigh, "How I regret my great fifties!!" She enjoyed leafing through his collection of photographs from the turn of the century, vividly recalling Liane de Pougy, la Belle Otéro, Emilienne d'Alençon, Sarah Bernhardt, as well as other actresses and opera singers she had known well. She would describe their dresses, their jewels and hairdos, recreating for her fascinated audience their vocabularies and mannerisms, recounting their loves and scandals. But the project to produce *Chéri* did not materialize.

By 1938 Saint-Tropez was overrun with tourists; the port was so crowded that cars parked everywhere cut off the view of the sea. Colette found intruders in her garden. Autograph seekers, photographers, and reporters knocked at the door and slipped into the house in spite of Pauline's angry protests. The situation was becoming unbearable, so Colette decided to sell and proceeded without delay; she could not bear procrastination, preferring to lose money. The first purchaser was the right one, and the seller's price was to be accepted at once. Indecision in any matter astonished Colette. In October she put La Treille Muscate up for sale; Charles Vanel, famous for his part in *The Salary of Fear,* made an offer that she accepted; the following year he sold the property at a handsome profit.

She did not want to resettle in the south, because "I have a terrible urge to go to Brittany"; Paris was "a little rancid," and the news in September 1938 was "pitch black." Renée Hamon had moved back to her native Brittany. Wasting no time, Colette asked Renée to send her brochures of the hotel where she was staying, "the rates, the food, the kind of clientele."[60] Was it near the sea? How was the beach? Rocks? Sand? On September 27, Renée made a special trip to Paris to convince Colette to move to Auray; Paris was growing feverish after Hitler's latest speech, and France had begun partial mobilization. She found Colette "serene, more beautiful and more dynamic than ever." She wore a haute-couture blue woolen ensemble and "around her neck one of those silky scarves, which are her own smart secret." Renée entreated her to leave Paris, since war was imminent. Colette retorted that everyone around her pleaded with her to leave, and that she might agree to go, "but not to be bored." Her daughter suggested Castel Novel, which seemed preposterous to Colette: "Why not bring all Jouvenel's ex-wives together?" The only place that tempted her was Auray. "Maurice, did you hear? There is a lilac room! Pauline, we will take two hot-water bottles and seven blankets. Yes, Chatte, you are coming."

To relax Renée, who was frightened, Colette bantered. "Good little Corsair, what do you think of Hitler? A vegetarian Monsieur, who eats only porridge at noon and, sometimes, an egg in the evening . . . a Monsieur who does not make love, even with men . . ." In spite of her lighthearted banter, Colette knew only too well that the storm was gathering; she was concerned about the fate of Erna, her translator, an Austrian refugee who had fled the Nazis — "her future worries me."[61] She wrote to the minister Albert Sarrault, asking him to take care of Erna's case.

*Duo* was a hit at the Théâtre Saint-Georges in October. Colette boasted to Germaine Patat that thanks to *Duo,* she was making money without having to work, since the theater gave her six percent of the box-office. She was elated and never failed to check the daily receipts.

All plans to go to Brittany were interrupted when *Paris-Soir* sent Colette and Goudeket to Morocco in October to report on the sensational trial of Moulay Hassen. Hassen had been a beautiful prostitute at the time of the French conquest; she had spied for the French, and "there was talk of great services rendered." In 1912 and 1925 she had saved the lives of several French officers threatened by the uprising of local populations against their colonial rulers. Allegedly, she had known the top brass; now, at fifty, she was operating a brothel near Fez. One day some children playing in a vacant lot came upon a big hamper full of human limbs that had been boiled. The hamper was traced back to Moulay Hassen's brothel, where three prostitutes had vanished and four others had died. Searching the house, the police heard faint cries; they tore down a wall and found four girls and a boy of fifteen, starved and bearing the marks of torture. They had been walled up for days. In Paris the story was expected to be flamboyant and sordid, with scandalous connections revealed and a general uproar. It turned out otherwise. Moulay Hassen's lawyer could not understand why *Paris-Soir* had bothered to send such a reporter as Colette and thought the French press was blowing it out of proportion. After all, it only had to do with "four mountain women" who did not even have a civil status. "Nobody here pays any attention,"[62] he said.

The crowd at the trial came only to see Colette. In an article published later in *Looking Backwards (Journal à Rebours)*, she explained the crime committed in cold blood by Moulay Hassen by the circumstances of her life: "what we call cruelty was the stuff her life was made of since childhood." Being a prostitute at the mercy of men, "where would she have learned that to punish women, that is to say, creatures of no real value, has any limitations?" The teenage girls brought to the witness stand, "beaten, starved, never attempted to run away"; Moulay Hassen crushed with one glance "the barely nubile little prostitutes . . . gracious chattel, but nevertheless chattel, their unshakable, ponderous stupidity makes one sick," wrote Colette. At the end of the trial Moulay Hassen broke down; she had waited in vain for "the deposition in her favor of the officers of the conquest." Hiding her face in her handkerchief, she wept for the only reason that could affect her — "they had all forsaken her."[63] She got off with fifteen years of hard labor.

From Fez, "immense and exactly the color of a caiman out of its silt and dry," Colette resumed her plans to go to Brittany, corrected the proofs of her short novel, *Le Toutounier,* and organized the trip. She would leave by car with Maurice. Moune and Luc-Albert Moreau would come by train, while Paul Géraldy and his lady friend would arrive on their own. Renée was to book a small suite and see if Colette could visit a school for deaf-mutes in Auray; it would be good matter for an article, and she had expressed a nostalgic wish, "may I see Belle-Isle one day!" Then as an afterthought, she added, "We shall go to the midnight mass."[64] But Colette came down with the flu and had to postpone her trip till February 7.

## I Never Thought That the Human
## Race Would Come to This Once More

At last they left for Auray. Colette felt sorry for her "twilight cat" — "If you had only seen poor, admirable Chatte muster her strength, be brave and cheerful for the trip, purr constantly . . . !"[65] Chatte could hop down on the road when needed but could not leap back into the car; she would beg for a lift with a pathetic glance. Wasting no time once she had arrived, Colette walked barefoot along the beach looking for shells, and four days later she could write, "I have picked up my courage, we will be back in Paris on the 14th."[66]

On the nineteenth Chatte died. Blue-gray as smoke, intelligent, and passionately attached to Colette, Chatte always sat next to her while she wrote. Colette's pain was as deep as it was discreet; she wrote to a friend that she could not stop thinking of Chatte, but would show an expressionless face to all. A month later to the very day, Souci, the twelve-year-old bulldog, went into convulsions; while Maurice and Pauline held her down, Colette frantically tried to reach a veterinarian — in vain, for it was Sunday. "Our perfect companions have never less than four paws,"[67] mused a distressed Colette. She was so upset that she locked herself up until she could control her emotions. She found it a strange coincidence that Chatte "had died on February 19 and Souci on March 19."[68]

Four years later, a clairvoyant came to her apartment. The first thing she said was that she saw a gray cat: ". . . she is here all the time. She does not want to leave you, you are everything for her." That evening all Colette could talk about was "the presence of Chatte . . . If her soul clad in gray still haunts our home after four years of death . . . we must have remained worthy of her."[69] Colette never called that psychic back, fearing she would tell her that Chatte had left them for good.

Eight years after the death of her last two pets, Colette still felt their loss; "only working hours can keep us forcefully away from the thought that comes back all the time. . . . The wisest — the most egoistical — rush to the most common remedy: "Quick! Quick! Another dog! Another pet!" She rejected that kind of solace, saying, "I never wanted another Chatte."[70]

In 1949 she enumerated the animals that "had sometimes enriched, sometimes saddened [her] life": her brother's boxer, who "knew several songs"; her bulldog Souci, who "knew an extravagant number of words";[71] Chatte, who had a favorite song, "Blue Heaven," which Colette often played on the record player for her. "When I will cease singing the praise of Chatte, I will have become silent forever." Having renounced the company of four-legged pets, she gave herself a new companion. "Now I exclusively own one single living creature, it is my fire. It is my guest, it is my creation . . . and I want to have the last word with it, my old habit to tame, gained through my involvement with animals."[72]

In March Colette reported on the trial of the serial killer Weidman for *Paris-Soir*. It was later published in *Les Cahiers de Colette* and in the

edition of her collected works, *Le Fleuron,* under the title "Monsters."
Here she described and compared several killers: "I have often speculated
in astonishment about the various kinds of men who take away human
lives." She wrote about Patrick Mahon, who murdered girls and young
women in the peaceful English countryside: he was young with "a winning appearance . . . the sweetest of voices. . . . One detail retains my attention, wild animals came to him, birds followed him." She noted that
Weidman "kissed the jail's little cat." Both murderers were "of a merry
disposition, sociable, they liked the outdoors, the sunshine, the moonlit
nights." Colette thought that "in spite of its name, a 'monster' is never
unique. . . . He is compared much too hastily to legendary monsters, he is
nothing but a failed undertaker."[73] A murderer, she said, be it Nero or
Caligula, is only someone whose passions have not been routed properly.

Ferenczi published *Le Toutounier,* a sequel to *Duo,* in which Hermine
and Colombe are both platonically involved with married men. Colombe
is happy to become the secretary of the man she loves and waits discreetly for the death of his sick wife. But Hermine does not want to
wait and tries to shoot her friend's wife, who then asks for a divorce.
Only passion could thrust life into a positive pattern and bring about
the courage to claim happiness at any cost.

In April Claude Chauvière died. "Part Persian cat, part Ophelia,"[74]
she was elusive, hard to size up, talented, and hypersensitive. She had
been Colette's secretary for three years and "proved very unsuited for
the job." Her goal, which she had made clear, was to write a biography
of Colette, which, according to Maurice Goudeket, was "a true picture
of Colette in her daily life." He also noted that as soon as Claude was
not under "the tonic influence of Colette," she turned to mysticism and
was devastated by "a secret despair."[75] Claude Chauvière had been married to Georges Lefèvre, a prominent reporter who had conducted the
first in-depth interview of Colette. Georges felt that Colette had subju-
gated his wife, and his colleagues gossiped. One day without warning, a
chauffeur-driven car stopped at the Lefèvres' door, and Georges picked
up his suitcases and sped away while Claude swooned in the maid's
arms. She turned the adventure into a novel, *Someone Stole My Love (On
m'a volé mon Amour).*

Colette entertained only a passing fancy for Claude Chauvière, who
found herself rejected by both husband and lover. She liquidated her
worldly possessions, converted to Catholicism, and left for an unknown

destination. After a period of semireclusion, she was baptized on July 2, 1928, with Colette standing as her godmother. Their friendship endured until Claude's death.

After selling La Treille Muscate, Colette declared that she would not own another house; this resolution lasted until April 1939. Driving home after the weekly dinner at Les Mesnils, Colette noticed a house sheltered by a magnificent old cedar; a wisteria covered eighty yards of stone wall, enclosing a vegetable garden and a flower garden. She made a split-second decision; she wanted that house now. Following her instructions, that very evening Maurice drove back to Méré, met the owner, and agreed to pay any price he wanted if he would sell Le Parc, which he did. Colette had the great blue cedar cut down because it blocked out the sunshine and burned it in the fireplace; but in spite of her *coup de foudre* for Le Parc, she still longed for Brittany.

Renée was preparing to sail back to Tahiti and asked Colette if her daughter would like to sail with her as a film assistant. Colette doubted she could "unhook Bel-Gazou from her habits" (she was living with a woman who was on drugs); however, she gave Renée a letter of recommendation for the Ministre des Colonies, and wrote on her behalf to the director of Radio-Mondial: Renée had shot two films in Tahiti, and her experience could be useful "for the colonial propaganda." As Colette was writing at her desk, Renée noticed that her face looked drawn. Suddenly Colette sighed, "If you knew how disgusted I am with myself . . . disgusted . . . disgusted. Yesterday, I was unable to walk." She had struggled all day with an incapacitating pain in her leg and "about midnight with Maurice's help," had managed to walk at last. With Moune and Luc-Albert Moreau, she headed straight for her familiar cure, a hearty meal: some goose with green peas and "a large slice of strawberry pie." She spoke merrily, but the unfamiliar expression of dismay fleetingly reappeared: "I could not walk."[76] It was the first time that the arthritis which would eventually cripple her had struck so unexpectedly and so overwhelmingly. Colette fought the pain. She went to Renée's lecture after coaching her, teaching her to speak "as if conversing." Activity and discipline were Colette's panacea. She would repeat as her mantra: "La Règle guérit de tout" ("Rule cures all").

Colette spent July in Brittany and August with Léo and Misz

Marchand in Dieppe, which had been a haven for nonconformists from across the channel in the Victorian Age, the favorite resort of Bloomsbury bohemians and still popular with English tourists. By the end of August they left, cutting short their vacation. War was imminent; all diplomatic efforts had failed; France had mobilized.

Maurice was fifty and not mobilized. He begged Colette to stay in Dieppe to await the turn of events, but she remained silent. They had an agreement never to intrude on one another's thoughts, but Maurice broke the rule and asked what she was thinking. Colette simply said, "same as you,"[77] and they drove back to the Palais Royal. War was declared on September 3. Gas masks were distributed, and people went about wearing the gray contraption with goggles and filter on a shoulder strap. One man suffocated while trying it on.

Cars were being requisitioned. Colette still had her Citroën when she received a call from her brother Léo from Levallois-Perret, where he had spent fifty years in a room on the sixth floor. The concierge had found him unconscious in the stairway. Colette, refusing to face the idea of Léo's death, found him "in a rather bad state, but in no immediate danger."[78] Anything she and Maurice had suggested to improve his living conditions had been rejected as a useless complication; a wooden dresser and a metallic washstand were all he needed. He liked to play pool, collect stamps, and play the piano. He would drop by unannounced for dinner and allow Pauline to trim his hair and drooping mustache. He chose to be a clerk "because, seated at a desk, he kept only a fallacious appearance of a man," while his true self flew back to the six-year-old boy he had never ceased to be. For over half a century he had roamed "a mental realm where everything suits the fancy and the dimension of a child."[79] He was a combination of common sense and madness, according to his mother, who "never saw such indifference to cleanliness."[80]

His red hands, which knew "neither hot water nor gloves," had kept an unexpected musical virtuosity; Colette felt that it was that eerie sound that she would miss most. "No more will I hear him playing with his chapped, clumsy fingers, from which flowed sounds of a scintillating and round quality."[81]

Léo had been her living archives of Saint-Sauveur since he had the rare gift of total recall; he could describe in detail and with photographic precision everything that had been part of their childhood. Like Julie de Carneilhan's brother, he was the living past. For several weeks,

Léo's heart beat slower and slower — twenty-nine, twenty-six, then twenty-four pulsations a minute; Colette was glad that he did not suffer and never knew he was dying. With the help of Geneviève, Achille's daughter, he was moved to Bleneau near Saint-Sauveur, his true home. He died on March 7, 1940. Geneviève sent Colette a letter, not a telegram, knowing that she would not come to the funeral. They were not on friendly terms, and Geneviève contested Léo's will; Colette vented her anger by writing to Moune that his inheritance amounted to a puny eighteen thousand francs but "that deranged creature would do the same if it was worth 18 millions."[82]

Another death rekindled unwelcome memories. Polaire had been found unconscious after an attempted suicide. Oversized headlines on the front page of the newspapers read: "Polaire wants to live" or "Yes, that night I wanted to die, says Polaire." Reporters rushed to interview her at the Hôpital Beaujon "in a small white room, in a small white bed, a little girl lost in the immense hospital . . . with a blue ribbon in her hair and a burning flame in her eyes." She wept as she told her story, "Yes, that horrid night, I tried to kill myself, I had enough of this dreadful life, so I lunged against the door, but first I had the strength to squeeze hard the neck of my little dog, my only friend, whom I did not want to leave behind. Then I tried to break my head against that horrible door. They found me before it was all over, they carried me away. I was so cold, cold to the heart. . . . Look through the window at all those roofs, imagine all those homes, that is what I missed so badly, a small place next to a fire-place."[83] Her attempted suicide was the result of bureaucratic bungling.

In 1928, while Polaire was performing in Paris, Internal Revenue seized her summer estate, the Villa Claudine at Agay on the Riviera, and auctioned it off with all its furniture, paintings, portraits of herself, and precious souvenirs. In 1925 Polaire had had her taxes assessed at one thousand, four hundred francs; the following year the assessment jumped to ten thousand, eight hundred francs. She filed a protest and the assessment was lowered to one thousand, eight hundred francs for 1927, but it was not retroactive — Polaire was still held responsible for the 1926 mishap. She asked for a delay and left the keys of her villa with an agency in order to rent it. Polaire's career was on the rebound; she had a four-month contract in Paris. One day she received a telegram from a friend warning her that the tax collector was to auction off her villa the following morning. She immediately sent a telegram promising to pay her taxes in a lump sum, but it was too late. The movers had gone on a rampage — the drawers had been opened and emptied onto the floor, and letters, photographs, and all her personal belongings had been thrown about. This vandalism terrified her. There was an uproar in the newspapers, and the administration admitted the ten thousand, eight hundred–franc figure was an error, but still refused to adjust retroactively. Polaire sued the administration in vain, and from that point on her life went downhill; she gambled and drank, felt threatened, and sank into a deep depression. She had to sell her *hôtel particulier* on the Rue Lord Byron, another building she owned in Paris, and her jewels.

In 1932 she wrote her memoirs and turned to Colette for a preface, but Colette had no kind feelings left for the dazzling Claudine, who was slipping out of favor with the younger public. "The poor creature is going to publish her memoirs and asks me to give her a preface. I will not write a preface for her," explained Colette, because Polaire had told her that she wanted to relieve her heart, to "scream," so everybody would be "on bad terms with her."[84] Actually, Colette feared Polaire's revelations. She decided to write "a little paper" on Polaire without mentioning her memoirs.

At the hospital Polaire found reassurance and compassion and no longer wanted to die; she told a reporter that she would like to write a play about a woman who wanted to kill herself, was saved at the last minute, and spent the rest of her life saving the lives of those who, like herself, were in total despair. "'Happiness' comes only from the happiness you give others." For two months she hovered between life and death; she died on October 11.

In 1949 Colette summed up Polaire's destiny in one page; she had given up on life on one of those dark rainy days "which brought tears to her eyes." When she was young, famous, and wealthy, she would sink into depression at sunset and weep unnoticed at a window. She felt lonely and suffered from "chronic anxiety." Colette mocked her ambition to write: "She imagined a scenario about a woman . . . who dies poor, horribly abandoned, that woman was Polaire herself. But we did not know it."[85]

In November Colette and Maurice joined the radio station Paris-Mondial, which was broadcasting official propaganda aimed at the

United States. Well-known writers and artists were invited to give talks and lectures. Because of the difference in time zones, the programs were scheduled from midnight to 4 AM; Colette spoke at 2:30 AM and Maurice presented a play in English at 3:20 AM every Monday.

Paris was under the shroud of a strict blackout; not one ray of light filtered through the windows and car headlights were painted dark blue. Maurice drove cautiously through the chilling fog to the Rue de Grenelle, passing a few ghostly cars, motorcycles, and bicycles. Policemen helped by signaling directions at crossroads with hasty beams of their flashlights. The studios shared a dark and foreboding building with a post office; as they groped their way in, Colette and Maurice bumped into the shadows of telegraph boys. Inside the flood of light was blinding, the bustle cheerful and noisy, "The tom-tom of a party . . . cruelly assails our unprepared eardrums and as we push the heavy door of Studio One, the *fortissimos* of Ray Ventura's orchestra grab us."[86] But the reality of the war could not be dismissed; men were in uniform.

Colette "spoke a few words in French, then handed her papers to Drew Leyton, who read the rest, translating as she went." Once in a while Colette spoke a few lines in English: "Maybe because of my accent, you did not realize that I spoke in English . . ."[87] She approached her American audience with her typical radio style: confidential and informal. "No, I will not speak of the war tonight, nor will I even speak about Paris. I would like to talk about America, or rather, about New York." She spoke as if revealing a secret: "Here I have never dared tell the truth about those three days I spent in New York."[88]

In the following weeks she underlined what she had in common with Americans: "a taste for simplicity, comfort, and no protocol." She took her audience on a tour of her own district, from the Palais Royal garden to a *crémerie*, where they served rustic meals. She spoke of the young seamstresses, who worked all day and knit socks and scarves for the soldiers in the evening, or skipped a meal to contribute money to a patriotic fund: "All around me arises that need to give, which burns in the heart of those who possess nothing." On Christmas Eve she spoke of midnight mass, of churches full of parishioners, of *Réveillon* in small villages; she reached out to her audience with nostalgia. Once a week until May 2, 1940, Colette appealed to the heart of America, then waited for Maurice in a canteen, eating "a hypothesis of ham between two mattresses of bread."[89]

The first air-raid warning occurred a few days after war was declared. The first time Colette went down to the cellar with Maurice and Pauline; her neighbor, Denise Tual, saw her seated in an armchair, wrapped in several plaids and a shawl. Maurice, in his pajamas, had a blanket around his shoulders and looked composed and cool. The cellar was small and musty; Colette thought of the vaulted cellars of the Hôtel Beaujolais next door and dispatched Pauline to prepare a comfortable nook with chairs, a table, and a few blankets.

Foreseeing future shortages, Colette systematically began to hoard everything that could be hoarded; she had her coal cellar filled, "she organized a system of parcels from all the friends we had outside Paris . . . these transactions necessitated a correspondence of ministerial proportions."[90] Thanks to her prudence, her household lacked neither food nor wine during the occupation of Paris.

The second alert was spent in the cloisterlike cellar of the Hôtel Beaujolais; but the third time Colette found the lack of air and the darkness so distressing that she decided, like many other Parisians, to stay in her apartment. As in 1914, when the sirens blared Colette opened all the windows, so that an explosion would not shatter the panes. To steady her nerves she decided to take up tapestry; "it is a vice that I can indulge in only during wars."[91] She kept busy making designs with threads she chose with the eye of a frustrated painter; if she hadn't written, she might have chosen painting as a career. In fact, she did paint, and had given some of her paintings to Anna de Noailles and to the princess de Polignac. The apartment in which she stored her other paintings burned during the war, and all were lost.

Her daughter came to visit and brought with her another cause for worry; Bel-Gazou's friend Françoise had turned into an alcoholic. She started the day at ten in the morning drinking Pernod, had half a bottle of cognac after lunch, Pernod again at six, port before dinner, and cocktails late in the night, yet managed to look composed. Colette feared that her daughter was doing the same on a lesser level.

It was increasingly difficult for Colette to walk; however, she kept a busy social agenda. She finished *Hotel Room (Chambre d'Hôtel)* and started a diary, *Looking Backwards*. Her doctor scolded her, "How could you have drained yourself to such a point!" To recuperate Colette went to the Hôtel Ruhl in Nice. Her daughter had made grandiose reservations for a whole suite, but Colette, with wartime spirit, retained only one room with a bathroom. She was recuperating slowly; "I feel better mentally, I am eating again but my hip and my leg hurt dreadfully."[92] She won five hundred and fifty-three francs at the lottery and spent them with Erna Redtenbacher and her lover Christiane de D——, who took Colette for long rides through the hills covered with mimosa in bloom. As soon as she was stronger, she returned to Paris, where she felt safe.

At the end of May the British Expeditionary Force and the French army were trapped at Dunkirk by the advancing German army. Two hundred thousand British and one hundred and thirty thousand French were taken to England in a desperate rescue operation involving all the ships and boats that could reach the beaches. Two French divisions protecting the embarkation were captured by the Germans.

Maurice wanted Colette to leave Paris immediately and settle in their newly acquired home in Méré. Colette resisted, then suddenly accepted, because "the time to break the string had come." They arrived to find that all empty houses had been assigned to regiments stationed in the area; Le Parc had been allocated to a regiment with fifteen horses. Colette wanted to turn back, but "Maurice was determined to stay, it took him one hour to have the place cleared." As he was escorting out the mayor, whom he had brought in to solve the situation, a major came in, planning to turn the house into a hospital "for the Moroccan troops, afflicted with lice." Colette intervened — "Maybe you will take the house, but I refuse to give it up."[93] The troops were moved to other vacant villas. Colette remained in Méré, while Maurice commuted every day to his offices at *Marie-Claire* and *Paris-Match*.

On the very first day at Le Parc, Christiane arrived in a taxi to ask for help. "A terrible error" had been made by the French administration and Erna, who was in France as an anti-Nazi refugee, had been sent to a concentration camp in the Pyrenees. Christiane de D—— tried to reach all her powerful friends; Colette immediately wrote to the minister of the colonies, Georges Mandel, on her behalf. A month later Erna was rescued from the concentration camp "like one snatched from the flames." Christiane had spent "all the money she had."[94] They returned to their home in Brittany, where they committed suicide. Renée Hamon, who also lived at Trinité-sur-Mer, informed Colette, who was deeply affected by the news. "A suicide leaves us indifferent when strangers are concerned. But I learn with consternation that these two pure creatures have chosen to terminate their lives."[95]

On June 3 the Paris region was under its first intense bombardment. Bel-Gazou left for Castel Novel, but "when a flood of rich refugees, relatives and friends, with nurses, children and governesses arrived,"[96] she fled to Curemonte. Colette learned that a neighbor, who was driving during the raid, was hit and lost a leg; that another one waited in his car while his wife rushed for the cover of a tree and was decapitated by an explosion. This did not keep Colette away from Paris altogether; whenever she had some business, she left for the city with Maurice. With a firm grip on her nerves, focusing on the normal in the midst of the abnormal, Colette wrote to Moune that chickadees were coming out of their nests, that a little nightingale had fallen from its nest and was safely put back, but added that a friend's cat had died of a heart attack during an air raid.

As Maurice reached Paris on June 11, he was struck by the strange aspect of the streets. People were loading their cars; there was smoke coming from the Quai d'Orsay, where they were burning the archives; all administrative services were being moved out of Paris. Maurice hurried to his office and to his bank, then returned at full speed to Méré to tell Colette that they should pack and leave. She refused, even when Maurice explained that the region was likely to become a battlefield. There was no point in arguing, for with Colette only seeing was believing; he suggested a drive and took her to the highway. Colette saw the cars overloaded with everything from mattresses to birdcages; she saw the slow oxcarts driven by peasants; she saw the wagons, the bicycles, the first wave of refugees. She described the exodus as "France slithering over herself." Maurice thought they should settle wherever *Paris-Soir* and *Paris-Match* decided to establish their wartime offices. In the meantime, he persuaded her to go to Curemonte — the center of France seemed the safest place in case of an invasion. On June 12, at four in the morning, "they left weighed down with luggage and cans of gasoline, Pauline on the backseat,"[97] joining the vanguard of fleeing French. They arrived at Curemonte at five in the afternoon; it had been a relatively easy journey, since they had gone ahead of the terrible congestion, which grew as the hours went by. Curemonte comprised two ruined medieval castles on a small hill. When the weather was rough, stones and beams kept rolling down, but there was a remodeled apartment over the stables. For three weeks Colette remained in that "green tomb" without letters, telephone, or radio. Curemonte was engulfed in silence. Colette complained that she felt a hundred years old and looked it! Safety, when it meant "total isolation to the point of nausea," was harder to bear than danger.[98] Common people had shown more common sense. "Why didn't we stay in Méré like our cleaning lady?"[99]

The exodus had cast hundreds of thousands of people on the roads; around Curemonte there were suddenly one hundred and sixty thousand persons in excess of the normal population. Colette learned that some of her friends had died: Vuillard the painter, Lugné-Poé the director. She expressed her dismay to Moune, "The shock has made them fall off the tree."[100] She wrote to Misz, "the day I see you again, I, who know so well how to keep myself from crying, I fear that I will break down."[101]

Two days after Colette and Maurice left Le Parc the German army marched into Paris, deserted by its inhabitants. The following day they reached Brest in Brittany. The Loire region was bombed. General de Gaulle, at forty-nine the youngest of the French generals, who had warned repeatedly about the limitations of the Maginot line, escaped to London, where he formed a government in exile. On June 18 he went to the studios of the BBC and made his famous speech. Four days later an armistice was signed, and France was divided into an Occupied Zone and a Free Zone. On July 3 the National Assembly voted Marshal Pétain full powers and adopted a new constitution; the government set up quarters in the fashionable spa of Vichy.

As Colette was growing restless at Curemonte, Maurice arranged for them to move to Lyons, where many newspapers had established their temporary headquarters; they managed to get enough gas to reach Lyons and settled in a hotel with a view of the river. It was an old hotel with large rooms, visited by a friendly mouse that Colette fed with bread crumbs. She insisted on driving to Paris, but gas was unavailable, so Colette went to see her old friend, Edouard Herriot, then mayor of Lyons, who facilitated things for her. Always preparing for the worst, she wrote to Edouard Bourdet that they had left in a hurry and had "nothing or too little. . . . And the money we took with us flows as fast as the Rhône. We still have some, but in Paris and not heaps of it as you can imagine." Bourdet immediately offered to send her whatever amount she needed. When Maurice learned of Colette's uncalled-for request, he almost lost his cool. He asked her to tell Bourdet that they did not need money, so she wrote immediately, "No! You are crazy! We don't need it now."[102]

In Lyons Colette contributed articles to the weekly *Candide,* but as soon as they had some gas they packed and drove to Paris. To go from the Free Zone to the Occupied Zone, they had to pass checkpoints manned by German patrols. When they reached the control post a German soldier, looking at Colette, said that she was Jewish; she denied it. Examining Pauline's black hair, yellow eyes, and dark complexion, he declared that she was Jewish also. Maurice said in German that he alone was Jewish; the soldier refused to let them pass and they drove back to Lyons. Colette wrote to Bourdet, "Alas! I have married an honest man."[103]

They tried again. Lyons was full of celebrities who had fled Paris and who were going back now that the government was urging people to resume a normal way of life. Mary Marquet, an actress with the Comédie Française who had been a protégée of Sarah Bernhardt's and mistress of Edmond Rostand, was going back. She had long been a friend to Otto Abetz, the German ambassador, so Colette gave her a letter to be hand-delivered to him, hoping that he could facilitate Maurice's return to Paris. Colette knew Abetz. He had been on friendly terms with Bertrand de Jouvenel and was well aware that Bertrand's mother was Jewish. Most people believed that the Germans would not deal with the French Jews the way they had with German Jews, and the affable Abetz, more than anyone, was responsible for that false sense of security.

Abetz was married to a Frenchwoman named Suzanne; he had spent years in Paris and had made many friends in the high circles of intellectuals and socialites. In the midthirties a group of right-wing intellectuals, headed by Charles Maurras, founded the association Rive Gauche to promote their ideas. Most were prominent writers, philosophers, and historians, among them Henry de Montherlant, Henri Massis, Pierre Gaxotte, Robert Brasillach, Jacques Bainville, and Bertrand de Jouvenel. Otto Abetz, who was then working to promote the cooperation of French and German youths in the framework of Nazi propaganda, was invited to give a lecture. Since the end of World War I there had been a strong belief in some right-wing intellectual and social circles that a rapprochement with Germany would maintain peace and be beneficial for both nations.

Colette explored every possibility of returning home. Invited to dinner by the Swedish consul, she told him what had happened at the checkpoint. Sweden was neutral, so the consul gave Colette a letter of recommendation; this time the letter touched off "much consideration and clicking of heels" at the same control post. Entering Paris on September 11, an exhausted Maurice ran a red light; a French police officer warned him in a subdued tone, "Walk on tiptoe in Paris, we have visitors."[104]

## Life in Occupied Paris

Back at the Palais Royal, Colette joined Le Petit Parisien. She was now looking backward; in Hotel Room she revived her past as a music-hall artist and in The Rain Moon (La Lune de Pluie) she explored her past jealousy, her deathless grudge against unfaithful Willy. The stories were published by Fayard, since her former publisher, Ferenczi, was Jewish and could no longer publish. Ferenczi's press was assigned to an administrator appointed by the Germans, Jean de la Hire, Colette's and Willy's first biographer turned collaborator. He was also put in charge of Le Matin. The Vichy government had fallen in step with the Nazis; by law, Jews were forbidden to work for the press, the radio, the theater, and the cinema. Goudeket could not work officially anymore. But to Colette Paris meant work, friends, news, everything that counted for her. She was ebullient.

Communications in Paris were difficult; cars were requisitioned and bicycles could only be found at a stiff price. Some of Colette's privileged friends kept their cars, notably the painter José Maria Sert, Generalissimo Franco's ambassador to the Vatican, who resided in Paris and was on good terms with the Germans. Colette kept in close contact with the Serts.

Rationing was strict. Personal allotment of staple foods was at a survival level: bread — 8.8 ounces per day, meat — 6.3 ounces per week, oil and butter — .05 ounce a day, cheese — 1.4 ounces a week. Shortages of material, clothing, wool, and shoes were getting worse; women dyed their legs with diluted iodine to fake stockings, and wooden clogs had replaced leather shoes. The winter was one of the coldest of the century; women started to wear slacks made out of their husband's pants. The Paris prefect of police declared that women were endangering the virtuous modesty endorsed by the Vichy regime and prohibited women to wear masculine attire under penalty of law.

Food was becoming an obsession. "Conversations about supplies are

reaching the intensity of a neurosis, alas a collective one,"[105] wrote
Colette. The black market flourished; one of Colette's providers was a
friend of Moréno's, Gaston Baheux, known as Tonton, owner of the
Liberty Bar in Pigalle. He was peddling food and news as well. Whenever
Colette went to his restaurant she left with a roast, a fowl, or a lobster,
cognac and wine. Pauline had friends at Les Halles, the city's central
food market. Denise Tual noticed that some days Colette would watch
from her window as Pauline walked cautiously under the arcades of the
Palais Royal, laden with a big, heavy bag. Colette reported upon "the
great events of life," the arrival of a few fresh eggs, her search "for cocoa
that tastes like cocoa," adding, "I have not seen the beautiful cat, which
came here to dine and sleep, he must have been eaten."[106]

Colette received a steady flow of victuals from Nantes, where two of
her admirers, Yvonne Brochard and Thérèse Sourisse, lived. They had resigned from their teaching positions and settled in on a farm they
owned. The "two little farmers" supplied Colette with eggs, sausage,
even beef. Only when their cow gave birth did the flow of butter stop
temporarily. Colette sent five hundred francs to Renée Hamon in
Brittany for potatoes. In November she asked for apples and chestnuts.
Renée was sending oysters, "a fortune in onions, priceless garlic," and
rutabagas. "We have become spoiled children, who scream and fuss
around a parcel." Life in Paris had become difficult but "as during the
other war, it is Paris I want, melancholy as it may be,"[107] confessed
Colette. With the efficiency of a true survivor, she never neglected her
supplies and bartered even with her close friends. She found jars of apple
and orange preserves for Moune and two other friends and announced
her plan to buy vegetables for the three of them.

Colette and Maurice were never without an invitation to dine out in
one of the city's secret gastronomic havens: with the minister Léon
Barthou, the writer Georges Duhamel, and the surgeon Dr. Mondor,
they had lunch at the Café de Paris. "The clandestine resources of Paris
are very interesting, we opened wide eyes (and wide mouths)!" when
lobsters and steaks were set on the table. The secret banquet took place
in one of the private dining rooms, which Colette called "sinister and
stuffy closets." The legal lunch at the Café de Paris comprised tuna salad
"without tuna," stewed tomatoes, and cherries.

On Pauline's day off Colette ate at the Mirliton: Bayonne ham,
tomato salad, and mutton chop, while Maurice had a steak with all the

trimmings. She also replenished their supplies, "and we bought there (hush!), a roast for today!" The prices were "indecent" but "one has to eat" and, affirmed Colette, "one has to know how to make use of one's connections."[108] During a lunch with the Préfet de la Seine, the high authority for the Paris region, Colette asked him for a daily pint of milk, a special ration alloted for the old. Her request was granted.

The round of dinners took Colette and Maurice to the sumptuous table of the American millionaire Florence Gould, whose guests one day included a high-ranking German officer, a Russian, and the director of *Gringoire,* Horace de Carbuccia. When Maurice started a conversation with the German, a deep silence fell over the dining table; Colette thought Maurice was "magnificent," but the atmosphere was electric.

An invitation by the director of the Musée du Louvre to dine on the top floor of the palace-museum, with a view of the Carrousel gardens, was a treat especially enhanced by an *aïoli,* a dish smothered in garlic sauce. But the most gargantuan and friendliest dinners took place in the apartment of José and Misia Sert; they received their supplies from neutral Spain and treated their less privileged Parisian friends lavishly. They also knew the well-kept addresses of the best black-market bistros. Marcel Boulestin was back from London, and he had the right connections. Colette commented that a mutual friend had lost forty pounds, "like everyone else except me."[109]

With everyone hoarding supplies, the mouse population thrived. Bel-Gazou had rented her apartment but her tenant had to move out of the bedroom, which was infested by mice. Colette's cleaning lady told her that in her building they had "a cat on duty." It was assigned to each tenant "for a night or two, according to the quantity of game."[110]

Doctor Ducroquet, a specialist treating Colette's arthritis, invited her and Maurice to dine "magnificently" with Musidora and her husband. The doctor had just bought a Manet at the flea market. Art, jewelry, and rare books were mysteriously appearing, so many homes had been plundered in the first weeks of the war; the black market was not limited to food. The spoils of Nazi victims were sold and bought, dispersed, destroyed. Maurice, barred from the press, decided to use his knowledge of rare editions and started to trade in books. Books had acquired "a price unknown to this day," and Colette admired him for working "with flair and passion . . . we may see him turn into a book dealer some day." Colette had "started something like a novel . . . I am advancing at an unusual speed without wanting to stop." Then, "after 75 pages," she hit a wall. "I have to demolish it or go around it."[111] A month later she was still perplexed: "I am scratching away at my novel and wondering which way it is heading." It was to become *Julie de Carneilhan,* a revenge novel aimed at her second husband.

February brought new anxiety, for Colette announced: "I am going to be jobless also!"[112] She had received an anonymous phone call; a trembling voice had informed her that the whole staff of *Le Petit Parisien* had resigned en masse. Colette looked elsewhere for what was available. She contributed monthly articles on fashion to *L'Officiel de la Couture* and wrote short chronicles for *Images de France:* "Paris," "Style," "Beauties of France," "Where Shall We Go Next Summer," and five other titles were collected in *Belles Saisons* in 1945.

In March Fayard published *Looking Backwards;* Colette wrote to Hélène Picard that the only reason for caring about the book was money. She was struggling to sell Le Parc, on which she still owed forty thousand francs, which were coming due. She had not paid her income tax since 1939, and a first installment of thirty-five thousand francs was due by the end of the year. But she had inherited half of the proceeds from the sale of Léo's stamp collection — thirteen thousand francs — and ironically announced that it made her feel rich. Maurice treated her as if she were still "in her beautiful fifties."[113] He was serene and trusted in the future; she was putting things in order, preparing for the unexpected.

She wrote two sketches for the Théâtre Michel. One of the sketches was about *La Pompadour;* the other was a return of *Claudine,* the still-famous schoolgirl of 1900. Colette wrote a song for the pretty singer, Parisys, in which Claudine teaches the new generation of young men how much life is worth living; it was timely in the general gloom of the second year of the occupation. The revue was a flop, and Colette had her name removed from the posters when it opened in another music hall.

Her last novel, *Julie de Carneilhan,* was finished in June. Julie, forty-five, is twice divorced; her second husband, the politician Herbert d'Espivant, has remarried a very wealthy woman. He has suffered a heart attack and asks Julie to come and see him. When they were married, the flamboyant count had lived beyond his means; Julie had sold her pearl necklace and given him one million francs for his political campaign. In jest he had given her a receipt, acknowledging that he owed her a million. Now he needed Julie's complicity to swindle his wife; he had devised a financial scheme, after which he could divorce her. He asked Julie to demand the repayment of the debt; since his wife hated debts, she would pay the million back immediately. Espivant would keep half of it and give the other half to Julie for the part she was to play. Julie, once passionately in love with d'Espivant, acquiesces to his plan. The scheme works but Espivant does not keep his word, giving Julie only a demeaning ten-percent commission. Insulted and angry, Julie turns to her brother, with whom she goes back to their rural family home. In this roman à clef Espivant is endowed with Jouvenel's charm, his flamboyant style, and his womanizing; there is also a seventeen-year-old boy, Espivant's wife's son by a previous marriage, who is in love with Julie and reminds one of Bertrand.

Colette did not consider her novel very good; she was even annoyed that Marguerite Moréno had read it. It created a stir in the inner circle of her friends; Claire Boas de Jouvenel considered the novel a vicious attack and thought she was the swindled wife, as did Isabelle de Comminges. The third baronne de Jouvenel could also see herself in the millionaire married for her money. As for Espivant, it was immediately rumored that Colette had depicted Henry de Jouvenel and that he had fared no better than Willy in *My Apprenticeships*.

Anatole de Monzie was appalled. He admired Colette, equating her with no less than Chateaubriand and Rousseau. He asked her if she meant to smear the reputation of "Bel-Gazou's father." He hoped for a public denial. None came. Colette sent a letter to Monzie written in the most ambiguous terms; she drove a dagger delicately through her old friend's heart by saying that, had he not been her old friend, she would not have bothered to answer his letter. Why did he have to inform her that some anonymous gossipmongers implied that Espivant, a vulgar crook, had anything to do with the man who had been Monzie's friend and her former husband? She told Monzie that only two people really knew Jouvenel, namely he and she; therefore, if Monzie did not recognize Jouvenel in Espivant, he was not Espivant. She reminded Monzie that she herself was not to be found all of a piece in her novels, and gossip should be treated for what it was. The answer was unclear; the novel hit the target.

*Julie de Carneilhan* was serialized in *Gringoire*. The June 4 issue announced Colette's novel; on the same page there was a caricature of the Statue of Liberty brandishing a menorah, and Uncle Sam was called

Uncle Sem. The first chapter of *Julie* appeared in the June 13 issue, which also carried excerpts from the diary of Anatole de Monzie, now a minister in the Vichy government. On the first page there was an article against England by Philippe Henriot, a collaborator who would be shot by a Resistance commando on June 28, 1944. In the same issue an article praised the decree that deprived naturalized Jewish refugees of their French citizenship, thus delivering them to the Nazis. Another collaborator requested the arrest of all British citizens living in the south of France. In the June 20 issue there was a denunciation of all Jewish businessmen living in North Africa. Many journalists and writers who contributed to *Gringoire* during the occupation were arrested and stood trial after the liberation; Colette could claim that her contributions were not political.

When Fayard published *Julie de Carneilhan,* on the back cover he announced the forthcoming publication of *Mein Kampf,* by Adolf Hitler.

In the issue dated December 1942 of *Les Lettres Françaises Clandestines,* an underground newspaper of the Resistance, Colette was criticized for having published in collaborating newspapers. But the author of the article added that there was no doubt that she did not know the company in which her text would appear; it only proved that in the press controlled by the occupying forces, any text, even nonpolitical, could involve an unsuspecting writer in the propaganda orchestrated by the Nazis. Many writers published their works during the occupation: Albert Camus published *L'Etranger,* Jean-Paul Sartre *L'Etre et le Néant,* Simone de Beauvoir *L'Invitée,* to name but a few. The ambiguity of Colette's situation was not exceptional; she had friends on the right and the left of the political spectrum, but remained uncommitted.

Colette was aware that the Germans' grip was tightening and the persecution of Jews intensifying. Julien Cain, director of the Bibliothèque Nationale, had been fired, arrested, and detained in a camp. "His wife does not move from her telephone; she is in a dreadful state, she hopes that it is some kind of mistake, that he will be back anytime," wrote Colette to Moune. Julien Cain's friends started a petition to free him, and Moune asked Colette to sign it. She immediately answered, "No, the first result of the petition would be to draw attention to Maurice."[114] However, she helped in the only way she thought safe — she sent food.

In August she received a preprinted card: "I have received your parcel. My sincere thanks" and the signature, "Julien Cain."

After the arctic winter came a tropical summer. As soon as the sale of Le Parc was secured by a down payment, Colette instructed Moune to harvest all the fruit and vegetables. But the caretakers had already left with the coal, the fruit, the vegetables, and the bottles of wine stacked in the cellar.

Fresh air was a necessity for Colette; as soon as the metro started running again, Colette and Maurice boarded it at 5:30 AM and went to walk in the Bois de Boulogne. Bicycles were at a premium and hard to find, so when La Fédération du Cyclisme asked Colette to write an article promoting cycling — "What do you think of bicycles?" — Colette seized her chance "to ask them for a deluxe bicycle"; in July she bought an Alcyon bicycle, and with Maurice, who had a "dragon," they went pedaling. "I can see the eulogy after my death: at age seventy, she committed herself to cycling, her performances will remain famous . . ."[115] To fight her arthritis, Colette tried a cure at the Ax-les-Thermes spa.

*Les Cahiers Colette* and *The Pure and the Impure* were published by Aux Armes de France, the new name of the century-old press, Calmann-Lévy, now under the direction of the collaborator Louis Thomas. She started a new book about her various homes and called it *A Set without Characters (Le Décor sans personnages),* before giving it its definitive title, *Trois-Six-Neuf* (in France a lease is generally signed for three, six, or nine years; the title of the English translation is *Places*).

## Monsieur, the Germans Have Come to Arrest Monsieur

The constant raids of the Luftwaffe over London were undermining hopes for victory; "Nothing came to cheer the dark days of 1941, until the astonishing news broke upon the world, that Hitler was attacking Russia." Maurice grasped the consequences of this attempt to conquer the land where "General Winter" had defeated Napoleon; he broke the news joyfully to Colette: "The war is over."

"You're mad."

"It may go on three or four years more, but for me . . . Hitler has already disappeared and the German soldiers you see passing by are no longer anything but ghosts."

But on December 12, at six-thirty in the morning, Pauline answered a knock at the door, then went to wake up Maurice in such a state of emotion that she addressed him in the third person: "Monsieur, the Germans have come to arrest Monsieur."

"A German officer, helmeted and wearing around his neck the chain of the *Feldgendarmerie*, had followed Pauline"; he politely told Goudeket what he was to take with him. Maurice sent Pauline to awaken Colette. He "had got used" to the idea that he could be arrested, but "had never shared these fears with Colette." She was up and "mistress of herself"; she helped him to pack his bag. "Colette accompanied me to the head of the staircase. We looked at each other. We were both smiling and exchanged a kiss. 'Don't worry,' I said, 'all will be well.' 'Off you go,' said she, . . . with a friendly tap on my shoulder.'"

In describing this scene, Maurice insisted upon their determination to dominate their feelings, because stoicism was "one of the essential traits of Colette's character, without knowing this her work . . . is not entirely understandable." The general perception is that of a Colette "free, uninhibited, given to the moment," but "her personality is more complex. . . . Not very aggressive in the ordinary things of life, mistrustful of heroes, Colette attained without effort the greatest possible firmness of soul . . . no one could be more virile in adversity."[116]

This moral strength shows in a sober note sent that same week to Hélène Picard. "They arrested Maurice, Friday at 6:30 AM in the dark. I will not inflict details upon you. He left very calm, I don't know for what destination, charged with the crime of being Jewish, of having fought in the previous war as a volunteer and having a citation." Without transition, Colette told her that the owner of a boutique at the Palais Royal who raised parakeets had agreed to board Hélène's birds, since she could no longer feed them. "It is no longer possible to keep dogs, cats, or birds. . . . My Hélène, pray to the god of poets for your Colette." Hélène, crippled by a bone disease, could barely walk, but she was ready to take the overcrowded metro to comfort Colette. "No, my Hélène, do not come to see me,"[117] she said. The sight of her old friend whom she had not seen for years would weaken her resolve and trigger her emotions, and Colette feared the danger of breaking down.

A thousand Jews were arrested the same morning as Goudeket. They were to be deported immediately to Germany to the death camps. But the trains had been reserved for the German troops heading home on their Christmas furlough, so the Jews were interned instead in Compiègne. Maurice observed that those who gave in to depression "were speedily in danger of dying." He could do nothing for Colette "except survive." He applied his reason and will to that single purpose; "the first thing to do was to accept the life in the camp . . . cleanliness, hygiene, and good humor became urgent obligations."[118]

For a whole week Colette did not know where they had taken Maurice. But on December 23 a sick old man released from the camp called her and told her that Maurice was in Compiègne, that his morale "was excellent," that he slept on straw and survived on soup, two hundred and fifty grams of bread, and a cup of herb tea a day. As the days dragged on Colette would sit at Maurice's desk for hours in the silent apartment, devastated by worry; Natalie Barney reported that Colette, seeing her own reflection unexpectedly in a mirror, did not recognize herself.

On January 31, Colette said to Marie Dormoy, who came to buy a manuscript for the Bibliothèque Doucet, that thanks to certain influences, Maurice would be free in a few days. On the first of February, Colette was informed that he would be released the following day; but he did not show up. Then a French writer, whom she does not identify in her recollections, was released. He came to tell Colette that he could obtain a job for Goudeket at Compiègne "as long as the war was to last." Colette asked what Goudeket's job would be in the camp. "Nothing much. Just give the Germans bits of information on the detainees." Colette refused.

"But it is either this job or death."

"I choose death," said Colette.

"But your husband has not been consulted."

"We both choose death," was Colette's chilling answer.[119]

As the news that Goudeket had been arrested spread, friends organized a relay to avoid leaving Colette alone. The entrance to 9 Rue de Beaujolais was jammed with bicycles. Hélène Morhange came with Antonia Lichwitz, Geneviève Leibovici, Doctor Marthe Lamy, and the only friend with a car, Simone Berriau; as soon as some left, others arrived. Colette, in total control of herself, never spoke of her anguish, but she was seeking an intervention on Maurice's behalf. She "knocked at doors" persistently. After three weeks she was able to establish clandestine contacts with him. "Colette never relaxed her efforts to have me freed . . . there was no step that she was not prepared to take . . . she saw collaborators and Germans,"[120] acknowledged Maurice. No one can tell whose intercession was decisive. Was it Drieu-La Rochelle? Was it Sacha Guitry, who later said he had threatened a high-ranking German officer with committing suicide on the spot, to show how the French were really treated by Germans who pretended to be friendly? Sacha had direct access to Otto Abetz and Fernand de Brinon, the official links between the Vichy Government and the Germans. Colette had another efficient friend, José-Maria Sert, but no one could do more than Suzanne Abetz.

On the morning of February 6, 1942, Maurice was summoned to the German Office and told, "*Sie sind entlassen*," "You are free." To get back to Paris he walked and took whatever transportation he could find; he was without money. When he reached the Palais Royal, Pauline opened the door and let out a scream. Colette was at the hairdresser, Pauline called her; Colette was so shaken that she asked a friend to walk her home. Meanwhile, Maurice stripped on the landing so as not to infest the apartment, since his clothes were full of lice and vermin. He weighed ninety-six pounds. Colette "had never seen on a human being extra-human colors, the green-white of the cheeks and forehead, the orange around the eyelids, the gray of the lips."[121]

After Goudeket's liberation Suzanne Abetz wrote to Colette, who had sent her flowers, "I am happy to know that you are happy." She sent over a chauffeur from the German Embassy with several of Colette's books for her to inscribe (the Italian ambassador, among others, was eager to have an autographed book), and invited Colette to have tea with her, hoping that Goudeket, "always prepared to take a plane" — that was a useful hint for caution — "would be in Paris, nevertheless." Suzanne wrote, "My" Colette (the quotation marks are hers), to wish her "dear protégée"[122] a merry Christmas.

It took Colette a week to summon up enough energy to write to Marguerite Moréno. "For eight weeks I had to bear something too heavy for words. . . . Maurice, 'absent' from December 12, has been given back to me . . . . now I indulge in the luxury of being very tired."[123] He soon felt "absolutely fit," but noticed that "Colette could not regain her nervous balance."[124] She was trying to resume her work but his presence was not enough "to make it easy."[125] She was crushed by fatigue and outraged to be at the occupying enemy's mercy. She was startled every time the doorbell rang; "the nervous tremor, the twitch of the lip and of the eyelid, the jerk of the shoulder toward the ear . . . doesn't one ever heal from that?" Many women had gone through the same ordeal, yet their nervous reflexes had slowly subsided. "But I . . . I have passed the age when one can heal."[126]

Maurice was not a free man; he was "banished from visible existence, from its pleasures, from its activities, barred from the theaters . . . from the restaurants, as if he had a contagious disease, barred from every kind of work, as if he were mentally retarded." She seethed with anger, but could not express her revolt. Her "best friend's" life "depended on a sort of insane bureaucracy."[127] His identity papers were stamped with the word "Jew," and he had to wear a yellow star sewn on his coat. Because arrests were made during the night, Maurice left at midnight and reappeared only at nine the following morning. Help came from many sides. At the Palais Royal the bookstore owner left the backdoor open and prepared a hiding place behind a stack of books, with a pillow and a lamp. The owner of the embroidery boutique gave Maurice a key to her backdoor. The tenant of the garret above Colette's apartment suggested that if the Germans came again to take Maurice away, he should rush to her room and slip into her bed; they would never look for him there. Never spending one night at the same place, Maurice went from garret to garret in the Palais Royal district or around the Etoile; he slept here and there "like a chimney swallow."[128]

Colette was waging another battle against arthritis. After a series of shots of Lipidol she suffered from side effects, crushing muscular pains. She tried x-rays, which "kept her flat" from five to midnight, then "daily shots of sulphuramide,"[129] which took away her appetite. These shots proved useless and incredibly unpleasant; it was "a truly new experience"; for thirty seconds she felt like "a blazing chimney . . . they shove fire into the depths of your lungs, into your nostrils . . . !"[130] Yet she chose to suffer, saying, "I will not stop the treatment."[131] Sometimes Misia Sert could drive her to her doctor. Whenever she could not, Colette, with stoic determination, called one of the rickshawlike contraptions devised with Parisian ingenuity: a small wooden box mounted on two bicycle wheels, pulled by a man on a bicycle. Colette was pedaled away in great discomfort to the merciless treatment. She suffered burns from her stomach to her knees. The violence of the treatment gave her some hope that it would work.

Renée Hamon was terminally ill with cancer. Unable to go up and down the steps of the metro, Colette sent Maurice to see her and put her personal doctor, Marthe Lamy, in charge of her friend. They agreed to conceal from Renée that she had cancer and told her instead that she had a rare tropical disease, elephantiasis, which was curable. Colette encouraged her to follow her example. "You, too, must go to the end of everything cruel that is prescribed"; for beyond the pain, there was still the fresh sea breeze, "the good sunlight." Renée wanted to write a book to keep her mind busy, and asked Colette for a plan. "A plan! Lord! I never knew what that was!" Her only advice was to "be more brief in the sentimental than in the picturesque." She was deeply moved by Renée's plight, more than she usually allowed herself to be. In letter after letter came the encouraging lie, "your cure is just a matter of patience." Because Renée had become very religious, Colette went to light "a pretty candle at Notre Dame des Victoires,"[132] and was pushing Fayard to hurry to publish her book.

To remain mobile Colette wanted to buy an electric wheelchair. As she communicated the idea to Moune, she added that a friend had just brought her a rabbit, and that she had written sixty-six pages, but would have preferred "to have planted sixty-six raspberry bushes, killed sixty-six potato beetles, or eaten sixty-six thousand strawberries."[133] Paris from *My Window (Paris de ma Fenêtre)* was published in May by Aux Armes de France; a second edition, published in 1944 by Milieu du Monde, was followed by a third in 1948 by Ferenczi. The first edition was a collection of articles dated from October 16, 1940, to September 25, 1941; the amended third edition, one-third longer, included additional texts written during the occupation. Colette referred to it as "my d—— volume of remembrance."[134] The chronicles were mostly aimed at a female readership; Colette reported on women's daily struggles to cope. Chemists were trying to create substitutes for wool and natural fiber, requisitioned by the Germans. In March of 1942 a decree was published in the *Journal Officiel*: all hair cut in hairdressers' salons was to be collected by an official service. The total "harvest" was shipped monthly to the Calvados region, where it was steamed and blended with twenty percent Fibranne, woven and made into cloth that shrank in the rain. By using paper with this blend, four hundred thousand pairs of slippers were manufactured.

Rabbit skin became the only one available for making gloves.

To keep warm, Colette suggested wearing gold jewelry because gold made her feel warm. Lining clothes with newspapers could also help, and she advocated going to bed at dusk, wearing sweater, socks, and bonnet. She noticed that the art of conversation was coming back, that the spirit of long provincial evenings, when no light was wasted, was renewing sociability in the urban blackout. She told of dark provincial kitchens in which the foot warmer was a live sheep lying on the ground. True or fictitious, Colette's bucolic recollections entertained her readers and her fan mail kept swelling. She gave out recipes fit for a time of scarcity; the *Flognarde* enjoyed an incredible success. "Two eggs, a cup of flour, a little water or whey, salt, and three teaspoons of powdered sugar."[135] Beat it like dough for a pancake, let it rise and bake it for twenty minutes. It swells into an air-filled puff.

During the war the French read avidly; statistics reveal that between 1939 and 1941 the number of readers tripled. On the *Quais* boxes usually full of secondhand books were empty; serious literature held a tremendous appeal. Montaigne, the sixteenth-century philosopher, was at the top of the chart; three thousand copies of his *Essays* sold every month. Jean Cocteau appealed to young writers not to let France's literary renown perish. In 1942 Sacha Guitry planned a book to glorify France in the face of defeat and occupation, *De Jeanne d'Arc à Philippe Pétain*. This was a collection of texts by established authors; Colette contributed a text on Balzac. The book had a limited edition of six hundred and fifty copies selling at twenty-five thousand francs each; Sacha gave twenty percent of the profit to the needy through the *Secours National*. Guitry also organized an exhibition of actors' paintings and photographs; when the German propaganda inspector spotted a picture of the great tragic actress, Rachel, and another of Sarah Bernhardt, he ordered Guitry to take down the pictures of the Jewish actresses. Sacha told him to do it himself and left. The picture of Sarah, with Sacha kissing her hand, was removed; the picture of Rachel became "Portrait of an Actress."

Colette carefully avoided political implications. *Paris from My Window* was noncommittal, as was a preface to the catalog of the exhibition *Fruits and Flowers Since the Romantic Period (Les Fleurs et les Fruits depuis le Romantisme)*. At the annual art show, the exhibition was centered around a series of portraits of Colette. There was Colette in her seductive twenties by Humbert, Colette slim and mischievous by Forain, and Colette as an eighteen-month-old toddler by Stéphane Baron. The latest portraits were by Segonzac and Luc-Albert Moreau.

It was during the dark hours of 1942 that Colette wrote *Gigi*. The story had been told to Colette in the winter of 1926 by two sisters who ran a hotel on the Riviera, having retired from the demimonde with a small fortune. One had been an opera singer. The two courtesans had raised their niece with the sole purpose of captivating a millionaire who came regularly to visit them. They taught her all the idiosyncrasies of the rich and idle young man and made her so attractive that he proposed to make her his mistress and set her up in style. To her aunts' dismay, their niece refused the offer, and to their utter surprise, the millionaire asked her to marry him. The girl brought up to be a kept woman became instead the wife of the man she truly loved. In 1918 it had been the talk and the envy of the demimonde.

Colette remembered this Cinderella-like fairy tale; she pushed it back in time. With *Gigi* she went back to her twenties when, with Willy, she had haunted the picturesque world of the courtesans. She wrote to Léon Barthou, "I am tangled in a short story that takes place in 1898–1900. With what political and financial personalities would a wealthy sugar manufacturer have dinner?"[136] Mixing facts and fiction, she put Barthou, the car manufacturer De Dion, and the playwright Feydeau in her story. Colette gave Henry de Jouvenel's mother's nickname "Mamita" to Gigi's grandmother. Aunt Alicia is a composite of Liane de Pougy and la Belle Otéro. Gigi reminds us of Colette at age fifteen, with the same slate-blue eyes, the high "little moujik's" cheekbones, and Claudine's free speech. She has a dress with rows of braids, similar to the dress Gabri wore in photographs taken at Châtillon. Colette bequeathed to the last avatar of her younger self, the true-to-life scene that prompted her marriage to Willy. Gigi, who at first refuses to become Gaston's mistress, reconsiders, realizing that she will miss him so much that "she prefers to be unhappy with him than happy without him."[137] *Gigi* was serialized in the weekly *Présent,* published in Lyons from September 28 to November 24. "I never saw its color or its shape, and I don't care,"[138] wrote Colette.

In July there was a roundup of all Jews of foreign origin living in France; twenty thousand people were arrested and deported to the extermination camps. On July 27 Misz Marchand, who was a Polish Jew, took her own life, fearing that she had become a threat to her husband. She swallowed three tubes of sleeping pills. For four nights and three days Doctor Marthe Lamy tried to save her, keeping in touch by telephone with Colette, who was very fond of Misz, "such a pure being, so far removed from ugly things." Colette was exhausted "without having accomplished anything. One has to accept this also."[139]

Maurice lived under constant threat and thought Colette needed a respite. He left for the Free Zone and took refuge in Saint-Tropez with Julio Van der Henst and his wife Vera, formerly a ballerina in Diaghilev's *Ballets Russes*. Colette sent a preprinted Interzone card every day, the only communication allowed between the Free and Occupied Zones. She worried: "For five days, not a single Interzone card and I know that he writes as I do every day."[140] Time dragged on; in September Colette wrote to Renée that Maurice was "still there, tanned and a little sad. He misses me as I miss him. When and how will our separation end, which in two segments has already lasted four months." The weather was lovely, "but gorgeous weather is not always conducive to happiness. Yet I am wise."[141] Years later she wrote: "The nightmare of separation . . . is, I believe, something that cannot be erased."[142]

There were a few welcome diversions. Adrienne Monnier, the lesbian owner of a bookstore on the Rue de l'Odéon that had been one of the centers of the Roaring Twenties' literary avant-garde, wrote articles about life in Paris during the occupation. She was a friend of Doctor Marthe Lamy and Doctor Paulette Gauthier-Villars, who invited her to meet Colette. Paulette was the first woman to hold a Chair of Medicine; she still called Colette "Aunt Colette." They had lunch in a little restaurant on the Rue de Babylone. Adrienne Monnier was startled by Colette's first glance; she described it as fierce, sharp, and wary, as if evaluating an enemy. By slow stages, these eyes took on another expression, first a tamer look, then a kind, warm gaze, as if Colette were giving something of herself. People who met her for the first time were surprised by the scrutiny and distrust in Colette's eyes: "She seemed to measure up the person, she saw through people. Her eyes were the color of the sea: they turned blue, or green or gray and were lightly speckled with gold. Those who met her agreed that no photograph gave an idea of the intensity of her gaze; when she looked at a stranger, he would feel himself sized up at his true worth and fell silent or stammered." When she was told what people felt in that first encounter, Colette had a revealing answer: "It is because I know what to put in my eyes."[143]

As Colette sat down, the restaurant owner came up with her cat and handed it over to her. Everybody knew Colette was fond of cats; her radio talks had made her popular. Sure to please Colette, the patronne offered her a typical Burgundian dish, escargots. "No," said Colette, she had never been able to swallow a snail. The patronne then served her chopped meat with garlic, an omelette followed by a chuck roast, and potatoes sautéed in butter. During this clandestine black-market lunch, once the topic of food had been exhausted, the conversation turned to haunted houses. Colette, in a flight of fancy, said she had owned one that had once belonged to a religious order; she sold it, because of the hostile ghosts who walked in procession down the hall and were unfriendly to laypeople. Colette knew an extraordinary soothsayer, Elise, who asked every client to wear a candle under her blouse and not to remove it until the next meeting, when she would whittle it into tiny scraps as she foretold the future. What she said always came to pass. Colette insisted that Elise was not reading her client's mind, because often she spoke without understanding what she was saying. Adrienne Monnier, an amateur palm reader, read Colette's hands, in which she saw a tendency to mysticism, kept in check by reason, and a mount of Venus that indicated an unusual sensuality. Her thumb betrayed enormous violence — it was a thumb better suited to a pirate. Colette laughed and admitted that she was very violent and sometimes wanted to kill, that she preferred knives, with their silent blades, to revolvers with their "absurd noise." When she demonstrated how to hold an imaginary knife, Monnier thought it was fortunate that her violence had gone into writing her books. After lunch they went to Doctor Lamy's for some "*real* prewar coffee." As they walked, passersby recognized Colette. After a pause at a bistro, they reached Marthe's apartment; Colette, who was there for the first time, examined everything with close attention and even caressed some objects, as if integrating the new space into her mental landscape. It was a ritual of hers that had astonished the proper Abbé Mugnier. Introduced to a garden, she would proceed with eagerness — as if it were an urgent task — separating flower petals, crumpling leaves and chewing them, licking poisonous berries or mushrooms, "pondering intensely over everything she had smelled or tasted."[144]

—⟋⟍—

Colette followed her self-imposed rule of working steadily; in the fall she started on a volume of four short stories. The major theme running through *The Cap* is deceit — appearance versus reality, the fine art of fallacy, of occulting the truth. It is, in a way, an illustration of the art of writing; Colette said, "I consider lying as the first duty of the novelist." She told Parinaud that from the very first *Claudine* she knew that to write was to transform reality. "I am not Claudine . . . she is me and she is not me. To lie so well was already the work of a true novelist."[145]

Colette herself is one of the protagonists in three of the short stories, which blend reality and fiction, matching people with imaginary characters. She had mastered this technique in *The Break of Day*, but she had used it skillfully to a lesser degree from the very beginning. In the first short story "The Cap," which gives its name to the volume, Colette brings back Paul Masson, the master deceiver whose memory still held her spellbound. To describe him she uses the words and phrases "camouflage," "his controlled impersonality," "his series of ingenious lies," which she enjoyed "as fantastic tales," and admits that she followed with excitement the verbal contests between Masson and Marcel Schwob, "those two refined and fallacious wits." In "The Cap" love is born from a hoax and dies when an illusion is dispelled. In "The Tender Shoot" the elderly narrator tells Colette how he was mystified by a teenager with whom he had a nightly rendezvous. In "The Green Sealing Wax" ("La Cire verte") deceit leads to madness. Colette intermingles Sido, the captain, and herself at the age of fifteen with fictitious characters. Old Mr. Hervouët is dead, and his will is missing. It was in an envelope sealed with a rare green wax. His young widow produces a will sealed with the uncommon wax. The green wax becomes a metaphor for deceit, for the widow Hervouët had stolen the green wax from Gabri's desk on the false pretense of borrowing some books. When the fabricated will is opened, the handwriting betrays the widow, who, unable to come up with a plausible lie, loses her mind and starts swirling madly, spinning like a dervish, confessing that she poisoned her husband. Sido draws the uncommon conclusion that "mad people should be judged only by mad judges. Yes, judges who could understand how much scheming there is in madness, who would look for that hidden, fraudulent spark of lucidity."[146] And Sido criticizes the widow, not for having poisoned her husband, but for her stupid way of trying to deceive "without genius."

The last story, "Armande," is set in a provincial town much like Châtillon. A doctor just out of medical school and a young heiress have been in love for years, suffering from the illusion that their social status was so different that love between them was impossible. This illusion is suddenly dispelled when a chandelier drops on the young doctor's head. The shock reveals the truth and brings about a happy ending.

As soon as her manuscript was ready, Colette found out how much the times had changed. She had to submit it to "the committee, the syndicate, the thing, the contraption, which decides because of the scarcity of paper, to publish or not to publish." She waited for two weeks; then "a female member of this contrivance" called her on the phone to let her know that she could count on her "benevolence" and that she "hoped" to give her good news soon. "She is twenty-four," seethed Colette. "This is the future Europe. We must say nothing. We must wait." *The Cap* was published the following year by Fayard.

Colette's patience was running out. She avoided her friends: "I am an animal who hides when I feel unworthy of the daylight." She wrote a few potboilers and a program for an exhibition at the Galeries Lafayette. "I am losing oxygen, physically and morally." And she gave the reason for her depressed mood: "Maurice writes to me every day, and I write to him. But so many days go by and I feel so old."[147]

In November of 1942 the Allies landed in North Africa; fearing an invasion of the south of France, the Germans occupied the Free Zone. The hunt for Jews intensified. Since the threat to his life had become the same everywhere, Maurice left Saint-Tropez to return to Paris. He hid for some time with Lecerf, a graphologist whom Colette mentions in *The Evening Star*. He and his wife without other help farmed forty-five acres in the Tarn. After a while Maurice left them and resumed his clandestine trip back home, carrying only a light attaché case. Someone sheltered him for a night; then a milkman on his rounds drove him close to the line, where a German patrol suddenly appeared. Maurice spotted an old peasant on the road, walked quickly up to him, grabbed him by the arm, and acted as if he were a lawyer discussing a sale with a client. The old man understood immediately and played his part; as they talked, the German patrol moved away. In Paris Colette was counting the days: "five months and five days without Maurice."[148]

On December 11 he made it back to Paris. For eighteen months by night Goudeket hid in a garret with a small skylight at the Palais Royal.

It was baking or freezing according to the weather; no one suspected his presence. He had to be especially on his guard for the shopkeeper with a passion for parakeets. He was in collusion with the Germans and tons of food passed through his innocent-looking shop. Colette stayed on good terms with him.

Three times a day Colette and Maurice were "buoyed up with hope" by the BBC, "but how slow all that was! Colette and I huddled even more closely together,"[149] remarked Maurice. And Colette thought, "What is there to do except to keep warm? . . . When will I breathe the odor of the tides and the salty breeze that comes from the west?"[150]

## Oh! It's Too Long and I Am Too Worn Out

January 28, 1943, was Colette's seventieth birthday. Two days later the Vichy government created a militia to fight alongside the Nazis against the French Resistance. In Paris posters announcing the execution of Frenchmen charged with sabotage or attacks against the Germans multiplied. For each German killed, a number of hostages were taken and shot. The British symbol of victory, "v," and the Gaullist emblem, the Cross of Lorraine, blossomed on the walls and in the corridors of the metro.

Maurice was in greater danger than ever. Colette was disheartened: "Oh! It's too long and I am too worn out. I shall be done before It is."[151] Her hip was getting worse, so she tried acupuncture. The specialist, Doctor Soulié de Morant, was also treating Jean Cocteau. Colette's friends, knowing how much she suffered from being confined to her room, circumvented the system to send her flowers. Renée sent her daphnes from Brittany; from Provence she received branches of almond trees in bloom. She was grateful; "I need these flowers, unavailable in Paris, to bear the weather, the waiting, and my work, without sinking." She was writing *Nudité,* "an unbearable little job" for the Mappemonde press in Brussels. She felt "sequestered" and wondered how Maurice, "a good companion, a brave companion, managed to show such serenity."[152]

In March La Galerie Charpentier asked Colette to write a text to be published with aquarelles by Laprade; the volume, *Flowers and Fruit (Flore et Pomone),* turned out to be a celebration of Colette's favorite gardens. She fed on her past. "I own almost everything I have lost, and even my beloved dead." She compared herself to a little horse she once had. One day she was driving her carriage when suddenly the horse had stopped, terrified at the sight of a harrow left in the middle of the road. She had had to turn back, for the little horse, overcome with panic, could not pass by the harrow. Summers later they came to the same spot; the horse stopped and refused to move. "On the empty road he saw so well the ghost of the harrow that in one minute he was drenched with sweat." Colette used the fable of the little horse to explain herself: "I have often been that visionary little horse. It is very difficult for life to dispossess me."[153]

After exploring the world of fruit and flowers, she turned to the animal kingdom with *From the Paw to the Wing (De La Patte à l'Aile)*, published by Correa. Then she wrote another discreetly nostalgic text, *The Photographer's Wife (La Dame du Photographe)*; once more she was the young narrator, reminiscing about "a village surrounded by woods, the autumn rain falling on heaps of apples . . . waiting to be taken to the press." This is one of the rare texts in which Colette looks kindly and with compassion at the apparent emptiness of a housewife's existence. The main character, the photographer's wife, attempts suicide because she has "a petty life" and desperately craves "something grand." She persuades herself that in dying "one has to experience sublime moments." Colette sees her "very petty life" as "feminine greatness . . ."[154] She vindicates the housewife's dreary chores and the invisible net of virtues that support an uneventful, dutiful life. The constant threat of losing Maurice led her to appreciate the peace of a humdrum existence.

As she was searching for a way to protect him, the thought occurred to her that by converting to Catholicism he would be less vulnerable, forgetting that the Nazi persecution was based on race, not on religion as it had been in the Middle Ages. It was a common mistake. According to Renaud de Jouvenel, Claire Boas de Jouvenel, feeling that Bertrand resented her for being Jewish because it put him at great risk, converted to Catholicism. Later Bertrand, too, converted.

Colette turned to the Catholic writer François Mauriac, a crusader always ready to convert his peers. In 1943 there was between Mauriac and Colette what Goudeket calls "a spiritual flirtation." Philosophically, they were as far apart as could be; for Mauriac, physical attraction was sinful, and his novels deal with lust, evil, and the problem of salvation. He was aware of Colette's impact on her readers, which prompted him to try to draw her to his side by proclaiming her writings moral by their very immorality. Colette enjoyed his comments, particularly when he sighed, "Where hasn't she managed to forage again, this big honeybee!"[155]

Mauriac was a charmer; Goudeket watched, fascinated, when he came to visit Colette. Most of the time she reclined on her large sofa bed — "her raft," as she called it — propped up by pillows, wrapped in shawls, a fur blanket thrown over her legs even in summer, her table placed like a bridge over her lap. Mauriac, slim and elegant at fifty-eight, would sit by Colette's "raft," leaning toward her. He had a muffled voice, a voice full of whispers, very special, very mesmerizing, the result of a throat cancer removed at a very young age. Goudeket thought that he would have been more convincing playing the part of the devil, the great seducer, than that of a missionary. Mauriac knew how to lead a mind along the path he chose; soon Colette was reading the Bible and the Epistles of Saint Paul. Colette asked him to find her a prayer book, bound in black leather and stamped with a cross like the one her mother used to have. The next day she received the prayer book she wanted. It had been left with the concierge. She thought Mauriac had sent it, but with the book came a letter from Princess Orbeliani, a deeply religious woman who had mystical visions; she was very ill and about to leave Paris in an ambulance. Before departing she phoned Colette, who asked her why she had sent her this prayer book. Princess Orbeliani replied that four days earlier she had seen Colette in a dream, asking her for that specific prayer book, so she had sent it to her.

A month later a messenger brought Colette a letter from the princess. She had written it as she lay dying, and the last sentence was unfinished; she had placed her pen on her night table and died peacefully. Colette was more impressed by this strange occurrence than by Mauriac's intellectual Catholicism. However, she was not the one to be converted; she wanted him to convert Maurice.

Maurice was ready to do anything to relieve her anxiety, but he knew that his "heterodox idea of God" was not acceptable. He was not opposed to the idea of a conversion to "the Christian Order"; he had long been "searching for a Superior Being." He told Mauriac that he was ready to start his instruction, so Mauriac set up an appointment at the Maison des Jésuites at 17 Rue Monsieur. Goudeket mistook one street for another and went to the Rue Monsieur-le-Prince, to a delapidated building bearing the number "17." He pushed the half-open door; a bell rang. He came face to face with a fat woman, outrageously made-up, wearing dangling earrings. Maurice asked her if Father Fessard lived there. The Jesuit's name was unfortunate, for it meant "Whipper"; the procuress promptly answered, "We have no Father Whipper, but we have a little Mother Whipper." Maurice reported his blunder to Mauriac, who "hissed between his teeth, you are on the right track." He was not. He went to the right address and told the Jesuit priest that "God for him was the highest idea he could conceive of Man, like an ever receding horizon," asking him if it was important to know "if God created Man or Man created God."[156] Father Fessard muttered that adult conversions were difficult, and that Maurice should pray for God's grace. It was a polite but firm dismissal.

In June there was a new production of *Duo* at the Théâtre des Ambassadeurs; Colette was able to attend the first night. Acupuncture was working; "three days of relief dazzled me!"[157] She made the most of it. The producer Robert Bresson drove her to see his latest film, and she was planning to see Moréno in her latest movie when suddenly she came down with an intestinal infection caused by "a protozoan which thrives mainly in South America. It is called trichomoniasis." Colette wondered where she could have caught a tropical disease. For ten weeks she was "truly ill, turning into liquid things which should be solid."[158] Doctor Marthe Lamy wanted to try a new medication "because it was purple." Colette, interested by the theory that "intestinal parasites die from the color purple," remembered that a long time ago she had been told "that in churches with stained-glass windows, the flies never fly in the violet or blue rays of light."[159]

Unable to go out or to write, Colette turned to soothing, repetitious crewelwork. "My rhythmic labor . . ." brought up music — Ravel, Honegger, the songs of French folklore — but beyond the songs, beyond unwelcome thoughts about absent friends, "surges an obsession half a century old," the desire to write; "an idea calls for the help of words." She had imagined that while she was adding stitches, she would be free of the written word, but, "like the trot of two horses harnessed by pairs, the need to work on a tapestry and the literary creation make friends, then part, then come together again."[160]

In the evening Colette played cards with Maurice. Her daughter came from Curemonte to buy a few pairs of shoes on the black market and left with three stoves, instead. There was a string of bad news. Marcel Boulestin's cook had found him dead in his bed. "He must have ended as he lived with no moral or physical pain,"[161] commented Colette. He was an opium smoker who cared only about his own well-being, but he did it with such good humor that everyone felt inclined to indulge him. In October another friend, Jean de Polignac, died, "leaving a wife and a cat, I don't know which one will survive, they loved him so much." A few days later Colette learned that Renée Hamon also had died, at the age of forty-four. Colette turned to Moréno for support: "Thank you for having written to me in those hours when I brood over the memories of beings who died too early . . . don't stop writing to me."

Another death hurt Colette even more deeply. In November Winnaretta, princesse de Polignac, died in London of a heart attack. Maurice did his best to help Colette bear her pain. Whenever she burst out "barking, meowing, and screaming insults,"[162] he would promise that tomorrow would bring good news. To console her, Moréno sent chestnuts from her estate in Touzac, knowing that Colette loved them. She gorged herself to the point of swelling, feeling stifled, her heart compressed. But how she loved chestnuts!

Colette was fighting to keep above the circumstances, morally and physically. On Saturday mornings she would go to the *Pasdeloup* concert with Jean Cocteau. Simone de Beauvoir noticed her, barefoot in her sandals. She could no longer hear the music exactly and perceived an inbalance in the instruments' sound. She decided that she needed a hearing aid. Daniel Dreyfus, the banker, had shown her a new device with a microphone, and she was going out of her way to get one. She asked Germaine Patat to come and not to expect her visits anymore, as it was difficult for her to negotiate stairs. She kept a pair of thick white gloves in her pockets, which she put on to climb the stairs, helping herself with her hands when she was not observed. But because she wanted a sixty-one-year-old farmer who had written a book to receive an award from the Ministère de l'Agriculture, she went, swayed the jury in Joseph Cressot's favor, and listened to "the tactful, ravishing speech of the peasant author. I did not regret the trouble, believe me!"[163] she said, although she caught a cold and a fever from the outing.

Colette started on a story that reflected her mood — *The Sick Child (L'Enfant Malade)* — in which Jean, a ten-year-old, has poliomyelitis. "The child who was expected to die . . ." escapes from his suffering by daydreaming and living in a magical world of shapes and colors. Finally he is cured and, as life takes him back into reality, he falls asleep "consenting, cured and disappointed."[164] Propped up on her "raft" at the window overlooking the Palais Royal garden, Colette worked at *The Sick Child,* which she "dragged for three months." She thought she had finished it but had to return "to her vomit" and rewrote the last page all over again. To celebrate the end of her "nightmare story," Colette was wheeled in a chair to the Comédie Française to see Paul Claudel's *Le Soulier de satin.* The Shakespearean play by the Catholic diplomat-poet-playwright lasted five hours; Colette, to her surprise, enjoyed it.

But few days went by without disturbing news. Pierre Moréno, active in the Resistance, had been denounced by neighbors and arrested. Colette was worried until Tonton, owner of *The Liberty Bar,* sent her a note that read, "Marguerite's emotions are over," meaning that Pierre had been released. "These days are neither safe, nor heartening,"[165] remarked Colette. Misia Sert was attacked in front of her home, coming out of the metro with Christian Berard and her secretary, Boulos. They had been to the opera, and she was wearing her jewels. Three men followed them, knocked Misia to the ground, and tore her earrings right off her ears. While Berard fought off one assailant, Boulos managed to reach the doorbell; the door swung open, lights came on, and the criminals fled. The next morning one of the earrings was found on the sidewalk. Misia called Colette to warn her to be on her guard. The mother of the playwright Claude-André Puget was approached by a man with a gun as she came out of a theater. No one intervened, everyone was scared; the man left with her diamond ring. Pierre Moréno was arrested for the second time by the Vichy government militia; the Germans were intensifying their fight against the *maquisards,* who were attacking German supply lines, then retreating to the mountains. She empathized with Marguerite, "yours is the most difficult part: to wait." Renaud de Jouvenel came with bad news; the militia had requisitioned Castel Novel. Renaud joined the Resistance.

In March the poet Max Jacob was arrested and taken to the camp at Drancy, where he died. He was one of Willy's friends and Colette knew him well; he had converted to Catholicism long before the war, but his friends were unable to have him released. Colette was also worried about the Bloch-Levallois. The Chihuahua lived in Monaco; now it was feared that, under German pressure, Monaco was going to expel its refugees. The Van der Henstes, who had sheltered Maurice, fled from Saint-Tropez "with little money, no home, no furniture, little luggage" and found shelter in maids' rooms just above Colette's apartment. She was appalled by "the dismaying sight" of once-wealthy people who had become "destitute homeless."

Maurice lost his crippled brother; he had long cared and provided for him and his wife. The government demanded that the widow turn in her husband's ration card immediately. Colette was outraged. Upset by these successive tragedies, she pushed herself to walk to Notre Dame des Victoires and lit candles — "There are times when one does not hesitate to intermingle amulets, beads, fetishes and one feels that they blend together without any resistance." She was doing her best to keep Marguerite from agonizing over Pierre's fate. "I tell you the little I know, to keep your mind busy a moment. Paris is crawling with stories, rumors, tragedies."[166] Tonton came with the news that a friendly priest believed there would be an intervention in Pierre Moréno's favor.

In April the Palais Royal shook as the bombs fell on La Chapelle district. There were raids night and day. Electricity was turned off from daybreak to nightfall. Professor Henri Mondor cheered Colette up by having sixty bottles of vintage wine sent to her, and Pierre Moréno was released on May 25, after ninety-nine days in prison. He went straight to Touzac to comfort Marguerite, then left to join the French clandestine forces.

*Paris from My Window* was published in Geneva by Milieu du Monde, *The Tender Shoot and Other Stories* by Les Editions Lumière in Brussels. La Guilde du Livre published *Gigi* in Lausanne.

Everything was dwarfed by the *Débarquement*, D-Day, on the sixth of June. "A noisy night, seven or eight alarms . . . and yesterday, the excitement of this landing. . . ."[167] But June, started in hope, ended in sadness: Missy committed suicide. She had tried to kill herself with a dagger, hara-kiri style, for she wanted to die the samurai's noble death. When this attempt failed, she tried again; this time she asphyxiated herself with a gas stove. She was eighty-one. Sacha Guitry took care of her and saw to it that she had enough to eat. After the publication of *The Pure and the Impure,* she had told Colette that she would see her no more; Colette was vexed that Missy rejected her and treated it as a childish whim. Missy's funeral was held in the Saint Honoré d'Eylau church. The hearse bore the Morny coat of arms; Guitry had taken care of all the arrangements and, with a dozen faithful friends, followed her to her last resting place. Colette wrote to Moréno that Maurice felt pity for Missy, whom he called "this incomplete being." Even to Moréno she did not mention how she herself felt.

From D-Day, June 6, 1944 on, everyone was riveted to the radio, listening to the BBC. Food was becoming even scarcer, the sound of sirens more frequent. Colette sat at her window and listened to the distant explosions; she noted that on the sixth of August the sky was "a ceiling of planes." She was trying another cure, extremely painful injections with foot-long syringes, for she did not want to die "before having seen it all."[168]

The two months following D-Day seemed interminable. Suddenly the Germans began to evacuate their administrative services and Paris grew restless. Handwritten posters were inciting Parisians to rise up against the Germans. On August 17 the French police went on strike. The next day Maurice decided to go through the Tuileries Gardens to the terrace overlooking the Place de la Concorde to see what was happening; he watched as a French police car was blocked by a German one. The French were searched and taken away; then another car full of French policemen veered into the Place de la Concorde and fired a shot towards the Ministère de la Marine. Immediately two Germans mounted a machine gun to defend the building. Maurice forgot all caution and watched as the machine gun opened fire, and a group of German soldiers moved to evacuate the Tuileries, stopping people, demanding to see their identification papers. Maurice could not produce his papers without being arrested, so he rushed into one of the two bomb shelters under the Tuileries. When he heard no more running and shouting, he came out to find the garden gates shut, the Rue de Rivoli barred, and sentries everywhere.

Maurice returned to the shelter, which he shared with an old gardener who lived there in a sort of recess. All day long he heard gunfire and the rumbling of heavy trucks. The gardener went out to pick a few unripe tomatoes from vines he had planted, gave Maurice one, and offered him a chair on which he fell asleep, cold and hungry. The next day the sound of gunfire did not subside; at nightfall, Maurice was offered another green tomato. Then some German soldiers came into the shelter to sleep. All night long Maurice could hear them to his left and his right in the dark, but they were not aware of his presence; they left at daybreak. The Swedish ambassador had negotiated a truce between

Germans and Parisians for a few hours. The sounds of gunfire ceased, and the gardener told Maurice that the Tuilerie gates were unlocked. Maurice sprinted home.

When Colette had not seen him by nine in the morning as usual, she panicked. Her friends, alerted by phone, searched through all the police stations, all the hospitals. At the crack of dawn on the third day, Maurice knocked at the door. Emotionally spent, Colette greeted him "like an angry cat"; then her anguish melted away in tenderness.

During the next few days, Colette, like everyone, followed the advance of the Allied and French troops: "They are at Antony . . . they are on the Châtillon hills . . . they are about to enter Paris . . . they have entered."[169] A French voice on the radio called upon all the priests to ring the church bells. Within minutes Colette heard the bells of Saint Germain l'Auxerrois, Notre Dame des Victoires, and then, at last, as an overwhelming emotion swept through the city, the bells of Notre Dame de Paris were filling the air with the deep sound of resounding bronze.

Now and then the voice of the speaker was covered by the noise of a German tank passing through the narrow Rue des Petits Champs. There were shots that made Colette's glass collection tinkle on the shelves and a louder gunshot that brought down a painting. This was, as Colette called it, "the night that rose like a dawn"; suddenly all the windows sprang open, alive with light and voices singing La Marseillaise; from every window fluttered makeshift tricolor flags. Paris wept, laughed, screamed, and sang; people hugged each other in the streets and danced in a frenzy of happiness. At her window Colette thought, "Happy are they who are beside themselves."[170]

Colette's fear for Maurice was so deeply engrained that on the morning after the Liberation she refused to believe that Paris was truly free and full of French and Allied troops. Maurice tried to convince her, but she replied that only if he brought a Scottish major to lunch would she believe him. There were British troops stationed in front of the Louvre, so Maurice went straight to a Scottish major with a toothbrush moustache and a kilt. He introduced himself, started a conversation, and invited him to lunch. His return was a triumph; Pauline opened a can of American corned beef bought on the black market.

On August 26 General de Gaulle marched down the Champs Elysées. Colette watched the historic parade from the balcony of José and Misia Sert, almost exactly above the shelter where Maurice had been trapped a few days earlier. There were still snipers on the roofs throughout Paris, collaborators who believed in the return of the Germans; suddenly, as the parade swept down the Champs Elysées, gunfire broke out and the windows were shattered. Sert and his guests retreated into the apartment, where the mirrors came crashing down. When the shooting was over, Misia calmly served her guests a feast of cold cuts imported from Spain and vintage French champagne, while steadying herself with shots of heroin.

With Paris liberated and Maurice safe, Colette had her usual reaction after a crisis: "Now I want to eat." She wanted *boeuf à la mode* and herring in white wine; "*merde* for tomato salad and pasta."[171]

But rationing became even stricter. The fall and winter of 1944 were very cold, and the war was not over; it lasted another eight months. Some of Colette's friends who had socialized with the Germans now felt threatened. She was worried about Tonton's fate; black marketeers were being arrested. Coco Chanel, who had had an affair with a German officer, was afraid. Envy and longstanding rivalry prompted denunciations. Maurice, who had been on the side of "the hunted," knew he owed his life to those who could obtain favors from the Germans. In his memoirs he wrote that he and Colette took the defense of "people for whom in our hearts we had little indulgence"[172] against those who were returning from the safety of America or Switzerland, loudly condemning those who had collaborated.

On October 5 Frenchwomen were granted the right to vote. Colette, who years ago had scornfully declared that suffragettes deserved to be locked up in harems, was now proud that Bel-Gazou had been elected mayor of Varetz. Her stepson Renaud had been elected first alderman at Brive. Colette called them her two *maquisards* and bragged about Bel-Gazou's work for the Resistance.

In December *Places* was published by Correa. The Liberation had delayed the publication, but things were returning to normal.

# V

## "AM I NOT A QUEEN?"

*"Colette's life. One scandal after another — then everything
changes and she becomes an idol. She ends her life of music halls,
beauty parlors, old lesbians in an apotheosis of respectability."*
JEAN COCTEAU

SOCIAL LIFE HAD A NEW set of hosts; "In three days,
we have had two meals at the British embassy." Colette found the ambassador, Duff Cooper, and his wife Diana "charming." The "Comus
band," as Diana Cooper called her inner circle, included Jean Cocteau,
his friend, the painter Christian Berard (whom everyone called "Bébé"),
Louise de Vilmorin, Cecil Beaton, the Aurics, and Denise Bourdet. They
often met at the Véfour, where Cocteau held open house. It had been
the favorite café of young Bonaparte, Balzac, and Baudelaire; now, with
Cocteau and Colette, it was enjoying a revival. Sometimes the electricity
failed; when the lights went out, Lady Diana Cooper sent her chauffeur
to the British embassy for twenty candelabra complete with candles. In
the growing euphoria, these social gatherings turned into sophomoric
celebrations; "Let Maurice tell you about yesterday's 'student party,'"
wrote Colette to Moune. Present were the playwright Yves Mirande, a
general, several pretty women, a few officers from the Allied Forces, and
a lawyer, who all happily danced the farandole. To disguise themselves

"they pillaged the high-fashion hats, the furs, the scarves . . . , all that under the leadership of Josephine Baker in her military French uniform. Does it not feel pleasantly like the end of a war?"[2]

The *Epuration* trials, the trials of those suspected of having collaborated with the Germans, had begun. Jean Cocteau had declared that a poet should stay aloof and remain far from the madness of war and politics, but he did attend parties at the Franco-German Institute, where Otto Abetz held receptions for visiting German dignitaries. There was some talk of indicting him, but influential friends prevailed — especially Louis Aragon, who had played an important part in the Resistance. Sacha Guitry was arrested but his trial was dismissed for lack of evidence. Robert Brasillach, thirty-five, was judged, found guilty, and sentenced to die by firing squad; he had openly collaborated with the Nazis, having been on the staff of the pro-German newspaper, *Je Suis Partout*. In 1935 he had written a study, *Colette ou la Sagesse de Sido,* for which she had thanked him, saying, "I expect other pages from you. I believe they will be even better — you go fast! I am happy to see that and give you a very friendly handshake."[3] Brasillach's lawyer, Isorni, started a petition to have the sentence commuted to life in prison; he approached Colette, who refused to sign, saying that she only knew the bright young author; "I do not know the Robert Brasillach of Je Suis Partout." When Isorni reported Colette's answer to his client, Brasillach told him that during the war Colette had phoned him, begging him to intercede on Maurice's behalf when he was in Compiègne, and that he had gone to see her at the Palais Royal; "she knew what I was doing . . . it is better to shrug it off."[4] When Cocteau heard that Colette had refused to sign the petition, he promised to make her change her mind. Even members of the Resistance like Albert Camus had signed the appeal to General de Gaulle, as did Paul Valéry, François Mauriac, and Paul Claudel. Cocteau succeeded, and the next day Isorni received Colette's signature. But the petition was to no avail; on February 6 Brasillach was executed. Drieu La Rochelle blew his brains out in prison. Colette wrote to Lucie Saglio that the *Epuration* trials "were sickening."[5]

Natalie Barney had spent most of the war in Italy; she shared Ezra Pound's views and had adopted the Fascist ideology. When she wanted to return to France, she was refused a *Permis de Séjour;* Colette intervened, and Natalie Barney came back to Paris.

Colette's daughter joined *Fraternité*, a political and literary weekly, as coeditor. She demanded more sanctions against the collaborators and wrote a blazing article, "Indulgence — Thoughts about a Bungled *Epuration*." Colette asked Charles Saglio, "Have you read the article ... of my daughter in *Fraternité*? Listen to the tone of this *Jouvenelle!*"[6] The newly assertive Bel-Gazou had turned into a militant journalist; she went to Germany to report on Dachau. Colette was shocked by what she learned about the camps. In the laconic way she used when she was upset, she wrote to Moréno that her daughter had friends who had been deported to Buchenwald; only one had returned so far, and "in front of a café, place des Ternes, a few survivors 'with expressionless' faces pulled up their skirts to show their scarred legs, devoured to the top of the thighs by the camp dogs." She was shaken, but "shaken or not, I have to work." Ferenczi was back in Paris and wanted a book as soon as possible. Colette had four previously published short stories: "the best of the four is *Gigi* (I caught meningitis trying to find a rare title, you see)."[7]

Colette's elation was shattered by a string of bad news. In January she lost her friend Edouard Bourdet; his death put an end to the prospect of producing *Chéri* at the Comédie Française. On January 27 Charles Maurras, whose review of *Claudine at School* had helped skyrocket the book to fame, was sentenced to life in prison for collaboration. That same day Marguerite d'Escola, a novelist who had contributed stories to *The Thousand and One Mornings (Les Mille et Un Matins)*, sent Colette a note telling her that Hélène Picard was dying. A crippling bone disease had hunched Hélène to the size of a dwarf; Marguerite was the only visitor she admitted. "I would kill myself if Colette walked in," she told her. Hélène's all-blue apartment with its blue vases and blue parakeets was the unreal set of a dreamworld centered around Colette. Her pictures and all her letters were affixed to the wall; it was a shrine dedicated to Colette. They had not seen each other in several years, so Colette immediately sent Hélène a telegram and asked Marguerite d'Escola to come to the Palais Royal, where she was "nailed to her couch by arthritis." D'Escola riveted Colette's attention as she described Hélène's love — "She truly lived with you and drew her life from you." She asked Colette for a letter to cheer Hélène up. Colette picked up a bar of hard chocolate from her table. "She seized it, broke it with her solid teeth — 'Take this piece to her from me.'"[8] It was a sort of mystic communion.

When Marguerite d'Escola arrived at the hospital, Hélène was dead.

On April 26 Lucie Delarue-Mardrus, whose life and career had paralleled Colette's, died. "Try to find two creatures having the same trade, who could even look as much alike as we do, you and I." Colette wondered at Lucie's creativity — "My God! How rich you are, and abundant and diverse!" She complained to her that she had "to sweat blood and ink" to create her characters. When Lucie reproached Colette for using rare words like *anatife,* Colette replied, "My dear creature, if you saw an *Anatife,* you would know you can only compare an *Anatife* to an *Anatife.*" Why not use "barnacle," asked Delarue-Mardrus. Colette enjoyed the argument and added, "I love it when you scold me." They fought over the word *chrysoprase,* over the color *prasin,* "the golden green of the cat's eye." Colette confessed to Lucie that she wished she knew Latin — "how many times in my life have I looked at it 'from the outside' with covetous eyes. Too high! Out of my reach."[9]

After forty years of friendship they were still playing with words. *Bugrane,* for instance, was the name of a flower in Saint-Sauveur. "My Darling, we used to call it like that when I was a child, in my native village." When Lucie learned that Maurice had left Colette for the relative safety of the Free Zone, she sent her a spray of freshly cut syringa and a female puppy. Colette kept the flowers, but returned the puppy, "Thank you, Dear, for treating me royally."

In 1944 Colette sent Lucie a letter, which was to be the last; she had the flu and was reading Lucie's poems. "Your verse, I can feel them, a refreshing reward, the best ... " She thought of Lucie, her brisk steps, her dark eyes. "We owe many visions to illness ... I never see you old or growing old ... I who have celebrated (!) my seventy-first birthday!" Colette added, "Listen, I have put in a short story ... a word only for you, to tease you and make you scold me."[10]

Colette was unanimously elected to the Académie Goncourt on May 2. Three academicians, accused of collaborating, had stopped attending the meetings; a fourth, Jean de La Varende, had resigned. Colette was elected to his *couvert* (table setting). To keep the Académie Goncourt as different as possible from the conservative Académie Française, its founder had limited the number of academicians to ten and had selected the restaurant Drouant, in the Place Gaillon, as their meeting place, specifying that each table setting was to be engraved with the names of the successive members. Colette was elected to the *Premier Couvert*, engraved with "Léon Daudet 1900," "Jean de la Varende 1942," "Colette 1945." Only one woman had been elected before her: Judith Gautier, who had succeeded her father. Colette enjoyed the interviews and photographs. In *The Blue Lantern* she wrote that it was "a very feminine pleasure, to be the only woman at the Goncourt lunches," to be surrounded by "authentic men — age has nothing to do with that,"[11] — Rosny was eighty-six, Descaves eighty-four. To celebrate her election, her colleague André Billy wrote that Colette was "the greatest artist who has ever existed," that she alone could rival "the resplendent pleiad of British and American woman writers."[12] Colette called it "a dazzling paper."

In April Colette and Maurice spent six weeks in the south of France at Simone Berriau's Mauvannes. After five years of war and cold Parisian winters, the balmy climate and relaxed atmosphere were a letdown for Colette, who found herself unable to write for a few days. Still, she enjoyed Simone Berriau's extravagant way of life among the vineyards and olive groves. There were never fewer than sixteen people present. The guest of honor was El Glaoui, pasha of Marrakesh. Every time she went for a ride, Simone brought back unexpected friends. Her diplomacy allowed her to keep supplies on a sumptuous level. She came back from one of her trips with a load of new friends and a live sheep, destined to be the main course at dinner. She owned two cars, which was exceptional; Colette gasped when she bought a third, then a fourth. One night someone hurled a hand grenade in the park. No one was hurt, and Colette commented that the preposterous just happens in certain lives, it is their natural element. While in Mauvannes, she learned that Paul Valéry had died. Charles de Gaulle personally insisted on a state funeral for the philosopher-poet-mathematician. Colette received an official invitation to attend the ceremony; she made fun of it by using it as stationery. On the back of it she wrote: "Bonjour, My Moune, I have received eight reservations for Valéry's funeral. My perfect understanding of savings is to put them to use, as you may see."[13]

Maurice and Simone's companion, Yves Mirande, coauthored a comedy, *Not a Word to the Queen Mother (Pas Un Mot à la Reine-Mère)*, which opened in Paris the following season. Theater was back in Colette's life. Rasimi was planning a new production of *Chéri*. Colette was working on *The Evening Star*, half memories, half diary. It was a new approach to memoirs, one that brought the reader closer to the author in a relaxed and confidential style. She was meandering leisurely through her past, asking herself where she would go next. Would she go "tonight to Martinique" to meet her ancestors, if only in dream? Like the Impressionists of her youth, she was adding little touches here and there to the story of her life. Colette had always refused her publisher's offer to write her memoirs; she did not want, she said, to be burnt at the stake.

In July Colette drew up her last will and testament, designating Maurice Goudeket as her *légataire universel,* her general legatee. She divided her estate between Maurice and her daughter; each was to receive half of the royalties. Maurice was to be her literary executor, his only obligation being to keep Colette's daughter informed of his decisions. Her will specified that Goudeket's share included all her manuscripts and all the books from her personal library, inscribed to her. Foreseeing some opposition from Bel-Gazou, she specified that if her daughter contested the will or Goudeket's administration of her estate, Goudeket was then to receive the full amount of the royalties. The will also stated that if Maurice died before Colette de Jouvenel, Bel-Gazou would have to put the manuscripts and books up for auction and designate them as "The Maurice Goudeket Collection."[14]

Maurice Goudeket thought it was time "to establish the definitive dimension" of Colette's work by publishing her *Oeuvres Complètes.* He created La Société du Fleuron with two associates and started "hunting out and grouping unpublished texts" and collections of chronicles such as *Prisons et Paradis, Journal à Rebours, La Jumelle Noire,* and *En Pays Connu.* He wrote bibliographical notes "sorting out the tangle of successive editions. Colette read and corrected all the texts."[15] For three years they worked, "correcting the proofs under the same lamp." Maurice prevented her from "using her scissors too briskly on her early writings."[16] She made heavy cuts in *Les Heures Longues* and *La Chambre Eclairée,* and refused to include many of her articles. As she went through almost six thousand pages, she would pause and ask, "Have I really written all that, Maurice, is it possible that I have written all that?" and commented, "It's not so badly done, this work, you know!"[17] In the preface Colette wrote that only when all her works had been gathered in a series of identical volumes did she realize exactly what she had accomplished. Her complete works were published in fifteen volumes between 1945 and 1948. Colette was not well known beyond the boundaries of the French-speaking world; Maurice sought out foreign publishers "who would bring out all of Colette's books."[18]

As soon as travel resumed across the Atlantic, the American intelligentsia was back in Paris, and a new public discovered Colette. After a five-year gap, New York was intensely curious about Paris — not only about new Parisian fashions and new couturiers like Dior, but about the culture. Newspaper correspondents fell on everything and everyone.

For some, Sartre, Camus, and de Beauvoir were the rising stars, Existentialism and the Absurd the new ideologies. Others sought a traditional image of France — provincial lore, legendary cuisine, the picturesque life of small villages, all of which could be found under the aegis of *Sido*, in the remembrance of Saint-Sauveur. Love in French society was certainly mirrored in Colette's works; periodicals aimed primarily at a feminine readership, such as *Vogue* and *Harper's Bazaar*, turned to Colette for articles. *Harper's Bazaar* translated and published *Gigi;* this romantic novella, eighty pages long, caught the American public's imagination. It had the charm of a fairy tale about a Cinderella, long ago and far away, in a world of Parisian courtesans and *boulevardiers*.

Attention was focused more and more on the Palais Royal, as it was becoming a "must" to see Colette. The first to come was Lee Miller from *Vogue*, who was surprised by the decrepit entrance, the absence of a doorbell, Pauline's hostile glance, and finally, by Colette herself, her sharp eyes lined with kohl, her furs, her crystal knickknacks. Colette showed her photographs going back to the days of Willy. Lee took pictures of Colette on her sofa, with her desk placed over her lap and her architect's lamp, its bulb covered with a shade made of a sheet of blue writing paper. In one corner stood a small mahogany piano. The bookshelves carried rare editions and some photographs of Sido and Captain Colette, whose medals were prominently displayed in a glass case.

*My Apprenticeships* had given readers the impression that Colette's past was a painful period, one to be forgotten. Cocteau, her daily visitor, was surprised that "she was inexhaustible on the *Claudine* period and seemed unaware of our own time, or gave it no importance." She treated the past as if it were still to be lived, "she was not content with recollections. She compared, pronounced judgment . . . and I have heard her make astonishing remarks about Bayreuth, Mallarmé and Verlaine."[19] In

*The Evening Star* she mentions her "virtuosity in remembering, which I alone do not judge as useless." She speaks of her "favorite paths in the past," of "mental exercise which has to serve her till her end." To remember, "that is my working method."[20]

By 1945 her arthritis had slowly progressed. She refused to take painkillers, even aspirin, because "It changes the color of my thoughts. It makes me gloomy. I would rather suffer cheerfully." She challenged herself: "I want to know just how far I can go." Pain became an object of investigation. She turned this ineradicable companion into the new object of her curiosity, finding in it a new way of magnifying or modifying reality. Paradoxically, pain kept her from thinking of death. "This pain, always young, active, which inspires amazement, anger, rhythm, challenges, this pain which hopes for relief, but does not forsee the end of life, fortunately I have pain."[21] She wrote to Carco, "How strange it is to suffer very much. Note, but keep it to yourself, that I do not believe it is totally useless. But I have not yet well understood how." To write was almost the same as to suffer, "but it is less strange."[22] She equated pain with "the super-feline inclination to challenge or to play." She remembered that as "the last Chatte was dying, she indicated with a paw . . . that a dangling string was still something to play with."[23] In January of 1946 Colette had "rewritten seven times the end"[24] of *The Evening Star,* yet she still worked on it throughout February. She closed this book of memoirs, which she thought was to be her last, with the ominous words, "From here I can see the end of the road."[25]

Maurice urged her to try a new cure in Geneva. She agreed to spend six months in Switzerland, but found the shots, massage, and electric treatment very painful. Lying in bed, she reflected on the meaning of love as she watched the sparrows who flew in through the windows, picked at crumbs on her tray, and perched on her bed, fearing the moment when she would discover "the preferred one." That was the danger: "to be chosen, to choose, to love." Such big words for a sparrow? wondered Colette, but answered herself, there is "no small object in love."[26] After Geneva a cure at Uriage was another disappointment. The pain grew worse and Colette had fainting spells, but for the sake of "poor, well-deserving Maurice," of "Saint Maurice," she managed "a sublime walk across the yard."[27] They left Uriage for Grasse. "The good news is that I am not allowed to work for two months," bragged Colette. Prince Pierre de Monaco came to see her, and they had long talks. While in Grasse, Colette learned that Bertrand de Jouvenel had lost his fourteen-year-old son. "He has another one, three months old, not by the same woman. How they keep up the tradition of disorder, these 'children of the Sultana!'"[28] She could not refrain from a posthumous barb at her long-deceased, philandering husband. In spite of her doctor's recommendation, Colette wrote a short story, "Florie," set in the music hall.

Back in Paris Colette's "bed-raft" was moved to Maurice's room and placed alongside the windows facing south; "Maurice wants me to be warmer this winter."[29] Colette's color was blue, but Maurice liked red; his room was hung with red wallpaper, and the doors and woodwork were white. Colette adopted the color, and soon the whole room turned scarlet: curtains, armchair, and the "raft" itself. The double door was covered with thick red satin. Since the Palais Royal was a historical building, it was forbidden to modify the facade, but Maurice obtained permission from the *Beaux Arts* administration to replace the masonry under the windows with glass so that Colette could see the garden.

Sitting on her "raft," her legs covered with an ermine rug, Colette kept two canes with crooked handles close by, which she used like hooks. In an azure blue porcelain vase on her table-desk she kept her fountain pens (one for correspondence, one to correct proofs, another to write), and a knife with a silver handle that looked like "a scorpion's tail." An ancient edition of Blaise Pascal's *Les Provinciales,* with its text deftly cut out, provided a secret box for a powder puff, rouge, and a comb. A blotting pad, scissors, eyeglasses, a telephone, one or two files, and a red folder had their permanent place on her table. There were shawls or fur wraps under every cushion; when friends came to dinner Colette forced them to wear them, because one should be warm while eating.

By now Colette depended on Maurice's total devotion and Pauline's undivided care. Pauline was thirteen when she entered Colette's service. There was an unexpected medieval flavor to their lady-and-servant relationship; Pauline remained Colette's maid for nearly forty years and, according to Maurice, served her as knights served their ladies in the days of King Arthur and "never had any other horizon than Colette." She supervised everything; she did the shopping, and the cooking when there was no cook; she took care of the pets, traveling with them by train while Colette and Maurice traveled by car. As the years went by she became guardian, nurse, messenger. Colette relied on her "at every moment day and night" and Colette valued her loyalty, treating her with affection and respect. When Colette decided to marry Maurice, she first asked Pauline what she thought, and Pauline gave her opinion: "Well, he isn't bad." She called Pauline "my child" and gave her Sido's jewels.

Every day there was the same ritual. Pauline came in to draw the curtains, Colette's first question was about the weather; she consulted her barometer, the thermometer, and her watch. Then Pauline brought in the breakfast tray with the newspaper and the mail. "Colette split open her croissant with a knife without ever dropping a crumb . . . buttered it slowly and salted the butter."[30] She poured a few drops of milk into her coffee, loaded it with sugar, then dipped her croissant with salted butter into the oversweetened brew. Then she worked, often through most of the night. "I notice less and less the difference between night and day."[31] When Pauline came in the morning, Colette would show her a thick pack of blue paper: "Look, Pauline, this is my work." When she had completed a text she would call Pauline in, hold the manuscript to her heart, and sigh with relief, "I have finished it, Pauline. Ah! I have finished it!" Then a little later she would ask Pauline to take the papers out from the cabinet where she had stored them, throw most of them away, and rewrite them all over again. When the volumes arrived from the printer, the first book was for Pauline, with an affectionate inscription: "To Pauline, my friend, my little one. . . . To Pauline, who for so many years has shown me as much affection as I feel for her."[32]

In November of 1946 Pauline came to Colette with an unexpected request: would she allow her to marry? She had been secretly engaged for several years, but said she would only marry if Colette approved; nothing would change in her daily service. She was forty-five. Colette was Pauline's witness at the town hall for the civil marriage and at the Church of Saint Roch for the religious ceremony; from then on she referred to Pauline's husband as "my son-in-law." He was a big, red-faced, placid fellow, whose sister was a baker in Montmartre. A memorable wedding feast took place in the bakery. In 1946 the restrictions had been lifted, but Paris was far from abundance. The couple's families arrived from Auvergne, Limousin, and Corrèze with a load of victuals that reminded Colette of the weddings in Saint-Sauveur. In the bakery, with its vaulted ceiling and gigantic table placed in front of the blazing oven, Colette enjoyed a gargantuan procession of venison, mutton, fowl prepared with berries, mushrooms, truffles, and chestnuts. The feast was enhanced by regional wines, her appetite whetted by the famous *trou Normand,* a shot of strong Calvados, between the courses. When, after several hours, the banquet was over, Colette, Maurice, and Bel-Gazou retired, leaving the guests to rest before dinner.

Going out became more and more of a problem, as there was no possibility of having an elevator built in the historic Palais Royal. Maurice devised a contraption made of tubes, which he and Pauline affixed to Colette's wheelchair with straps, and two men were hired to carry Colette up and down the narrow stairway. Gradually long journeys by car became too tiring, corridors in trains were too narrow for a wheelchair, and only travel by air remained. A trip required precise planning, beginning in Colette's room: she had to be carried downstairs, and another chair was needed at the airport with two men at one point and four somewhere else. Pauline, who was afraid to fly, took the train, or Julien, the chauffeur drove her to their destination.

International fame brought piles of letters to Colette's table and a tide of autograph seekers to her door; Maurice felt he had to protect her from unwelcome fans and reporters. He screened the visitors and was dubbed "The Great Inquisitor" or, as Bel-Gazou called him, "The Crocodile." Old friends especially resented Maurice's watchfulness. Even Barney and Moréno would phone Pauline to make sure Goudeket was out before attempting a visit to Colette. Natalie, always in the midst of multifarious love affairs, defined her lasting friendship with Colette as a haven against life's tempests and applied to their love the saying, "Love Me Little, Love Me Long."

Fame had its windfalls; the Bibliothèque Nationale mobilized its experts to find a rare book on Scottish tartans she wanted for a tapestry design. In turn, Colette donated *The Muscat Vine (La Treille Muscate),* illustrated by Dunoyer de Segonzac, "to my great and glorious neighbor, la Bibliothèque Nationale that . . . chimes for me the hours of the day and the night." Raymond Oliver, the new chef-owner of Le Véfour, created dishes specially for her; she composed a brochure for the launching of his restaurant. Le Véfour became an annex to Colette's apartment, and she invited her friends there. On such occasions two waiters in white coats were dispatched to carry Colette in her chromium wheelchair mounted on tubes and take her down the Rue de Beaujolais to Le Véfour, like some Oriental princess on her palanquin. All the boutique owners and all the passersby greeted the procession with warm and cheerful remarks; "Madame Colette" was the uncrowned queen of the Palais Royal.

A crowned queen, Elizabeth of Belgium, would climb its steep steps with her arms full of flowers, followed by an attendant laden with honey from the queen's beehives. The dowager queen would sit at the foot of the "raft" to chat; she and Colette had known the same generation of artists and writers. On one of the queen's visits, in March of 1949, Pauline remembered that two waiters had been hired from a catering service, while Pauline was to cook her specialty, a *gigot*. The waiters wanted to serve the leg of lamb on a silver platter, but Pauline strongly objected — the lamb was to be served in the dish in which it had been cooked, or it would lose its aroma. Colette heard the heated discussion and consulted the queen, who agreed with Pauline. The dish was served as it would have been on any French provincial table and Colette carved it herself. Once, as the queen was taking her leave, she said she wanted to give Colette a present she would really like. Colette asked for a case of Kriek-Lambik, a strong beer made from cherries; the queen needed an explanation, for she did not know what it was. "I don't know in what slums of Brussels they were found," recalled Goudeket, but the embassy car "solemnly brought us six bottles of this unmentionable beverage."[33]

In his quest for a new cure, Maurice begged Colette to try one more Swiss doctor. To make the trip more comfortable he drove her in one of the few American cars to be found in France; she was delighted. "The trip in such a car is a dream . . . you hear nothing, you feel nothing, you drive on a cloud." In Geneva the new doctor was awed by his responsibility toward his famous patient; "Dr. Menkes is a fat, dark cherub and he does not like to see me suffer." So eager was he to see her get better that Colette was inclined to lie and exclaim, "Yes! Yes! I am cured." Sometimes she felt like telling him to forget about her arthritis and start up a friendship, "It would be a success greater than the physical cure." She was exhausted by the therapy, suffered dizzy spells, and remained deaf for hours. She dragged herself to the dining room; for Maurice's sake, she kept to her diet of salads, radishes, raw onions, steak, and fruit, saying, "Maurice deserves to be canonized." He was commuting between Geneva and Paris; "How he works so we do not lack money too much!"[34] Colette wrote to Moréno that what she longed for was to rest with her in her country estate, to receive "what children put into the hands of handicapped persons, an empty nest, a flower, a dragonfly." Twice she wrote to her daughter, but had no answer. "This I cannot understand," complained Colette.

In June she suddenly felt better, although she knew she would never walk again. She kept this knowledge to herself because of Maurice, "who takes care of me with such passion that I am almost sad for his sake." Back in Paris, Colette asked Moréno to ship her some of the wine produced on her estate. "It has been so long since I felt on my physical and mental tastebuds, the spirited taste of a merry and witty wine! And what a purple robe!" With Marguerite she frankly vented her frustration: "My d——leg, it's terrible. M——, let's not talk about it." She added a postscript, "Wine? It soothes my many pains and no one forbids me to drink wine."[35]

In spite of her doctor's advice, Maurice drove her to Beaujolais, in the heart of the wine country. "The supreme decision of my best friend,"[36] wrote Colette, created an enchanting experience. They visited the cellars of a prestigious winery carved out of a hillside where, wheeled through endless cellars, Colette watched the wine making. The visit was so elating that Maurice saw it as an antidote; he took her to another winery, to a courtyard covered by a giant wisteria. In the yard, lit up by the car's headlights, forty grape harvesters were about to have their dinner. In *The Blue Lantern* she celebrated the beauty of that night, the magic of the vineyards, the glory of wine.

An association of Lyons' merchants asked Colette to write a promotional brochure to publicize French products; she chose to speak of Madame Marneffe, one of Balzac's characters. Her text was a eulogy of French fashion and taste, of luxury and elegance. The Swiss publisher Mermod found a unique way of tempting her to write a book. Twice a week he sent her a bouquet of different flowers, asking her to describe a flower of her choice whenever she felt like it; the result was *For an Herbal (Pour un Herbier)*, published in October 1948.

She sold the film rights for *The Ripening Seed*. The cinema had only paid casual attention to Colette's works, as neither *The Vagabond* in the twenties nor *Claudine at School* in the thirties had been a success. Then came *Gigi*. Pathé bought the rights to *Gigi*, and in 1948 sold them to a young producer named Jacqueline Audry. Colette wrote the dialogues, and "the film came out obscurely in the provinces."[37] The actress Danielle Delorme was unknown, as was the director, but the movie was a hit. Colette's name drew crowds to the box office. Overnight, producers offered to buy the film rights to Colette's every novel.

Meanwhile, feminists were becoming aware of Colette's status and reclaiming her. Janine Jacoupy produced a semibiographical film directed by Yannick Bellon. The film followed Colette from Saint-Sauveur to the Palais Royal. Colette read some texts and spoke with Jean Cocteau, Maurice, and Pauline. There were plans to broadcast *Chéri;* her first play, *En Camarades,* was published in *Le Monde Illustré Théâtral et Littéraire.* In June of 1948 she recorded five fifteen-minute-long discs in one week.

She spent the summer at Mauvannes. The first morning, to cheer her up, Simone put a live cicada on Colette's breakfast tray. "I examined her, I stroked her, I admired her, she was singing in my hand like a goat." Two sons of the pasha of Marrakesh arrived, followed by a truckload of luggage. For lunch Simone drove her guests through the hills to a village with immense sycamores and ancient fountains to a "magnificent meal." The elder of the two young Arab princes was so pleased that he walked straight into the kitchen and gave the cook a five-thousand-franc tip; the cook screamed out in ecstasy: "Now I can retire straightaway!"[38] Colette was just recuperating in this lively atmosphere, when she learned that Marguerite Moréno was ill. A few days later on July 14, as France was celebrating Bastille Day with fireworks, parades, and street concerts, Marguerite died. Pierre Moréno immediately wrote to Colette, "I am in her room at her desk. She is next to me, lying on her bed . . . our Marguerite died looking at me with love and anguish, a glance I will never forget." Colette wrote back, "Pierre . . . we did not deserve this." He had a word for Colette's and Marguerite's uncommon relationship; he called them "each other's parallel": both androgynes sexually and mentally, both at ease in incestuous love affairs, both having a moral code of their own.

Colette kept stumbling upon Marguerite's absence "and hurting herself." Every time she thought of her, she felt a pang she had never experienced before, something that made her react with a sort of wonder, "Oh dear! Marguerite is dead again." In an article for *Le Figaro* Colette recreated Moréno: the sound of her voice, the music of her diction, the permanent glow of her cigarette, her captivating fragrance, which always moved Colette, who greeted her with a special kiss of welcome on her slender neck, just under the ear. During the "bad nights" of pain Colette "nestled" against her memories. She had lost many friends, "but nothing resembles the shock"[39] of having lost her dear Soul.

Back in her scarlet room, Colette edited a collection of short texts, *Other Animals (Autres Bêtes)*, published by Le Fleuron; *The Blue Lantern* was published by Ferenczi. It was Colette's last extensive work, the last original one, part portraits, part journal, part memoirs. Goudeket was impressed by her decision to stop writing novels — "The fact that after *Gigi* Colette created no more characters was deliberate. 'After seventy,' she said to me, 'the mind loses the necessary force for inventing and sustaining a character to the end. It is time for me to give this up!'"[40] Yet in the last page of *The Blue Lantern* Colette admits, "Humbly, I will still write, for writing only leads to more writing. There is no other destiny for me." She wonders when one really stops writing. "I used to think that writing was like any other work"; the tool is set down, the worker rubs his hands and exclaims, "Finished!" But for the writer there is no end; it is always "to be continued."[41]

In September the cast of *Chéri,* scheduled to open in October at Le Théâtre de la Madeleine, came to rehearse in her room. Colette, enlivened by the actors' presence, modified the text to better suit them. Cocteau attended the rehearsals on stage. She asked him to proofread her new dialogue before she released it.

The version of 1921 had been a success, but the 1949 revival was an event. On opening night Colette suffered from stage fright, "with cold hands and trembling chin." When the last curtain dropped, Jean Cocteau went on stage. He defined the uniqueness of Colette's art: "She belongs to no literary school . . . she has charmed them all." The next day Colette sent him a note, saying, "Dear Jean, yesterday you threw me to the crowd. I was much too moved to say 'thank you.'" She called him "my young brother, who in everything is my elder in a magical way." Whenever she was tempted by laziness, she looked up to that "immaterial young man, who worked constantly as if for sheer pleasure."[42] They did a radio interview together. Cocteau came almost daily and sat at the foot of her "raft." He was impressed by Colette's stoic attitude: "Her courage makes her look quite fit." He noted in his diary, "She prefers this pain to good health,"[43] for it kept Maurice at home. Cocteau realized that Colette could not bear solitude.

In the fall the president of the Académie Goncourt died. According to the seniority rule Roland Dorgeles was to succeed him, but he declined

in favor of Colette, who was unanimously elected. Thus was she acknowledged as the greatest French writer of the day.

Maurice stubbornly took Colette to try another new cure in Monte
Carlo, where a doctor claimed he could successfully treat arthritis with
injections. For five years they returned to Monte Carlo for longer and
longer periods, as the quest for an elusive cure was replaced by the pleasure of a sunny climate. At the Hôtel de Paris she always had the same
ground-floor suite: two bedrooms, a drawing room, a room for Pauline,
and a private garden overlooking the sea. The first time Maurice pushed
her wheelchair into the hall the people who were there spontaneously
rose and bowed. Prince Pierre de Monaco nominated Colette honorary
president of Le Conseil Littéraire de la Principauté de Monaco, which,
like the Académie Goncourt, awarded an annual literary prize. Even
Monsieur Victor, the head bartender, prepared a special drink of barley
water and selected fresh radishes for her every day. Someone smuggled
into Colette's private garden, to which only Goudeket had the key, a
snow-white cat with four kittens; they became the most welcome
denizens in her little kingdom. Léo Marchand arrived to work on a play
based on *The Other One,* and Colette thought it a paradox that she
should be resting while Léo and Maurice were working hard on the dialogues. Maurice was turning into her ghostwriter. For the first time in
her life she was not writing, only wandering through the gardens in her
wheelchair. Young Prince Rainier brought her profusions of flowers
"and excellent candies." But she could not remain idle very long. "I will
have to leap into the work," wrote Colette to Moune, and indeed she
did: "I caught *The Other One* by the tail and cling to the third act." She
worked for seven hours at a stretch, then was glad to have a break when
Jean Cocteau came to visit with his lover Jean Marais. Goudeket left
to spend three days in Paris for the release of the fifteen volumes of
Colette's collected works. He returned to take her home. "Maurice is
equal to Maurice, which is really something." He was now suggesting a
new doctor, "a black doctor, who if I understand, is sent to me from
America." Colette was intrigued. She was so perked up that she worked
on *The Other One* "seven hours and twenty minutes without a stop,"
then was wheeled to dinner with Julien Cain. She was challenging herself with gusto, "As I suffer wildly, I pick the occasion to be cheerful and

friendly for the sake of challenge"; however, she quoted Sido's words, "O hideous old age!"[44]

One of the last witnesses of Colette's life before the *Claudines,* Misia Sert died on October 15. Chanel, Misia's closest friend, had her body placed on Sert's canopied bed and lovingly restored her beauty. When she opened the door to waiting friends, Misia, who had spent her last years dazed by drugs, was as beautiful as in her youth, dressed in white, wearing her jewels, lying on a bed of white flowers, with a pale pink ribbon across her breast and a pale pink rose placed on the ribbon. Colette thought, "Earth knows neither death nor rest . . . everything changes and does not die. . . . Winter has no end, nor has Spring a beginning."[45] To André Billy she said, "I have no fear of my deathbed, even in my imagination."[46] Once in Dauville she casually told Pauline, "I would like to be buried in Le Père Lachaise". No less casually, Pauline answered, "That's a cemetery I don't know." Colette smiled. "You will learn to know it."[47]

When the rehearsals for *The Other One* started at Le Théâtre de la Madeleine, Maurice substituted for Colette. However, for several rehearsals the actors came to Colette's room, where she gave them directions. On opening night, January 23, 1950, there was an endless standing ovation for Colette when the actors announced the author. In February Colette, Maurice, and Pauline headed for Monaco. Goudeket was in charge of an intense correspondence with Anita Loos, who was adapting *Gigi* for Broadway. It was scheduled to open in the fall and there was still no one to play the part of Gigi. Anita Loos and Gilbert Miller were scouring America and England for a very young actress with enough talent to compensate for lack of experience. At the Hôtel de Paris a film crew was shooting *Rendez-Vous à Monte Carlo,* the French title for *The Monte Carlo Baby.* On a particular day the crew was still shooting a sequence at one o'clock, when they should have cleared the hall by lunchtime. Colette arrived in her wheelchair, pushed by Maurice, and stopped to watch "a very charming and very young English girl who was struggling, half in English half in French, under the spotlights." Colette turned to Maurice and said, "There is our Gigi for America." "All right," said Maurice, "I will try to arrange that."[48] That same afternoon he met with Audrey Hepburn. Born in 1929 in Brussels, like Maurice, she was half-Dutch. Her father was an English bank director, her mother a Dutch baroness. During the war her uncle and a cousin were executed by the Nazis, while Audrey suffered from fear and even starvation. After the war she made her film debut in Holland, then moved to London with her mother, where she got the small part that had brought her to Monte Carlo.

Colette perceived the seriousness behind her smile, the sadness in her eyes, the strong will, winning charm, and perfect upbringing of the young actress who was to be the incarnation of the complex and dazzling Gigi. Colette, "with a mere glance and a word, made a star rise in the theatrical firmament." Goudeket immediately cabled Anita Loos that she was not to sign up anyone before meeting the actress chosen by Colette. As Audrey was fluent in French, Colette explained Gigi to her. Throughout her life Hepburn displayed lovingly — in her dressing rooms, in the hotels where she stayed, and in her successive homes — a photograph showing Colette reading *Gigi* with an eloquent gesture of her hand while Audrey listens, her head resting on Colette's shoulder. It was inscribed, "To Audrey Hepburn, the treasure I found on the beach" — Colette.[49]

Under Goudeket's stewardship Colette's financial affairs prospered. In 1949 her royalties for foreign rights amounted to one hundred and twenty-five thousand francs; they reached eight hundred thousand francs in 1952. Le Fleuron not only published Colette's *Oeuvres Complètes,* it also published limited editions for collectors. The company bought the apartment Colette and Maurice rented in the Palais Royal for one million, three hundred thousand francs. Financial order and method had come into her life.

Maurice did everything he could to keep her in good spirits; in August he took her to Versailles to avoid the summer heat, and for two summers he took her to Dauville on the Atlantic, where she could easily move about in her wheelchair, attend ballet performances, and go to the cinema. With unflinching resolve, she kept as mobile as she could, sending out invitations to dinners: "If you are not ashamed of my stretcher, oh let's go to my neighbor, Le Véfour." "Oh, let's return to Le Véfour for lunch! Whenever you want, since you do not blush at my disability,"[50] she wrote to Professor Mondor. She welcomed visitors. Julien Green noted in his journal, ". . . one cannot see her without loving her. Her large eyes are the most beautiful of any woman's eyes I know, beautiful as those of an animal brimming with soul and sadness."

She showed him piles of fans' letters, which would remain unanswered, and some collector's books on ornithology. "Oh these birds, how beautiful they are! Do look . . ." An elderly friend dropped by and spoke excitedly of pornographic literature. When he left, Colette looked pensive, then commented: "Old people are lousy."[51]

Her life never lacked startling occurrences. In the summer of 1951 she was finishing lunch with Maurice and Bel-Gazou when a fire started in the mezzanine below the apartment. To avoid panic, Maurice quietly told Pauline, "Put Madame in the wheelchair, we will take her out, there is a fire downstairs." He put some precious manuscripts in a suitcase and hurried back to Colette, only to find that nothing had been done. His cool had been disastrous; Pauline had not believed him. Raymond Oliver came running from Le Véfour to lend a hand; they unfolded the wheelchair and put Colette into it, but it was too late to carry her out — the stairway was full of smoke. They knew that if the fire reached their floor, the wooden structure of the Palais Royal would go up in flames like a torch; people in the garden urged them to jump out of the windows, screaming, "We can see your floors giving way!" Bel-Gazou, Maurice, Raymond Oliver, and Pauline stared at each other, knowing that Colette could not be lowered through a window; coolly she said, "Anyhow, there is no reason why we should not have our coffee."[52] Coffee was served. The firemen arrived, there were noises of crashing windows and gushing water, and the fire was put out.

In 1952 Colette left for Monte Carlo in January. Cocteau had dinner with her and found her "separated from the world." He watched as Maurice routinely pushed the wheelchair to the bar, then to the dining room. The Gypsy of the orchestra came to play for Colette; he seemed to come from another era, "to form a sort of phantom group with Colette, his violin and the *Gigi* tune."[53]

That summer *Le Figaro* started a referendum on the spelling reform proposed by the government. Colette had just left Monte Carlo for Dauville and the cool Atlantic breezes, where reporters approached her in the hall of the Royal Hotel to learn her reaction to the proposed simplification. She brandished the paper, "No! No! No! I want a picturesque, thorny spelling, for me it is a landscape. Nothing should be taken out, more should be added: consonants, some *y*s, *h*s, all sorts of exaggerations. It is much prettier. You see, I am a partisan of the spelling reform, but the other way round. . . . Do we tire children with spelling? Of course not.

We give them something to hang on to, we must attract them with things that capture the eye and the ear . . . and it entertains them! . . . it is through its difficulties that a word becomes a being . . . I don't want words to be spoiled, to be deprived of their shape and their pride."[54]

In the fall Colette wrote to Kurt Rossner, "don't pity me too much, physical pain is a habit, which the body accepts without too much difficulty." She added that she was trying to work at "the adaptation of a foreign play with my extraordinary husband,"[55] They were adapting Jan de Hartog's *The Bed Canopy*. The Dutch author was unknown, so the three codirectors of the Théâtre de la Micholdière decided to splash a famous name on the poster. They hoped Colette would sign the play. François Perrier went to the Palais Royal to persuade her to agree, knowing that Maurice Goudeket would do most of the work. On his way to the Palais Royal, he thought it ironic that Goudeket was now increasingly Colette's ghostwriter, the way she had been Willy's. Perrier proposed a schedule of writing sessions in her "museum-apartment." She told him to come early, just when Pauline returned from her morning shopping and brought fruit and vegetables to her bed. "This was a great performance," reported Perrier, who watched Colette's masterful showmanship with an actor's eye. She reviewed, in detail, the contents of her maid's basket and found a striking sentence about the color, shape, and texture of each fruit and every vegetable. "At the very gates of death, she still knew how to discover the poetry of an apple or a cauliflower." When the private show was over, Colette produced typed pages with a trembling hand, "There you are. It is ready. I had the scene typed, I think you will be pleased."[56] Perrier respected this innocent lie. But one day, Colette, in her throaty voice, suddenly started to improvise the dialogue, all her talent magnificently present. Perrier could not jot it down fast enough; as soon as he left, he rushed to the first café and scribbled down as fast as he could the words he remembered, trying to faithfully repeat the dazzling dialogue Colette had improvised.

### Hail to Colette!

On January 28, 1953, the Académie Goncourt celebrated their president's eightieth birthday. Two maître d's were dispatched from Drouant with two heavy baskets of fresh oysters, followed by waiters with large silver platters set on warmers and covered with silver domes. Nine academicians, Bel-Gazou, and Maurice crowded into the dining room around Colette; a cake with eighty candles was brought in, and she blew them out. Colette laughed, told stories, and enjoyed the company.

The French press paid homage to "the greatest woman writer since George Sand." Anonymous readers brought gifts to her door. Someone sent her a bottle of Bordeaux dated 1873, "which still kept a little fire, a faded color, a good fragrance of violets." Pauline would not tolerate anyone offering "more beautiful fruit than hers on such a day," but she had to compete with Prince Rainier of Monaco, who sent a basket of fruit and flowers. Goudeket gave her a bracelet; "my best friend circled my wrist with the yellow metal for which I confess my preference." Bel-Gazou brought orchids. Two American admirers, one from the East Coast, one from the West, sent "two of those American parcels that delight the sight as well as the palate." The Académie Goncourt fenced in Colette's "raft" with a full edge of red azaleas. The newspapers celebrated "Our Colette"; she loved that possessive, which made her an "undivided possession" of all the French. She loved the warmth, the "abundance of laughter and tears."[57] She knew she had become a national treasure.

Claude Roy enquired, "Who is a classic for contemporary readers?" There was a consensus: "It is Colette. Indeed she is perhaps the only classic of our time." He gave a modern definition of a classic, different from the traditional one, which deals with humanity in its essence and with permanent values. Colette touched the particular. "She is the writer who receives the most personal messages, her readers address her their confidences, their problems." Claude Roy, who belonged in spirit to "the ME generation," felt that "one always wants to write to Virgil, Cervantes, Stendhal or Proust to know what they would do in our place ... the classics are those from whom one expects practical answers."[58]

There were other definitions of Colette's unique position in twentieth-century French literature. Gérard Bauer, who met her when she was literary editor at Le Matin, remembered, "She used to say to me, 'There are days when you have to write your article about nothing and these are the best.' That is Colette's way, nothing with her becomes everything, in other words, life itself. It is the dog asleep, the cat crossing the garden on its mysterious quest, the flower leaning out of the vase, the aroma of a dish prepared in the kitchen, all blended with the expectation of someone's return, the anxiety of a threatening departure." It is the daily happening, the very stuff of life. Bauer calls her style "her pantheistic grace."[59] Henry de Montherlant explained that there was as much difference between Colette and André Gide as between Saint Simon and Anatole France. "Critics don't know what to do with Colette, because there is nothing to critize, only to admire."[60]

The *New Yorker* of February 7, 1953 joined in with an article:

> To honor the eightieth birthday of France's writing genius, Madame Sidonie Gabrielle Colette, born in Saint-Sauveur-en-Puisaye, Yonne, January 28, 1873 and still writing today in her apartment in the Palais-Royal, literary weeklies here all fêted her with photographs of herself and with the compliments of others that have accrued over her lifetime. Facsimiles of letters addressed to her over the years were printed, among them a typical one from André Gide presenting "praise you certainly did not expect. I, too, am astonished at my writing to you" and a letter from Marcel Proust in his wavering, evasive handwriting: "I wept a little this evening on reading *Mitsou*. Humbly I compare your restaurant scene with those of my Swann, whom you do not yet know." Paul Claudel, Paul Valéry, Francis Carco, Jacques de Lacretelle, André Dunoyer de Segonzac and Pierre Fresnay, along with Rebecca West, Katherine Anne Porter and Rosamund Lehmann contributed praise from near and far. Intimate letters from fifty years ago from Colette's provincial earth-loving mother, the terrestial Sido of *La Naissance du Jour* have been published by the literary weeklies for the first time and also, like a third link in the female line of family sensibility, a paragraph from Colette's daughter, which terminates by quoting Saint Louis the King: "Merci, Mon Dieu, de m'avoir prêté Madame ma Mère" (I thank you, Lord, for having lent me Madame My Mother).

To Curnonsky, also about to turn eighty, Colette wrote, "It is true we are octogenarians . . . swear that you have not forgotten the Rue Jacob." She ended her letter with a pang of nostalgia: "Today you are the only one who belongs to the time of my first novel."[61]

She continued to be showered with honors. The president of the municipal council came to the Palais Royal with La Grande Medaille de la Ville de Paris. On March 30 Colette was promoted to the rank of

Grand Officier de la Légion d'Honneur, the first woman writer to achieve this high distinction. On May 29 Douglas Dillon, the American ambassador, presented Colette with the diploma of the National Institute of Arts and Letters of the United States of America. "If I had legs, or even just one, I would be Queen of the World."[62] Cocteau noted in his diary in the fall of 1952 that the Nobel Prize was to be awarded either to Colette or Sartre, but it went in fact to François Mauriac. Cocteau marveled at her charisma: "She lived as if fame did not exist and fame fell into her trap." He noted that, like Sand, she "had the ability to call the tune and accept life on its own terms." She too abandoned "her androgynous garments." Cocteau asserted that "Colette was the first who was not ashamed of her body . . . the first to model herself on nature and its countless attacks on modesty." Colette's inability to distinguish between good and evil "placed her in a state of innocence," and Cocteau insisted that this was what made her great. He compared her purity to the "terrifying purity of Nature"; and according to him, "she refused nothing of the rich corruption of life." He compared her life to a garden. Films in slow motion have revealed that "a garden engages in fierce struggles, erotic gestures, and murders; if a country priest as he waters his flowers could observe all this at a human tempo, he would take to his heels." He marveled that Colette could maintain a protective cloud around her person, and that she "retired into her cloud like a god who knows more about things than we do."[63]

The film *The Ripening Seed* was released in January 1954; the proceeds of the opening night were to go to the Caisse de Solidarité des Etudiants, a fund for needy students. Colette recorded a message that was broadcast as a prelude to the movie; when her voice came through the loud-speakers, the silent audience was gripped by emotion. If this was a farewell, it was brimming with love for life. She had watched the un-folding of life; it is in the beginning, she said, that the essential drama lies, not in death, which is only a commonplace defeat. What message of wisdom was she to leave to the students? Did they imagine that between their youth and her eighty years there was a heavy load of experience? "Let me reveal to you that experience amounts to nothing."[64] This is what astonished her when she was young, and what astonished her even more now. She declared that no clock ever chimes the hour in which discovery is over; for her the world was new every morning, and this daily new beginning would only stop the day she ceased to live. This was Colette's message to the new generation.

In February *Gigi,* in an adaptation by Goudeket, opened at Le Théâtre des Arts; the director and actors begged him to bring Colette to the first night. But in her recent appearances at the first nights of *Chéri* and *The Other One,* "the whole audience rushed toward her box, followed her to the sidewalk and surrounded her car." She was too weak for such crowds, "glory had become too strong a drink for her." The French televison arranged a conversation "in duplex" between Colette and the academicians of the Académie Goncourt, who were gathered at the theater: "she improvised a few phrases about love and youth . . . all the more moving because of the weariness in her voice."[65]

Bertrand de Jouvenel, now an international celebrity and a prominent philosopher and political economist, came to see her; he handed her a bouquet of *strelizias;* Colette had taught him the name of these flowers during their trip to Algeria. She asked him if he remembered the *Ouled-Naïl,* "the dance of their fingers." She gave him a copy of *The Earthly Paradise,* inscribing it, "To Bertrand, the Earthly Paradise, do I make my meaning clear?" He left very moved. She wrote him a short letter — "So you came back, my boy?" — and asked him to send her some pictures of his home and children, since "I am a little responsible for so many good things." She told him that Maurice was taking her to Monte Carlo; that after that trip "the mirror will tell me if I may call you. But will you still be young enough?"[66]

While they were in Monte Carlo in March, a scandal started in Normandy and spread like brushfire; the clergy had mobilized against the movie *The Ripening Seed.* In one theater the president of the reserve officers' local chapter stood up as soon as the first images appeared on the screen and blew a whistle as loud as he could; twenty priests led a procession of two hundred demonstrators to picket the movie house where the film was being shown. Met by a police squad, they shouted that they wanted the movie suppressed and passed out leaflets that proclaimed "Clean Movies for Our Children," signed "Indignant Fathers." Ten people were arrested in Caen.

The demonstration had been carefully planned; the bishop of Bayeux had instructed his parish pastors to forbid their flocks to see *The Ripening Seed.* In his sermon at Notre Dame de Caen, the priest told his parishioners that not only were they not to go, but they were to express their indignation as strongly as they could. Ten organizations petitioned the mayor, asking him to ban the movie. But the University of Caen students gave it a standing ovation, and Claude Autan-Lara, the movie's director, was cheered. After the show, at midnight, the students demonstrated in the streets in favor of the film. Almost at life's end, Colette was having yet another brush with the Catholics; her novels were on the index of forbidden books. In 1928, Abbé Bethléem had branded Colette's novels as "the excesses of the most scandalous literature, be it the *Claudines* or *The Break of Day*."[67] The Catholic critic Charles Bourdon spoke of "unhealthy seduction . . . of evil conduct," for Colette thrives on evil "like a worm in the mud. . . . Let us stay away from the sewer in which she swims for we could be splattered." The Catholic philosopher Gabriel Marcel wrote, when *Duo* was published, "Nothing but the wretched problems of the bedroom. . . . What makes the atmosphere almost unbearable for me is the author's clear connivance with her characters. . . . There is a book by her called *The Innocent Libertine,* this title sheds its light on everything, the contradiction displayed in the title lies at the heart of all her work and gnaws away at it like a cancer."[68]

In April Colette presided for the last time at the annual meeting of Le Conseil Littéraire de Monaco; André Maurois lunched at the prince's table with Colette. He thought her beautiful eyes seemed to look into another world, but she struggled to show her friends more affection than ever, "like a traveler on a ship moving out of the harbor makes signs scarcely visible to his friends still standing on the quay . . . it was devastating."[69]

Daisy Fellowes invited Colette to lunch with James Lees-Milne, the English historian, who left a portrait of the octogenarian writer. "Under a fuzz of thin, greyish hair, she has an oval, piquant little face, very pretty. Large eyes, expressive, beautiful and mascara'd . . . neatly shaped little nose, plump, expressive hands and two large amethyst rings on her left hand on the little finger and the next." She wore the star of the Légion d'Honneur pinned on a blue coat with gold braid. Although the menu was "exquisite," Colette asked for tea and cheese. "She is very frail and touchingly childlike," commented Lees-Milne. "Yet sharp, she came out with pertinent phrases and rather poetic expressions in a deep

Burgundian voice. Her speech like her style of writing is clipped, economical and exact." He noted that the conversation did not flow easily. Colette "kept interrupting us with little birdlike cries of complaint about the spoon, or the salt, while looking bewildered and muddled. . . . She talked of fish and of the superior intellect of the pike." Then Colette's mind wandered back to her childhood and she said that her mother had a tortoise called Charlotte, which slept through the winter. "There came a day every year when she heard her mother call out, *'Charlotte s'éveille! C'est le printemps!'*" (Charlotte woke up! It is spring!) To Lees-Milne, Colette seemed to be "the ghost from a departed era more idyllic, more earthy even than ours."[70]

Meanwhile, Colette wrote to Moune that she did not write to anyone else, not even to her daughter, "who does not write either," because she now had arthritis in her forearms; "paper is one more thing I have to deprive myself of . . . a writer who can no longer write . . . strange pain."[71]

Maurice took Colette back to Paris early in May. They went for a ride around Paris, and she enjoyed it, bending forward to see better. She would raise her hands "in a gesture of wonder," but returned to her scarlet room tired out. By June Colette no longer read the newspapers Maurice brought her every morning; she did not open her letters. She began to sleep in the daytime. When she woke up, she would lift her watch that struck the hours and the quarters and put it to her ear, consult her barometer and her thermometer, and note the sun's position. She asked Pauline for her cases of butterflies or illustrated books and, with a magnifying glass, looked at insects, birds, and plants. Neither Colette nor Maurice understood "those terrors that man creates for himself concerning his death . . ." nor "that belief in survival which man has worked out for himself; we never decided what was more astonishing, his arrogance or his faintheartedness." Besides, for Colette this would have meant "admitting a fundamental difference between animals and men, which she saw no reason to believe."

Toward the end of July Maurice hired a nurse to help Pauline, who for months had lifted Colette, placed her in her bath, brought her back to her "raft," given her whatever she asked for all day, gotten up three or four times at night, "and remained on the alert at her door . . . Pauline had become the arm one gropes for in the half-shadows." Colette was leaving life without suffering, "like a setting sun . . . at peace with herself and with all that surrounded her." Maurice remembered a page she had written long ago: "If before your last dawn the dust of the world has not sealed your eyes from the marvelous light, if right to the end you have kept in your hand the friendly hand which guides you, lie down smiling, sleep happily, and sleep privileged."

Maurice bought a rare album of colored lithographs of birds, plants, and insects. He sat on the floor next to her and they looked at the album together. The window was open; swallows were flying very close; Maurice leaned his head against Colette, and she bent over him. "She pointed to the boxes of butterflies, . . . to the book and the birds . . ." She was aware of her own weakness and knew that the end was close; she leaned closer to Maurice; "her hands fluttered like wings," in one gesture she showed the butterflies, the album, the birds flying across the garden, and said, "Look, Maurice, look!" She spoke no more, and sank into a slumber. The next day she woke with "a radiant visage," and seemed extremely happy. She was speaking; her lips were forming words, but there was no sound; she lifted up her hands and spoke in absolute silence with an invisible presence. Maurice was convinced that the presence that made her face radiate such happiness was Sido.

Maurice stood next to Pauline and watched Colette as her breath became raucous. This lasted fifteen minutes, then "suddenly there was a silence and Colette's head bent slowly to one side with a movement of infinite grace."[72] It was August 3, Maurice's birthday. He would die in 1977, on Colette's birthday, January 28.

### Scandal to the Last

The government declared that Colette would be given a state funeral. Maurice also wanted a religious ceremony. The parish priest of Saint-Roch refused, and his refusal was upheld by Cardinal Feltin, archbishop of Paris. Colette had never expressed a wish to have a religious funeral, but Maurice was certain she would have approved his request. In a last attempt to sway the church, he asked "if the fervent love given by Colette to all things created did not please the Creator?" The answer was clear — that was beside the point; "if only Colette at the last moment had shown repentance for her sins! Even if from the hall, through a

doorway, a priest could have made the gesture which was required!"
Maurice had to resign himself not to have a cross on the pink and black
granite tomb he erected for her in the Père Lachaise cemetery. The
tomb bears only three words: "Here lies Colette."[73]

Colette was the first woman writer to have a state funeral. George
Sand had been granted the posthumous honors, but her daughter had
refused this tribute to her mother's talent and requested instead a private
religious service in a small chapel. This was authorized by the archdio-
cese, despite the fact that George Sand had been a freethinker. Her liberated life and unorthodox philosophy were overlooked or forgiven. Not
so in Colette's case.

In the garden of the Palais Royal Colette lay in a catafalque draped
with the tricolor billowing in the wind, surrounded by a floral hedge
that stretched across the court. There were wreaths from the prince of
Monaco; the French Parliament; the city of Lyons and its mayor,
Edouard Herriot; a garland of roses with ribbons in the Belgian colors
marked with one name, Elizabeth; a sheaf of lilies from the Association
of the Music Halls; a big country bouquet from her Compatriotes de
Saint-Sauveur; and flowers from the minister of education, the Préfet de
la Seine, the Préfet de Police, the municipal council, the Comédie
Française, the press, the publishers ...

Under the watchful eyes of the police officers controlling the flow of
admirers, six thousand people filed by Colette from 8:15 AM to 10:30 AM;
at 10:30, the gates of the Palais Royal were closed to the public. Facing
the catafalque sat Maurice Goudeket, Colette de Jouvenel, and Pauline.
They were flanked by the members of the Académie Goncourt, La
Société des Gens de Lettres, and other French notables. Because of her
rank in La Légion d'Honneur, Colette was given military honors, and
an honor guard of the Garde Républicaine took up its position.

The minister of education eulogized Colette; he qualified her literature as sensuous, pagan, "dionysiac," "full of rustic health in the midst of
the feverish chills of human misery." He praised Colette for the lesson
that could be gathered from her works. "The miracle of Colette," said
the minister of education, "is that although she seems to describe despair, she is never truly desperate." He concluded, "she avoided darkness
and preferred the blue of vibrant atmosphere, the green of shimmering
foliage, the red of palpitating blood."[74] The minister saw her as deeply
rooted in the French soil, rejecting the philosophical systems and subtle

reasonings that paralyze hope; she made everything simple, he said, with a healthy peasant's common sense. That was Colette's official image.

Other eulogies followed. Then the band of the Garde Républicaine struck up Chopin's slow "Funeral March," and the coffin was loaded onto the hearse and driven to the Père Lachaise cemetery. Some were not happy with the conformity of the whole ceremony. "For this lover of forests, they should have placed the coffin among rocks and tall, dark trees. . . . This woman had a great soul, a chief's soul, she should have left her Palais Royal to the grandiose sound of the Valkyrie's funeral. Only Wagner would have been right to sweep her away in the glory of the *Götterdämmerung*."[75]

Colette had barely been laid to rest when another scandal erupted. After attending the funeral two writers — a Frenchwoman, Edmonde Charles-Roux, and an Irishman, Graham Greene — went to dine together; Graham Greene, a devout Catholic, was furious that the archbishop of Paris had denied Colette a religious funeral. He decided to express his feelings in an open letter. On a corner of the dinner table, he wrote his letter in English, carefully weighing his words, producing a deliberately insolent address to Cardinal Feltin. Edmonde Charles-Roux, who shared Greene's indignation, translated his letter. The following morning it was submitted to another writer, Maurice Druon, who approved it and sent it to *Le Figaro,* which published it on the front page seven days after the funeral. The letter was aggressive:

> In our faith, the deceased are never abandoned. It is the right of every baptized Catholic to be accompanied to the grave by a priest. This right we cannot lose, even by a crime, because no human being is capable of judging another, nor deciding where his sins begin and his merits stop.
>
> But today by your decision, no priest offered public prayers at Colette's funeral . . . are two civil marriages so unforgivable? The lives of certain Saints offer worse examples. . . .
>
> To non-Catholics, it may seem that the Church lacks in charity, the Church refuses its prayers in the time of the greatest need. How differently the Protestant Church treated André Gide after his death! Of course Catholics may esteem that the voice of an Archbishop is not necessarily the voice of the Church, but

many Catholics in France, in England, in America will greatly resent as a personal wound the fact that your Eminence by such a
strict interpretation of the rule seems to deny all hope of the final
intervention of God's Grace, which we depend upon in our last
hour, your Eminence as well as all of us.[76]

The following week *Le Figaro* published Cardinal Feltin's answer:

Sir,
You have forgotten that the Catholic, Apostolic and Roman
church is a Society that, as such, has its rules. You seem not to
know the rule concerning religious funerals.[77]

The archbishop reminded Graham Greene that when a person had
left the church freely and of her own will, the church did not want to
impose its rites on her. In Colette's case, a religious funeral would have
been seen by many as a scandal.

Immediately a bellicose passion seized Greene's partisans as well as
the archbishop's supporters; *Le Figaro* opened its pages to its readers.
Most approved the archbishop's decision and thought that giving
Colette a religious funeral would have been imposing it on her. But
many considered the refusal a lack of Christian charity and declared that
her two divorces and two civil marriages were not enough to deprive
her of a religious funeral. Some argued that Colette's love for God's creation was so great that it was enough to open the gates of Paradise. Some
thought the whole controversy was healthy and useful, since it brought
up the questions of repentance, sin, strict Catholicism, faith, charity, and
freethinking, and brought to light Colette's communion with life
through unrepentant love.

# APPENDIX

## BEYOND COLETTE

COLETTE HAD EXPIRED WITH a serenity that surpassed Maurice's hope for a gentle death. At first, the shock gave him a sort of immunity to pain, as a severe wound temporarily knocks out all feeling; then the pain of absence crept over him. Solitude and loneliness are different; absence, the absence of the essential being, is the worst of miseries. Maurice felt that his life should now be devoted to Colette's works; he supervised the publication of four volumes of her correspondence, encouraged translators, reached out to scholars, welcomed researchers, and helped biographers. Nothing was moved in the Palais Royal apartment; Pauline stayed in Maurice's service.

One year after Colette's death, he started to write the story of their life together. Having finished the volume, he then took steps to have a plaque placed on the Palais Royal façade; he also petitioned to have a street named after her. He was convinced that later he would be buried next to her and entrusted friends with the task of having a few words engraved on the tombstone: "Here her 'best friend' has come to join her."[1]

In 1957 he found out that this was not to be his destiny. During a summer in Biarritz he met an old friend, Lucien Lelong, and his third wife, Sanda, thirty years younger than he. Like Maurice, he was sixty-eight. (The Lelongs had had lunch twice with Colette and Maurice, who noticed that Colette paid a lot of attention to Sanda, but was not very friendly.) Maurice felt an attraction slowly growing between himself and Sanda, and decided to travel in Italy for a while to break the spell. When he came back, Lucien had died. A few months later Maurice and Sanda married. They had a son in 1960, Maurice was seventy-one.

The Palais Royal apartment belonged to Goudeket's company, Le Fleuron; he thought Colette's daughter should live in it, so he rented it to Bel-Gazou.

First and foremost, however, Bel-Gazou was Jouvenel's daughter; she did not live in awe of "The Madonna of the Palais Royal"; she wanted to give all its luster to her father's image — tarnished, according to her, by her resentful and unforgiving mother. In conversation she would recurrently switch to an argument in praise of her father: he was magnificent, generous, a genius in politics, a great diplomat, but, more than anything, she insisted he was a great writer. This was the crucial point of Bel-Gazou's obsession; she had convinced herself that her father was as great a writer as her mother.

Her friend, the writer Michel del Castillo, was driving her home when their taxi passed the spot where Jouvenel had died of a heart attack. Suddenly Bel-Gazou said, "It is not true that my father died in the company of a prostitute in the bushes of the Rue Gabriel."[2] This was a pathetic denial of her mother's vindictive remarks. Natalie Barney thought that Bel-Gazou's "resemblance to the detested father may have put Colette's maternal love to the test."[3] Colette de Jouvenel, feeling inessential to her mother, imitated her father's grand style. She lived in a sumptuous apartment on the Left Bank, whose drawing-room walls were covered with red damask silk. There were imperial sprays of flowers in precious vases; the furniture was imposing and heavy; the paintings on the walls were overwhelmed by elaborate gilt frames; the tables were loaded with valuable period knickknacks. Colette de Jouvenel welcomed her friends dressed in pants and a turtleneck, with a permanent cigarette at the corner of her round, sensuous mouth. She was always filling her guests' glasses faster than necessary, as if to avoid genuine relationships, as if to remain hidden, protected by the museumlike set, the flowing alcohol, the cigarette smoke. When she came to spend a summer with del Castillo and his friends in the ancient rectory they rented on the outskirts of Paris, she filled it with crates of whisky and champagne, flowers by the ton, silk from Dior, perfume from Guérlain.

She lived abroad most of the time. Michel del Castillo remembered her standing on the terrace of her house in Anacapri, Italy, waiting for the woman she loved, who was arriving on the evening *aliscafo*. He thought that she was constantly fleeing a shadow that haunted her; she felt thrown back into nothingness; whatever she tried to do had been done much better by her mother. Why should she raise a pet? Colette had made hers a permanent part of literature. Why should she care for a garden? Colette was the goddess of all gardens. Words? What could Bel-Gazou do with words when her work would be inevitably crushed by her mother's?

She knew that the "Bel-Gazou" in her mother's books was not herself, but a literary creation of an extraordinary child bursting with life, running around barefoot with scars on her knees and bloody elbows, dominating the peasant children around Castel Novel. Early in life Bel-Gazou had found out that tears, sighs, and sweetness were despised; she described how she had lived in fear in the dark halls of Castel Novel, crying every time her parents left, which was most of the time. She grew up feeling that no one wanted her, that she was nowhere in her place, her sexuality denied, her intelligence undervalued.

Cocteau remarked that he always saw mother and daughter calling one another from a distance, as in a loving game of blind man's bluff, or hide-and-seek. Bel-Gazou was caught in a double bind; she was overwhelmed by her admiration for Colette and paralyzed by her resentment. Her frustration found an outlet in what became a *cause célèbre*. She contested Colette's will and filed a lawsuit against Maurice Goudeket: "It took on Homeric proportions. She hired ten, twenty lawyers and stunned them with a flood of letters as witty as they were hairsplitting. Besides, to whom did she not write?"[4] The judge ruled in Colette de Jouvenel's favor. Bel-Gazou won control over her mother's literary legacy; from then on, she alone could authorize a publication or grant access to Colette's manuscripts.

She settled in the Palais Royal, where she complained that she felt disturbing presences and even heard footsteps at night. She began to feel that she had a mission. The money that swelled her bank account as Colette's international fame grew and royalties poured in left her with the feeling that she had not earned it and, maybe, did not deserve it. So she made it her duty to justify such a windfall; she supervised all new editions and adaptations, wanting to become worthy of her mother's greatness, which she now promoted. After a few years she would even pretend to be surprised when a friend reminded her of her previous life. She would say, "Really? Whisky? Nightclubs? Casual love affairs? Well, indeed! How bizarre!"[5]

She began to idealize her mother and reshape her image. Missy? Colette's lesbian love affairs? Her heterosexual love affairs? Her philandering husbands? Her ruthless way of getting even with them in her books? All that was incidental and deprived of reality.

After gaining control of her mother's works, a metamorphosis took place — Colette de Jouvenel became less and less "Jouvenel," more and more "Colette"; she reclaimed her mother to the point of mimicry. She was so concerned with the image of her mother as the Colette of the Palais Royal — a Madonna in a halo of honors worshiped as the incarnation of French culture, a national monument — that she coaxed researchers into submitting their work to her by baiting them with promises of unpublished material. She contended that Colette's great love had been Henry de Jouvenel, that Willy was an old man who abused her, and Goudeket no more than a gigolo. Every essay, every study, every biography concerning her mother had to make her points or was declared worthless or poorly written. She expressed her disappointment loftily in ferocious letters that stunned their recipients. She traveled extensively, made friends from Rome to New York, and kept up an enormous correspondence with dignitaries, artists, and intellectuals.

Mimicking Colette, she was always ready to give out recipes and advice, and she started to grow vegetables and herbs on her estate. She would pick up a famished stray, take it to dinner at a restaurant, feed it foie gras and salmon and, carried away by her sense of righteousness, admonish diners sitting at the next table to give their four-legged companions the best morsels. According to Michel del Castillo, she would go to extremes, plucking the morsel herself from the flabbergasted stranger's plate and feeding it to their pet. If they expressed displeasure, Bel-Gazou simply called them selfish imbeciles.

It was hazardous to invite her out, as an absurd argument could flare up anytime: the white wine was not properly chilled; the crêpe was not *flambée* the way it should be; the omelette was not fluffy. She would graciously impart her imaginary country wisdom to butlers and maîtres d'hôtel. She had developed an expertise in healthy living and spread her newly acquired science around; at last this made her feel like Colette, who, with equal ease, could give the recipe of pot-au-feu or the secrets of cactus-growing. Bel-Gazou enjoyed her vicarious life, adapting her mother's reality to her dream.

At the Bibliothèque Nationale there are a few of Colette's love letters obviously addressed to Missy, but an inexpert pen has drawn lines over the *M*s to turn them into *W*s and the *ss*s have been elongated to look like *ll*s; the name "Missy" has been turned into a clumsy "Willy." The only reasonable guess about these amateurish corrections is that they may have been meant to abolish expressions of love addressed to the marquise de Morny and to turn them into respectable love letters addressed to a husband.

After Maurice Goudeket's death in January of 1977 Sanda Goudeket decided to sell the apartment owned by the Société Le Fleuron, which was now under her administration. She also decided to sell off, at the Hôtel Drouot, Colette's manuscripts and eighty volumes by other authors, all inscribed to Colette, following exactly what Colette had specified in her will: if Goudeket died before Bel-Gazou, all her manuscripts and library were to be auctioned off as "Maurice Goudeket's collection."

The Bibliothèque Nationale, which had the right of preemption on every sale of manuscripts, acquired *The Ripening Seed, The Other One, Looking Backwards, Gigi, For an Herbal,* and the typescript and first galleys of *My Apprenticeships.* Then an agreement with Sanda Goudeket allowed it to buy twenty-six complete and forty-seven fragmentary manuscripts in folders. In 1963 Maurice had already donated the manuscripts of *Claudine Married, Claude and Annie,* and *Retreat from Love* to the Bibliothèque Nationale.

Colette de Jouvenel started a flamboyant campaign — "The widow of my mother's widower wants to sell Colette's apartment." She wrote to Jacques Chirac, then mayor of Paris, and to the minister of culture, asking them "to rescue" not only the apartment but the manuscripts and books from Colette's library, saying, "This amounts to ransacking the apartment and since Paris has given Colette's name to the square near the Palais Royal, Paris should turn her apartment into a museum,"[6] which, in itself, was a judicious request.

In February of 1978 Sanda Goudeket wrote to *Le Figaro* protesting the campaign led by Bel-Gazou and asking why Colette de Jouvenel had sold the lower apartment at 9 Rue de Beaujolais, where her mother had lived for four years, instead of turning it into a "Musée Colette."

Sanda Goudeket remarked that Bel-Gazou did not contest her mother's will in 1954, but attacked it later on the grounds that it deprived her of her inheritance, while receiving fifty percent of the royalties. Now she wanted the apartment to become the "Musée Colette"; if the city of Paris bought it to make it such, "nothing could please me more," protested Sanda. She specified that before auctioning off the books and manuscripts, she had consulted the administration of the Bibliothèque Nationale and had the administrator's full agreement.

Bel-Gazou sent a reply to *Le Figaro,* accusing Sanda Goudeket in insulting terms of trying to make a profit. She protested against an action in "which common profit held more place than the soul's greatness . . . and sales, which offend good taste and feeling." She even questioned her mother's wisdom; according to her, Colette's will was reckless. She blamed Colette's "lack of prudence" for being convinced that Maurice would never remarry. She added that she expected "neither gifts nor restitution" from Sanda Goudeket. As for herself, she said, she would never have "sold" any manuscript or book to the Bibliothèque Nationale, forcefully underlining Madame Goudeket's greedy "commerce." She concluded lyrically: "Oh crime! I have sold the mezzanine apartment! Legitimate children! Keep the mezzanine and leave 'the noble floor' to widows and widowers! . . . A museum in the apartment my mother called a tunnel! But it could not hold one-tenth of the substance of a museum!" And Bel-Gazou ended with a flourish, "If it can satisfy the avenger, let her know I have two books from her sale of October 28."[7]

She appealed to the minister of culture, and *Le Figaro* published his answer. In restrained and polite terms, he reassured Colette de Jouvenel that he understood her concern and had informed the administrations of the university and the Bibliothèque Nationale of the interest presented by the manuscripts that were to be auctioned off. Then Bel-Gazou called upon the president of the Académie Goncourt, where she found more empathy; Hervé Bazin concurred that it was "scandalous" that the second wife of Colette's last husband, a person quite removed from Colette, should inherit what would normally go to Colette's daughter "or to France."[8] He wisely suggested that the writers' guild, the impartial Société des Gens de Lettres, should have control over a writer's literary legacy.

When Colette de Jouvenel died in 1981 her half-brothers inherited the rights to Colette's works. Renaud de Jouvenel died in 1983 and

Bertrand de Jouvenel in 1987, leaving Colette's inheritance to their children. Thus the legacy so carefully made by Colette to Maurice Goudeket, "her best friend," ironically reverted to Henry de Jouvenel's descendants by Claire Boas and Isabelle de Comminges.

# ABBREVIATIONS

*Works frequently cited are referred to by author or abbreviated title after the full citation.*

*Colette.* 3 vols. Paris: Robert Laffont, 1989.
— EACH VOLUME IS REFERRED TO BY ★, ★★, ★★★ FOLLOWED BY THE PAGE NUMBER.
*Colette.* NRF La Pléiade. 3 vols. Paris: Gallimard, 1984–91.
— EACH VOLUME IS REFERRED TO BY PLI, PLII, PLIII FOLLOWED BY THE PAGE NUMBER.
*DV* : Goudeket, Maurice. *La Douceur de vieillir.* Paris: Flammarion, 1955.
*LHP* : ———. *Lettres à Hélène Picard.* Paris: Flammarion, 1958.
*LM* : ———. *Lettres à Marguerite Moréno.* Paris: Flammarion, 1959.
*LMT* : ———. *Lettres à Moune et au Toutounet.* Paris: Des Femmes, 1985.
*LP* : ———. *Lettres à ses pairs.* Paris: Flammarion, 1973.
*LPB* : ———. *Lettres à Annie de Pène et Germaine Beaumont.* Paris: Flammarion, 1995.
*LPC* : ———. *Lettres au Petit Corsaire.* Paris: Flammarion, 1963.
*LV* : ———. *Lettres de la Vagabonde.* Paris: Flammarion, 1961.
*LS* : *Lettres de Sido à sa fille, précédées de Lettres inédites de Colette.* Paris: des Femmes, 1984.
*PC* : Goudeket, Maurice. *Près de Colette,* Paris: Flammarion, 1955.

*Note: Whenever there are several quotes from the same work, the note is indicated at the last quote with all the relevant pages.*

# NOTES

## I — THE DEATH OF A MOTHER

1. *LS,* 440.
2. *LS,* 445.
3. *LS,* 30 July 1912, 446.
4. *LS,* 467.
5. *LV,* to G. Wague, 75–76.
6. *LV,* to Hamel, 81.
7. *LV,* to Hamel, 83.
8. *LV,* note 2.
9. *LV,* to A. Mendelys, 86.

## II — BARONNE DE JOUVENEL

1. Dans la Foule, ★, 1297.
2. Bibliothèque Marguerite Durand, dossier Colette.
3. "L'Ouvroir", *Le Matin,* 19 March 1914.
4. "Les Belles Ecouteuses," ★, 1327.
5. *LV,* to Wague, 87.
6. *LV,* to Hamel, 89.
7. *LV,* to Hamel, 90.
8. Kolb, Philippe. *Correspondance de Marcel Proust* (Paris: Plon, 1980), 12: 337, 353.
9. *L'Entrave,* ★, 1026–28.
10. *Le Petit Niçois,* 10 February 1913.
11. *L'Etoile Vesper,* ★★★, 677.
12. PLII, 324, 372.
13. *L'Etoile Vesper,* ★★★, 675.
14. Ibid., 678.
15. *Impressions d'Italie,* ★, 1243.
16. Gold, Arthur and Robert Fizdale. *Misia* (New York: Knopf, 1980), 151.
17. *LV,* 90.
18. *LV,* to Wague, January 1913.
19. *LV,* to Paul Barlet, 184, to Paul Barlet.
20. *L'Etoile Vesper,* ★★★, 680.

21.   *LV,* to Hamel, 94.
22.   *L'Etoile Vesper,* ★★★, 680.
23.   *LV,* to Hamel, 95.
24.   *L'Etoile Vesper,* ★★★, 680.
25.   *L'Entrave,* ★★, 1132–33.
26.   Ibid., 1066.
27.   Ibid., 1089.
28.   Ibid., 1126.

"*Sigh no more, ladies, sigh no more.*"
Shakespeare. Much Ado About Nothing. Act II, Scene 3.
29.   *LM,* 11 February 1914.
30.   *LM,* 37.
31.   Pozzi, Catherine. *Journal* (Paris: Ed. Ramsay, 1987), 52–53, 74–76.
32.   Ibid., 53.
33.   Ibid., 76.
34.   Musidora. *Mémoires* (Paris: Mercure de France, nd), 72.
35.   Ibid.; *Dossiers Musidora,* Bibliothèque de l'Arsenal.
36.   *L'Entrave,* PLII, ★, 462.
37.   Musidora, 186.
38.   *LV,* to Hamel, 1914.

*World War I*
39.   Moréno, Marguerite. *Souvenirs de ma vie* (Paris: Editions de Flore, 1968), 231–32.
40.   Gold and Fitzdale, 163.
41.   Carrière, J. P. *Mémoires* (Paris: Gallimard, 1985), 183.
42.   Musidora, 188.
43.   Pozzi, 81.
44.   *LV,* III.
45.   *Le Matin,* 2–3 September 1914.
46.   *Les Heures longues,* ★, 1210.
47.   Moréno, 235.
48.   Dormann, Geneviève. *Amoureuse Colette* (Paris: Albin Michel, 1986), 187.
49.   Ibid.
50.   Ibid., 188.
51.   PLI, XXVI; Dormann, 189.
52.   Dormann, 169.
53.   Dormann, 187.
54.   *Les Heures longues,* ★, 1220–21.
55.   Dormann, 188.
56.   Ibid., 187.
57.   Exposition Colette. Bibliothèque Nationale, Catalogue no. 269.
58.   Dormann, 189.
59.   Ibid.
60.   Ibid., 189–190.
61.   *Mitsou,* ★, 1386.

62.  *LV,* to Hamel, 1915.
63.  "Lac de Come," ★, 1270.
64.  Dormann, 190.
65.  *Trois-Six-Neuf,* ★★★, 384.
66.  Ibid., 385–386.
67.  Léautaud, Paul. *Journal Littéraire,* 25 January 1916, Paris, *Mercure de France* 1954–1966.
68.  *LV,* to Hamel, 1916.
69.  Ibid.

#### Cinema
70.  Letter to Annie de Pène *in* Dormann, 188.
71.  *Le Cri,* 9 June 1918.
72.  *Le Figaro,* 5 March 1920.
73.  Virmaux, Alain et Colette. *Colette au cinéma* (Paris: Flammarion, 1975), 11.
74.  Ibid., 10.
75.  Ibid., 55.

#### You See . . . Plus Ça Change
76.  Caradec, François. *Feu Willy* (Paris: Ed. Carrère-Pauvert, 1984), 275.
77.  *Cinéma,* 1 March 1917.
78.  *Comoedia,* 15 January 1911.
79.  *Excelsior,* 20 November 1917.
80.  Caradec, 264.
81.  Ibid., 269.
82.  Apollinaire, Guillaume. *Oeuvres en prose complètes* (Paris: Gallimard, 1991), 921–22.
83.  Musidora, 194.
84.  *LV,* to Hamel, 22 March 1917, 125.
85.  *LV,* to Wague, October 1918, 129.
86.  Ibid.
87.  PLII, XXXII.
88.  Binion, Rudolf. *Defeated Leaders: Caillaux, Jouvenel, Tardieu* (New York: University Press, 1966), 12; Lefèvre, Frédéric, "Une heure avec Henri de Jouvenel," *Les Nouvelles Littéraires,* 24 March 1928.
89.  *LV,* 126.
90.  *LV,* to Wague, 14 July 1918.
91.  *LV,* 14 October 1918.
92.  de Pougy, Liane. *Mes Cahiers bleus* (Paris: Plon, 1977), 109.
93.  *Sido,* ★★, 787.
94.  Chauvière, Claude. *Colette* (Paris: Firmin-Didot, 1931), 25.
95.  Carco, Francis. *Colette mon amie* (Paris: Ed. Rive Gauche, 1955), 11.
96.  Ibid.
97.  *LP,* to Carco, 207.
98.  Ibid., 205.
99.  Ibid., 204.
100.  Carco, 11.

101.   Ibid., 38–39.
102.   Carco, 145.
103.   Carco, 16.
104.   Musidora, 190.
105.   Carco, 116.
106.   Ibid., 109.
107.   Beaumont, Germaine, quoted in Claude Chauvière, 119.
108.   Binion, 135.
109.   Martin du Gard, H. *Les Mémorables* (Paris: Flammarion, 1957), 140.
110.   Ibid.
111.   Chauvière, 121–122.
112.   *LPC,* 1 April 1929.
113.   *LP,* to Hélène Picard, 108–109.
114.   Chauvière, 122.
115.   Ibid., 87.

*The genius who wrote Chéri*
       Proust, *LP,* 40.
116.   *LP,* 38.
117.   *L'Etoile Vesper,* ★★★, 651–52.
118.   *LP,* 40.
119.   PLII, 1550.
120.   Ibid.
121.   de Pierrefeu, Jean. *Le Journal des Débats,* 13 October 1920.
122.   de Jouvenel, Henry. "Pourquoi je suis socialiste," *Revue des Vivants,* Nov–Dec 1935.
123.   Lyon, Lawrence. *The Pomp of Power* (London: Hutchinson, 1922), 175.
124.   Fanges, Jean. "Henry de Jouvenel en Corrèze," *La Revue des Vivants,* Nov–Dec 1935, 1708.
125.   Binion, 135–136.
126.   Willy. Preface in *Ginette la Rêveuse* (Paris: Albin Michel, 1919).
127.   de Pougy, 108–109.
128.   de Jouvenel, Bertrand. *Un Voyageur dans le siècle* (Paris: Laffond, 1979), 291.
129.   *LM,* 4 April 1920.
130.   de Jouvenel, *Un Voyageur,* 57–58.
131.   de Jouvenel, Bertrand. "La vérité sur Chéri," PLII, LV–LVIII; Dormann, 227–228.
132.   "Lettres de Colette à Renaud de Jouvenel," *La Revue de Paris,* December 1966.
133.   *LHP,* 31.
134.   Richardson, Joanna. *Colette* (New York: Franklin Watts, 1986), 86.
135.   *Journal intermittent, Oeuvres complétes.* Edition du Fleuron. (Paris: Flammarion, 1950) 15: 246.
136.   *Aventures quotidiennes,* ★★, 447.
137.   Ibid., 258.
138.   Lefèvre, Frédéric. *Une heure avec Colette* (Paris: NRF., Gallimard, 1927), 133.
139.   Chauvière, 210–12.
140.   Lefèvre, 135.
141.   Chauvière, 3, 65.

142.   Chauvière, 176.

*The perversity of gratifying an adolescent lover does not devastate a woman,*
*quite to the contrary*
La Naissance du Jour, ★★, 593.
143.   LM, 49.
144.   LP, to Proust, 85.
145.   LM, 53.
146.   de Jouvenel. Un Voyageur, 56.
147.   Ibid.
148.   LM, 58.
149.   Ibid., 1921
150.   Larousse Mensuel, April 1921; Nouvelles Revue Française, 1 September 1922.
151.   Les Nouvelles Littéraires, October 1922.
152.   LP, to L. Marchand, 9.
153.   LM, 57.
154.   Savoir, Alfred. Le Journal, 10 December 1921.
155.   Chauvière, 209.
156.   Bonmariage, Sylvain. Willy, Colette et moi (Paris: Charles Frémanger, 1954), 40.
157.   Ibid., 42–44.
158.   Le Voyage Egoiste, PLII, 1096.
159.   LM, 59.

*Colette, Parisian Hostess*
160.   Chauvière, 64.
161.   Ibid., 65.
162.   Painter, George, O. Marcel Proust (Paris: Mercure de France, 1959), 2: 276.
163.   Mugnier, Abbé. Journal (Paris: Mercure de France, 1985), 299.
164.   Ibid., 394, 396, June 21, 1922, 407, July 1, 1922.
165.   LV, 148.
166.   LV, 155.
167.   LV, 152.
168.   Mugnier, 395.
169.   Eliacheff, Boris. Ma carrière autour du monde (Paris: Les Presses de la Cité, 1972), 110–111.
170.   de Diesbach, Ghislain. La Princesse Bibesco (Paris: Perrin, 1986), 324.
171.   Dossier Colette with the permission of the Société des Manuscrits et Autographes français.
172.   Diesbach, 326–27.

*I Am Divorcing*
LV, 171, 6 January 1924.
173.   Ibid.
174.   LV, 171, 6 January 1924.
175.   Colrat, Maurice, quoted in Guitard, Louis. La Petite Histoire, de la IIIe République: Souvenirs de Maurice Colrat (Paris: Les Sept Couleurs, 1959), 111.

176.   *LM*, 80.
177.   *LP,* to Carco.
178.   *LM*, 2 July 1924, 81.
179.   *LM*, 93.
180.   *LM*, 94.
181.   PLII, VIII.
182.   Chauvière, 75, 112.
183.   *Le Journal Littéraire,* April 1925.
184.   Paillet, Léo. *Dans la Ménagerie Littéraire* (Paris: Baudinière, 1925).
185.   Caradec, 296.
186.   Colette interviewd by Alain Parinaud, 1949. Archives Sonores, Institut national de l'audiovisuel, 1991.
187.   *LHP,* 72–73.

## III — FOURIERIST COLETTE

1.   *Comoedia,* 5 May 1925.
2.   LM, 100–110.
3.   LHP, 73.
4.   LM, 114–116.

### Maurice Goudeket
5.   *DV,* 33.
6.   *DV,* 93.
7.   *DV,* 95.
8.   *LM,* 111
9.   La Société des Amis de Colette. *Cahiers Colette* (Paris: Flammarion, 1977) 11: 207–208.
10.   Ibid.
11.   Diesbach, 377.
12.   Ibid.

### The Writer-Actress
13.   *LM*, 120–122.
14.   *LM*, 122.
15.   *Aux Ecoutes,* 15 February 1925.
16.   *LHP,* 76.
17.   *Aux Ecoutes,* 15 February 1925.
18.   Phelps, Robert. *Belles Saisons* (New York: Farrar, Straus and Giroux, 1978) 167.
19.   *LM*, 126.
20.   *LM*, 126.
21.   *LHP,* 80.
22.   *Aux Ecoutes,* 9 December 1925.
23.   *LHP,* 80.
24.   *LHP,* 82.

25.  *LM*, 129.

26.  *LM*, 129.

27.  *Cahiers Colette*, Letters to & from d'Annunzio.

28.  *LM*, 128.

29.  *LM*, 135, The italicized word is in English.

30.  *LP*, to Léo Marchand, 194.

31.  *L'Eventail*, November 6, 1926.

32.  Quoted in Phelps, 125.

*I am heading for my empty house brimming with promises and ambition*
    *LM*, 132.

33.  *LM*, 14 June 1928.

34.  *LM*, 141.

*As a writer Colette is still to be discovered*
    Goudeket, *Près de Colette*, 23.

35.  *PC*, 44.

36.  PLII, letters to G. Patat, quoted by Pichois, XVI.

37.  *LM*, 9 July 1927, 145.

38.  *LM*, 5 January 1928, 154.

39.  *DV*, 105, 117.

40.  *La Naissance du Jour*, ★★, 594.

41.  *LS*, 151.

42.  *La Naissance du Jour*, ★★, 646; *Sido*, ★★, 770.

43.  *La Naissance du Jour*, ★★, 651, 624.

44.  *Sido*, ★★, 774.

45.  *La Naissance du Jour*, 651.

46.  Ibid., 647–48.

47.  Ibid., 589.

48.  Fourier, *O.C.*, 1:72.

49.  *Le Voyage égoiste*, ★★, 152.

50.  *Sido*, ★★, 769.

51.  *La Naissance du Jour*, ★★, 610–11.

52.  *Le Pur et L'Impur*, ★★, 938.

53.  *La Naissance du Jour*, ★★, 588.

54.  *La Maison de Claudine*, ★★, 224.

55.  *Sido*, ★★, 770.

56.  *La Naissance du Jour*, ★★, 646.

57.  Fourier, *O.C.*, 7:228.

58.  *Paysages et Portraits*, 40.

59.  *La Vagabonde*, ★, 898–99.

60.  *Paysages et Portraits*, 41–42.

61.  *La Naissance du Jour*, ★★, 590–91.

62.  Fourier, *O.C.*, 13:622.

63.  *La Femme cachée*, ★★, 391.

64.  *Aventures Quotidiennes*, ★★, 453.

65. *L'Entrave,* ★, 1055.
66. *Claudine s'en va,* ★, 480.
67. Ibid., 591–592.
68. Fourier, *O.C.,* 11:25–28.
69. *Claudine s'en va,* ★, 592.
70. Ibid., ★★, 592.
71. Fourier, *Le Nouveau Monde amoureux,* Paris, Editions Anthropos, 1967, 366; *O.C.,* 7:558–564.
72. *La Naissance du Jour,* ★★, 592.
73. *Le Blé en herbe,* ★★, 336, 339.
74. Ibid., 351.
75. *L'Etoile Vesper,* ★★★, 665.
76. *La Naissance du Jour,* 623–24.
77. Ibid.
78. Ibid., 665.
79. *Chéri,* ★★, 77.
80. "Le Tendron," ★★★, 327; "La Fleur de l'Age," 931–932–933.
81. "Le Tendron," ★★★, 322.
82. *Le Pur et l'Impur,* ★★, 894.
83. *LM,* 81, 90.
84. *LM,* 97.
85. *La Naissance du Jour,* ★★, 598–600.

*I like to look at people at the precise moment when they signify something*
Letter to Renée Hamon, *LPC.*
86. de Cossart, Michael. *The Food of Love* (London: Hamish Hamilton, 1978), 198.
87. Ibid., 156.
88. Tréfusis, Violet. *Don't Look Around* (London: Hutchinson, 1952), 198.
89. Mugnier, 438–39.
90. Mugnier, 481.
91. *PC,* 140.
92. *La Jumelle noire,* ★★★, 1253.
93. "Des deux côtés de la rampe," *Cahiers Colette,* 13:127.
94. Colette. *Oeuvres complétes.* Edition du Fleuron. (Paris: Flammarion, 1950) 13:412.
95. Colette. *Mes Cahiers* (Paris: Aux armes de France, 1941), 414.
96. *LM,* 19.
97. *LP,* 336.
98. *DV,* 123.
99. *La Jumelle noire,* ★★★, 1087.
100. *DV,* 130.
101. Ibid., 129.
102. *L'Etoile Vesper,* ★★★, 651.
103. *Les Nouvelles Littéraires,* January 1929; Le Figaro, 16 April 1929; *Les Annales,* 15 April 1929; *Excelsior,* 10 April 1929.
104. *Les Annales,* 1 December 1928.
105. *La Seconde,* ★★, 728, 745, 748.

106.    Fourier, *O.C.*, 7: 260–71.

107.    *La Seconde,* **, 749, 737.

108.    *Le Pur et l'Impur,* **, 954–955.

109.    PLIII 1581–82.

110.    *PC,* 62.

111.    *LM,* 206.

112.    *PC,* 106.

113.    *LM,* 13 July 1930.

114.    *PC,* 110.

115.    *LP,* to Anna de Noailles, 77.

116.    *LM,* 210–11.

117.    *Dossiers Colette,* to Radcliffe Hall and Una Troubridge, Bibliothèque Nationale.

118.    *La Jumelle noire,* ***, 1183.

119.    *La Revue de Paris,* 14, Colette to Renaud de Jouvenel.

120.    *Aux Ecoutes,* 5 July 1925.

### The Last of Willy

121.    Caradec, 284–85.

122.    Rachilde. *Portraits d'Hommes* (Paris: Mornay, 1929), 36.

123.    Caradec, 306.

### The Pure and the Impure

124.    *Trois-Six-Neuf,* ***, 391.

125.    Ibid., 393.

126.    Ibid., 394.

127.    Audry, Marc. *Chère Colette* (Paris: Plon, 1972), 154.

128.    *Le Blé en herbe,* **, 347.

129.    *Le Pur et l'Impur,* ***, 901.

130.    *La Naissance du Jour,* **, 590.

131.    Fourier, *O.C.*, 6: 157, 7: 2–3.

132.    *PC,* 74.

133.    *Le Pur et l'Impur,* **, 886–87.

134.    "Mes idées sur le roman," Le Figaro, October 1937.

135.    *L'Etoile Vesper,* ***, 670.

136.    *La Naissance du Jour,* **, 583.

137.    Flanner, Janet. Preface to *The Pure and the Impure: A Case Book of Love* (New York: Farrar & Rinehart, 1933); Richardson, Joanna. *Colette* (New York: Franklin Watts, 1984), 218.

138.    *PC,* 74.

139.    Lefèvre, *Une heure avec Colette. Nouvelle Revue Française,* March 27, 1926.

140.    Ibid.

141.    *Les Nouvelles Littéraires,* 28 June 1930.

142.    *La Revue Parisienne,* 25 August 1840, quoted in *Honoré de Balzac: Oeuvres diverses* (Paris: Louis Conard, 1938), 3: 314.

143.    Colette. *Trait pour Trait* (Paris: Le Fleuron, 1949), 238.

144.    *La Naissance du Jour,* **, 601.

145.  Ibid., 610.
146.  *Paysages et Portraits,* ★★★, 43.
147.  Ibid.
148.  Pozzi, 656.
149.  Paul Géraldy, in Beaumont, Germaine et Parinaud, André. *Colette* (Paris: Le Seuil, coll. "Ecrivains de toujours, 1951), 71.
150.  *L'Etoile Vesper,* ★★★, 649.
151.  Ibid., 640.
152.  *La Naissance du Jour,* ★★, 603.
153.  *Claudine en Ménage,* 368.
154.  *Paysages et Portraits,* ★★★, 38.
155.  Fourier, *O.C.,* 6: 47.
156.  *Le Pur et l'Impur,* ★★, 884–86.
157.  *En Pays connu,* ★★★, 987.
158.  Ibid., 988.
159.  Fourier, *O.C.,* 7: 97–98.
160.  Fourier, *O.C.,* 7: 439–445.
161.  *Le Pur et l'Impur,* ★★, 884.
162.  Ibid., 919, 921.
163.  Ibid., 889.
164.  Ibid., 901.
165.  Fourier, *Le Nouveau Monde amoureux,* 272, 285.
166.  *Harmonian Man,* selected writing of Charles Fourier. Edited by Marc Poster (New York: Anchor Book Doubleday, 1971), 222–24.
167.  *LP,* to Saint-John Perse, 398.
168.  *Le Pur et l'Impur,* ★★, 903.
169.  Ibid., 905.
170.  Ibid.
171.  *La Fin de Chéri,* ★★, 528; *Le Blé en herbe,* 343–44.
172.  *Le Pur et l'Impur,* ★★, 911.
173.  Fourier, *O.C.,* 8: 101–104.
174.  *Le Pur et l'Impur,* ★★, 911.
175.  Ibid., 934.
176.  Ibid., 933.
177.  *Paysages et Portraits,* ★★★, 51.
178.  Ibid., 44.
179.  *Le Pur et l'Impur,* ★★, 922.
180.  Ibid., 927.
181.  *LM,* 216, 13 June 1931.
182.  *Le Pur et l'Impur,* ★★, 927–35.
183.  *LP,* 42–43.
184.  *PC,* 26.
185.  *Le Pur et l'Impur,* ★★, 935.
186.  Ibid.
187.  Ibid., 943.
188.  Ibid., 935–36.

189. Ibid., 923.
190. *Le Pur et l'Impur,* **, 963.
191. Fourier, *O.C.*, 7: 386–90.
192. *La Jumelle noire,* ***, 1198.
193. *Bella Vista,* **, 1367.
194. Proust, Marcel. *A la Recherche du Temps perdu.* La Pléiade edition (Paris: Gallimard, 1954), 3: 686.
195. *Le Pur et l'Impur,* **, 955; PLIII, 1581–82.
196. Fourier, *Le Nouveau Monde Amoureux,* 309–329.
197. *La Naissance du Jour,* **, 608.
198. *PC,* 26–27.

## IV — MADAME MAURICE GOUDEKET

1. *PC,* 69–71.
2. *LM,* 12 December 1931, 225.
3. Catalogue Exposition Colette, Bibliothèque Nationale.
4. Malige, Jeanine. *Colette, qui êtes-vous?* (Paris: La Manufacture, 1987), 99.
5. *LMT,* 52.
6. *LHP,* 159–160.
7. *LMT,* 52.
8. Ibid., 75–76.
9. Ibid., 25 July 1933.
10. *LM,* 233.
11. Richardson, 154.
12. Cossard, 196.
13. *LHP,* 165–66.
14. *LHP,* 166.
15. *La Jumelle noire,* ***, 1198.
16. *Duo,* **, 1138–47.
17. Fourier, *O.C.,* 7: 439–44, 97–98.
18. *Duo,* **, 1150–52, 1144, 1184–85.

*He has a charming way of asking: Do you need me?*
*LMT,* 276.

19. *DV,* 121.
20. de Rothschild, Philippe and Joan Littlewood. *The Very Candid Autobiography of Baron Philippe de Rothschild* (New York: Crown, 1984), 110.
21. Malige, 137–141.
22. *PC,* 87.
23. Ibid.
24. Malige, 141.
25. *Le Journal,* 30 May 1935.
26. Virmaux, 219–22.
27. *LP,* to Misz Marchand, August 1935, 241.

28. Ibid.
29. Richardson, 150–51; 159.
30. *LHP,* 8 October 1935.

*But none of his letters ever asked me to turn back*
  *Mes Apprentissages,* ★★, 1271.
31. *Le Pur et l'Impur,* ★★, 906.
32. *Mes Apprentissages,* ★★, 1204.
33. Ibid., 1201.
34. *Aux Ecoutes,* 22 August 1926; PLIII, 987.
35. *Mes Apprentissages,* ★★, 1209.
36. Ibid.
37. PL, Notes, 1041.
38. Ibid.
39. Léautaud, *Journal Littéraire,* vol. XI, 140–141.
40. Ibid.; Caradec, 312.
41. Mugnier, 558.
42. *PC,* 136–137.
43. Colette interview with Parinaud, 1949.
44. Blanquet, Marc. *Le Journal,* 8 February 1936.
45. Ibid.
46. *PC,* 136–37.
47. Gille, Valère. *Discours* (Brussels: Académie Royale de Langue et de Littérature françaises de Belgique, 1936), 7.
48. *Le Matin d'Anvers,* 24 July 1929.
49. *Pourquoi Pas,* 27 March 1936.
50. *LV,* to Misz Marchand, 1936.
51. Renaud de Jouvenel in *La Revue de Paris*; ibid, December 1966.

*Palais Royal*
52. *Close to Colette,* 123–124; *De ma fenêtre,* ★★★, 243.
53. *LPC,* preface, 8–9.
54. *LPC,* 144.
55. *Journal de Renée Hamon,* 6 April 1938; *LPC,* 147.
56. Ibid.
57. *PC,* 237–39.
58. *DV,* 163–165.
59. Del Castillo, Michel. *Cahiers Colette* (Saint-Sauveur-en-Puisaye, 1988), vol. 10: 5–14.
60. *LPC,* 53–54.
61. *LPC,* 55.
62. *PC,* 120–121.
63. *Journal à Rebours,* ★★★, 37; 41–43.
64. *LPC,* 10 November 1938.

*I never thought that the human race would come to this once more*
Colette, to Hélène Picard, *LHP,* September 1939.

65.  *LMT,* 4 July 1939, 149.
66.  *LMT,* 12 February 1940, 193.
67.  *Dossier Colette,* letters to Mlle Bernard-Fleury, Bibliothèque Nationale; *LP,* to Eliane Carco, 240.
68.  *LPC,* 65.
69.  *L'Etoile Vesper,* ★★★, 645–48.
70.  *LP,* 252.
71.  *Le Fanal bleu,* ★★★, 792.
72.  Ibid., 803.
73.  *Oeuvres complètes,* edition du Fleuron, 13: 435–41.
74.  Bonmariage, 243.
75.  *PC,* 59.
76.  *LPC,* 1 June 1939, 71–72.
77.  *PC,* 151.
78.  *LMT,* 162.
79.  *Sido,* ★★, 791.
80.  *LS,* 97, 163.
81.  *LHP,* 201, March 1940.
82.  *LMT,* to Moune, 207.
83.  *Paris-Soir,* 25 May 1938.
84.  *LMT,* to Moune, 58.
85.  *Trait pour Trait,* ★★★, 882–83.
86.  *Journal intermittent,* ★★★, 920–21.
87.  *PC,* 154; Malige, 187.
88.  Malige, 144.
89.  *En Pays connu,* ★★★, 922.
90.  *PC,* 153.
91.  *LMT,* 164.
92.  *LHP,* 200.
93.  *LP,* to Misz Marchand, 274–75.
94.  *LMT,* to Luc Albert Moreau, 181.
95.  *LPC,* to Renée Hamon, 88–89.
96.  *LV,* 274–75.
97.  *PC,* 159.
98.  *LP,* to Léo Marchand, 277
99.  *LMT,* to Moune, 183.
100.  Ibid., 184.
101.  *LP,* to Misz Marchand, 277.
102.  *LP,* to Bourdet, 403–404.
103.  *LP,* to Bourdet, 402.
104.  *PC,* 116.

**Life in Occupied Paris**
105.  *LMT,* to Moune, 191.

106.    Ibid., 190; *LM,* to Moréno, 243.
107.    *LPC,* to Renée Hamon, 100.
108.    *LMT,* to Moune, 203, 206.
109.    Ibid., 207.
110.    Ibid., 223.
111.    *LPC,* to Renée Hamon, 98–100.
112.    *LMT,* to Moune, 193.
113.    Ibid., 200.
114.    Ibid., 195–198.
115.    Ibid., 30 July 1941, 217.

   ***Monsieur, the Germans have come to arrest Monsieur***
        PC, 194.
116.    *PC,* 171–72.
117.    *LHP,* to Hélène Picard, 204.
118.    *PC,* 176; *Cahiers Colette,* "Lettres aux petites fermières." 10: 1988, 15–34.
119.    *PC,* 177.
120.    Ibid.; *LP,* 179–180.
121.    *L'Etoile Vesper,* ★★★, 597–98.
122.    Lottman, Herbert. *Colette* (Paris: Fayard, 1990), 372.
123.    *LM,* to Moréno, 241.
124.    *PC,* 177–80.
125.    *LHP,* 206.
126.    *L'Etoile Vesper,* ★★★, 596. 604.
127.    *LPC,* to Renée Hamon, 112–13.
128.    *L'Etoile Vesper,* ★★★, 602.
129.    *LPC,* to Renée Hamon, 128–129.
130.    *LMT,* to Moune, 227.
131.    *LPC,* to Renée Hamon, 115.
132.    Ibid., 116.
133.    *LMT,* to Moune, 228–29.
134.    *LP,* to Eliane Carco, 243.
135.    *De ma fenêtre,* ★★★, 214, 259–260.
136.    *LP,* to Léon Barthou, 420.
137.    *Gigi,* ★★★, 427, 440.
138.    *LPC,* to Renée Hamon, 121.
139.    Ibid., 119, August 14, 1942.
140.    Ibid., 120.
141.    Ibid., 120–21.
142.    *L'Etoile Vesper,* ★★★, 596.
143.    Monnier, Adrienne. *Les Gazettes d'Adrienne Monnier, 1925–1945* (Paris: Julliard, 1953), 289–293; *PC,* 25–27.
144.    Mugnier, 395.
145.    Colette interview with Parinaud, 1949.
146.    *Le Képi,* ★★, 338, 344.
147.    *LPC,* to Renée Hamon, 121, 6 November 1942.

148.   *LPC,* 29 November 1942, 124.
149.   *LPC,* Goudeket to Hamon, 125.
150.   *LPC,* to Renée Hamon, 125.

> *Oh it's too long and I am too worn out*
> *PC,* 175.

151.   *PC,* 175.
152.   *LPC,* to Renée Hamon, 126.
153.   *Flore et Pomone,* ★★★, 462.
154.   *La Dame du photographe,* ★★★, 492.
155.   *PC,* 169–170; *LM,* to Pierre Moréno, 247.
156.   *PC,* 172.
157.   *LM,* to Moréno, 249–250.
158.   *LPC,* to Renée Hamon, 143.
159.   *LM,* 261.
160.   *Belles Saisons,* ★★★, 548.
161.   *LM,* 21 September 1943, 254.
162.   *LM,* 258–59.
163.   *LM,* 261.
164.   *L'Enfant malade,* ★★★, 513.
165.   *LM,* 266.
166.   *LM,* 273, 270, 274.
167.   *LM,* 287.
168.   *DV,* 213.
169.   *L'Etoile Vesper,* ★★★, 601.
170.   Ibid.
171.   *LM,* 295.
172.   *DV,* 215.

## V — AM I NOT A QUEEN?

Cocteau, Jean. *Le Passé défini* (Paris: Gallimard, 1985), 2: 42.
1.    *LMT,* to Moune, 246–47, March 1945.
2.    Ibid., 247.
3.    *LP,* 376.
4.    Isorni, Jacques. *Le Procés de Brasillach* (Paris: Flammarion, 1946), 167; Isorni, Jacques. *Mémoires* (Paris, Flammarion, 1946), 285–286, 308–309.
5.    *LP,* to Lucie Saglio, 138.
6.    Ibid., 139.
7.    *LM,* 304.
8.    *LHP,* 249, 216–19.
9.    *LP,* to Lucie Delarue-Mardrus, 169, 176–77.
10.   Ibid., 182.
11.   *Le Fanal bleu,* ★★★, 799.
12.   *LP,* to de Billy, 197.

13. *LMT,* to Moune, 255–56.
14. Lottman, 396–97.
15. *PC,* 209–10; *DV,* 179–80.
16. 180.
17. Goudeket, in preface, *Oeuvres complètes,* edition du Fleuron, 6–7.
18. *PC,* 212.
19. Cocteau, 49.
20. *L'Etoile Vesper,* ★★★, 593.
21. *Le Fanal bleu,* ★★★, 729.
22. *LP,* 262.
23. *Le Fanal bleu,* ★★★, 730.
24. *LM,* 312.
25. *L'Etoile Vesper,* ★★★, 684.
26. *Le Fanal bleu,* ★★★, 731, 736.
27. *LM,* 313; *LMT,* 268.
28. *LM,* 315.
29. *LMT,* 275.
30. *PC,* 76.
31. *Le Fanal bleu,* ★★★, 752–753.
32. Védrine, Pauline. "10 ans de Souvenirs," Fonds Colette, Médiathèque de la ville de Nantes.
33. Goudeket, 236.
34. *LMT,* to Moune, 283–284.
35. *LM,* 323, 334, November 1947.
36. *Le Fanal bleu,* ★★★, 747.
37. *PC,* 37.
38. *LMT,* to Moune, 298–304.
39. *LM,* 344–345, 353.
40. *PC,* 215, 193.
41. *Le Fanal bleu,* ★★★, 805.
42. *LP,* 442, to Cocteau, October 1949.
43. Cocteau, 279, 364.
44. *LMT,* to Moune, 322–30.
45. *Belles Saisons,* ★★★, 521–23.
46. *LP,* to Billy, May 1950, 201.
47. *Dossier Pauline Védrine,* Nantes.
48. *PC,* 221.
49. *PC,* 222; LMT, to Moune, 345.
50. *LP,* to Professor H. Mondor, 394–95.
51. Green, Julien. *Journal* (Paris, Gallimard, Coll. La Pléiade, 4 December 1951), 2: 983.
52. *PC,* 230.
53. Cocteau, 166.
54. *Le Figaro Littéraire,* 2 August 1952.
55. *LP,* to Kurt Rossner, 368.
56. Perrier, François. *Profession menteur* (Paris: Le Pré aux Clercs, 1990), 202–203.

*Hail to Colette!*

57. *Le Fanal bleu,* ★★★, 759.
58. Roy, Claude. "Classique Colette," *Le Point,* 34 (1951): 25.
59. Bauer, quoted in Richardson, 215.
60. Montherlant, Henri. *Carnets 1930–1944* (Paris: Gallimard, 1957).
61. *LP,* to Curnonsky, 444.
62. *LMT,* to Moune, February 1953, 371.
63. Cocteau, 134–136, 163.
64. *Le Figaro,* 20 January 1954.
65. *PC,* 240–41.
66. *LS,* 23.
67. Bethléem, Abbé. "Romans à lire et à proscrire," *Revue des Lectures,* 1928, 103.
68. Trahard, Pierre. *L'Art de Colette* (Geneva: Slatkine Reprints, 1971), 104.
69. Maurois, André. *Mémoires, 1885–1967* (Paris: Flammarion, 1948), 382.
70. Richardson, 224–25.
71. *LMT,* to Moune, 1 March 1954, 379–80.
72. *PC,* 238, 242.

*Scandal to the Last*

73. Ibid., 243–45.
74. Druon, Maurice. "Autant que son oeuvre son destin est admirable," *Les Lettres Françaises,* 12–17 August 1954; and *Le Figaro, Le Monde, Paris-Match, Paris-Soir l'Instransigeant* on Colette's death, August 1954.
75. Thétard, Henry. La Revue des Deux Mondes 17 (Sept–Oct 1954).
76. Greene, Graham, "A propos des obsèques de Colette," *Le Figaro Littéraire,* 14 August 1954; *Carrefour,* 18 August 1954, 1, 5.
77. *Le Figaro Littéraire,* 21 August 1954, 1, 5, 8; Tesson, R. P. Eugène. "L'Eglise et le refus de funérailles religieuses," *Revue de Paris,* October 1954, 108–12.

## APPENDIX — BEYOND COLETTE

1. *DV,* 193.
2. Del Castillo, 10: 5–14.
3. Barney, Natalie, *Souvenirs Indiscrets,* Paris, Flammarion, 1960, 194.
4. Del Castillo, *Cahiers Colette,* 10:8.
5. Ibid., 10.
6. *Le Monde,* 22 October 1977.
7. *Le Figaro,* 5 February 1978.
8. Ibid.

# SELECT BIBLIOGRAPHY

Andry, Marc. *Chère Colette*. Paris: Plon, 1984.

Apollinaire, Guillaume. *Oeuvres en prose complètes*. Paris: Gallimard, 1991.

Barney, Natalie. *Souvenirs Indiscrets*. Paris: Flammarion, 1960.

Binion, Rudolf. *Defeated Leaders: Caillaux, Jouvenel, Tardieu*. New York: University Press, 1966.

Bonmariage, Sylvain. *Willy, Colette et moi*. Paris: Charles Frémanger, 1954.

Caradec, François. *Feu Willy*. Paris: Ed. Carrère-Pauvert, 1984.

Carco, Francis. *Colette mon ami*. Paris: Ed. Rive Gauche, 1965.

Carrière, J. P. *Mémoires*. Paris: Gallimard, 1985.

Catalogue Exposition Colette, Bibliothèque Nationale.

Chauvière, Claude. *Colette*. Paris: Firmin-Didot, 1931.

Cocteau, Jean. *Le Passé défini*. Paris: Gallimard, 1985.

Colette, Sidonie-Gabrielle interviewed by Alain Parinaud, 1949. Archives Sonores, Institut national de l'audiovisuel, 1991.

Colette. *Lettres à Annie de Pène et Germaine Beaumont*. Paris: Flammarion, 1995.

———. *Lettres à Hélène Picard*. Paris: Flammarion, 1958.

———. *Lettres à Marguerite Moréno*. Paris: Flammarion, 1959.

———. *Lettres à Moune et au Toutounet*. Paris: Des Femmes, 1985.

———. *Lettres à ses pairs*. Paris: Flammarion, 1973.

———. *Lettres au Petit Corsaire*. Paris: Flammarion, 1963.

———. *Lettres de la Vagabonde*. Paris: Flammarion, 1961.

———. *Mes Cahiers*. Paris: Aux armes de France, 1941.

———. *Oeuvres complètes*. Edition du Fleuron. 15 vols. Paris: Flammarion, 1948–50.

de Cossart, Michael. *The Food of Love*. London: Hamish Hamilton, 1978.

Del Castillo, Michel. *Cahiers Colette*. Saint-Sauveur-en-Puisaye, 1988.

de Diesbach, Ghislain. *La Princesse Bibesco*. Paris: Perrin, 1986.

Dormann, Geneviève. *Amoureuse Colette*. Paris: Albin Michel, 1986.

*Dossier Colette Willy*, Bibliothéque Nationale, Paris.

*Dossier Colette*, Bibliothèque Marguerite Durand.

*Dossiers Colette*, Bibliothéque Nationale, Paris.

*Dossiers Colette*, Bibliothèque Royale de Belgique.

*Dossiers Musidora*, Bibliothèque de l'Arsenal, Paris.

*Dossiers Renée Hamon*, Bibliothèque Nationale, MSNAF 18711.

Eliacheff, Boris. *Ma carrière autour du monde*. Paris: Les Presses de la Cité, 1972.

Exposition Colette. Bibliothèque Nationale, 1973.

Flanner, Janet. Preface to *The Pure and the Impure: A Case Book of Love*. New York: Farrar & Rinehart, 1933.

Fourier, Charles. *Oeuvres complétes*. xx vols. Paris: Editions Antrhopos, 1966.

Gold, Arthur and Robert Fizdale. *Misia*. New York: Knopf, 1980.

Goudeket, Maurice. *La Douceur de vieillir*. Paris: Flammarion, 1955.

———. *Près de Colette*. Paris: Flammarion, 1955.

Guitard, Louis. *La Petite Histoire, de la IIIe République: Souvenirs de Maurice Colrat*. Paris: Les Sept Couleurs, 1959.

de Jouvenel, Bertrand. *Un Voyageur dans le siècle*. Paris: Laffond, 1979.

Landoy, Adèle Sidonie. Lettres de Sido à sa fille, précédées de Lettres inédites de Colette. Paris: des Femmes, 1984.

Léautaud, Paul. *Journal Littéraire* (Paris, Mercure de France 1916), 1954–66.

Lefèvre, Frédéric. *Une heure avec Colette*. Paris: NRF, Gallimard, 1927.

Lottman, Herbert. *Colette*. Paris: Fayard, 1990.

Lyon, Lawrence. *The Pomp of Power*. London: Hutchinson, 1922.

Malige, Jeanine. *Colette, qui êtes-vous?* Paris: La Manufacture, 1987.

Martin du Gard, H. *Les Mémorables*. Paris: Flammarion, 1957.

Maurois, André. *Mémoires, 1885–1967*. Paris: Flammarion, 1948.

Monnier, Adrienne. *Les Gazettes d'Adrienne Monnier, 1925–1945*. Paris: Julliard, 1953.

Montherlant, Henri. *Carnets, 1930–1944*. Paris: Gallimard, 1957.

Moréno, Marguerite. *Souvenirs de ma vie*. Paris: Editions de Flore, 1948.

Mugnier, Abbé. *Journal*. Paris: Mercure de France, 1985.

Musidora. *Mémoires*. Paris: Meraire de France.

Paillet, Léo. *Dans la Ménagerie Littéraire*. Paris: Baudière, 1925.

Painter, George O. *Marcel Proust*. Paris: Mercure de France, 1959.

Perrier, François. *Profession menteur*. Paris: Le Pré aux Clercs, 1990.

Phelps, Robert. *Belles Saisons*. New York: Farrar, Straus and Giroux, 1978.

de Pougy, Liane. *Mes Cahiers bleus*. Paris: Plon, 1977.

Pozzi, Catherine. *Journal*. Paris: Ed. Ramsay, 1987.

Proust, Marcel. *A la Recherche du Temps perdu*. Paris: Gallimard, 1954.

Kolb, Philippe. *Correspondance de Marcel Proust*. Paris: Plon, 1980.

Rachilde. *Portraits d'Hommes*. Paris: Mornay, 1929.

Richardson, Joanna. *Colette*. New York: Franklin Watts, 1986.

de Rothschild, Philippe, and Joan Littlewood. *The Very Candid Autobiography of Baron Philippe de Rothschild*. New York: Crown, 1984.

Trahard, Pierre. *L'Art de Colette*. Geneva: Slatkine Reprints, 1971.

Tréfusis, Violet. *Don't Look Around*. London: Hutchinson, 1952.

Virmaux, Alain et Colette. *Colette au cinéma*. Paris: Flammarion, 1975.

# ACKNOWLEDGMENTS

$W$E ARE ESPECIALLY INDEBTED to the archivists and librarians without whose full cooperation this book could not have been written. We have received valuable assistance as we consulted in France:

les Archives de la Ville de Paris, les Archives de la Ville du Havre, le Minutier central des notaires de Paris, les Archives nationales: Etats généraux des Fonds: Marine et Outre-Mer, les Archives des ports: état civil des gens de couleur, les Archives juridiques de la Ville de Versailles, les Archives du Rectorat de Paris, les Archives de la Gironde, les Archives départementales de l'Yonne, la bibliothèque de l'Arsenal, la bibliothèque de l'Opéra, le musée de la Légion d'Honneur.

In Belgium:

les Archives de la Ville de Bruxelles, les Archives notariales de la province de Brabant, la Bibliothèque royale de Belgique, les services démographiques.

In the United States:

the libraries of the University of California at Los Angeles, the University of Texas-Austin, and Princeton University.

We most gratefully acknowledge the assistance of Claude Giraud, la Société des manuscrits et autographes français; Frans de Haes and Madame Grunhard, Musée de la Littérature, Brussels; Hubert Collin, Archives départementales et communales de Charleville; Michèle Le Pavec, curator of the département des manuscrits de la Bibliothèque Nationale; Marguerite Boivin, secretary of the Bibliothèque des Amis de Colette à Saint-Sauveur, and Agnès Marcetteau, archivist-paleologist of the Médiathèque de la Ville de Nantes.

We wish to thank Gladys Fowler-Dixon and Roger Fowler-Dixon for their unstinting help over the past years.

We are grateful for the steadfast support of Steerforth Press. We are especially grateful to Robin Dutcher. We want to thank Helga Schmidt. We would like to express our sincere appreciation to Tami Calliope for her meticulous editing and unwavering enthusiasm.

# INDEX

A NOTE ON THE AUTHORS

CLAUDE FRANCIS and FERNANDE GONTIER have co-
authored biographies of Marcel Proust and Simone de
Beauvoir. Their books in English include *The Book of
Honey* and a translation of de Beauvoir's *Who Shall Die.*

A NOTE ON THE BOOK

This book was composed by Steerforth Press using a digital version of Bembo, a typeface produced by Monotype in 1929 and based on the designs of Francesco Griffo, Venice 1499. All Steerforth books are printed on acid free papers and this book was bound using traditional smythe-sewing by Quebecor Printing/ Book Press Inc. of North Brattleboro, Vermont.